FASHIONING
JAMES BOND

FASHIONING JAMES BOND

Costume, gender and identity in the world of 007

Llewella Chapman

BLOOMSBURY ACADEMIC
LONDON • NEW YORK • OXFORD • NEW DELHI • SYDNEY

BLOOMSBURY ACADEMIC
Bloomsbury Publishing Plc
50 Bedford Square, London, WC1B 3DP, UK
1385 Broadway, New York, NY 10018, USA
29 Earlsfort Terrace, Dublin 2, Ireland

BLOOMSBURY, BLOOMSBURY ACADEMIC and the Diana logo are trademarks
of Bloomsbury Publishing Plc

First published in Great Britain 2022
Reprinted in 2022

Cover design: Jade Barnett
Cover image: Suit For Bond © United Artists/Handout/Getty Images

A catalogue record for this book is available from the British Library.

Library of Congress Cataloging-in-Publication Data
Names: Chapman, Llewella, author.
Title: Fashioning James Bond : costume, gender & identity in the world of 007 /
Llewella Chapman.
Description: [New York] : [Bloomsbury Academic], [2022] |
Includes bibliographical references, filmography, and index. |
Identifiers: LCCN 2021005421 (print) | LCCN 2021005422 (ebook) |
ISBN 9781350145481 (hardback) | ISBN 9781350258488 (paperback) |
ISBN 9781350164666 (epub) | ISBN 9781350164659 (pdf)
Subjects: LCSH: Bond, James (Fictitious character)–In motion pictures. | James Bond films–
History and criticism. | Clothing and dress in motion pictures. | Fashion in motion pictures. |
Costume–Great Britain. | Costume design–Great Britain.
Classification: LCC PN1995.9.J3 C47 2022 (print) | LCC PN1995.9.J3 (ebook) |
DDC 791.4302/6—dc23
LC record available at https://lccn.loc.gov/2021005421
LC ebook record available at https://lccn.loc.gov/2021005422

ISBN: HB: 978-1-3501-4548-1
        PB: 978-1-3502-5848-8
        ePDF: 978-1-3501-6465-9
        eBook: 978-1-3501-6466-6

Typeset by RefineCatch Limited, Bungay, Suffolk
Printed and bound in Great Britain

James . . . You simply are the best

CONTENTS

ILLUSTRATIONS

Figures

Plates

Tables

ACKNOWLEDGEMENTS

Just as a film costume involves a design, fabric selection, pattern-cut, sewing, and is impossible to create without a wardrobe team to produce or source it, nor would this book have been written without the help, support and encouragement from the following 'advisory wardrobe department'. First and foremost, my thanks go to Philippa Brewster, commissioning editor at I.B. Tauris, Rebecca Barden, commissioning editor at Bloomsbury, and Veidehi Hans, editorial assistant at Bloomsbury, who oversaw the beginning and end of this project.

As part of my research, I have been privileged to access many resources held by various repositories, and I would like to thank the following staff for their help and extensive knowledge of the collections they curate to assist me: Nigel Arthur, Jonny Davies and Victoria Bennett based at the British Film Institute; Mary Hudson, the librarian in charge of the Consumer Culture Collection at Southampton Solent University; James Shiras, Thoko Malvowane and Charles Drazin, who kindly permitted me to access the materials held by Film Finances Inc.; Stéphanie Desvaux, Margaux Berthier and Camille Fimbel at Galeries Lafayette; Anne Coco, archivist at the Margaret Herrick Library, Los Angeles; Françoise Lemerige, archivist at the Cinémathèque Française. I have also been very fortunate to speak with family members and colleagues of people involved with costuming the James Bond films, including Natalie Watson, Polly Westmacott-Hayward, Glenys Roberts, Del Smith, and Samantha and Mary Frank.

I have discussed my thoughts about this book with many friends and fellow academics during conferences and events, including Melanie Williams, James Chapman, Claire Monk, Sue Harper, Claire Hines, Ellen Cheshire, Danielle Sprecher, Elizabeth Castaldo Lundèn, Victoria Haddock, Katherina Niemeyer, Melanie Bell, Richard Farmer, Lisa Stead, Justin Smith, Steven Gerrard, Mark Glancy and Roger Law, Andrew Spicer, Jeremy Strong, Lawrence Napper, Sarah Street, Christine Geraghty, Nicholas J. Cull, Tobias Hochscherf, Cynthia J. Miller, Ciara Chambers, Laura Mayne, Mark Fryers, Carolyn Rickards, Jenny Stewart, Ed Vollans, Guy Barefoot, Katie Godman, Jo Brandon and the late David Culbert.

This book could not have been written without the invaluable knowledge of my 'Bond fan' friends, including Gary J. Firuta and Susan Edwards, who not only generously shared parts of their personal Bond collection with me, but also plied me with encouragement in the form of many vodka Martinis in the American Bar at the Savoy. Similarly, Mark Edlitz was kind enough to share transcripts of his interviews with me, and Matthew Field and Ajay Chowdhury provided me with advice and assistance as fellow Bond researchers. Furthermore, Melanie and Reg Ruse have both offered their analysis of the Bond films over dinner and drinks, and in Reg's case, a preference for the characters Pussy Galore and Fiona Volpe, as well as the guilty pleasure to be derived from Plenty O'Toole. Thanks go as well to Mark Ashby and Sharon Nicholas, who discussed all things Bond with me at the Royal Albert Hall, as well as Kevin Bertrande Collette, Mark O'Connell, Andrew Lycett, Tom Zelinski, Bill Koenig, Philip Whitfield and many others forming parts of the James Bond fan groups who have offered me advice when writing this book.

My family, too, have offered their love and encouragement throughout this project. My passion for viewing James Bond was instilled at an early age when watching the films on ITV with my parents, Richard and Dawn Burton. This was further encouraged by my late grandmother, Dorothy Burton, whose love of Sean Connery led to my brother, Michael Burton, and I sending her yearly Valentine's Day cards on behalf of the man himself: 'From Russia with Love.' Michael, his girlfriend, Katie Ford, and their son Alexander have also supported me to write this book, as have my parents-in-law, Colin and Anne Chapman.

Ultimately, though, there is one person whose love and encouragement has assisted me to research and write this book: my husband, and fount of James Bond knowledge, James Chapman. James's enthusiasm for my book, willingly provided throughout the heady days of batting fours and sixes, and equally during the more torrid times of feeling that I was out for a golden duck, have been invaluable, especially in his staunch belief that Roger Moore is the best James Bond (I politely disagree: it's Sean Connery). This book is dedicated to him.

INTRODUCTION

Introducing himself as 'Bond ... James Bond' to Sylvia Trench (Eunice Gayson) from across the baccarat table in Les Ambassadeurs Club, London, this is the first scene in which the British Secret Service agent, codenamed 007 and played by Sean Connery, appears in *Dr. No*, the first James Bond film. Sheathed in the 'armour of choice' for his profession, namely a midnight blue dinner suit tailored by Anthony Sinclair that is revealed piece by piece as the camera focuses on Bond's jacket sleeve and the 'cocktail' cuff of his shirt, left shoulder, back, silk-faced jacket lapels and pleated shirt placket, before his face is finally revealed on screen, the audience is slowly introduced to the character, framed and defined by his costume, with a penchant for quality, whether it be in women, cars, casinos or indeed, clothes. Seated opposite Bond, Sylvia is dressed in a glamorous scarlet georgette evening gown reminiscent of the dresses designed by the Paris fashion house, Worth, and both are surrounded by men and women in luxurious evening clothes in sumptuous surroundings. In what would come to be the most expensive costume scene in *Dr. No*, costing around £412, or 20 per cent of the final wardrobe cost, the casino scene is emblematic of what viewers would come to expect of a franchise spanning nearly sixty years and producing twenty-five films: a lavish spectacle of the highest quality dress.

The recent emergence of research around costume design and wardrobe in film has proved to be a fruitful avenue, allowing for an understanding of the wardrobe department's role in the production of a film, and how the realized costumes work to enhance character, narrative and mise en scène. However, the work conducted into this area remains a small amount of the research being produced in wider film scholarship. It is also, perhaps unsurprisingly, gendered: skewered towards the perception that costume is considered 'women's work', 'whether practiced by women or by men' as Deborah Nadoolman Landis has acknowledged, and indeed much of the scholarship being conducted in this area is by women.[1] Writing in 1998, Stella Bruzzi recognized that: 'Discussions of costume have tended to exclude men and masculine identities, as if attention to dress is an inherently feminine trait.'[2] Similarly, Pamela Church Gibson notes that 'the assumption, held by many academics, [is that] that fashion is a frivolous, feminine field'.[3] In 1976, Elizabeth Leese published her survey of 157 costume personnel, mainly designers, working in Britain and Hollywood, republished in 1991.[4] Since then, more focused and nuanced analysis of the role of the costume designer and the impact of costume and fashion in film has been produced besides Bruzzi and Church Gibson, in particular by Jane M. Gaines and Charlotte Herzog, Elizabeth Nielson, Pam Cook, Sue Harper, Sarah Street, Rachel Moseley, Tamar Jeffers McDonald and Melanie Williams, all of whom have adopted different approaches and methods with which to analyse and understand the importance of this design element in the production of film.[5]

Curiously, the opposite is true when reviewing the interest aroused by analysing costume and fashion in relation to the Bond films. With a few notable exceptions, including Pam Cook and Claire Hines writing on Connery's developing star persona in relation to his suits worn in his Bond films, Sarah Gilligan on Daniel Craig's masculinity in the role of Bond and his relationship with fashion brands, and Monica Germanà analysing how fashion enhances the gendered presentation of the 'Bond girls', the bulk of the writing dedicated towards the Bond films and costume is written by men, and predominantly focused on menswear, in particular on the character of Bond and his tailored suits.[6] For example, prior to Germanà's monograph which focuses on how fashion enhances the psychological characterization of the 'Bond girls' in the novels and the films, the main text concerned with Bond, fashion and costume was the collection *Dressed to Kill: James Bond The Suited Hero*, co-written by Jay McInerney, Nick Foulkes, Neil Norman and Nick Sullivan, which focuses solely on Bond's sartorial choices.[7] Since the production of this lavishly illustrated book, work conducted on menswear in the Bond films has been continued largely by male fans of the franchise, most prominently by Matt Spaiser in his online blog, *The Suits of James Bond*, which offers a superior analysis of the structure, style and shape of the tailored suits worn by cinematic James Bonds, and who has subsequently produced a regular podcast, *From Tailors with Love* with Peter Brooker, analysing menswear in the franchise and interviewing relevant guests.[8]

This book offers the first sustained analysis of both the male and female wardrobes designed, produced and sourced over the course of the James Bond franchise. Specifically, it focuses on three key and interrelated research themes: agency, labour and costumes. The first theme, agency, will map the authorial control and potential tensions that arise over the costume specification and key wardrobe decisions that are made to contribute to the overall look of each Bond film. It will focus in particular on the wardrobe department, the director, producer and scriptwriter, the actors and actresses, and the tailors, stylists and costumiers, each of whom have a connected yet individual remit in the production of an individual film.

The second theme, labour, connects to the theme of agency in understanding who is involved in making costume decisions, and to the third theme of the book, the costumes themselves, specifically in regard to the process behind the creation of costume from the initial designs based on the script and filming locations, to the realized item of clothing as it appears on screen. This involves understanding not only *how* costumes get from page to screen, but also the production line and *who* is involved. It is intrinsically linked to the voice afforded to those working to create and source costumes, and the different roles held within a wardrobe department in a film's production beyond a costume designer, such as wardrobe supervisors, wardrobe masters, wardrobe mistresses, wardrobe assistants, stylists and costumiers. As recognized by Williams, there is 'a larger absence in scholarship on screen costume, that of the labour of the entire wardrobe department as well as the number of outsourced laborers who also contribute to the clothing that appears on-screen but whose work is rendered doubly invisible'.[9] On researching this book, I have found that costume designers' voices, albeit minor in comparison to other crew members such as the cinematographer, art designer and set designer, were more represented than that of other wardrobe staff, although the individual roles would be sometimes interchangeable and the department would work together to achieve the overall specification and visual presence of costume within the Bond films. Williams notes that the costume designer Julie Harris, who designed the costumes for *Live and Let Die*, was once described as 'the girl you don't see ... the girl whose job it is to make other women look their best', and if this is true of the invisible role of the costume designer, it is all the more so with the labour of the wardrobe team to realize the work of said designer.[10]

The understanding of the agency and labour behind realizing costumes for the Bond films also reveals itself when closely analysing the costume designs, where available, and the costumes as they appear in the final film. This leads on to the final theme of this book: the costumes themselves. Firstly, this involves understanding how the costumes articulate the character groupings evident within the Bond films, and I have predominantly focused on the costumes afforded to Bond, the 'girls', the villains and the henchmen, which have been analysed in the context of how the costumes define a particular characterization in reference to gender and psychology, and how they work to support an individual film's design, colour scheme and mise en scène. As proposed by Harper: 'The clothes characters wear can provide an index to their class, politics and sexuality, and thus access to the intentions of the director/producer. They also provide evidence about the resources available to the company, and about the cultural competence of the costume designer'.[11] Furthermore, Street explains that 'studying films "through the clothes" enhances an appreciation of cinema which is primarily visual. It also draws attention to complex and often contradictory narrative structures; questions of stardom [...] and to representations of gender on screen'.[12] Secondly, the book will analyse how the costumes are promoted and marketed to consumers beyond viewing the film, which, as Street understands, is important 'to recognise that film costumes not only relate to the characters that wear them but also the audiences who watch them'.[13]

To research these themes, I have adopted an empirical methodology that draws upon a range of archive sources in order to inform the book's overall analysis of costume, fashion and gender within the Bond films. Approaching the research for this book was rather like attempting to sift through a variety of materials in order to complete a large jigsaw puzzle where some of the pieces were missing: either due to lack of access or because they had unfortunately been destroyed. Sources that I have analysed for this book include scripts, costume designs, correspondence, call sheets, daily progress reports, cost reports, trade papers, critical reception, press clippings, marketing and publicity materials. The repositories included the Archives Galeries Lafayette, the British Library, the British Film Institute (BFI), the Cinémathèque Française, the Film Finances Archive (FFA), the History of Advertising Trust, the Margaret Herrick Library, the National Archives (TNA), the Stanley Kubrick Archive, the Consumer Culture Collection at Southampton Solent University and the West Yorkshire Archives Service (WYAS). Alongside these sources, I have also employed textual analysis methods with which to closely analyse the realized film costumes in terms of colour, structure and cut as they appear in each Bond film to assist in understanding how they enhance character, narrative and mise en scène. As Harper argues, 'a satisfying account needs to combine such methods with textual analysis, and to be unafraid of making judgements of aesthetic quality'.[14] In support of and to enhance my analysis of these written and visual sources, I have interviewed family members and colleagues of those involved in tailoring menswear for the Bond films in order to further understand the process and labour involved, including Natalie Watson, the daughter of Anthony Sinclair, Polly Westmacott-Hayward and Glenys Roberts, the daughter and former wife of Douglas Hayward, Del Smith, who worked for Hayward, and Samantha and Mary Frank, daughter and wife of shirtmaker Frank Foster.

Thus, *Fashioning James Bond* lends itself to be written in a chronological fashion, allowing readers to understand the importance of costume within the Eon Productions film franchise as a whole. The book focuses on these Bond films, however it should be acknowledged that there are other screen adaptations of Fleming's novels, including the live television drama, *Casino Royale* (1954), and the non-Eon Productions films, *Casino Royale* (1967) and *Never Say Never Again* (1983). These offer further avenues for research in the future. Through researching the key themes of agency, labour and costume, the overall purpose of *Fashioning James Bond* is to understand how costume functions to support the cultural legacy of the longest-running cinematic franchise within British film history and its wider impact on consumer culture. As Albert R. 'Cubby' Broccoli, producer of the Eon Productions Bond films, once said: 'Regimes may rise and fall, lapels may widen or narrow [...] but ultimately, Bond remains the old-fashioned, suited hero'.[15]

Notes

1 Deborah Naḍoolman Landis, *Film Craft: Costume Design* (Lewis: Ilix, 2012), 12.

2 Stella Bruzzi, *Undressing Cinema: Clothing and Identity in the Movies* (London and New York: Routledge, 1997), xv.

3 Pamela Church Gibson, 'Film Costume' in John Hill and Pamela Church Gibson (eds), *The Oxford Guide to Film Studies* (Oxford: Oxford University Press, 1998), 36.

4 Elizabeth Leese, *Costume Design in the Movies: An Illustrated Guide to the Work of 157 Great Designers*, 2nd edn (London and New York: Dover Publications, 1991).

5 Jane M. Gaines and Charlotte Herzog (eds), *Fabrications: Costume and the Female Body* (New York and London: Routledge, 1990); Elizabeth Nielsen, 'Handmaidens of the Glamour Culture: Costumes in the Hollywood Studio System', in Gaines and Herzog (eds), 160–79; Pam Cook, *Fashioning the Nation: Costume and Identity in British Cinema* (London: British Film Institute, 1996); Sue Harper, *Women in British Cinema: Mad, Bad and Dangerous to Know* (London and New York: Continuum, 2000); Stella Bruzzi and Pamela Church Gibson (eds), *Fashion Cultures: Theories, Explorations and Analysis* (London and New York: Routledge, 2000); Sarah Street, *Costume and Cinema: Dress Codes in Popular Cinema* (London: Wallflower Press, 2001); Rachel Moseley (ed.), *Fashioning Film Stars: Dress, Culture, Identity* (London: British Film Institute, 2005); Tamar Jeffers McDonald, *Hollywood Catwalk: Exploring Costume and Transformation in American Film* (London: I.B. Tauris, 2010); Melanie Williams, 'The Girl You Don't See: Julie Harris and the Costume Designer in British Cinema', *Feminist Media Histories* 2, issue 2 (2016), 62–74.

6 Pam Cook and Claire Hines, 'Sean Connery *Is* James Bond: Re-fashioning British masculinity in the 1960s' in Moseley (ed.), *Fashioning Film Stars*, 147–59; Sarah Gilligan, 'Branding the new Bond: Daniel Craig and designer fashion', in Robert G. Weiner, B. Lynn Whitfield and Jack Becker (eds), *James Bond in World and Popular Culture: The Films Are Not Enough*, 2nd edn (Newcastle upon Tyne: Cambridge Scholars Publishing, 2011), 76–85; Monica Germanà, *Bond Girls: Body, Fashion and Gender* (London and New York: Bloomsbury, 2020).

7 Jay McInerney, Nick Foulkes, Neil Norman and Nick Sullivan, *Dressed to Kill: The Suited Hero* (Paris and New York: Flammarion, 1995).

8 Matt Spaiser, *The Suits of James Bond*. Available online: www.bondsuits.com/ (accessed 30 September 2020); Matt Spaiser and Pete Brooker, *From Tailors With Love*. Available online: https://fromtailorswithlove.co.uk/ (accessed 30 September 2020).

9 Williams, 104.

10 'She's the girl you don't see', *Evening News*, 7 December 1956.

11 Harper, 213.

12 Street, 11, 12.

10 Ibid., 7.

14 Harper, 2.

15 Albert R. Broccoli, 'Forward', in McInerney, Foulkes, Norman and Sullivan, 11.

1 'MY TAILOR . . . SAVILE ROW': SEAN CONNERY AND *DR. NO* (1962)

Albert R. Broccoli was one of the few film producers to recognize the potential appeal that Ian Fleming's James Bond novels might have for film audiences, explaining: 'From the very beginning I believed that 007 had enormous screen potential.'[1] Harry Saltzman, who had been involved with Woodfall Productions Limited, the company that had produced the critically acclaimed British New Wave films such as *Look Back in Anger* (1958), *The Entertainer* (1960) and *Saturday Night and Sunday Morning* (1960), also recognized the potential of Fleming's novels, and purchased an option to adapt them into film. A partnership was subsequently formed between Broccoli and Saltzman to produce the Bond films, and the question arose over which Fleming novel to adapt first. *Casino Royale* could not be produced, due to the rights being separately owned by the producer Gregory Ratoff to make a film based on this novel. Instead, *Thunderball* was intended to be the first Bond film produced by Eon Productions; however owing to an injunction brought by Kevin McClory against Fleming, Saltzman and Broccoli decided to adapt *Dr. No* instead.

Casting and clothing James Bond

After setting Wolf Mankowitz and Richard Maibaum to work on the script, and hiring Terence Young to direct *Dr. No*, Broccoli and Saltzman turned to one of the most important pre-production decisions to be made: which actor to cast in the role of James Bond. According to Broccoli, various names were briefly considered: Patrick McGoohan and James Fox, both of whom were reluctant to play Bond due to their religious principles, Michael Redgrave, David Niven, Trevor Howard, and allegedly Roger Moore. During the casting discussions, Broccoli remembered Sean

Connery, whom he had been introduced to by Lana Turner during the filming of *Another Time, Another Place* (1958). As Broccoli put it, Connery was 'a handsome, personable guy, projecting a kind of animal virility. He was tall, with a strong physical presence, and there was just the right hint of threat behind that hard smile and faint Scottish burr'.[2] *Another Time, Another Place* also revealed Connery's other potential that was important to the producers, namely 'a flair for wearing stylish clothes and an easy, confident style in front of the cameras'. Invited to meet with the producers, Connery walked in to Broccoli and Saltzman's London office based at 3 Audley Square wearing 'a brown open-necked shirt and suede shoes', and possessed 'a strength and energy' that Broccoli found 'riveting':

> Physically, and in his general persona, he was too much of a rough-cut to be a replica of Fleming's upper-class agent. This suited us fine, because we were looking to give our 007 a much broader box-office appeal: a sexual athlete who would look good in Savile Row suits, but with the lean midriff of a character who starts his day with twenty push-ups [...] Our search for James Bond was over.[3]

Although Broccoli and Saltzman were convinced by Connery, not everyone shared the pair's enthusiasm. According to Broccoli, Young's initial reaction to Connery was: 'Oh, disaster, disaster, disaster!'[4] A memorandum sent from Broccoli to Saltzman stated: '[Robert F.] Blumofe [studio executive at United Artists] reports New York did not care for Connery – feels we can do better', after David and Arnold Picker, the chief executives of United Artists, viewed footage of the actor with some of the actresses being considered for *Dr. No*.[5] Beyond Young and United Artists, the popular narrative supports the myth that Fleming also had misgivings about Connery, however this is disputed following the publication of a private letter that the author wrote to his mistress, Blanche Blackwell, in October 1961: 'The producer [*sic*] Terence Young, seems very nice and the man they have chosen for Bond, Sean Connery, is a real charmer – fairly unknown but a good actor with the right looks and physique.'[6]

After Connery signed his contract around the end of October 1961, Broccoli, Saltzman and Young 'threw everything into grooming' the actor for the part, recognizing that: 'The way Bond dressed was intrinsic to the character. We're talking about an ex-Eton type who mixed with the aristocracy, belonged to the most exclusive clubs, gambled at Monte Carlo and wore handmade silk shirts and Sea Island cotton pyjamas.'[7] Broccoli explained that they wanted to work the 'features which are the unmistakable James Bond hallmark' into 'Sean's macho image', namely: 'The casual but well-cut suits, the black, soft leather moccasins – 007 would never tie a shoe lace – the silk kimonos.'[8]

It is widely acknowledged that Young, regardless of his initial qualms, can be credited with assisting Connery in adapting into the sartorially stylish role demanded for the films. On his role of styling Bond from page to screen, Young stated that Connery 'had to be dressed impeccably' and trained him in style and etiquette.[9] Young took Connery to both his London-based tailor, Anthony Sinclair of Conduit Street, and his shirtmaker Turnbull & Asser, based on Jermyn Street. Of the director 'training' Connery, Steven Jay Rubin writes: 'With *Dr. No* in mind, Young immediately went to work on Connery. He realised first that the actor must feel comfortable in the role of Bond. If Connery was going to order a bottle of Dom Pérignon and some Beluga caviar, he had to do it with conviction.'[10] Ken Adam, production designer for *Dr. No*, affirmed: 'You have to remember that Sean was a pretty rough diamond [...] Terence taught him everything he knew.'[11] This popular myth of Connery's 'rough diamond' image, and that he needed assistance in dressing for the part, is somewhat exaggerated. As with Broccoli realizing Connery's sartorial potential in *Another Time, Another Place*, Connery played Paddy Damion in *The Frightened City* (1961) prior to the production of *Dr. No*, in which his character is dressed in two suits that are not dissimilar to the tailored look that Connery would subsequently sport in his Bond films (Figure 1.1). In his Bond films, Connery acts in similar ways when wearing a suit to how he does in *The Frightened City*, for example placing his hands in the pockets of his jacket and pulling up the legs of his trousers before sitting down.

Natalie Watson explains that her father, Anthony Sinclair, became a tailor because it was the family business. After spending four years in the army, Sinclair decided to start up his own bespoke tailoring business, located at 4 Gerrard Street in London, in 1946. *Tailor & Cutter* reported: 'From the start [Sinclair]

FIGURE 1.1 Sean Connery wearing a suit in *The Frightened City*. Directed by John Lemont © Anglo-Amalgamated Film Distributors 1961. All rights reserved.

concentrated on making clothes for the cinema and theatrical profession.'[12] Watson affirms: 'He came to know various film people, like Harry Fowler, Duncan Lamont and Bonar Colleano.'[13] From Gerrard Street, Sinclair moved to more spacious premises at 29 Conduit Street, and won the prestigious *Tailor & Cutter* 'Dandy' Award in 1957. Around the time of making Sean Connery's suits for James Bond, Watson explains that Sinclair 'also had a fair amount of American clients, one being Channing Pollock, a magician whose act involved releasing many doves which were concealed in the tail suit which he wore'.

On being employed by Eon Productions to tailor Connery's suits for *Dr. No*, Sinclair made all the suits for Connery and for his stuntman, Bob Simmons. In terms of the number of suits required, Watson believes that it 'would have depended on the scenes in the film, but probably two or three of each one' for Connery, with matching ones for Simmons. On the cost and amount of time it would have taken to tailor Connery's suits for the Bond films, Watson recalls:

> Back in the early 1960s the price of suits was then around £60 and the suit was 90 per cent hand-made and would have taken around three weeks which would have included two fittings at least. Anthony Sinclair would be told what scenes the various suits were needed for [with] appropriate patterns shown and chosen, and various weights of the cloth [selected] according to which countries they were [going to be] worn in.

Watson believes that Connery 'was not a difficult man to fit: he was tall, broad-shouldered and had a good figure!' Based on the measurements taken by Sinclair for Connery, Table 1.1 outlines the structure of Connery's suits for *Dr. No*.[14] Connery's suits were tailored in the particular style Sinclair offered to every client: an unstructured suit, which, as Matt Spaiser puts it, was 'neither with the structure of English equestrian tailors nor with the exaggerated drape of the English drape tailors. Sinclair's cut was unassuming but undeniably British.'[15]

Watson explains that many incorrectly attribute the term 'Conduit Cut' to Sinclair's style of tailoring, particularly when discussing the suits that he tailored for Connery, stating that her father did not 'invent or design, at any time, the "Conduit Cut" suit for James Bond – the suits that were made were the suits that every client got. Completely bespoke with each client having an individual pattern cut to his requirements.' Del Smith concurs with Watson's assessment, and agrees that there is no such cut in existence.[16] It is merely a journalistic term: London-made suits are either cut in 'Savile Row' style or 'West End' style, the main difference between the two being in price, not necessarily in quality, although suits tailored by a Savile Row firm are globally understood to provide the benchmark in terms of quality. It is worth pointing out that, to date, no actor playing the role of James Bond has ever worn a Savile Row suit in the Eon Productions franchise. This is in keeping with Fleming's character: although Bond of the novels dressed well, he did

TABLE 1.1 Sean Connery's suit measurements as taken by Anthony Sinclair in 1961/1962

Suit measurement term	Measurement (in inches)	Posture/figuration
Nape to waist	19	'Upright'
Jacket length	31¼	
Cross-back	9	
Chest	46½	'Prominent chest'
Jacket waist	37	'Hollow waist'
Seat	42½	'Prominent seat'
Shoulder	7	'Drop right shoulder'
Sleeve length	32	
Trouser waist	36	
Inside leg	32	
Outside leg	43½	'Prominent calves'

Source: Natalie Watson

not wear Savile Row suits, as Fleming explained to Michael Howard, the editorial director for Jonathan Cape Limited: 'In the present copy [for a Courtelle advertisement] I don't think they should suggest that Bond wears suits from Savile Row, which he doesn't.'[17] Furthermore, in a letter sent from Fleming's secretary to Arthur Paul, the art director of *Playboy*, dated 11 December 1962, the following description of Bond's attire was offered: 'Wears two-button single-breasted suit in dark blue tropical worsted. Black leather belt. White Sea Island cotton shirt, sleeveless. Black casual shoes, square toed. Thin black knitted silk tie, no pin. Dark blue socks, cotton lisle. No handkerchief in breast pocket. Wears Rolex Oyster Perpetual watch.'[18]

Sinclair cut the jacket of Connery's suits fuller than normal in order to allow him room to carry a gun under his left shoulder while still allowing the suit to drape attractively over his frame and retain the contours of the body. Following the release of *Dr. No*, Sinclair explained in an interview with *ABC News* that: 'The only gimmick, if I may call it such, is the one where [Bond] carries his gun, and the whole art of it is to cut the suit in such a way to which it's just that little bit fuller so that it follows the contours of the figure.'[19] The suits were also specially designed for the action sequences in the film. Sinclair stated: 'You've got to put your guts into that so whatever you do to the suit, you see [pulls up his jacket collar] any well-made suit, you'd be able to take it into a ball, crush it, stamp on it, sleep in it, then there you are [flattens collar down], you see, back again.'[20] Anne Hollander explains how the lounge suit developed sartorially: 'After the Second World War, the expensive made-to-measure version was refined, dimmed and smoothed out, and generally enhanced in the public mind as the new standard image of the elegant male.'[21] Hollander notes that the popular modern equivalent of the lounge suit 'now skimmed the surface and moved in counterpart to the body's movement, making a mobile work of art out of the combination.'[22]

Sinclair tailored six outfits for Connery in *Dr. No*: a midnight blue shawl-collared dinner suit, a Chesterfield overcoat, three lounge suits made from dark grey mohair, light grey mohair and a plain-weave glen check, and a navy blazer with grey flannel trousers. Of these costumes, Simmons wore two: the dark grey mohair and the light grey mohair lounge suits. Of the three lounge suits Connery wore in *Dr. No*, Spaiser notes that the jackets have two-button fastenings, the notched lapels are of a medium-narrow width, and they are cut with natural shoulders, roped sleeve-heads, a full chest and a gently suppressed waist. They include double vents, straight jetted pockets with no flaps, a breast pocket set at a low stance and four buttons on each sleeve cuff. Furthermore, the suit trousers 'have a traditionally English cut with a high rise to the natural waist and double-forward pleats. The trouser legs taper to a moderately narrow hem with turn-ups.'[23] Connery did not wear a belt or braces, as this would have broken the line of the suit; instead, his trousers were tailored to include 'Daks tops', a device created by Simpsons of Piccadilly, London. 'Daks tops' are button tabs that tighten the waist of the trouser to ensure the garment remains in place. Bond's navy serge single-breasted blazer was cut in the same style as the suit jackets, except it includes three open patch pockets, and the buttons were made from silver metal.

The midnight blue shawl collar dinner suit (Figure 1.2), or tuxedo in American parlance, worn by Connery in his opening scene in *Dr. No* is a suit that was designed in America in the early 1900s. It was originally intended as an informal coat to accompany black evening trousers and something to be worn casually in private. Over the following decades the dinner jacket saw a rise in its popularity and was worn at public events. By the 1960s it 'had become publicly formal evening dress, somewhat austere and ceremonial.'[24] Sinclair tailored the dinner jacket with one black silk-covered button fastening and silk gauntlet cuffs with four silk-covered buttons. It has a back vent, although this is an unusual design for a dinner jacket as it would not normally include them. The trousers include a black silk stripe down both outside legs. The Chesterfield overcoat was described by Christie's Auction House as: 'A single-breasted overcoat of navy wool trimmed with a navy velvet collar, lined in navy satin.'[25] The label included a handwritten note in blue biro: 'January 1962. S Connery Esq F252/14728', indicating that this would have been one of the last items to be tailored before Connery travelled to Jamaica to begin filming. In a press photograph taken of Connery, Young, Clive Reed, the

FIGURE 1.2 Sean Connery as James Bond wearing his midnight blue dinner suit. *Dr. No* directed by Terence Young © Eon Productions/United Artists 1962.

assistant director, L. C. Rudkin, the production manager, and Roy McGregor, the film's publicist, boarding the Eon Productions-chartered BOAC flight to Jamaica, Connery is wearing the overcoat and the dark grey mohair lounge suit, both of which would be worn in the film.[26] However, the overcoat would not be worn in the scenes filmed in Jamaica, and would instead feature in the scenes shot at Pinewood Studios.

Michael Fish, working for Turnbull & Asser, was employed to design and tailor some of the shirts for Connery's Bond. Fish supplied double-cuffed, or 'cocktail-cuffed', shirts using mother-of-pearl buttons rather than cufflinks in order for Connery to perform in his role as Bond with ease. This style of cuff was described by Nick Foulkes as 'spreading away from the wrist like a shirt collar'.[27] Simon Hobbs, of Turnbull & Asser, affirmed: 'What we did for Bond was design a very stylish sartorial shirt, double-cuff, that instead of using cufflinks to fasten the cuff we put two buttons on the cuff. This made it easier for Bond to put on the shirt and just as easy for Bond to take the shirt off.'[28] Table 1.2 displays Connery's shirt measurements taken by Fish, and the measurements directly correspond with his suit measurements taken by Sinclair.[29] On visiting Turnbull & Asser, Connery was reportedly impressed and admired 'the distinctive sartorial flourish' of the shirts according to Bronwen Cosgrave, who posits that 'around a week's worth of shirts' would have been made for the early Bond productions.[30]

Frank Foster, too, made shirts for Connery in *Dr. No*, and would subsequently work on all of the Eon Productions Bond films until Roger Moore's final film, *A View to a Kill*. As well as making shirts for Bond, Foster also made shirts and other

TABLE 1.2 Turnbull & Asser's shirt measurements for Sean Connery

Sean Connery	
Measurement term	Measurement (in inches)
Collar Size	17
Chest	44
Waist	36
Hips	41½
FT [Front] Yoke	6¼
BK [Back] Yoke	9½
Sleeves	35½
Length	31
Drop	14L

Source: *Inside Dr. No*, directed by John Cork (USA: MGM Home Entertainment, 2000).

costumes for many of the other leads and secondary characters in the films. The Appendix sets out Foster's filmography, including some of the actors for whom he produced shirts and costumes.[31] Prior to making shirts, Foster designed hand-made silk scarves made using rubber blocks that were sold by the London-based luxury stores Harrods and Galeries Lafayette. He came to shirt making by chance around 1949 – when asked by a friend to recommend someone to make a shirt, Foster put himself forward for the job. Foster explained that he had little experience of making shirts, however: 'I un-ripped some good ones and looked at the structure. As an artist, I understand structure. I then taught myself to cut the patterns.'[32] The starting price for a Foster-made shirt was £4.4s, and his premises were based at Bond Street, Henrietta Place and Clifford Street before Foster settled at 40 Pall Mall. On the art of making shirts, Foster explained:

> The secret of making a good shirt is skill, patience and knowing about textiles. Every piece of cloth we sell is high quality [...] I love making shirts. I can look at an individual and when I measure him I can see all the problems and the build [...] first you measure the neck. You have to notice the space between the shoulder and the bottom of the ear [...] You then measure the front shoulder to see how wide that is and from there you go down to the half-chest, across the top of the chest. From there you go to the abdomen and then to the hips and then to the waist. We don't use shirt tails, we cut shirts with square bottoms and

side vents [. . .] Then you do the cuffs, and cuffs have to be measured according to wrists.[33]

It was reported that by 1957 Foster had become a shirtmaker to the famous, with a company turnover of '£10,000 a year', and that he had recently obtained a contract to make shirts on behalf of Bermans and Nathans, the film and theatrical costumiers.[34] The first film Foster worked on was making shirts for Paddy Stone and Irving Davies in *The Good Companions* (1957). After working on many productions, both as a freelancer and through his contract with Bermans and Nathans, he stopped making film costumes in the mid-1980s, due to it being 'too much work', however Foster continued to provide textiles for various productions.[35]

Connery's shoes were purchased from John Lobb. It was later revealed by Young in a somewhat tongue-in-cheek interview with Elspeth Grant that 'he gets his shoes off-the-peg! I've tried to talk him into handmade shoes – but he just won't have 'em!'[36] Based on the estimates provided by Watson that it would take around three weeks to make a suit, and the consistent accounts of Young's so-called 'training' of Connery in bon-vivantism from the beginning of November 1961, it is likely that the suits would have tailored by mid-December to early January, before principal photography began in Jamaica on 16 January 1962. Broccoli stated that Young persuaded Connery to 'go out in the evenings wearing the clothes, so that he'd feel more and more at ease in them [. . .] Sean, sensibly, preferred to go around in jeans and bomber jackets. But we wanted him to get used to his Savile Row gear the way any good actor gets to know his costume', again embellishing the myth that Connery was not used to wearing a suit.[37]

Financing the wardrobe of *Dr. No*

With Connery 'in training' to prepare for his role as Bond by dining in fine restaurants wearing his tailored suits, Broccoli and Saltzman were busy preparing for the production of *Dr. No*. As part of the financing agreement between Danjaq SA and United Artists, one of the conditions was that the producers would seek a contract with the completion guarantor Film Finances Limited. Founded in 1950 by Robert Garrett, a film producer, and Peter Hope, an insurance broker for Lloyd's of London, Film Finances specializes in providing guarantees of completion on film productions to lending banks and distributors. The company employed John Croydon, an independent film producer and highly experienced studio manager, as a consultant to assess the script, budget and schedule and report on the viability of offering a guarantee on a proposed film production.[38] Though Film Finances' relationship between Eon Productions and United Artists was focused on the financial aspects of *Dr. No*, the papers held in the company's archive nonetheless reveals many of the details relating to the costumes that were created and sourced for the film.

Film Finances received the fourth draft screenplay, a production budget and a schedule to review the project. The total budget for the film was calculated at £317,359, of which 'Costumes and Wigs' was calculated at costing £1,250 (0.4 per cent). Broken down, £720 was listed against 'location', £480 listed for 'main shooting studio and lot', totalling £1,200.[39] For the wigs, £30 was assigned for location and £20 for studio. Of the production unit salaries, £1,400 was budgeted for the 'Wardrobe Designer and Staff' category. No wardrobe designer was named in the budget, and John Brady was named as the wardrobe master and Eileen Sullivan the wardrobe mistress. A later budget was slightly recalculated, and the costume and wig budget allocation was reduced to £1,050, despite the overall budget being increased to £322,069 (0.32 per cent). The salary costs for Brady and Sullivan remained the same, as demonstrated in Table 1.3. It displays the consistent gender difference between pay rates during the 1960s in relation to wardrobe salaries.

In Croydon's report on *Dr. No*, he explained to Garrett that: 'I had liked the script and the look of the papers until I heard that Terence Young was to be the director!'[40] On the budget allowance for costumes and wigs, Croydon noted that 'costume costs seem to lie in an "in between" category. If no "House" was to be employed to dress the women, then the figure seemed high, but if "creations" were expected, the amount did not seem enough. We must remember the propensity of Saltzman and Young to go rushing off to the Paris "houses" in such circumstances!'

Croydon's assessment of the budget allocation for costume was based upon his belief that it would be the female wardrobe that would prove to be the main cost, although as can be understood from the arrangements to prepare Connery for the

TABLE 1.3 Budget breakdown for John Brady and Eileen Sullivan's salaries

	Rate	Preparation and Tests		Locations		Main Shooting and Studio Lot		Finishing Costs		Total
		Weeks	Amount	Weeks	Amount	Weeks	Amount	Weeks	Amount	
John Brady	£35	4	£140	5 ½	£192	4	£140	1	£35	£507
Overtime					£170		£100			£270
Eileen Sullivan	£25	4	£100	5 ½	£137	4	£100			£337
Overtime					£120		£70			£190
Location Allowance					£96					£96

Source: Film Finances Archive (FFA), Realized Film Box 328: *Dr. No* Production Budget, n.d.

role of Bond, it was actually his tailored items which would ultimately be the most significant wardrobe cost. Cosgrave explains that because of the film's modest budget, the remaining wardrobe budget allocation was minimal for the rest of the cast, and indeed, on viewing the film this is most certainly true.[41] As Ursula Andress, who was cast in the role of Honey Ryder, put it: 'The clothes? I had no clothes. I had a swimming costume, a bathrobe, a Chinese-style blouse and a pair of trousers, which I lost in a chase scene.'[42] Lois Maxwell, playing Moneypenny, Bernard Lee, cast as M, and other minor cast members wore their own clothes. By collating the data from the film's weekly cost reports, it can be understood that Connery's and Simmons' suits tailored by Anthony Sinclair equate to 37 per cent of the overall final cost of the costume and wig expenditure, £2,254, calculated at approximately £840.[43] This also means that the rest of the calculated final cost of the costumes, £1,414, had to have been spent somewhere, if not on Andress or the minor cast members. Indeed, by analysing the dates in relation to the higher levels of costume expenditure that occurred during *Dr. No*'s production in the weekly cost reports, compared alongside the call sheets and daily progress reports, it can be ascertained when and where the money on costumes was being spent, as indicated in Table 1.4.

Production began in Jamaica on 16 January 1962 at Palisadoes Airport with scenes 39–48 being shot. The first call sheet demonstrates which costume was assigned to whom, namely the dark grey mohair suit for Bond, a tropical beige wool suit for Felix Leiter (Jack Lord), a Hawaiian shirt and straw hat with a black grosgrain ribbon for Quarrel (John Kitzmiller), a beige uniform for the 'Chauffeur' (Reggie Carter), and a short green sleeveless dress for the 'Girl Photographer' (Margaret Lewis).

Later call sheets do not allocate costumes by number, however the suit Connery wears at the airport labelled costume '2' is the second suit he wears in the film, and therefore his costumes were likely to be numbered in the order of which they were intended to appear:

1   Midnight blue shawl collar dinner suit and Chesterfield overcoat.

2   Dark grey mohair lounge suit.

3   Light grey mohair lounge suit.

4   Navy blazer and grey flannel trousers.

5   Plain-weave glen check lounge suit.

6   Polo shirt and cotton trousers.

7   Towelling bath robe.

8   Nehru jacket and trousers.

9   Vest and trousers.

10   Decontamination suit.

TABLE 1.4 Collated weekly cost report data for 'Costumes and Wigs'

Date	Total committed cost to date	Estimate to complete	Estimated final cost	Over budget	Expenditure
22 January 1962	£264	£786	£1,050	_____	£264
28 January 1962	£449	£601	£1,050	_____	£185
3 February 1962	£487	£563	£1,050	_____	£38
10 February 1962	£493	£557	£1,050	_____	£6
17 February 1962	£497	£553	£1,050	_____	£4
24 February 1962	£809	£241	£1,050	_____	£312
9 March 1962	£968	£500	£1,468	£418	£159
16 March 1962	£1,002	£500	£1,468	£418	£134
23 March 1962	£1,029	£700	£1,729	£679	£27
30 March 1962	£1,168	£700	£1,868	£818	£139
6 April 1962	£1,655	£200	£1,855	£805	£487
20 April 1962	£1,958	_____	£1,958	£908	£303
31 August 1962	£2,254	_____	£2,254	£1,204	£296

Source: FFA: Realized Film Box 328: Data collected from weekly cost reports dated between 22 January 1962 and 31 August 1962.

Andress arrived in Jamaica on 30 January and began her role on 2 February, filming her very last scenes in the film when Bond and Honey find themselves adrift on a boat after escaping from Dr. No's (Joseph Wiseman) Crab Key Island, wearing the 'little Chinese dress'. Andress's famous entrance scene with the actress emerging from the sea in an ivory bikini was shot at the Laughing Waters location six days later.[44] The creation of Andress's bikini happened during this brief period, with Andress recalling that on her arrival 'we had no wardrobe, so we had to get right on with the bikini. [...] And it was so strange – there was a girl who had a boutique, and she was also making dresses, and she was a friend of mine from Rome – Tessa Prendergast [...] and we made the bikini together.'[45] In another interview, Andress explained that a different bikini had been sourced before her arrival, but she disliked the 'traditional Jamaican style' of it: 'I didn't like the palm trees or the leaves or the tropical flowers on the print of the fabric. I wanted something very simple [...] I had a very special idea of how I wanted the bikini [...] I chose the material. I didn't sew it, but I helped to cut it!'[46] Following Andress's arrival, Broccoli sent a telegram to David Picker on 31 January

TABLE 1.5 Excerpt from Call Sheet No. 1, 16 January 1962

Artist	Character	Costume No.	M/U	Hair	W/Robe	Lv Hotel	On Set
Sean Connery	James Bond	2	7.15	7.30	7.00	8.00	8.30
Margaret Lewis	Girl Photographer	1	6.00	6.45	-	8.00	8.30
Reggie Carter	Chauffeur	1	6.45	-	7.15	8.00	8.30
Jack Lord	Felix Leiter	1	As Available				
John Kitzmiller	Quarrel	1	On Set Dr. No's		-	8.00	8.30

Source: FFA: Realized Film Box 328: Call Sheet no. 1, 16 January 1962.

requesting: 'Please have someone obtain from Saks Fifth Avenue three white bras Hollywood Vassarette style 1245 size 34B padded. Send soonest.'[47] The bikini was made from ivory cotton, and is described by the auction house Christie's as a 'two-piece costume comprising a top, constructed from Andress' own under-wired *brassière*, covered in ivory cotton [. . .] [it] had been designed to be a practical working "action" garment suitable to withstand the rigours Andress' role imposed on it'.[48] Owing to this description, as well as the various anecdotal evidence, this suggests that the three *brassières* ordered from Saks may have either not arrived on time, or that they were perhaps deemed unsuitable. It should be noted that although Prendergast received a costume design credit in the film, there is no evidence to suggest that she was employed on the production beyond the consistent reports that she assisted Andress in the creation of the bikini, especially as her name does not appear either in the call sheets or the daily progress reports. Therefore, it can be surmised that Broccoli, Saltzman and/or Young likely offered Prendergast a credit in return for her assistance in creating the bikini on location in Jamaica.

By comparing the dates when the bikini would have been constructed against the dates of the weekly cost reports outlined in Table 1.4, £6 of the costume and wig budget was spent during this period, and on the balance of probability this money would have been spent on creating the bikini using the structure of Andress's own *brassière*. The 'broad leather belt' that Andress wore with the bikini was reportedly provided by Gordon Joslin, then a 28-year-old Royal Navy Acting Petty Officer on HMS *Troubridge*.[49] Joslin recalled that a member of the production crew approached the naval officers who were watching the filming and asked for their assistance: 'The Petty Officer looked at me and said, "Let's have your webbing belt." He grabbed it off me and it was wrapped around Ursula Andress's hips. I didn't get it back.' The ammunition belt was written off as lost overboard.

Until 24 February, the expenditure for the wardrobe appeared to be on target and within budget, although production was eight days over schedule and reports had begun to emerge from Jamaica that Young had enjoyed spending money on luxuries, including costume: 'The only thing about Terence that hasn't changed is his "grand seigneur" way of living. He has spent money personally like water and has charmed us out of over £500 in cash advances and we still don't know what his various bills around the island will come to,' Saltzman complained.[50] One of these costs was Miss Taro's (Zena Marshall) dressing gown. Marshall incorrectly believed that Young lent her his own dressing gown.[51] In actual fact, the gown was purchased from Sulka, an exclusive haberdashery store, whose clients included the Rockefellers, Clark Gable and Edward, Duke of Windsor.[52] The ivory silk *peignoir* and corresponding belt, labelled 'S399', was adapted during the filming. In the scenes when Taro speaks to Bond on the telephone, the robe is slashed at the side seams and has turned-back sleeves, whereas in later scenes the seams have been stitched together.[53] Furthermore, the unit also had to retake one day's work according to the film's production diary because: 'faulty wardrobe was the reason for ½ day of this.'[54]

The production unit returned to London to complete filming at Pinewood Studios which started on 26 February. It was at this point that Croydon's astute prediction that the lure of the Paris fashion 'houses' would prove irresistible to Broccoli, Saltzman and Young came true, and the collated weekly cost report figures in Table 1.4 reveal that spending on costume began almost immediately after the crew's flights had landed at London Airport at Heathrow. Within two weeks, £471 had been spent on wardrobe costs, and had almost reached the total amount spent on costumes when the production was being shot in Jamaica (£497). The costume costs continued to escalate. From reviewing the call sheets and daily progress reports it is evident that the money was being spent on costuming the Les Ambassadeurs Club scenes. As listed in the call sheet dated 2 March for scenes 29 and 30, the named actors included Connery, Eunice Gayson, cast as Sylvia Trench, Stanley Morgan and Simon Martin, as well as the following crowd with specific wardrobe requirements listed:

10 men	Evening dress
25 men	Lounge suits
2 men	Waiters
2 men	Croupiers
10 women	Evening dress
15 women	Cocktail dresses
1 man	Cashier [55]

The script describes the set, atmosphere, mise en scène and costumes that were to be used in the scenes to capture such luxurious surroundings:

29. INT. LE CERCLE CASINO. GAMING ROOM. BACCARAT TABLE. MED SHOT. NIGHT.
A large high-ceilinged rococo room crowded with obvious café society. Most of the MEN are dressed in dinner jackets. The WOMEN in evening gowns. The *Chemin-de-fer* tables are full and surrounded by onlookers. There is a glitter of expensive jewellery; the tense atmosphere and subdued conversational hum characteristic of places where people gamble for high stakes.[56]

Sylvia is described as 'willowy, exquisitely gowned, with a classic, deceptively cold beauty' in these scenes. Beyond such expenditure for these two lavishly costumed scenes, a wardrobe disaster struck when they were about to be shot.

Gayson recalled that she was originally supposed to wear a gold and brown silk dress for the scene, however on arriving on set she was 'horror-struck. The set was gold and brown and I just disappeared into it.'[57] Young wasn't impressed either, exclaiming: 'No, no, no [...] This scene is absolutely pivotal to the whole film, as we're introduced to James Bond for the very first time, and I can't see her! It's important she wears something striking that stands out.'[58] The director immediately sent Gayson to Pinewood's wardrobe department, 'but they simply didn't have anything suitable off-the-peg', nor was there time to make another dress. Therefore, Gayson and Sullivan went on a mission to find a replacement. On arriving at what was known to have been a local dress shop, Gayson and Sullivan discovered that it had since become a wool shop. As they were leaving, Gayson noticed 'a beautiful bright red georgette dress hanging on the back of a door', however although the colour was 'perfect', the dress was a size 20 and Gayson was a size 8. Sullivan replied: 'Never mind, the colour's good against the brown – we'll take it!' On set, Sullivan 'cut a chunk out of the fabric' for the dress to fit Gayson, and it was held together during the filming of the casino scenes with pins down the left-hand side: 'Which was fine when I was sitting at the card table, but the cameraman, Ted Moore, pointed out that when I was standing I couldn't turn far one way or the other or they would be in shot,' Gayson explained. This is evident in the scene that appears in the film, particularly when Gayson stands up from the table and turns to pick up her coat, and a gentleman in evening dress strategically moves to cover the part of the dress fastened with pins. As Gayson recalled: 'So there I am on the set of a $1 million film, in a beautiful red gown held together by pegs. But it was a beautiful tight fit and I thoroughly recommend it to anyone in need of urgent costume alterations!'

The remainder of production ran relatively smoothly in relation to costume and wardrobe. Patricia Baden was employed by the production from 2 March until 16 March for eight days as a wardrobe assistant and was paid £4.10s.0d. per day when the casino and Dr. No's apartment scenes were being filmed.[59] On 6 March Joseph Wiseman arrived on set for make-up, hair and wardrobe tests for his cream Nehru jacket and trousers. By 3 April the principal photography of *Dr. No* was complete and post-production synching and pick-up shots began. In Eon Productions schedule to complete this, Connery was expected to undertake six costume changes to achieve this in one day, as can be understood from Table 1.6. These shots were taken on 26 April.

As can be understood from the collated cost report data, £1,086 was paid on costume and wigs after the completion of filming. This was likely due to monies being owed to Bermans and Nathans for the renting of costumes and any outstanding receipts for various individual items. It could also be posited that Broccoli and Young may have paid Sinclair in instalments. According to the final

TABLE 1.6 'Proposed further shooting to completion' schedule noting Sean Connery's costume changes

Friday 27 April	R/T LIMOUSINE (B.P.) Sc.54 (Bond wearing hat, grey flannel suit, blue shirt, blue tie)	Tunnel
	R/T ALPINE (B.P.) Sc. 114–121 (Bond wearing blue blazer, blue tie and shirt)	"
	QUARREL'S CANOE (B.P.) Sc. 142 (Bond wearing blue sweater, shirt and jeans)	"
	CAPE CANAVERAL (B.P.) REACTOR ROOM CONSOLE Sc. 220	"
	INT. REACTOR ROOM DOOR – VERY CLOSE SHOT BOND'S ENTRANCE REACTION – Sc. 218 (Bond in decontamination suit)	"
	INT. SHAFT R/T. BOND'S first reaction to hot tunnel – Sc. 212 (Bond wearing torn brown silk jacket and strips round hands)	"
	DRAGON SCENE – BOND BEING HIT Sc. 196	"
	HOTEL BEDROOM – C.S. BOND'S REACTION to TARANTULA on shoulder – Sc. 99	"
	INSERT GEOLOGICAL BOOK & DENT'S RECEIPT	"

Source: FFA: Realized Film Box 328: *Dr. No* Proposed further shooting to completion, 18 April 1962.

cost report dated 31 December 1962, after the film had been released in October, the final amount paid on costumes and wigs was £2253.9s.10d, an overcost of £1,204 (53 per cent).[60] For the wardrobe salary costs, the final cost was £986.17s.3d, one of the few areas where the film came in under budget at £413. Overall, the film went over budget by £69,953, and came to an overall final cost of £392,022.2s.3d.

Dr. No costume analysis

The viewer's introduction to Bond comes in Les Ambassadeurs Club, wearing his midnight blue shawl-collared dinner jacket, which would become a recurring costume for the character in the twenty-four Eon Productions Bond films that have followed to date. On analysing the effectiveness of the on-screen suit worn by Bond, Neil Norman argues that 'the well-tailored suit is to Bond the armour of his profession. And the better the tailoring, the more effective the armour.'[61] These elements of how fashion is used to promote Bond as an action hero while still befitted in the highest quality of gentleman's dress conforms to what Hollander describes as the ultimate purpose of male suits: 'The whole costume may thus settle itself naturally when the body stops moving, so that its own poise is effortlessly resumed after a swift dash or sudden struggle.'[62] After being requested by M to meet at Universal Exports, Bond arrives wearing his Chesterfield coat over his evening clothes and a homburg hat. This scene would become one of the running jokes within the later films of the franchise: Bond aiming and throwing his hat on the hat stand in front of Moneypenny. After being sent by M to Jamaica, Bond leaves the airport wearing his dark grey lounge suit. Although this suit would be too hot for the Jamaican climate, it works for continuity as Bond would have boarded his flight in the colder London weather. The script offers a small amount of information on the construction of this suit: '[Bond] transfers Walther from trouser bank (NOTE: There is an in-built concealed clip there) to shoulder holster.'[63] Following this, Bond wears the light grey suit throughout his scenes in the Colonial Club, meeting with Quarrel and Felix Leiter, and at the Puss-Fellers Club. Again, the script indicates a description of the suit which is incorporated into the scene: 'BOND, standing in front of mirror, is putting finishing touches to tie. He is in shirt-sleeves, and a tropical jacket hangs ready on back of chair.'[64] This is adapted from Fleming's brief description of Bond's attire in the novel: 'He went into his room and dressed in his old dark blue tropical worsted suit, a sleeveless white cotton shirt and a black knitted tie.'[65]

When Bond meets Leiter for the first time, the script begins what would become a running wardrobe-related jest throughout the later Bond films in relation to humorous references to tailors and tailoring, although it ironically claims that Bond's suits have been tailored in Savile Row, working to establish the myth:

LEITER
(moving around so he can see BOND
CLEARLY)
Interesting. Where were you measured for this, bud?

BOND
My tailor . . . Savile Row.

LEITER
That so? Mine's a guy in Washington.[66]

Bond visits Professor Dent's (Anthony Dawson) office wearing the navy blazer and grey flannel trousers, before changing into his plain-weave glen check suit to wear to Government House and aboard Quarrel's boat. Bond wears the blazer and grey flannel trouser combination again when visiting Miss Taro's house. After this point, Bond takes on a more casual look for his excursion to Crab Key Island with Quarrel, wearing a blue polo shirt and denim jeans before being captured by Dr. No.

As with Bond's suits, the first Bond film also establishes the costume prototypes for the Bond villain and the 'Bond girl'. Dr. No appears in the film wearing a Nehru jacket (Figure 1.3). This style is popular in South East Asia and is named after Jawaharlal Nehru, the first Prime Minister of India (1947–64), and derives from a *Sherwani*. A shorter, less formal style of the *Sherwani* emerged in the early 1940s known as a *band gale ka* (closed-neck) coat, and both were cut close to the body with a suppressed waist and flared skirt. The Nehru suit's distinguishing feature is

FIGURE 1.3 Dr. No in his cream Nehru jacket and trousers. *Dr. No* directed by Terence Young © Eon Productions/United Artists 1962. All rights reserved.

the 'Mandarin' collar, a short stand-up collar of one or two inches, that is turned up with no lapel alluding to Western military jackets. Apart from the collar, the rest of the suit is unembellished and simply tailored. The jacket can have single or double vents, and the collar is fastened with a hook to give a clean cut to the overall ensemble. The sleeves of the jacket normally include buttoned cuffs. The jacket effectively hides the shirt worn underneath except the shirt cuffs and a small amount of the collar.

Due to the tight cut of the suit, the most suitable shirt to wear with it would be a tunic-collared shirt to retain the smoothness of the suit fabric against the body. It can be paired with trousers of either matching or different fabric. A range of fabrics can be used, from khadi hand-spun cotton to heavier merino tweeds. Dr. No's jacket is tailored from cream shantung silk with one back vent. This is worn with matching cream trousers with double forward pleats. Dr. No first appears in this costume framed in the doorway to Bond's suite in his compound on Crab Key Island, of which only his silhouette is visible. As the camera tracks Dr. No walking across to where Bond sleeps, the audience is afforded tantalizing views that depict separate elements of his costume, similar to how Bond is introduced: the bottom half of his trousers and then his white socks and shoes. To add to the sinister silhouette created from such close tailoring, the audience watches as Dr. No lifts the duvet covering Bond with his black steel mechanical hands. Little is written in the script specifically on Dr. No's costume, however scene 205 offers the following description: 'He is impeccably dressed in a tussore suit.'[67] 'Tussore' refers to a coarse silk from the larvae of the tussore moth and is normally brown in colour. This colour, of course, was changed for the film.

After Bond is summoned to dine with Dr. No, he also dresses in a Nehru suit made of brown shantung silk that has the unusual touch of a white pocket square in the breast pocket of the jacket; an element that would not normally be included as traditionally the Nehru jacket does not have pockets. Effectively, the switching of the colours works as a visual irony: light colours are typically associated with 'good' and being the hero. It is fastened with five brass buttons on the front which are visible unlike Dr. No's, and it has no back vent. Bond's trousers are also cream with double-forward pleats although his are finished with a cuffed hem. The Nehru ensemble that Bond wears is therefore more Western in design than Dr. No's. This film begins what would become a common theme in future Bond films later in this decade, namely the influence of Asian dress which is used as a visual signifier to represent the cultural politics of Bond villainy. As James Chapman believes, the character of Dr. No 'set the standard for all the later megalomaniacs bent on world domination'.[68]

As the film's main female lead, Andress is afforded the iconic image of the first 'Bond girl' through the statement of her character's costume, or rather, lack of it (Plate 1). Honey's costume works in direct contrast with Sylvia's evening gown worn during the casino scenes that has a silhouette reminiscent of the haute couture dresses designed by the Paris fashion house Worth. The script describes Honey's outfit in detail:

> HONEY, standing at the water's edge, her back to him. She is naked except for a wisp of home-made bikini and a broad leather belt with an <u>undersea</u> knife in a sheath. (Undersea knife differs from a conventional hunting one in that it has a rather bulky cork handle which causes it slowly to surface if dropped underwater. This is rather important as they are characteristic.)[69]

Christie's described the bikini: 'the cups [are] decorated with a dart detail, gathered at the centre and decorated with a bow detail, the bikini briefs, cut across the grain, gathered at the hips and embellished with decorative straps, fastening at the left-hand side and lined in cotton.'[70] The modern bikini dates from 1946, the design of which was accredited to mechanical engineer Louis Réard. Réard's design was a string bikini that included four triangles made from thirty square inches of fabric, and was perceived to be an obscene display of sexuality at the time. Despite its initial reception, Brigitte Bardot wore a bikini during the Cannes Film Festival in 1953 after the release of the film *The Girl in the Bikini* (1952), which helped to popularize its image in Europe and create a market for the item of clothing in America. During this period, however, the bikini was not without controversy. The Vatican declared it as 'sinful' and the bikini was banned in Italy, Portugal and Spain as well as some US states. The American *Modern Girl Magazine* wrote in 1957: 'It is hardly necessary to waste words over the so-called bikini since it is inconceivable that any girl with tact and decency would ever wear such a thing.'[71] Versions were created in America to be a more 'acceptable' compromise, where none of the navel could be seen.

Therefore, Honey's wearing of a bikini in *Dr. No* heightens the sexualized female body beyond what was normally on display in society at the time. This costume works in one of two ways for the character's entrance: firstly, Honey is positioned as the epitome of sexualized femininity and unashamed to be so. Oliver Saillard has argued that the bikini works to promote 'the power of women and not the power of fashion', and it contributed to the sexual revolution dominating society in the early 1960s.[72] Secondly, this costume reflects the power of her character. Honey is alone as she emerges in her bikini which works initially to portray her as the weaker sex. Based on Laura Mulvey's theory of 'to-be-looked-at-ness', Chapman argues that 'women in the Bond films were there purely for decoration is reinforced in so much as Andress [. . .] was dubbed; denied her own voice, the girl is, literally, reduced to the object only to be looked at'.[73] However, the inclusion of a weapon in Honey's webbing belt displays that she is capable of acts of violence and can look after herself: she threatens Bond with the knife on the beach after he frightens her. In a later scene, Honey informs Bond that she is an orphan whose marine zoologist father cared for her before his mysterious death which Honey attributes to Dr. No.

In this scene, she displays a shrewd intelligence and encyclopaedic knowledge, revealing to Bond that she revenged a man who raped her by killing him, slowly and painfully, via a bite from a black widow spider. Due to the image of Honey in her bikini, sales of the item rose after *Dr. No* was released.[74] Andress has also explained how it assisted her future career and economic independence stating: 'This bikini made me into a success. As a result of starring in *Dr. No* as the first "Bond girl" I was given the freedom to take my pick of future roles and to become financially independent.'[75] Andress's performance as Honey, therefore, is presented in the film in a similar way in terms of costume to that of the film's villain Dr. No. Honey becomes synonymous with the way in which 'Bond girls' of the 1960s are presented and how they reflect a certain socio-political type. Chapman notes that the general perception of the 'Bond girls' is that they are two-dimensional: 'Women are commodities, to be consumed by Bond and then discarded, often meeting grisly ends [...] The Bond starlets represented a *Playboy* male-fantasy image of female sexuality: well-scrubbed, big-breasted, long-haired and sexually available.'[76] This is a rather sweeping generalization, given the portrayal of Tatiana Romanova (Daniela Bianchi) in *From Russia With Love*, as well as Tilly Masterson (Tania Mallet) and Pussy Galore (Honor Blackman) in *Goldfinger*, and arguably Tracy di Vincenzo (Diana Rigg) in *On Her Majesty's Secret Service*, who does not appear as 'sexually available' in the traditional sense of the term, albeit while wearing a padded *brassière* to enhance her cleavage.

Reception

In terms of the critical reception for *Dr. No*, the film received mixed reviews, generally split between two distinct camps. The larger camp generally felt that the film was good entertainment and likely to be successful as the first of a series of Bond films, however there was a significant camp who believed the film was 'grotesque' and lacked the talented direction of either Alfred Hitchcock or Fritz Lang.[77] Most believed Connery to be well cast in the role of Bond, however some were confused as to where his accent came from: quite a few suggested that Connery was either American, Irish, or a mixture of both. A few reviewers specifically mentioned, or made passing reference to, Connery's Sinclair-tailored suits, although often inaccurately claimed that the suits were tailored by a Savile Row firm. Margaret Hinxman reviewed: 'While deploring its sadism, its ethics and its amorality, I admit I enjoyed every depraved and dazzling moment of it [...] Sean Connery is a flawless choice for the snob hero Bond: virile, tough, perfectly tailored and faultlessly knowing about everything from dry vodka Martinis to *chemin de fer*.'[78] Ernest Betts did not like the film: 'I expected something better than this', though referred to his suits as 'immaculate' with 'his special gun hitched to special braces'.[79] Betts also quipped that Andress 'wears so little she ought to be called Andrea Undress'. Alexander Walker was more positive, and on Connery wrote: 'this is Ian Fleming's Secret Serviceman James Bond down to the 60-guinea tailor's label.'[80] Although Thomas Wiseman found it 'disturbing that we should be offered as a hero – as someone we are supposed to admire – a man whose methods and morals are indistinguishable from those of the villain', he nonetheless thought of Connery: 'In the first James Bond film *Dr. No*, Ian Fleming's famous and *tres chic* Special Agent 007 (even his shoulder-holster is specially tailored for him in Savile Row) is played by Mr. Sean Connery. He is a strapping fellow who manages the mayhem very nicely.'[81] The *Motion Picture Herald* believed of Connery: 'The search for the exciting figure who was designed to set masculine pulses hammering and feminine hearts throbbing ended with the selection of Sean Connery, youngish British actor with a strong background in films and television, who succeeds in fitting the James Bond specifications with approximately the precision of a hand in the proverbial glove.'[82] Not everyone was enthralled with Connery's suits in his Bond films, however. In perhaps one of the earliest cases of what is termed in this book as 'tailoring wars', the Italian tailor Domenico Caraceni believed that while Fleming had dressed Bond correctly, the film producers had not:

> There is a great difference between the clothes of Sean Connery in the films and those of James Bond in the novels. In the films the secret agent is dressed with a hint of vulgarity in the American style. In the novels, apart from the inadmissible lapse of sandals with a blue suit and the raincoat for driving, Bond is dressed very correctly without display [...] I will go further: [in the novels] that black-and-white suit, probably from Donegal, with dark-blue shirt, shows a fine appreciation of modern fashion, and indubitably an elegant idea. Bond's manner of dressing might appear doubtful to a certain Italian taste: but, taking into account the Anglo-Saxon taste and his particular form of activity, he is absolutely faultless.[83]

Nonetheless, most were impressed with Connery and his suits, with the *News of the World* putting it most succinctly when stating, albeit inaccurately: 'Sean Connery fits Fleming's hero like a Savile Row suit.'[84] The costumes from *Dr. No* have proved irresistible to collectors: in 2001, for example, Andress's bikini sold for £41,125.[85] Not a bad return for £6.

Notes

1   Albert R. Broccoli with Donald Zec, *When the Snow Melts: The Autobiography of Cubby Broccoli* (London and Basingstoke: Boxtree, 1998), 126.

2   Ibid., 165.

3 Ibid., 168. The perception that Fleming's Bond was upper-class, or indeed wore Savile Row suits is a myth.

4 Ibid., 170.

5 *Inside Dr. No*, documentary, directed by John Cork (USA: MGM Home Entertainment, 2000).

6 Fleming to Blanche Blackwell, 25 October 1961, published in Fergus Fleming (ed.), *The Man with the Golden Typewriter: Ian Fleming's James Bond Letters* (London and New York: Bloomsbury Publishing, 2015), 257.

7 Broccoli with Zec, 169.

8 Ibid., 170.

9 *Inside Dr. No*.

10 Steven Jay Rubin, *The James Bond Films: A Behind the Scenes History* (London: Talisman Books, 1981), 17.

11 *Inside Dr. No*.

12 'Sinclair signs for Burton's: Another multiple seeks the Savile Row image', *Tailor & Cutter*, 26 March 1965, 413.

13 Natalie Watson interviewed by the author, 26 November 2018. All quotations from Watson that are included in the monograph were taken from this interview.

14 Thank you to Natalie Watson for providing the author with an image of Sean Connery's measurements taken by Anthony Sinclair in late 1961/early 1962 for Eon Productions, and to Del Smith for helping the author to interpret them.

15 Matt Spaiser, 'A Dark Grey Flannel Suit in Jamaica in *Dr. No*', *The Suits of James Bond*, 18 June 2018, www.bondsuits.com/dark-grey-flannel-suit-jamaica-dr-no/ (accessed 11 January 2019).

16 Del Smith, interviewed by the author, 14 November 2019. All quotations from Smith included in the monograph were taken from this interview.

17 Fleming to Michael Howard, 16 August 1961, in Fergus Fleming, 290.

18 Henry Chancellor, *James Bond: The Man and His World* (London: John Murray, 2005), 58.

19 *Inside Dr. No*.

20 Ibid.

21 Anne Hollander, *Sex and Suits: The Evolution of Modern Dress* (New York: Alfred A. Knoff, 1995), 110.

22 Ibid., 54.

23 Spaiser, 18 June 2018.

24 Hollander, 110.

25 Christie's, 'Lot 266: *Dr. No*, 1962', *James Bond 007*, 17 September 1998, www.christies. com/lotfinder/lot/dr-no-1962-1290251-details.aspx?from=salesummery&intObjectID =1290251&sid=71c65a83-6fda-4200-9c3b-fca4747b93e2 (accessed 17 January 2019).

26 *Dr. No* Special Edition, *Cinema Retro* 4, no. 9 (December 2012), 25.

27 Sullivan, *Dressed to Kill*, 174.

28 *Inside Dr. No*.

29 Ibid.

30 Bronwen Cosgrave, 'Agent of Style: James Bond and Turnbull & Asser', *turnbullandasser*, 1 October 2014, http://turnbullandasser.co.uk/agent-of-style-james-bond-and-turnbull-asser (accessed 11 January 2019).

31 With thanks to Mary and Sam Foster for assisting the author with this Appendix and confirming which films Frank Foster worked on and which actors he produced shirts and other costumes for.

32 'Gentle Author', 'Frank Foster: Shirtmaker to the stars', *Spitalfields Life*, 19 November 2015, https://spitalfieldslife.com/2015/11/19/frank-foster-shirt-maker/ (accessed 27 June 2020).

33 Ibid.

34 Tony Miles, 'Frank put his shirt on – SHIRTS!' *Daily Mirror*, 17 April 1957, 2.

35 'Master chemisier in love with shirts', *Savile Row Style Magazine*, Winter 2010, https://savilerow-style.com/archive/issue021/style06.htm (accessed 27 June 2020).

36 Elspeth Grant, 'On Films: The Best for Bond and Bette', *Tatler*, 2 October 1963, 62.

37 Broccoli with Zec, 171.

38 Both James Chapman and Charles Drazin offer an in-depth analysis of Film Finances contribution towards the production of *Dr. No* in Chapman, 'The Trouble with Harry: The Difficult Relationship of Harry Saltzman and Film Finances', *Historical Journal of Film, Radio and Television* 34, no. 1 (March 2014), 43–71, and Drazin, *A Bond for Bond: Film Finances and Dr. No* (London: Film Finances Limited, 2011).

39 Film Finances Archive (FFA), Realized Film Box 328: *Dr. No* Production Budget, n.d.

40 Ibid.: John Croydon to Robert Garrett, 11 December 1961.

41 Cosgrave, 'Golden Style', in Cosgrave, Lindy Hemming and Neil McConnon (eds), *Designing 007: 50 Years of Bond Style* (London: Barbican International Enterprises, 2012), 11.

42 Ibid.

43 Figure based on calculating the items tailored by Anthony Sinclair, including a dinner suit, an overcoat, three lounge suits and a blazer and trousers, of which two of each item would have been made for Connery (£720) and two duplicate lounge suits made for Bob Simmons (£120).

44 FFA: Realized Film Box 328: Call Sheet no. 16, 2 February 1962 and Call Sheet no. 21, 8 February 1962.

45 'Commentary', *Dr. No*, DVD, directed by Terence Young (1962; UK and USA: MGM Home Entertainment, 2000).

46 '*Dr. No* Special Edition', 123.

47 Paul Duncan (ed.), *The James Bond Archives* (London: Taschen, 2015), 38.

48 Christie's, 'Lot 291: *Dr. No*, 1962', *James Bond*, 14 February 2001, www.christies.com/lotfinder/Lot/dr-no-1962-1992074-details.aspx (accessed 12 January 2019).

49 Chris Hastings and Laura Elvin, 'For her thighs only: Iconic belt used to dress sultry Ms Andress in first Bond film *Dr. No* belonged to Navy sailor . . .', *Mail on Sunday*, 30 June 2018, www.dailymail.co.uk/news/article-5904859/The-belt-used-dress-Ms-Andress-reveals-Navy-officer.html (accessed 12 January 2019).

50 FFA: Realized Film Box 328: Harry Saltzman to Garrett, 18 February 1962.

51 'Commentary', *Dr. No.*

52 Christie's, 'Lot 280: *Dr. No*, 1962', *James Bond*, 14 February 2001, 140.

53 Ibid.

54 FFA: Realized Film Box 328: *Dr. No* Summary of Location Shooting, n.d.

55 Ibid.: Call Sheet no. 5, 2 March 1962.

56 British Film Institute (BFI), S18574: Richard Maibaum, Wolf Mankowitz and J. M. Harwood, *Dr. No*, fifth draft screenplay, 8 January 1962, 9a–10.

57 Tim Masters, 'James Bond: How *Dr. No*'s Eunice Gayson made film history', *BBC News*, 1 October 2012, www.bbc.co.uk/news/entertainment-arts-19756033 (accessed 12 January 2019).

58 Eunice Gayson with Andrew Boyle and Gareth Owen, *The First Lady of Bond* (Cambridge: Signum Books, 2012), 149.

59 FFA, Realized Film Box 328: Daily Progress Report, nos. 5, 6, 9, 10, 11, 12, 14, 15; 5–16 March 1962.

60 FFA: Realized Film Box 328: Final cost of production of *Dr. No*, 31 December 1962.

61 Norman, *Dressed to Kill*, 117.

62 Hollander, 8.

63 BFI, S18574: 28.

64 Ibid.

65 Fleming, *Dr. No* (1958; London: Penguin Books, 2009), 48.

66 BFI, S18574: 41.

67 Ibid., 111.

68 James Chapman, *Licence to Thrill: A Cultural History of the James Bond Films*, 2nd edn (London: I.B. Tauris, 2007), 66.

69 BFI, S18574: 78.

70 Christie's, 'Lot 291: *Dr. No*, 1962'.

71 *Modern Girl Magazine* (c. 1957), quoted in Audrey Stanton, 'The scandalous history of the bikini', *The Good Trade*, www.thegoodtrade.com/features/history-of-the-bikini (accessed 27 June 2020).

72 Kathryn Westcott, 'The bikini: Not a brief affair', *BBC News*, http://news.bbc.co.uk/1/hi/in_depth/5130460.stm (accessed 27 June 2020).

73 Chapman, *Licence to Thrill*, 66.

74 Stephanie Pedersen, *Bra: A Thousand Years of Style, Support and Seduction* (Newton Abbot: David and Charles, 2004), 69.

75 Will Bennett, 'Former Bond girl to sell *Dr. No* bikini, *Telegraph*, 12 January 2001, www.telegraph.co.uk/news/uknews/1314376/Former-Bond-girl-to-sell-Dr-No-bikini.html (accessed 17 January 2019).

76 Chapman, *Licence to Thrill*, 95.

77 *Monthly Film Bulletin*, 29/345, October 1962, 136; *Spectator*, 12 October 1962.

78 Margaret Hinxman, 'New Films: *Dr. No*', *Daily Herald*, 6 October 1962.

79 Ernest Betts, 'Oh No! This is NOT the way to make a good thriller', *People*, 7 October 1962.

80 Alexander Walker, 'So many beauties in one picture: They're all for James Bond, of course', *Evening Standard*, 4 October 1962.

81 Thomas Wiseman, 'Is Mr. Bond your idea of a hero?', *Sunday Express*, 7 October 1962.

82 '*Dr. No*', *Motion Picture Herald*, 3 April 1963.

83 Lietta Tornabuoni, 'A popular phenomenon', in Oreste Del Buono and Umberto Eco (eds), *The Bond Affair* (London: Macdonald, 1966), 33.

84 'Girls, Mayhem and Mr. Bond', *News of the World*, 7 October 1962.

85 Christie's, 'Lot 291: *Dr. No*, 1962'.

2 'FITTING FLEMING'S HERO': SEAN CONNERY (1963–67)

By the time that *Dr. No* was released, Broccoli and Saltzman were already planning the next Bond film, which they had decided would be adapted from Fleming's novel *From Russia With Love*. For this film, the budget doubled and was reportedly $1.9 million (£678,000).[1] Therefore, this allowed for more money to be allocated to wardrobe staff as well as costume and wigs. Unlike Tessa Prendergast's limited contribution as the 'costume designer' for *Dr. No*, Jocelyn Rickards was employed as the costume designer for *From Russia With Love* and was much more involved in designing the costumes for the female wardrobe, notably Tatiana Romanova (Daniela Bianchi) and Rosa Klebb (Lotte Lenya). In terms of salary, Rickards was paid £1,120, Eileen Sullivan, returning as the wardrobe mistress, £1,298, and Ernie Farrer £1,358 as the wardrobe master.[2] As with *Dr. No*, these costs highlight the gender pay difference between the male and female crew members working on wardrobe.

Sue Harper believes that Rickards 'was the most interesting newcomer' working in British costume design over the 1960s, and had 'the most impressive portfolio [...] whose connections with the intellectual avant-garde were very productive. Rickards instinctively understood artistic innovation. She was primarily an interpreter of the inner actor.'[3] Rickards herself explained that she liked to 'work with directors with whom she had an immediate rapport and chose her projects on that basis.'[4] Harper notes that as a costume designer, Rickards 'unusually trusted actresses' instinct for appropriate clothes.'[5] On designing costumes, Rickards outlined:

Designing clothes or costumes for films is not a self-serving device to make the audience stop and wonder at the beauty of your invention. It is rather a means of conveying by a visual signpost the background of each character. If clothes are well designed, they are probably unnoticeable, but should carry with them a number of messages, like what kind of school the character went to, what newspapers he or she reads, what political affiliation he has, what his sexual inclinations are, whether or not his financial position is secure – and if insecure whether or not he cares. All this saves valuable minutes of screen time by getting points across for the eyes rather than verbally.[6]

Rickards was employed on *From Russia With Love* due to previously working with Saltzman on *Look Back in Anger* and *The Entertainer*, recalling: 'I loved him, he was just divine. He was an engaging man [. . .] in those early days he was smashing.'[7] Rickards further explained:

> Harry Saltzman rang me one day and said: 'I'm doing an Ian Fleming film.' He'd done *Dr. No* which I'd seen and liked, and he said: 'I want you to do the costumes,' and I said: 'Harry, I haven't got a union ticket. They'll all go mad,' because it was being shot at Pinewood [Studios], and he said: 'Leave that to me. You just get on with the costumes and I'll get you a ticket as soon as there's no one on the books.' [. . .] And, well, he got me a ticket very quickly. He just rang everyday . . . I'd been trying before, to no avail, but within a week I had a ticket.[8]

Rickards joined the Association of Cinematograph Television and Allied Technicians (ACTT) on 26 March 1963 with a listed weekly pay rate of £50.[9] As a director, Rickards believed that Terence Young was 'extremely good, sort of very thoughtful director. He worked it out amazingly and I think that might be why it [*From Russia With Love*] stands up so well,' though Rickards admitted that she preferred *Dr. No* as a film.[10]

As with *Dr. No*, Anthony Sinclair tailored Connery's suits for *From Russia With Love*, and continued to do so for all of Connery's Eon Productions Bond films. Connery was afforded more tailored costumes in this film: he wears seven lounge suits, one dinner suit and one coat. The seven lounge suits alone in *From Russia With Love* would have cost around £960 ($2,600) presuming that two of each of the suits were made. John Cork explains that the Turnbull & Asser shirts for *From Russia With Love* cost $30 (£10) each.[11]

In the pre-title sequence, 'Bond' is seen in a midnight blue shawl collar dinner suit similar to the one he wears for his introductory scene in *Dr. No*. This suit has narrower lapels than the *Dr. No* dinner jacket, and thus appears more modern and in-line with tailoring of the 1960s. The bowtie that Bond wears is slightly different to the one worn in *Dr. No*, as noted by Spaiser: it remains the narrow standard batwing shape, although the one worn here has straight ends.[12] The use of a similar dinner jacket, albeit with slight differences, works to support the narrative of the opening scene and hints to the viewer that the wearer is not the 'real' Bond, but a stand-in for a SPECTRE training exercise. Costume in this scene works to define the character of Bond. It conforms to what both the audience and his enemies expect Bond to be dressed in, setting a template for later films.

The 'real' Bond is first viewed in *From Russia With Love* during a riverside picnic scene with Sylvia Trench (Eunice Gayson). Bond is attired in the most casual wear he appears in throughout the film: a loose cotton shirt with a large indigo and gingham check pattern and pale blue polyester swimming trunks. This costume works in direct visual irony with the scene that follows, when he is called for a meeting in M's office. This is the first time in the Bond films when the character wears a monochrome dark navy suit. It is most likely made from worsted flannel and is cut in the typical Sinclair style. Q (Desmond Llewellyn) is introduced here, and he provides Bond with a 'smart piece of equipment': a black leather attaché briefcase that includes twenty rounds of ammunition, a flat throwing knife and AR7 folding snipers' rifle, fifty gold sovereigns, and a teargas cartridge disguised as talcum powder. This briefcase, as with other stylish gadgets introduced in this film, begin the reoccurring theme of 'fashionable' weapons in future Bond films. The briefcase works in direct contrast to the weapons hidden in the clothing of the villainous henchmen and women in the film.

When Bond arrives in Istanbul, he is wearing a charcoal grey dupioni silk suit with a pale blue shirt and navy grenadine tie. It is also this scene in which Blofeld's henchman, Red Grant (Robert Shaw), spies on Bond outside of the airport. Grant wears the same suit throughout the film. In contrast to Bond, Grant's suit is made from heavier and more traditional cloth in grey and brown stripes with white pinstripes in a brown windowpane pattern. Whereas Bond's suit jackets are mostly fastened with two buttons, Grant's jacket includes three. The cufflinks Grant wears attach him to his association with SPECTRE and are square with a silver case and purple stone centre. The trousers are tailored the same as Bond's with double-forward pleats which taper down towards the ankles and finish with cuffed bottoms. Bond wears the first of his Glen Urquhart check lounge suits on visiting Ali Kerim Bey (Pedro Armendáriz) after the latter's office has been destroyed. On accompanying Kerim Bey to the gypsy camp, Bond wears a charcoal grey flannel suit. When Bond meets Tatiana on the boat to obtain information from her about the Lektor cryptographic device, he wears his second Glen Urquhart suit. Aboard the Orient Express, Bond and Tatiana purport to be husband and wife under the pseudonym of 'Mr. and Mrs. Somerset'. As Somerset, Bond wears a charcoal grey sharkskin suit. Following the Orient Express scenes when Bond and Tatiana escape in a boat, Bond wears a short navy wool coat and black peaked cap with a gold anchor motif on the front that he has acquired from a SPECTRE agent who had been waiting for Grant. Bond's costume references the naval background afforded to the character by Fleming in his novels. In the film's final scenes when Bond and Tatiana are staying in a Venetian hotel, Bond is dressed in a heavy navy flannel chalk-stripe suit. It is more old-fashioned in terms of style than Bond's other suits in this film although it also appears more relaxed and less structured in its tailoring.

Following the opening credits, the head of SPECTRE, Ernst Stavro Blofeld (Anthony Dawson), who is credited only as '?', is viewed in a similar illusion to that of

Connery's Bond in *Dr. No*: from a variety of camera angles that only reveals parts of his costume and never his face.[13] From what can be viewed, Blofeld is dressed in a black two-piece suit with four buttons on the sleeve cuffs and a folded white pocket square in the breast pocket as he strokes his white Persian cat. He wears a white shirt with gold diamond-shaped cufflinks and a black grenadine tie. The script notes in this scene that Blofeld is to wear 'a distinctive ring' on his hand which includes the SPECTRE symbol.[14] Rosa Klebb is also introduced in this scene. Rickards designed a masculine olive green two-piece suit for the character which lends its design features and shape to that of the Mao suit, which would be adopted in *You Only Live Twice* and become synonymous with Blofeld's character in later Bond films. According to John Cork, Lenya's costumes were originally to be made with padding as the actress weighed around 100 pounds, however Lenya 'baulked at the idea, saying that she could play the part in such a way that she would not look weak or small.'[15]

The Chinese Mao tunic suit is a descendant of the Eastern tunic with Mandarin collar, although combines the jacket with Western styles that can be traced back to the styles of the British Army uniforms during World War I and the American Army uniforms during the Spanish–American Philippine War. It was an attempt in 1949 to provide a Chinese counterpart to the Western business suit and is known in China as the *Zhongshan* suit. It is named after Dr Sun Yat-sen (Mandarin translation: Sun Zhongshan) who, as the founder of the Republic of China, wanted to create a form of national dress and advocated the wearing of functional clothes. 'Mao' is a Western term for the suit so-called after Mao Zedong, the Chinese leader who had an affinity for wearing them in public and arguably contributed to the perception in the West that they were representative of the Chinese Communist regime. The traditional Mao suit differs from the Nehru jacket in that it does not have a Mandarin collar and instead has a turndown collar and four flapped patch pockets with one inner pocket. Klebb's feminized version is of a similar cut, however it has no collar and her lilac sheer silk blouse is visible underneath. It has four large fabric-covered buttons. She wears the jacket with a knee-length pleated skirt and brown leather court shoes.

During Klebb's meeting with Tatiana, Klebb's costume here is comparable with her description in the novel: 'A toad-like figure in an olive green uniform which bore the single red ribbon of the Order of Lenin came into the room.'[16] She wears a khaki Russian military uniform so as to convince Tatiana that she is still an agent working for SMERSH, deluding the latter into seducing Bond. With this costume, Klebb wears thick black circular spectacles to adopt the illusion of a toad as described by Fleming. On the Russian uniform, Rickards recalled:

> I went into Berman's and said: '[Lenya's playing a] KGB Colonel and I want a really smart uniform.' And there was a man called Tiny [Nicholls] in charge of military costumes and he said: 'Oh, I can't make one for you,' and produced such a moody-looking thing, I walked around the corner and said to Monty

[Berman]: 'Look, she's coming from America. You know her name, I know her name, she's someone to be reckoned with. I wouldn't put her in that rubbish that Tiny's put out for me and he refused to make.'[17]

On being asked why Nicholls wouldn't make the Russian uniform, Rickards believed: 'He was just being obstinate. Monty was furious [...] and eventually sacked him over this.'[18] Ironically, given Rickards's complaint, Nicholls was later employed as the wardrobe master on *The Man with the Golden Gun* and *For Your Eyes Only*, and as the costume supervisor for *Octopussy*, *A View to a Kill* and *The Living Daylights*.

Tatiana was dressed conservatively by Rickards, which reflects her professional status as working for the Russian government. On Bianchi, Rickards believes that she was: 'Pretty as a flower. She was so shy that she couldn't even bear to strip for a fitting.'[19] The script directs the approach towards clothing Tatiana: 'Her simple business apparel somehow looks smart and attractive.'[20] Arguably, Tatiana reflects a certain type of 'Bond girl' in that they dress in a slightly masculine and assertive fashion with little make-up, for example Tilly Masterson (Tania Mallet) and Pussy Galore (Honor Blackman) in *Goldfinger*. In Tatiana's first scene, she wears a tawny brown suit with a gold weave. The jacket has wide notched lapels and is hip-length, with a four gold button fastening and one gold button on the cuff. With the jacket she wears a knee-length skirt. Beneath the jacket, Tatiana wears a white sheer silk blouse with spread collar, her *brassière* just visible beneath the blouse fabric. This conveniently assists the narrative construct in this scene that positions Klebb as having a lesbian sexuality when she attempts to flirt with Tatiana. The subtle gesturing to Klebb's lesbianism is hinted at later in the film, when Klebb watches Bond and Tatiana in bed through a two-way mirror heightening the voyeuristic gaze that is a common theme throughout the Bond films.

The Orient Express scenes are interesting in the ways that the costumes assist in developing character and the continuation of narrative, including a 'fashion show' by Tatiana (Figure 2.1). The script also builds upon the tailor-based humour which began with *Dr. No*, outlining:

223. INT. COMPARTMENT 6. TATIANA
Opening door. BOND comes in, closes it and locks it.

TATIANA
So we are really on the train together – !

BOND
With a lovely four-day honeymoon before us.

TATIANA
(reproachfully)

Honeymoon! I have nothing to wear –

BOND
(taking her black ribbon out of his pocket,
handing it to her)
Your trousseau –

TATIANA
James!

He smiles, turns around, goes into Compartment 6/7, comes back a moment later with another suitcase, sets it down, opens it. She looks at the contents, gasps. It is packed with obviously expensive women's apparel. She throws her arms around him delightfully.[21]

In the scene that follows, Tatiana has changed from her conservative suit into a revealing pale blue chiffon nightgown with white embroidered lace appliquéd onto the bust and sleeves. It has a blue chiffon overskirt that is parted in the centre and is cut in an empire line with a back yoke and six small fabric-covered buttons. Based on Bianchi's shyness, Rickards devised rubber nipple covers to shield the actress's modesty: 'Harry [Saltzman] came to me in a state of high excitement after watching rushes of one love scene between her and Sean. "Jocelyn, it's not true what you say about Daniella. She is showing her nipples." I showed him the blue chiffon nightdress she'd worn and said, "look, all rubber".'[22] The script includes verbal humour in reference to her costume:

FIGURE 2.1 Tatiana Romanova's 'fashion show' in *From Russia With Love*. Directed by Terence Young © Eon Productions/United Artists 1963. All rights reserved.

226. INT. COMPARTMENT 6. TATIANA. BOND

TATIANA is 'modelling' her new wardrobe for him. He watches her, smiling.

TATIANA
I will wear this in Piccadilly.

BOND
You won't. They've got some new laws there now.[23]

Bond then goes with Kerim Bey to capture Benz (Peter Bayliss), a Soviet security officer who followed them onto the train after recognizing Tatiana. On leaving the compartment, Bond says to Tatiana: 'Excuse us, Tania. We'll continue the fashion show later.' Entering Benz's compartment, Bond takes the navy silk pocket square from the breast pocket of Benz's jacket and stuffs it in his mouth. As Kerim Bey threatens Benz with a gun, Bond pulls the latter's suit jacket down over his shoulders and arms from behind to prevent him from escaping. Benz is dressed in a poorly-fitted light grey lounge suit with dark grey chalk stripes and two jetted pockets. With this, he wears a cream shirt fastened with a black worsted tie. As Bond exits the compartment, he states to Kerim Bey: 'Not mad about his tailor, are you?', an improvised line which was not included in the script. On re-entering his compartment, Tatiana has changed her clothes, continuing with the 'fashion show'. Here, she wears a blue chiffon knee-length dress with spaghetti straps and ruched decoration around the cleavage. The dress is again cut in an empire-line with a ribbon tie under the bust which is knotted on the left-hand side and her hair is tied up with a blue hair ribbon. The dialogue follows:

Tatiana   You like it?

Bond   Yes. It does rather suit you.

Tatiana   I will save everything else for England.

Bond   Er, it *is* four o' clock, you know.

Tatiana   This is not *kulturny* [cultured] in the afternoon? Even on a honeymoon? Then I will . . . take it off.

Bond   I think we're talking at cross purposes again.

Similar to Bond's line about Benz's tailor, this dialogue works as a signifier to the visual humour employed by costume in Bond films.

It is in Venice after tracking down Bond and Tatiana that Klebb, costumed in a grey dress with a white apron to masquerade as a hotel maid, makes use of the first costume-based weapon in a Bond film, namely the poison-tipped, flick-knife shoes. They were adapted from the poisoned knitting needles that Klebb attempts to kill Bond with at the end of Fleming's novel, and are described in the following way in the script: 'CAMERA ZOOMS IN TO KLEBB'S FEET as she presses button on one shoe with toe of other to slide blade out.'[24] The shoes, designed by the film's art director, Syd Cain, are black leather brogues that include a two-inch blade that flicks out from the capped toe. Luxford realized Cain's design, and 'devised a simple, spring-loaded mechanism in the sole of the shoe. Klebb simply had to click her heels to press a pin that set the dagger into action.'[25] As with Bond's attaché briefcase, the 'costume weapon' would be continued in *Goldfinger*.

Goldfinger (1964)

The third James Bond film, *Goldfinger*, went into production in March 1964. James Chapman explains that *From Russia With Love* was chosen to 'consolidate Bond's popularity in Europe', whereas *Goldfinger* 'represented a strategy whereby the producers hoped to establish Bond in the American market'.[26] The film was budgeted at £700,000 ($1.9 million).[27] However, others dispute this amount, and it has been suggested that *Goldfinger* cost around $3 million (£1.1 million), nearly the cost of *Dr. No* and *From Russia With Love* combined.[28] Young began pre-production work on *Goldfinger*, however he decided to direct *The Amorous Adventures of Moll Flanders* (1965) instead, and so Guy Hamilton was hired to direct *Goldfinger*. It is debateable how much agency Hamilton had over the costume decisions for *Goldfinger*. Ken Adam, who had returned to design the sets for *Goldfinger*, was not impressed with the choice of director, writing privately to Stanley Kubrick in August 1964 after the film's completion:

> I also miss the stimulus of your company, though it could be trying at times. No stimulus from Guy Hamilton, and although I have known him for years, very little contact. A strange, conflicted individual, without any visual concept. If the film [*Goldfinger*] will be good, which I hope it will be, it must be due to the peculiar chemistry associated with Bond, the sort of 20th Century spectacular.[29]

Eon Productions' press release stated that after starring in *Woman of Straw* (1964) and *Marnie* (1964), Connery was 'back at his dapper best as Fleming's sartorially-elegant British agent'.[30] Honor Blackman, whose previous credits included playing Cathy Gale in *The Avengers*, was cast in the lead female role of Pussy Galore, and German actor Gert Fröbe was cast as the film's titular villain. Changes to the wardrobe crew also occurred with *Goldfinger*: Eileen Sullivan returned as the wardrobe mistress, but John Hilling replaced Ernie Farrer as the wardrobe master. A wardrobe supervisor was hired for the first time on a Bond film: Elsa Fennell.

No costume designer is credited in the film, however a small amount of costume concepts survive that were designed by Beatrice 'Bumble' Dawson, using black felt tip, watercolour and metallic gold paint on fine paper, for Pussy Galore, Pussy Galore's Flying Circus and Mei-Lei (Mai Ling).[31] Dawson began her film career during the Second World War by designing the jewellery for *Caesar and Cleopatra* (1945), and at the same time designed the female wardrobe for the theatre play *The Duchess of Malfi* (1945). Following this, the designer worked on both British and Hollywood-financed productions, including as the dress designer for *London Belongs to Me* (1948). Her costume designs for *The Pickwick Papers* (1952) received an Academy Award nomination for 'Best Costume Design – Black and White' in 1956, and Dawson subsequently worked on *Espresso Bongo* (1959), *The Challenge* (1960), *The L-Shaped Room* (1962) and *The Servant* (1963). On designing costumes, Dawson believed that: 'You must start with a colour scheme and stick to it [...] in films all the dresses must look right together, no matter how they are combined in groups.'[32] Meg Simmonds explains that 'Bumble Dawson incorporated the gold theme into many of the film's costumes including a gold tuxedo for Goldfinger and a gold waistcoat for Pussy Galore. Her costume concepts are the oldest in the Eon Productions Archive.'[33] Harper observes that during the 1950s, Dawson's designs were 'audacious and expressive', of which her approach to *Trottie True* (1948) 'took real risks with colour and historical verisimilitude'.[34] By the 1960s, Dawson 'had developed a precise design manner' that was particularly witty.[35] This is demonstrated by her spiky and determined staccato sketches provided for *Goldfinger* using flamboyant two-tone colours rendered in felt-tip pen. Frank Foster realized Dawson's designs for the Flying Circus pilots.

Connery wears eight Sinclair-tailored suits in the film, however through his close analysis of the suit structure and fabric, Spaiser argues convincingly that six out of the eight tailored outfits were made for Connery in *Woman of Straw*, which had been shot before *Goldfinger* in 1963.[36] The suits worn by Connery in both films include the ivory dinner jacket and black trousers, a brown houndstooth suit (two-piece in *Woman of Straw* and with a waistcoat in *Goldfinger*), a blue herringbone flannel suit (three-piece in *Woman of Straw* and two-piece in *Goldfinger*), a barleycorn hacking jacket and cavalry twill trousers (three-piece in *Woman of Straw* and two-piece in *Goldfinger*), a grey Prince of Wales glen check suit (two-piece in *Woman of Straw* and three-piece in *Goldfinger*) and a charcoal grey three-piece suit. The suits specifically tailored for Connery in *Goldfinger* included a notched-lapel black dinner jacket and a dark brown two-piece suit with shadow stripes. If it is indeed the case that six out of eight suits were reused for *Goldfinger*, this would have significantly reduced the costume costs normally allocated to Connery's outfits, allowing for more money to be spent elsewhere on costumes for other characters. It is notable that Goldfinger, for example, has more costume changes than villains in previous Bond films, and Oddjob's (Harold Sakata) costume is a tailored black lounge jacket, waistcoat and cashmere trousers, resplendent with a dangerous black bowler hat customized with a metal rim, similar to the 'costume weapon' of Klebb's shoe. The hat was designed by Adam. Three copies were made of the hat, realized by special effects designer John Stears.

The film includes a visually humorous pre-credit sequence in relation to costume: Hamilton believed that the scene was 'a wonderful piece of nonsense. I mean, where you can go swimming with a seagull on top of your head and you can unzip your suit and have a white tuxedo underneath?'[37] Bond initially wears a black frogman's wetsuit as he breaks into the Ramirez Export Company. As he leaves, Bond literally transforms as he nonchalantly removes the wetsuit to reveal a dinner suit, with ivory jacket complete with red carnation. As Peter Lamont, the film's draughtsman, recalled: 'John Hilling had to get Sean out of that supposed wet suit which was really a nylon suit made to look like a wetsuit, so he could just unzip it and he had the evening dress underneath. It was a very popular shot that.'[38] This suit is particularly striking as it is the first time the audience views Bond dressed in an ivory jacket. Thus, the suit is positioned to be as iconic as Bond's midnight blue version that the character wears in *Dr. No* and *From Russia With Love*. The jacket includes peak lapels that are self-faced: typically, a black dinner jacket would have silk facings, not an ivory one. The jacket has mother-of-pearl buttons, is fastened with one button, and has four buttons on each sleeve cuff. Bond's trousers are midnight blue in colour. As with his previous dinner suits, Bond does not wear a cummerbund. His shirt is made of white cotton and includes a white satin stripe, and has a pleated front, spread collar and double cuffs. The batwing shaped bowtie is made from black satin. This costume demonstrates that Bond is a man with the confidence to bend the normal rules of style as well as Connery's ability into being able to make an unusual choice of suit look good. There is, however, one exception.

Though *Goldfinger* is the most fashion-promoting of the Bond films thus far, it is also appropriate to afford it the dubious accolade of allowing Bond's first fashion faux pas. It comes in the form of the towelled blue playsuit. In the script, the playsuit is described merely as 'combination robe-trousers' which a member of the wardrobe department interpreted as a playsuit.[39] Typically worn by women, Bond's playsuit effectively takes its shape from the jumpsuit albeit with short legs. It has a camp collar, a front zip fastening, and a belt attached at the back. Although the suit may be unbecoming when compared to the usual standard of costume that Bond is dressed in, it does however contribute to two recurring themes in Bond films: dress and undress, and the use of towelling fabric in costumes for the Bond films of the 1960s. Its blue colouring is of note here as this is a popular colour to dress Bond in due to his naval background. Though it is appropriate in this scene for the purposes of both theme and narrative, it has seemingly been lost at the back of Bond's wardrobe as this costume has not appeared in any Bond film since. It has, however, since been recreated by Orlebar Brown, aimed at fans of the franchise and retailing at £395 in 2019.

Making up for this faux pas, Bond later dresses in a particularly stylish three-piece suit in *Goldfinger* (Figure 2.2), previously worn by Connery in *Woman of Straw*. Spaiser believes that the suit is made of tropical-weight wool woven in a grey and white glen plaid known as 'Prince of Wales' check, where the fabric is

FIGURE 2.2 James Bond's three-piece 'Prince of Wales' check suit. *Goldfinger* directed by Guy Hamilton © Eon Productions/United Artists 1964.

woven in a 2x2 hopsack (basket) weave with a high number of ends and picks per square inch.[40] The trousers conform to the others worn by Connery in the Bond films, however this time the bottoms are plain-hemmed rather than cuffed. The waistcoat has six buttons, of which Bond only fastens five. Bond's tie is a navy silk knit with a square-cut bottom. In 2013, Matthew Priest writing for *Esquire* placed this suit second in his list of the 'greatest suits in films', the winner being Cary Grant's mid-grey glen check two-piece suit that he wore when performing as Roger Thornhill in Alfred Hitchcock's *North by Northwest* (1959). Grant's suit was supposedly tailored by the Savile Row firm Kilgour, although this is debated.[41]

It is *Goldfinger* which offers the most distinct literary adaptation in terms of costume in Fleming's novels, particularly in relation to Auric Goldfinger. Arguably the most lavishly costumed of the 1960s Bond villains, Goldfinger wears the most costumes of any villain in the Bond films during this decade. He is costumed with flair and panache, and all of his suits include the colour gold in a variety of colour tones and fabrics. Creatively, they are used to promote his character and his overwhelming desire and love for gold in every form. Elisabeth Ladenson describes Goldfinger as 'a walking tautology' that displays his overreaching powers of spreading gold through his dress and other characters' clothing in Fleming's novel.[42] This can be seen throughout the film from Goldfinger's entrance, which also coincides in the scene with Bond's playsuit. Goldfinger is dressed in a gold shot-silk shirt with a shawl collar that is made from white terrycloth below the collar's notch. It has short sleeves with a plain hem and is fastened with five widely-placed gold buttons. He wears gold shorts in the same fabric as the shirt and bright gold slip-on shoes. These items slightly differ from the description of Goldfinger's clothing for this scene in the script: '[Goldfinger] wears an incongruous yellow cap, finger-tip length gold terrycloth robe and gold sandals. With his majestic paunch he looks, except for a conspicuous hearing-aid in one ear, like a decadent Roman Emperor.'[43]

In the golf scene between Bond and Goldfinger, we can see how costume, Goldfinger's in particular, was adapted directly from Fleming's writing (Plate 2). For the film, Bond wears a wine-coloured Slazenger jumper with a light grey polo shirt underneath and charcoal wool trousers. Bond uses a red and white-coloured glove for his left hand which is placed in his trouser pocket when not in use. Although Connery's Bond doesn't necessarily fit Fleming's description in terms of dress, the film does choose to adapt Goldfinger's rather absurd and humorously described golf suit from the novel. Fleming explains in the novel that for golf 'people often wear bizarre clothes to the game', and Goldfinger's outfit is no exception:

> Everything matched in a blaze of rust-coloured tweed from the buttoned 'golfer's cap' centred on the huge, flaming red hair, to the brilliantly polished, almost orange shoes. The plus-four suit was too well cut and the plus-fours themselves had been pressed down the sides. The stockings were of a matching heather mixture and had green garter tabs. It was as if Goldfinger had gone to his tailor and said 'Dress me for golf – you know, like they wear in Scotland'.[44]

The golf scene promotes Goldfinger's malevolent golden aura in similar ways to that of the novel. Connery's costume here is reflective of 'Goldfinger affect', which Ladenson argues contributes to the yellowing of Bond's clothes in the novel.[45] Fleming describes Bond as changing in to a 'yellowing black and white hound's tooth suit' for the golf game.[46] The script describes Goldfinger's costume as: 'GOLDFINGER approaches the entrance of the shop, wearing yellow brogues, rust-coloured plus-fours (pressed down sides), matching tweed jacket and buttoned "golfers" cap.'[47] Goldfinger is costumed in the film as wearing a brown wool shawl-collared jacket with a notched narrow lapel, a one-button fastening and one back vent. The white shirt has a short and rounded point collar and is fastened with a silk grenadine tie with diagonal stripe detail in the colours of gold, light brown, dark brown and black. This is teamed with a gold wool cardigan. His matching brown trousers are calf-length, and look particularly ridiculous, to display his cream socks and brown leather Oxfords. Completing the look is a brown flat cap.

Later in this scene, there is a similar semantic fashion code between the novel and the film. As Goldfinger prepares to leave in his black and gold Phantom III 1937 Rolls-Royce, Bond appears wearing a tweed hacking jacket with a brown weave. Underneath the jacket, Bond wears an ecru shirt with double cuffs and a dark brown grenadine tie. These are worn with light brown, narrow-cut trousers woven in a cavalry twill weave. By way of comparison, Goldfinger wears a darker brown two-piece checked suit in this scene which is made from tweed cloth with a golden-brown base with checked black and green thread intersected with a red over-check. The jacket is worn with a yellow shirt that is fastened with a narrow dark brown satin-silk tie. Though Bond's suit is lighter than Goldfinger's in this scene, there is a form of mirroring and reflection here in terms of dress between the hero and the villain.

In Geneva, Goldfinger appears in his key costume: a shawl-collared dinner suit, described in the script as a 'gold smoking jacket'.[48] The *Gentlemen's Magazine of London* defines the smoking jacket as a 'kind of short *robe de chambre*, [made] of velvet, cashmere, plush, merino or printed flannel, lined with bright colours, ornamented with *brandebourgs*, olives or large buttons', and is a jacket traditionally worn after dinner.[49] Spaiser explains that the suit is 'made of a shiny silk dupioni in a two-tone dark brown and gold weave. The dark brown is in the warp and the gold is in the weft, which is easily visible in crosswise [weaves].'[50] This forms a fine pinstripe weave which creates sheen across the camera lens as Goldfinger moves about the set. The suit includes narrow gold silk lapels with a gold button fastening with two gold buttons on the cuffs. Underneath the jacket Goldfinger wears a white shirt fastened with gold buttons and a black batwing bowtie. The costume is completed with high-waisted black trousers.

On his Kentucky ranch, Goldfinger is dressed in a similar style to that of his previous suits, however there are subtle differences. Goldfinger wears a woollen brown jacket with lighter brown trousers with cuffed bottoms. The jacket has a shawl collar lapel with one notch, a two-button fastening and two jetted pockets. Underneath the jacket Goldfinger wears a woollen yellow waistcoat which includes the detail of wide red and white checks, and is tailored with a narrow lapel, two jetted pockets and six gold buttons. On his head he wears a yellow flat cap which matches the checks woven in the fabric of the waistcoat. This ensemble includes a narrow dark brown satin-silk tie and tawny leather gloves. In the Fort Knox scenes, Goldfinger begins by wearing a brown Chesterfield coat with wide notched lapels, one ticket pocket and two gold buttons on the cuff. During the US Army's attempt to retake Fort Knox, Goldfinger takes off his coat that reveals he is wearing a khaki green US Army jacket underneath. The theme of gold continues and Goldfinger is costumed in a gold shirt which is just visible beneath the jacket. By comparison, Bond wears a tailored suit in dark chocolate brown, with a subtle detail of closely spaced pinstripe in darker brown, again working to create mirroring between the villain and hero in *Goldfinger*. Bond's suit works in harmony with the surrounding gold when he is placed inside the Fort Knox vaults, which displays the effect that Goldfinger is having on Bond as per the novel. After thwarting Goldfinger's plan, Bond is dressed in his final suit, made from charcoal grey woollen flannel fabric, and this demonstrates a distancing from Goldfinger's malevolent aura through costume.

There are three 'Bond girls' present in *Goldfinger*, which would also form the approach of *You Only Live Twice*. Bond first meets Jill Masterson (Shirley Eaton), dressed in matching black satin-silk lingerie as she lies on a chaise longue covered in a blue towel. The script offers two suggestions of what Jill might wear. It was decided to go with the latter, in reference to Fleming's novel which describes Jill as being 'naked except for a black *brassière* and black silk briefs': 'She is almost naked except for the briefest of bikinis. (ALTERNATE SHOT in black bra and panties).'[51] Bond offers to take her for dinner, which transpires as taking her back to his hotel room. Bond initially wears light blue cotton pyjama bottoms with an elastic waistband which is tied with a white drawstring as he lies on the bed with Jill. She wears his matching pyjama top. As Bond goes to retrieve champagne from the fridge, he slips on a black and white nail-head silk dressing gown which has turnback cuffs and a shawl collar with black piping around the edge. It is hemmed below his knee and is tied at the waist with a belt in matching fabric. As Bond reaches into the fridge, he is attacked from behind. After Bond recovers, he discovers Goldfinger's creatively cruel assassination of Jill with her body painted gold in a visually stunning scene that is developed through fashion in terms of the film's post-production marketing strategy.

On Bond pursuing Goldfinger in Geneva in his battleship grey Aston Martin DB5, the viewer is introduced to the second 'Bond girl' in the film, Tilly Masterson, who is seeking revenge for the death of her sister Jill. Like Tatiana in *From Russia With Love*, Tilly is conservative in her dress and she wears a cream spread collar shirt with a thickly-knitted cream woollen cardigan. With this, she is costumed in a grey knee-length pencil skirt fastened with a square brown and gold leather belt and square-toed brown leather court shoes. Her hair is neatly tied with a brown chiffon scarf in a chignon. This costume works in direct contrast to her sister's attire in the film's opening scenes, and thus positions her as being on a mission. It also reflects Fleming's description of the character in the novel: 'She wore a white, rather masculine cut, heavy silk shirt. It was open at the neck, but it would button up to a narrow military collar [and] a very wide black stitched leather belt with double brass buckles [...] Her short skirt was charcoal-grey and pleated looking. Her shoes were expensive looking black sandals.'[52]

During Bond's flight to in Baltimore, the script includes a visual fashion joke when the co-pilot 'takes off her earphones [and] picks up a copy of *Vogue*'; the 'E' of the magazine's title can briefly be viewed in the film.[53] The quip relating to fashion and lifestyle magazines would be repeated in *On Her Majesty's Secret Service*. These scenes introduce the final 'Bond girl' in *Goldfinger*: Pussy Galore. Her costume is also reflective, as with the other characters, of Goldfinger's overarching influence and she is positioned as working for Goldfinger's operation through the running of her flying school. On the flight, Galore is dressed in a black crushed velvet trouser suit. The jacket includes narrow lapels and its sleeves are cut just above the wrists to reveal gold square turnback cuffs fastened with a gold metal cufflink. Galore wears a gold leatherette waistcoat underneath the jacket with a gold four-button fastening. She wears gold nail polish and black leather low-heeled boots.

On arrival at Goldfinger's ranch, Galore changes into a dark brown suede jacket with notched lapels and flapped pockets. It is fastened with three fabric buttons and Galore wears a long-sleeved brown polo-neck jumper underneath the jacket. With this, she wears light brown trousers that have a high-rise waist and brown leather ankle boots. When she sits drinking a mint julep cocktail with Goldfinger, he suggests that Galore 'change into something more suitable' to be more sexually appealing to Bond. For this, she changes into a lilac wrap-around long sleeve blouse and plum high-waisted trousers, a colour that reflects her distancing from Goldfinger and closeness to Bond in the scenes that follow. The blouse, made of sheer silk, is designed with a wide spread collar and square turnback cuffs with one gold cufflink. Galore's costume in this scene is easily her most effeminate. Her previous costumes reflect Fleming's description of her character in the novel, a lesbian with a capital L, of which her sexuality was defined after Galore was sexually abused by her uncle at the age of twelve.[54] The film avoids being as explicit as the novel, although she does briefly allude to her sexuality when she states to Bond: 'You can turn off the charm. I'm immune.' It is also in these scenes between Bond and Galore that costume is used as verbal humour as well as visual, with Bond asking: 'Where do you hide your gold knuckles in this outfit?' to which Galore replies: 'Oh, I never carry my weapons after business hours.' At the end of the film, Galore wears a similar costume to the one she has previously worn on Goldfinger's plane, however this time the suit is made of white silk. This works as a reference to her being 'seduced' in the barn of Goldfinger's ranch by Bond to become good, and her switching of allegiance from Goldfinger to Bond.

For the London premiere of the film, Charles de Temple designed a special piece of jewellery for Blackman to wear. As reported by the *Newcastle Journal*:

> A solid gold finger modelled from one of Miss Blackman's and valued at £10,000, has been made by American sculptor-jeweller, Charles de Temple, to commemorate the film. The model bears not only the fingerprints, but every wrinkle of the original. It is finished off with a swathe of diamonds around the bottom and a six-carat diamond swinging from one side.[55]

The producers were apparently impressed with de Temple's workmanship and he was later employed to design the wedding ring for *On Her Majesty's Secret Service*. As well as Blackman's jewellery at the premiere of *Goldfinger*, Eon Productions commissioned Furs Renée of London to create a lavish evening coat made of gold leather and trimmed with mink fur for Eaton to wear on a three-week publicity tour in America. The coat was knee-length with three-quarter length sleeves, lined in a checked gold *lamé*. It was worn again by Eaton at the premiere of *Tomorrow Never Dies*.

Thunderball (1965)

Directed by Young, *Thunderball* was budgeted at $5.5 million (£1.9 million), almost double that of *Goldfinger*. Principal photography for *Thunderball* began on 16 February 1965 at Pinewood Studios with an eighteen-week production schedule, the intention being to release the film in time for Christmas. Eileen Sullivan returned as the wardrobe mistress, and John Brady was employed as the wardrobe master, having previously held this role on *Dr. No*. Anthony Mendleson was employed as the costume designer. By this time, Mendleson was an established and successful British costume designer whose previous credits had included *Kind Hearts and Coronets* (1949), *The Ladykillers* (1955), *The Mouse on the Moon* (1963) and *The Yellow Rolls-Royce* (1964). Mendleson enjoyed working on the production of *Thunderball*, explaining: 'Oh, that was great fun! Out in Nassau for about two months, that was no hardship. I got quite nice clothes for Claudine Auger and the other girl, Luciana [Paluzzi].'[56]

It is in *Thunderball* that Sinclair received a credit in a Bond film for the only time, and the tailor was invited by Eon Productions to a special press preview in December 1965 in the Bahamas.[57] In the film, Bond wears a mix of tailored clothing and casual wear appropriate for the location's climate. Of the tailored items, the first suit Bond wears is a dark grey flannel three-piece suit at the funeral of Colonel Jacques Boitier (Bob Simmons) in France. Bond wears a mid-blue shirt beneath his jacket, fastened with a black grenadine tie. Also present is Boitier's widow, Madame Boitier (Rose Alba), dressed in black clothing with a large hat and long veil. After the funeral, the camera follows Madame Boitier entering her home to which Bond lies in waiting. When Bond punches Madame Boitier, it is revealed that it is actually Boitier posing as his widow, offering a visually humorous fight between Bond in his tailored suit and Boitier, heavily made up with blue eyeshadow, mascara, red lipstick and blonde wig, dressed in a sheer black satin blouse, black satin pencil skirt and black high-heeled black court shoes. This is the first time in a Bond film when cross-dressing is used for humour and would later be adopted for similar effect in *Diamonds Are Forever*. Bond escapes from Boitier's home using a jet pack, and this allows for the first costume-related quip in the film on Bond's landing: 'No well-dressed man should be without one.' There is also a minor costume continuity error in this scene: when Bond puts on the jet pack his shirt has double cuffs and when he lands, he is wearing a shirt with cocktail cuffs.

On Bond's arrival at the Shrublands health clinic, he wears the barleycorn hacking jacket and cavalry twill trousers that were previously worn in *Goldfinger*. Other costumes worn by Connery in these scenes include a blue terrycloth robe provided by the clinic, a navy silk dressing gown and a short-sleeved black polo shirt with cavalry twill trousers to sneak around the clinic. On leaving the clinic, Bond wears a brown herringbone tweed knee-length topcoat. Underneath the topcoat, Bond wears a navy blazer with dark grey flannel trousers. The blazer is similar to the one Bond wore in *Dr. No*, however the buttons on this blazer are made from brass rather than gun metal, and there are four buttons on the cuff rather than two. Bond later appears in M's office wearing a brown and black blended worsted-mohair three-piece suit and a cream shirt that is fastened with a brown grenadine tie. After being sent to Nassau, Bond meets Dominique 'Domino' Derval (Claudine Auger) when wearing a rose-coloured linen shirt and light blue Jantzen swimming trunks. Other casual shirt and shorts combinations worn by Bond in *Thunderball* include a matching blue shirt and trousers and a straw pork pie hat with a blue and white checked grosgrain ribbon, a navy cotton Fred Perry polo shirt with white swimming trunks, a red wetsuit, a blue and white striped butcher shirt with cream linen trousers, a blue and white gingham-checked shirt with blue Jantzen shorts, and a pink and white gingham shirt paired with the same shorts he wears on meeting Domino for the first time.

Emilio Largo (Adolfo Celi) does not have as many costume changes as Goldfinger, but he is the most stylishly dressed villain of all Connery's Bond films. On arriving at SPECTRE's headquarters he wears a three-quarter length camel coat over a dark charcoal grey three-piece suit, possibly Italian-tailored owing to the Cifonelli shoulder structure that includes a highly stylized construction with a concave contour sloping from the collar and rising up towards the arm with strongly roped sleeve-heads. The jacket has a clean chest, and fastens with three buttons, and is cut with narrow notched lapels and no vent. Beneath it, Largo wears a cream-coloured shirt fastened with a black tie with white polka dots. The tie is a flamboyant choice, but also one which may have been selected as a reference to Largo's connection with Domino that is revealed later in the film. When Largo appears on his boat, the *Disco Volante*, he wears a naval-style double-breasted navy blazer with eight shanked buttons made of polished brass. Spaiser points out that throughout the film Largo tends to wear the blazer as if a dressing gown: most of the time he wears it with black diving trousers and a burgundy silk cravat with no shirt underneath.[58] The only time he wears it with other clothes, specifically a white shirt and a pair of stone-coloured trousers, is during a short daytime scene later in the film. Other costume items Largo wears include a white and silver striped linen shirt with light brown linen trousers, a grey silk dressing gown and a white shirt with charcoal grey linen trousers. His wetsuit is black, in contrast to Bond's red version.

For the female leads, Domino is dressed as a walking embodiment of her unique moniker throughout the film in black and white, mostly in a variety of bikinis and swimsuits. In the black and white photograph of her sitting with her brother that is included in the dossier Bond reads at Universal Exports, Domino is dressed in a zebra print bikini. This bikini is worn later in the film, and includes a small amount of pink piping on the edges of the ties on the briefs. When Bond meets Domino for the first time, she wears a black nylon off-shoulder one-piece swimming costume, with meshed fabric in a lattice pattern that swirls around her body. On leaving the sea and lunching with Bond, she wears a white chiffon unfastened jacket with a one-inch collar over the swimsuit, which has black satin piping around the sleeves and a black ribbon tie knotted in a bow at the shoulder. For Domino's other bikini, the top is designed in a *brassière* style and the bottoms are briefs. The bikini is most likely made from nylon and is two-toned in black and white. The style of the *brassière* is influenced by the yin and yang symbol and reflects Domino's characterization in that she is conflicted between Largo and Bond. The briefs are black at the front and white at the back, the white draping around the top and knotted in the centre. The development of her characterization and switching of allegiance from Largo to Bond is evident through her black and white costuming: on Bond first meeting her she is dressed in an all-black swimsuit and by the end of the film is costumed in a white dress after agreeing to assist Bond in defeating Largo. With the swimwear, Domino often wears a wide cotton headband in a variety of colours including white, pink, white and blue.

The black and white colour scheme afforded to Domino's costumes is at its most dominant during the scenes based at the casino when Bond meets Largo for the first time at the *chemin de fer* table, and it is likely that it was the most expensive scene of the film's wardrobe budget. These scenes also offer a visual code switch between Bond, who is dressed in a midnight blue dinner suit, and Largo, who is dressed in an ivory dinner jacket with black trousers. Unlike Bond's other Sinclair suits in the film, the dinner suit is believed to have been created by the costumier Bermans and Nathans, and it is lined with a burgundy satin.[59] By comparison, Largo's ivory inner jacket works as a flipped visual irony between the hero and the villain, similar to *Dr. No*. The camera also focuses on Largo's SPECTRE ring worn on the fourth finger of his right hand as Largo and Bond insinuate their backgrounds to one another. The black and white theme of the costumes is also highlighted by a woman behind Largo's left shoulder wearing a dress with a semi-sweetheart neckline, of which the bust is covered with a block of white silk fabric with black flowers. Behind Bond's right shoulder there is a woman wearing a black satin dress with a sweetheart neckline with a diamante detail on the bust and a black chiffon jacket fastened at the neck with white silk floral detailing. Domino wears an A-Line white silk evening gown and white chiffon shawl with ermine trim. The gown is hemmed at the knee, with spaghetti straps and a scooped neckline. The fabric includes ruched detail in a wrap pattern over the bust to the waist and is gathered at the waist with a diamond clip. The silk fabric extends from the waist to the knee in a train at the left-hand side. She wears white stiletto shoes. Domino's jewellery includes 'a pair of ear-clips by Trifari and an unsigned necklace, the oval cluster ear clips with central cabochon imitation emerald in a two-row border of imitation diamonds, the necklace of imitation emerald and diamonds, the flower head and ribbon cluster and drops in an "antique" style'.[60]

The most interesting character in *Thunderball* is that of the femme-fatale and SPECTRE Agent, Fiona Volpe (Luciana Paluzzi). In an early draft of the script, Volpe is a 'red-headed' Irish woman named Fiona Kelly, and described as 'the most beautiful accomplished young witch since Morgan Le Fey'.[61] It is in this film that the bad 'Bond girl' character becomes cemented in the franchise and is a recurring feature in most of the Bond films since. Her costumes, too, are very much reflective of her characterization, and they have been designed to emphasize her sexuality that she uses as a weapon, working to mirror the characterization of Bond and highlight the contradictory nature of gender, namely through the use of different shades of blue, the colour that is normally assigned to Bond's costumes. The script for *Thunderball* directs that Volpe's costumes reflect expensive fashions of the day, and notes that the character be 'strikingly dressed as though turned out by Balenciaga', the Spanish luxury fashion house.[62] The viewer is introduced to Volpe in bed with François Derval, Domino's brother. In this scene, Volpe is dressed in a floor-length pale blue chiffon and silk-lined nightdress, of which the scooped neckline is extremely low-cut. The cut of the dress is empire line, with the chiffon fabric pleated and gathered at the bust to which the fabric fans out beneath. Silk ribbon flows from the straps, which have small bows attached at the back, and gathers in a centrally tied bow underneath the bust. From there, the ribbons wrap around to the back of the dress and flow to the ground. The hem of the nightdress includes a pattern made from silk strands rising upwards in a wave pattern, which is reflective of the film's water theme. Her shoes are flat silk-covered ballet pumps in the same shade of blue. Volpe next appears in the film as a masked motorcyclist wearing black leather, who chases down and kills Count Lippe with a rocket projectile grenade on the orders of Blofeld. As the costume is ungendered in this scene, viewers would likely assume that the assassin is male until Volpe deposits the bike in a river and removes her helmet – revealing her face and a mane of long red hair.

Two of Mendleson's costume sketches for Volpe, using the medium of pastel on paper, have been published by Eon Productions. The first is the dress that Volpe wears on her first meeting with Bond. Meg Simmonds describes the design: 'This demure pastel dress with diaphanous scarf belies the true nature of assassin Fiona Volpe [...] This non-confrontational costume works well to set Bond up for an unexpected high-speed lift back to his hotel in her baby blue mustang convertible.'[63] Typical of Mendleson's artistic renderings, the design embodies his lyrical and imaginative style in capturing a dream-like and whimsical quality through a combination of sketchy and light pencil lines and textured pastel layers. The diaphanous scarf is likely made from silk, and it includes a blue paisley pattern detail. It is clipped to her dress with an imitation sapphire and diamond brooch sourced from Christian Dior.[64] The dress is made from silk and cut in an A-Line pattern, made from fabric that has a pale blue base and is dyed over the top with a dark blue wave pattern, again foregrounding the theme of water recurrent throughout *Thunderball*.

The dress Volpe changes into after she has sexual intercourse with Bond before she is subsequently killed is the second Mendleson design published by Eon Productions, again capturing the designer's whimsical style. Simmonds describes it: 'As Fiona Volpe begins to reveal her true nature to Bond, Mendleson adorns her in this exotic ostrich feather boa. The ice blue colour of her cocktail dress hints at the cold-blooded killer she really is and also contrasts well with the trickle of red blood from the bullet in her back that kills her.'[65] As with Volpe's previous costume, the diamond and sapphire jewellery was provided by Christian Dior. The dress is sheath-shaped and waisted with a boat neckline ruched at the bust, emphasizing Volpe's hourglass figure. The ice-blue dress sparkles slightly in the light and is likely made from a glitter stretch mesh Lycra fabric.

In this scene, Bond changes into a light grey sharkskin suit, with a mid-blue cotton shirt and a midnight blue grenadine tie. The blue hues of the costumes work to underline their similar personalities: both Bond and Volpe are hired as agents of their respective organizations, both kill without remorse, and both use sex as a weapon in order to persuade or coerce victims into achieving their end goal (Plate 3). For Bond, this is something that was particularly highlighted in the previous film, *Goldfinger*, when Bond forces Pussy Galore into kissing him in a barn before she relents, has sexual intercourse with him, turns heterosexual, and informs Leiter of Goldfinger's plans. As a reward, Bond sleeps with her at the end of the film, and thus sex works to ideologically reposition her character. The irony between Bond and Volpe lies in their gender: Bond is positioned as a hero and Volpe as a villain who is killed by a bullet meant for Bond. As John Cork explains on the gender inequality present in the early Bond films:

> The filmic incarnation of James Bond created a male character who is just as capable of using sex as a weapon, whilst still maintaining a ferocious appetite. The difference is that most of the fictional women who have used sex as a weapon have been portrayed as villainesses, with Bond meant to remain just a hero. Therein lies the true double standard.[66]

After Bond points out to Volpe that he knew of her work as a SPECTRE Agent due to her ring with the SPECTRE logo on it, the dialogue follows:

Volpe   It's a ring I like to wear.

Bond   Vanity has its dangers.

Volpe   Vanity, Mr. Bond, is something you know so much about.

Bond   My dear girl, don't flatter yourself, What I did was for King and country. You don't think it gave me pleasure, do you?

Volpe   But of course! I forgot your ego, Mr. Bond. James Bond, who only has to sleep with a woman and she starts to hear heavenly choirs singing. She repents and immediately returns to the side of right and virtue. But not this one. [Straightens Bond's tie] What a blow it must have been, *you* having a failure.

Bond   Well, can't win them all.

A minor point of note in the dialogue between them is that Bond refers to 'King and country' rather than 'Queen and country'. This might be meant as a general line, yet it also works to highlight the gendered nature of the exchange: Bond is speaking in the masculine and Volpe in the feminine. Bond sleeps with women to ideologically recondition them, notably Galore, but also later in *Thunderball* when Bond has sexual intercourse with Domino, whereas Volpe plays a 'cat and mouse' game, and has sex before the pleasure of killing her prey and cannot be ideologically repositioned. Furthermore, Volpe is a character included in the film who does not appear in Fleming's novel, and as such her character, in particular her dialogue in this scene, works to foreground the filmmakers' awareness of the gendered inequality present in the early Bond films.[67] This is also true of the inclusion of a female 00 Agent included in the publicity shots for *Thunderball* of the meeting between the nine agents in Universal Exports, however the woman is not visible in the film.

You Only Live Twice (1967)

Lewis Gilbert was hired to direct *You Only Live Twice*, which was reportedly budgeted at $9.5 million (£3.3 million). Roald Dahl was hired by Broccoli and Saltzman to revise the script initially drafted by Sydney Boehm and subsequently worked on by Harold Jack Bloom. By *Thunderball*, the films had established distinct 'Bond girl' archetypes, and Dahl revealed to *Playboy* that he was told by the producers: 'You can come up with anything you like so far as the story goes,' but not to alter the character of Bond or 'the girl formula', particularly reminiscent of *Goldfinger*.[68] The producers explained to Dahl:

> 'So you put in three girls. No more and no less. Girl number one is pro-Bond. She stays around roughly for the first reel of the picture. Then she is bumped off by the enemy, preferably in Bond's arms.'
> 'In bed or not in bed?' I asked.
> 'Wherever you like, so long as it's in good taste. Girl number two is anti-Bond. She works for the enemy and stays around throughout the middle third of the picture. She must capture Bond, and Bond must save himself by bowling her over with sheer sexual magnetism. The girl should also be bumped off, preferably in an original fashion.'
> 'There aren't many of those left,' I said.
> 'We'll find one,' they answered. 'Girl number three is violently pro-Bond. She occupies the final-third of the picture and she must on no account be killed. Nor must she permit Bond to take any lecherous liberties with her until the end of the story. We keep that for the fade-out.'

Unlike Maibaum's previous Bond scripts, there is little description afforded by Dahl in the way of costume and dress, likely because Dahl's script had little in common with Fleming's novel. Furthermore, there was no costume designer assigned to *You Only Live Twice*. Eileen Sullivan returned as the wardrobe mistress, and Brian Owen Smith replaced John Brady as the wardrobe master. Roy Ponting employed as the wardrobe supervisor for the second unit in Japan. As Bond's tailored wardrobe was already well established by *You Only Live Twice*, it was for Bond's casual wardrobe, the villain, the women, the secondary characters and extras that needed costume decisions to be made by the wardrobe department. In the following order, Bond's costumes for *You Only Live Twice* include: a Royal Navy Commander's uniform, a dark herringbone suit with ecru-coloured shirt and navy grenadine tie, over which he later wears a double-breasted olive green trench coat, a black fedora hat and distinctive black and white leather shoes, a casual cotton *yukata* (bathing) kimono, a dark blue mohair wool blend suit, unusual in that the jacket has a one-button fastening, worn with a light blue shirt and navy knitted silk tie, an ecru linen sports shirt and dark brown trousers without pleats, a soft pink shirt worn with grey tropical wool trousers, a variety of Japanese costumes when undercover, and a grey knitted jumper with a polo-neck collar, loose fitting grey trousers, gloves and a ninja mask.

It is notable that this is the first Bond film to directly recognize Bond's naval rank as a Commander of the Royal Navy directly through costume. The Commander dress uniform would later be worn by Roger Moore in *The Spy Who Loved Me* and Pierce Brosnan in *Tomorrow Never Dies*. The provenance of Connery's uniform remains unknown, however it is likely that it was created by Bermans and Nathans, as with Rosa Klebb's military uniform. Although it is unlikely that military tailor Gieves & Hawkes was involved with tailoring Bond's naval costume, they have confirmed that their company later tailored suits for Connery's personal wardrobe.[69] In *You Only Live Twice*, Bond's uniform is made from navy wool. The jacket is double-breasted, includes eight gilt buttons with a crown and anchor motif, jetted pockets, and double vents. The sleeves of the jacket include the rank insignia of the Commander, namely three rings of gold braid and an executive curl in the upper braid. The trousers are high-waisted with double-forward pleats. Underneath the jacket, Bond wears a white shirt with a pointed collar and double cuffs. The shirt cuffs are fastened with a pair of gold-plated cufflinks sourced from Simpsons of Piccadilly that have oval-plates with an engine-turned decoration and chain-link connection.

Bond's casual *yukata* kimono, worn in Tiger Tanaka's (Tetsurô Tamba) villa is traditionally worn during the summer months in Japan, and is made from cotton, or *futomono* (thick materials) in Japanese parlance. It includes a grey and indigo pattern of bamboo leaves and pine trees that have been printed using the traditional *yūzen* dye resist technique and a stencil. In Japanese culture, the inclusion of bamboo leaves is indicative of prosperity and strength, believed to ward off evil and pine trees, which are normally included on more formal kimonos, symbolize youth, strength and longevity, and represent rebirth, renewal and a bright future. This motif is later repeated in the film on Kissy Suzuki's (Mie Hama) Japanese wedding outfit. Bon's *yukata* has a shawl collar, and is wrapped over his body and fastened with a black *obi* (belt) in a *heko* style (soft and sash-like).

Similarly, Tanaka is also robed in a *yukata* kimono, however Tanaka's includes a grey colour base and a lengthwise tiger-stripe print in indigo blue. The stripes are a direct referencing of the character's name, of course, and in Japanese folklore represent strength and courage, as well as protection from evil spirits and bad luck, an appropriate motif given Tanaka's position as the head of the Japanese Secret Intelligence Service and the equivalent of M. On Tanaka's early scenes in *You Only Live Twice*, he dresses in tailored suits cut in a style that is more comparable with Bond's suits than that of Tanaka's British opposite, M. On his initial meeting with Bond, Tanaka wears a two-piece suit made from a lightweight woollen cloth in charcoal grey. Later in the film, he wears another two-piece suit, this time in a lighter shade of grey. Both suits have a two-button fastening, with notched and narrow lapels and are cut with a full chest, suppressed waist and have straight jetted pockets. The charcoal grey jacket has a single vent at the back, whereas the light grey suit has no vent. Tanaka's suits differ from Bond's in that they have a stronger, more structured shoulder that is cut straight. Both suits include straight-legged trousers with a single-reverse pleat and plain hems, and Tanaka wears a white shirt with a spread collar and double cuffs. With the charcoal grey suit, Tanaka wears a burgundy silk tie and with the light grey suit, a silver tie with a grey geometric print. Both suits include a folded white pocket square in the breast pocket.

It is in *You Only Live Twice* that Donald Pleasence is costumed in the look and style that becomes synonymous with Blofeld's character, which would be returned to in *Diamonds Are Forever* and *For Your Eyes Only* and subsequently parodied by Dr Evil (Mike Myers) in the Austin Powers films (1997–2002). Unlike Blofeld's previous appearances in from *From Russia With Love* until *Thunderball*, it is in *You Only Live Twice* that the audience sees the character fully-garbed for the first time. When Bond meets Blofeld in his volcanic lair, the latter is dressed in a version of the Chinese Mao suit. The cut and fabric of the suits were dictated by class and rank, and was normally tailored in colours of either muted blue, green or grey. As Clarissa Sebag Montefiore notes, lower-ranking officials wore tunics made from 'itchy grey cloth', middle-ranking officials wore polyester, and those at the top wore wool.[70] The choice of cavalry twill fabric and the colour of the suit can be understood as reflecting Blofeld's position as the head of SPECTRE. Unlike the traditional Mao suit however, Blofeld's version only includes two pockets, indicative of it being a Westernized version of the Chinese suit.

After receiving the producers' mandate on how the women in Bond films should be depicted, Dahl followed this religiously, and the characters' costumes are sourced to be a direct reflection of this. 'Pro-Bond girl number one', Aki (Akiko Wakabayashi), an agent and Bond's opposite number in the Japanese Secret Service, is mostly dressed for the first half of the film in costumes influenced by the West, as is the case with her superior Tanaka. Aki's first costume is an unstructured A-line dress in powder blue that is reminiscent of Mary Quant's jersey shift-dress designs of the 1960s that became synonymous with the British supermodel Twiggy. Aki's dress is made from silk organza and is sleeveless and knee-length. It includes a chiffon overlay panel at the front and back of the dress that is connected at the boat-shaped neckline and is made in the same shade of powder blue. The chiffon overlay has a matching wide silk panel stitched at the armholes and at the bottom hem, and it overlaps the A-line dress hem underneath by one inch. On her left shoulder Aki wears an imitation aquamarine 'spray' brooch purchased from Trifoli with a scrolling frond design.

Later, after Aki takes Bond to meet Henderson at his apartment, she wears a white chiffon headscarf with the dress when driving her Toyota 2000 GT Roadster. This costume contrasts with and refracts away from Volpe's similarly coloured costume worn in *Thunderball* when she picks up a hitch-hiking Bond in her Ford Mustang convertible, and Aki's dress re-aligns the colour shade of pale blue to the good 'Bond girl' who works with the hero rather than against him. When Bond is taken to Tanaka's villa, Aki wears silk sports *brassière* and hot pants with an elasticated waistband that are similar to the Japanese masseuse costumes in the previous scene except are made in an aqua blue fabric as opposed to pink to differentiate her from the other women. In the later scenes that take place at Tanaka's villa, Aki wears a pink lawn knee-length dress in a similar style and shape to that of the powder blue dress worn on first meeting Bond. This dress differs slightly in that it has a high, round collar and is made from jersey silk fabric. It has decorative stitch detailing across the yoke and down the centre seam, and includes long, flared bell-shaped sleeves. The dress includes an overlay in the same pink lawn jersey silk fabric.

Following Bond's arrival at Tanaka's ninja school, Aki wears Asian dress for the first time, namely a kimono made from silk (*gofuku*). It is a *furisode* (swinging sleeve); a more formal kimono than the *yukata* worn by Bond and Tanaka in the latter's villa. The *furisode* is normally worn by young, unmarried women such as Aki. The base colour of the fabric is white and includes a pattern in the shape of paulownia leaves and flowers in various shades of blue. This patterning is closely associated with femininity and female identity in Japanese culture, especially for unmarried women, and works in harmony with Aki wearing a *furisode*. The colour blue, derived from indigo, is understood to act as a repellent to snakes and insects in Japanese mythology, and therefore works as a visual irony given her death by poison. With the kimono, Aki wears an embroidered *hanhaba* (half-width) *obi* with red, blue and gold threads styled in a symmetrical *seigaiha* (blue ocean wave) fan pattern that represents a desire for peaceful living and a symbol of peace and prosperity, furthering the visual irony, especially given her job role. Similarly, her later *yukata*, worn before she is 'bumped off by the enemy', is made from a white fabric base with blue patterning, this time made from *futomono* as with Bond's and Tanaka's earlier costumes. It includes a maple leaf motif, and as with the previous paulownia symbols, suggests elegance, grace and beauty. According to the traditional Japanese reading, when maple leaves are sent by a woman to a man, it poetically symbolizes the ending of a relationship. Normally this would be read as the woman's love is waning, however by including this motif on Aki's costume, it adds poignancy to her death that is caused by her sleeping next to Bond and being killed after drinking poison intended for him.

'Girl number two' is Helga Brandt (Karin Dor), working on behalf of SPECTRE. With her red hair, dark eyes and fair complexion, Brandt appears as a femme-fatale and Fiona Volpe Mark II in *You Only Live Twice*. Unlike Volpe, who uses her sexuality as a weapon and is positioned as Bond's opposite in *Thunderball*, Brandt does not receive the same treatment in *You Only Live Twice*. Brandt appears as a more menial employee than that of Volpe, namely adopting the role of personal assistant to Mr. Osato (Teru Shimada) and a waitress delivering champagne, which conflicts with her also being a torturer and an assassin. In her role as Osato's secretary, the character wears clothing that is reflective of 1960s fashions as with Aki's Westernized costumes. In these scenes, Brandt wears an orange blouse made from a silk gauze fabric with notched lapels that is fastened with small fabric-covered buttons. It has three-quarter length sleeves with turned-up cuffs. With the blouse, Brandt wears a high-waisted white A-line skirt with a centre seamline, hemmed at the knee, that includes two flapped patch pockets on the hip. To emphasize her waist, Brandt wears a matching white patent leather belt with twelve studded punch-holes and a flat silver-plated buckle.

After Bond is captured by Osato's henchmen and taken to Brandt's cabin on the *Ning-Po*, Brandt has been directed to torture Bond for information and then assassinate him. Unlike Volpe, who is positioned in *Thunderball* as choosing to have sex with Bond for her own pleasure before she attempts to kill him in a 'cat and mouse' game, Brandt is supposed to torture and kill Bond by using cosmetic surgical implements, however chooses instead to be seduced by him after Bond offers Brandt $150,000 to help him escape back to Tokyo. This is in keeping with the mandate given to Dahl that Bond 'bowls [girl number two] over with sheer sexual magnetism' in order to save himself. Regardless, Brandt still attempts to kill Bond the following morning, however she is not afforded the speech made by Volpe that effectively positions her as being Bond's opposite. Brandt's knee-length evening gown has been selected to accentuate her figure and channel Rita Hayworth's image in *Gilda* (1946) when the actress wore a black evening gown designed by Jean Louis. Brandt's gown is made from a silk dupioni fabric in russet and chocolate brown colour tones that is covered in sequins. It is cut as an asymmetric sheath dress, with a straight camisole neckline and spaghetti straps.

The left-hand strap has a sleeve panel of chocolate brown chiffon attached, stitched to the back of the gown along a diagonally placed zip that fastens over the hips. The sleeve includes hand-stitched amber hanging glass crystals shaped in the form of icicle pendants. The asymmetrical zip fastening is accentuated when Bond uses the surgical knife to remove the straps and pull the zip of the dress down Brandt's back after he seduces her.

For Brandt's final scenes when she is 'bumped off' in Blofeld's piranha-filled pool, she wears a scarlet costume, reminiscent in the style and shape of her first outfit that she wears as Osato's secretary. The blouse and matching A-line skirt are made from a heavy silk dupioni fabric. The shoulder yoke of the blouse includes the stylish addition of epaulettes with a gold-plated button fastened on each and a matching button placed on either side of the slanted hems. The skirt is hemmed at the knee and worn underneath the blouse. Brandt's outfit is cinched at the waist with a wide belt made from matching scarlet fabric, fastened at the centre with a thick rectangular gold-plated clasp.

Kissy Suzuki is 'Girl number three'. Her costumes work in opposition to that of Aki, in that Kissy begins by wearing Japanese clothing for her fake wedding to Bond, and in later scenes wears Westernized clothing as she takes part in the infiltration of Blofeld's lair. For the wedding, Kissy wears a kimono termed a *shiromuku* (white, pure and innocent), that is worn as part of a traditional Japanese *Shinto* wedding ceremony. Kissy's white *shiromuku* is made of heavy silk, likely made from Japanese *Chirimen* silk, and includes gold embroidery sewn the shape of bamboo leaves and pine trees in a similar connection with the patterns printed onto Bond's *yukata* in earlier scenes. With the *shiromuku*, Kissy wears a gold-embroidered *tsunokakushi* (wedding headpiece). There are different Japanese theories relating to the shape and style of the headpiece, including that the headdress reflects the bride becoming obedient to her husband, or that it covers the bride's long hair wherein bad spirits may be hiding. Other theories claim that the hood serves the purpose of shielding the bride's face from the wedding party until she is revealed to her groom at the altar, similar to that of a Western wedding veil. This latter theory is in keeping with the staged wedding scene in *You Only Live Twice*, when Bond worries over what the face of his bride will look like after Tanaka derogatively jests that she has 'a face like a pig'. Along with the *tsunokakushi*, Kissy's wedding costume includes *kanzashi* tortoiseshell hair ornaments and a *sensu* fan made from gold leaf which is tucked into her *obi*.

On visiting the cave near Blofeld's lair, Kissy wears an ivory cotton string bikini that invites direct comparison between herself and Honey Ryder in *Dr. No*. Similarly fashioned to Honey's bikini, the cups are structured with a dart detail and are gathered at the sternum with a small bow and the briefs are cut across the grain and gathered at the hips, which are embellished with decorative straps. After Kissy arrives back at Blofeld's lair with Tanaka and his ninja team, she wears a short, hip-length, wrap-around tunic fastened with a bow at the right-hand side over her bikini. It is sleeveless, and made from cotton patterned with pink, tan, brown and white stripes. The tunic and bikini costumes appear particularly out of place, especially given that Bond, Tanaka and the ninjas are dressed in grey combat outfits that are appropriate for the action sequences. The only purpose of Kissy's tunic appears to be an attempt to provide a modicum of decency during the fight between Blofeld's henchmen and the ninjas, and this costume item is swiftly abandoned before Kissy escapes the lair with Bond. In reality, the discarding of the tunic is to ensure that Kissy's bikini is correctly in place and on display for the audience when she and Bond escape in the dinghy at the end of the film, so that Bond can take his 'lecherous liberties' with her in the film's fade-out.

Following the release of *You Only Live Twice*, Connery decided to hang up his Sinclair-tailored suits owing to his tiredness with the gruelling production schedule needed to regularly release the Bond films, his wariness of being typecast within the role, his salary, and the attention he received on promotional tours since the release of *Goldfinger*. On fame, Connery would later complain of the attention:

> I'd been an actor since I was twenty-five, but the image that the press put out was that I just fell into this tuxedo and started mixing vodka Martinis. And, of course, it was nothing like that at all. I'd done television, theatre, a whole slew of things. But it was more dramatic to present me as someone who had just stepped off the street.[71]

He would later reprise the role in *Diamonds Are Forever* after being lured back by United Artists.

Notes

1   Chapman, *Licence to Thrill*, 72.
2   The National Archives (TNA): BT 64/5262: Salary Costs for *From Russia With Love*.
3   Harper, *Women in British Cinema*, 216, 217.
4   'Jocelyn Rickards', *The Stage*, 28 July 1965, 13.
5   Harper, 216.
6   Jocelyn Rickards, *The Painted Banquet: My Life and Loves* (London: Weidenfeld, 1987), 58.
7   BUFVC: Roy Fowler, 'Women's Work in British Film and Television', Jocelyn Rickards, interview 493, http://bufvc.ac.uk/hectu/oral histories/bectu-oh (accessed: 25 June 2020).
8   Ibid.
9   BUFVC: Rickards, Application for ACTT membership form, membership number 25326, 26 March 1963.
10 Fowler.

11 'Commentary', *From Russia With Love*, DVD, directed by Terence Young (1963; UK and USA: MGM Home Entertainment, 2000).

12 Spaiser, 'The Second Dinner Suit – Stalking in *From Russia With Love*', *The Suits of James Bond*, 18 June 2012, www.bondsuits.com/the-second-dinner-suit/ (accessed: 17 January 2019).

13 Blofeld was voiced by Eric Pohlmann in *From Russia With Love*.

14 *Inside From Russia With Love*, documentary, directed by John Cork (USA: MGM Home Entertainment, 2000).

15 'Commentary', *From Russia With Love*.

16 Fleming, *From Russia With Love* (1957; London: Penguin Books, 2009), 47.

17 Fowler.

18 Ibid.

19 Ibid.

20 BFI, S6501: Richard Maibaum, *From Russia With Love*, final draft screenplay, 18 March 1963, 8.

21 Ibid., 78.

22 Rickards, 81.

23 BFI, S6501: 79.

24 Ibid., 124.

25 Meg Simmonds, *Bond by Design: The art of the James Bond films* (London: Dorling Kindersley, 2015), 20.

26 Chapman, 79.

27 BFI: Eon Productions Press Release for *Goldfinger*, n.d.

28 *The Goldfinger Phenomenon*, documentary, directed by John Cork (USA: MGM Home Entertainment, 2000).

29 Stanley Kubrick Archive (SKA), SK/11/9/19: 'Cables – MISC': Ken Adam to Stanley Kubrick, 22 August 1964.

30 'Press release for *Goldfinger*'.

31 Cosgrave, Hemming and McConnon, *Designing 007: 50 Years of Bond Style*, 28.

32 Cecil Wilson, 'Designs on Marilyn', *Daily Mail*, 4 May 1956, 10.

33 Simmonds, 314.

34 Harper, 214.

35 Ibid., 216.

36 Spaiser, 'Sean Connery's Suits in *Woman of Straw* vs. *Goldfinger*', *The Suits of James Bond*, 29 October 2018, www.bondsuits.com/sean-connerys-suits-in-woman-of-straw-vs goldfinger/ (accessed 18 January 2019).

37 *The Making of Goldfinger*, documentary, directed by John Cork (USA: MGM/UA Home Entertainment, 1995).

38 'Commentary', *Goldfinger*, DVD, directed by Guy Hamilton (1964; UK and USA: MGM Home Entertainment, 2000).

39 BFI, S6508: Richard Maibaum and Paul Dehn, *Goldfinger*, final draft screenplay, 26 February 1964, 10.

40 Spaiser, 'The *Goldfinger* Suit: A Three-piece Glen Check', *The Suits of James Bond*, www. bondsuits.com/the-goldfinger-suit/ (accessed 19 January 2019).

41 Matthew Priest, 'The Greatest Suits in Films', *Esquire*, 3 September 2015, www. esquireme.com/style/greatest-suits-film (accessed 19 January 2019).

42 Elisabeth Ladenson, 'Pussy Galore', in Christoph Lindner (ed.), *The James Bond Phenomenon: A Critical Reader* (Manchester and New York: Manchester University Press, 2003), 186.

43 BFI, S6508: 8.

44 Fleming, *Goldfinger* (1959; London: Penguin Books, 2009), 76

45 Ladenson, 188.

46 Fleming, *Goldfinger*, 73.

47 BFI, S6508: 24.

48 Ibid., 42.

49 António Sérgio Rosa de Carvalho, 'The smoking jacket', *Tweedland: The Gentleman's Club*, 4 January 2016, http://tweedlandthegentlemansclub.blogspot.com/2016/01/ the-smoking-jacket.html (accessed 21 June 2020).

50 Spaiser, 'Auric Goldfinger: The Brown and Gold Silk Dinner Jacket', *The Suits of James Bond*, 26 August 2014, www.bondsuits.com/auric-goldfinger-the-brown-and-gold-silk-dinner-jacket/ (accessed: 19 January 2019).

51 Fleming, *Goldfinger*, 47; BFI, S6508: 11.

52 Fleming, *Goldfinger*, 194.

53 BFI, S6508: 57.

54 Fleming, 223.

55 'There's gold in that finger', *Newcastle Journal*, 7 October 1964, 6.

56 BUFVC: Linda Wood and Dave Robson, Anthony Mendleson, interview 280, https:// historyproject.org.uk/interview/anthony-mendleson (accessed 26 June 2020).

57 'Bahamas scene', *Tailor & Cutter*, 7 January 1966, 2.

58 Spaiser, 'Emilio Largo: The Eight-Button Blazer', *The Suits of James Bond*, 4 July 2013, www.bondsuits.com/emilio-largo-the-eight-button-blazer/ (accessed 20 January 2019).

59 Bonhams, 'Lot 198: Sean Connery from *Thunderball*, 1965', *The Angels Star Collection of Film & TV Costumes*, 6 March 2007, www.bonhams.com/auctions/15337/lot/198/ (accessed 25 June 2020).

60 Christie's, 'Lot 205A: *Thunderball*, 1965', *James Bond 007*, 17 September 1998, www. christies.com/lotfinder/lot/thunderball-1965-1290188-details.aspx?from=searchresults &intObjectID=1290188 (accessed 25 June 2020).

61 Richard Maibaum and John Hopkins, *Thunderball*, Draft Screenplay, n.d., 25a.

62 BFI, S8910: Richard Maibaum, *Thunderball*, Shooting Script, 30 November 1964, 4?

63 Simmonds, 64

64 Christie's, 'Lot 210A: *Thunderball*, 1965', *James Bond 007*, 17 September 1998, www. christies.com/lotfinder/lot/thunderball-1965-1290195-details.aspx?from=searchresults &intObjectID=1290195 (accessed 25 June 2020).

65 Simmonds, 65.

66 'Commentary', *You Only Live Twice,* DVD, directed by Lewis Gilbert (1967; UK and USA: MGM Home Entertainment, 2000).

67 In an early treatment of *Thunderball* written by Fleming, Jack Whittingham and Kevin McClory, Fleming suggested that a 'beautiful' female double agent named Fatima Blush be included, with Fleming writing: 'Her appearance in tight-fitting black rubber suiting will make the audiences swoon.' However, as Robert Sellers explains, Blush was subsequently dropped from all subsequent treatments and scripts in *The Battle for Bond: The genesis of cinema's greatest hero* (Sheffield: Tomahawk Press, 2007), 23.

68 '007's Oriental Eyefuls', *Playboy*, June 1967, 87.

69 Author email correspondence with Jules Walker, Military Department, Gieves & Hawkes, 29 June 2020.

70 Clarissa Sebag Montefiore, 'From Red Guards to Bond villains: Why the Mao suit endures', 2 November 2015, *BBC*, www.bbc.com/culture/article/20151007-from-red-guards-to-bond-villains-why-the-mao-suit-endures (accessed 26 June 2020).

71 Kurt Loder, 'Great Scot', *Rolling Stone*, 27 October 1983.

3 'THE MAN WITH THE MIDAS TOUCH': LIFESTYLE, FASHION AND MARKETING IN THE 1960S

Termed retrospectively as 'Bonditis' by Lietta Tornabuoni, the 'Bondanza' by Drew Moniot and as the 'Bond phenomenon' by Tony Bennett and Janet Woollacott, this chapter will analyse how the James Bond novels and 1960s Eon Productions films were culturally important in relation to their influence upon fashion and lifestyle in a wider cultural sphere, specifically in relation to marketing and brand promotion.[1] It was during the early 1960s that James Bond began to be referenced in fashion marketing campaigns, with Bennett and Woollacott explaining that the early part of the decade 'saw Bond take off into a semi-independent existence as a figure used widely in advertising and commodity design', and that the character's cultural presence 'was overwhelming, impossible to avoid'.[2] The allure of Bond was summed up by Hugh Gaitskell in a letter to Fleming: 'The combination of sex, violence, alcohol, and – at intervals – good food and nice clothes is, to one who lives such a circumscribed life as I do, irresistible.'[3] The use of Bond in advertising and the marketing of brands 'tended to work alongside the films': Bennett and Woollacott argue that products would modify 'the associations Bond served to orchestrate as to place him at the centre of a significantly reorganised set of ideological and cultural concerns'.[4] The 1960s 'constitutes *the* moment of Bond', which was a 'peculiarly concentrated one' in that the character was 'omnipresent' in advertising and commodity design.[5] Therefore, this chapter will analyse early forms of Bond-themed marketing from 1960 prior to the release of *Dr. No* in September 1962, leading up to the 'boom' period of 1965 when America, Britain, France and Japan were particularly quick in attempting to capitalize on Bond's popularity in order to sell a variety of themed merchandise.[6]

Dressed to sell: The 'James Bond Look'

Prior to casting Connery in the role of Bond, a small number of British fashion retailers and cloth manufacturers recognized the branding and marketing potential of Fleming's published novels. Fleming did not mind this, although he clarified in a letter to Michael Howard that although he was potentially happy for Booths, the gin manufacturer, to use his name in their marketing, 'I couldn't bear shirts. I don't mind James Bond's name being used but I'm afraid I don't want my name to appear in promotional stuff.'[7] One of the earliest uses of the Bond name to market clothing was by Courtaulds, one of Britain's largest textile companies, who produced a range of synthetic clothing and used Bond to promote these products in April 1961, though apparently without obtaining the relevant permission. Fleming was irritated, writing to Howard:

> Rather surprised about Courtaulds. What are the arrangements & what the reward? I was asking Booths £5,000 for the privilege – not that they were willing to pay it – but Courtaulds is a £50,000,000 company. They should definitely not trade on my handiwork no matter whatever publicity my books get. And I shall also want many dozens of shirts made to measure from their stuff! Would you ask Elaine Greene of M.C.A. [Management Consultancies Association] to get in touch with them and screw them good and proper.[8]

The use of James Bond in fashion-related marketing evidently took off, regardless of whether Fleming received payment or his shirts, and in May 1961 Iris Keenan announced that: 'Men's fashions have a new trendsetter … James Bond.'[9] Referring to the trend as the 'James Bond Look', Keenan explained that it combined 'ruggedness and sophistication. It demands clothes with a no-nonsense elegance; clothes which remain impeccable in any of the desperate situations in which an undercover man is likely to find himself; clothes which are easy to care for.' Notably, this is a sentence that attempts to combine the exoticism of Bond's exploits with the perceived 'everyday' image and average male desire for clothes which needed little care yet remained stylish. Indeed, as Joyce McKinnell noted two months later, Bond was becoming a 'new trend-setter for men', and was 'surprised that it hasn't happened before', arguing that: 'During the past few weeks there has been a slant of advertisements for men's wear à la Bond [. . .] If this Bond trend catches on like women's trends do, I can see a welcome revival of male interest in no-nonsense elegance clothes and the finer arts of food.'[10]

This type of Bond-related fashion marketing as observed by Keenan and McKinnell is evidenced by the advertisement for Courtelle entitled 'M is worried – send for Bond!' published in September 1961. Unlike Courtaulds, Fleming endorsed the use of the James Bond name for Courtelle. However, in August 1961 the author outlined the issues that he had with the wording of the advert regarding a reference to Savile Row-tailored clothes that Bond does not wear, and that Courtelle had not returned his generosity in permitting them to use James Bond for marketing their brand:

I really don't mind these [advertisements] but they rather annoyed me by writing a patronising letter offering me <u>one</u> sweater, <u>one</u> pair of slacks, or indeed any <u>one</u> object from their collection instead of begging me to come in and take my pick of their stuff – which I naturally wouldn't have done but which would have sounded rather handsomer. In fact I would like them to invite me round some Tuesday or Wednesday afternoon to have a look at the stuff I am sponsoring. I have absolutely no idea what it looks like.[11]

In regard to this early form of fashion marketing, the branding is particularly gendered, and aimed at attracting the male market by attempting to inspire men to harness their 'inner Bond' and the character's overtly masculine qualities through the wearing of branded clothing, and at the same time dually marketing the items towards a female audience. McKinnell noted: 'Come to think of it – this Bond influence would make our men far more interesting and certainly more masculine,' with women consumers understood to influence what 'their' men chose to wear. This attempt at a dual-gendered marketing campaign was to be capitalized upon later in the decade after the release of the first three Eon Productions Bond films.

In *The Sunday Times Magazine*'s inaugural issue published in March 1962, two relevant articles appear relating to James Bond and the character's cultural influence: the first being the publication of Fleming's short story 'The Living Daylights'; and the second an article, 'Renaissance of the British Girl', written by Fleur Cowles, who described the current London fashion scene thus:

the British male is completely changed: he is now noticeably fashion conscious [...] That Teddy Boy adolescent, with his extravagant appeal for attention, has fallen into line. He is employed. He need give very little money for family maintenance. He has plenty to spend for himself [...] Between them, boys and girls spend *all* their money. They are not putting it in the bank. They spend it in unthought-of ways [...] forming bright clutches in crowded restaurants everywhere; they spend a lot on regular visits to the theatre and the cinema. They want things *now*. The boys want their cars, they both want their holidays, and the girls want expensive perfumes, lots of cosmetics and clothes – even a fur stole – *now*.[12]

Although Cowles does not directly reference the 'James Bond phenomenon' in popular culture, it can be understood from her article that consumerism was changing: the perception that the 'London young', of whom the 'darling' dress designer Mary Quant was an inspiration, wished to spend their earnings in a frivolous and expendable way as opposed to saving money. Furthermore, over the course of the decade it becomes very much evident on reviewing *The Sunday Times Magazine* that it actively promoted fashion, drinking and travel to excess;

something of which Fleming promoted in his novels and Eon Productions developed in their films.

A later contribution to the 'James Bond Look' was promoted by the trade paper *Style Weekly* in November 1962 following the release of *Dr. No* in a two-page spread that was dedicated to men's rainwear. Including direct references to James Bond and other famous characters from popular culture such as Chief Inspector Jules Maigret, Philip Marlowe and Simon Templar, *Style Weekly* answered that men wanted 'a style that suggests qualities he admires in "heroes" in contemporary fact and fiction [...] A man who lives dangerously – cool, hard, detached, sceptical, self-reliant, clear-headed – one or more of these impressions is what the raincoat must convey.'[13] The 'James Bond Look' was described as: 'a fly-fronted, belted style in a Terylene/cotton mixture fabric, available from Dannimac in navy and four other shades to retail at 10 guineas. It has a front and back yoke, diagonal welted pockets and a short centre vent.' Certainly, the navy colour was in keeping with what Bond himself would likely choose to wear, and in *The Man with the Golden Gun*, Fleming describes Bond as wearing a raincoat that was 'bought yesterday from Burberry's.'[14]

There is little evidence to suggest that specific Bond-branded marketing really caught on until after the British release of *Goldfinger* in September 1964. However, in May 1963, between the release of *Dr. No* and *From Russia With Love*, the cosmetics company Pond's launched a thirty-second, black-and-white advertising campaign for their Angel Face 'Double-0-Seven'-branded lipstick, which also contained personnel involved in later Eon Productions Bond films. The advertisement was directed by Guy Hamilton, the future director of *Goldfinger*, and the two artists who featured in the advertisement were Imogen Woodford and Charles Gray, who also provided the voice-over commentary.[15] Gray's later acting credits included playing Dikko Henderson in *You Only Live Twice* and Blofeld in *Diamonds Are Forever*. The advertisement begins with a close-up shot of Woodford's lips as she swipes Angel Face lipstick over them, accompanied by jazz music. The camera pulls back to reveal her face, and then pans across to the mirror on the left of Woodford. It then focuses on Woodford writing '00' on the mirror with the lipstick as Gray's voice-over questions: 'Are you brave enough to wear Double-0 colours?' A shot from a gun can then be heard as the camera jump-cuts to the '00' on the mirror, now including a bullet-hole in the top-left of the second '0'. As this happens, Gray states: 'The sheer murder, shameless, passionate colours that stay soft, smooth all day.' The camera then pulls back to frame Woodford, who now turns away from the mirror to provide a full-on face shot, before the camera switches back to a close-up of Woodford's lips, drawing out once again to reveal the entrance of Gray with his back to the camera. As Gray leans in to kiss Woodford's cheek, the camera pans back to the mirror as it captures Woodford adding '7' next to the '00' in lipstick. Gray then suggests: 'Tomorrow, wear 007, in the most *ruthless* pink.' The camera then cuts to a medium-shot including a row of Angel Face-branded lipsticks in the foreground with Woodford and Gray framed in soft focus in the background. As the camera pans across the row of the lipstick range, Gray states: 'Double-0-Seven colours . . . By Angel Face.'[16]

In *Television Mail*'s 'Production View', it asked: 'Why the silly hat and all the get up for the model? Still, it was intriguing and glamorous in a way, but possibly too high above the level of the teenage market.'[17] By way of comparison, the 'Agency View' noted that 'in passing, I liked the esoteric humour of 007 Angel Face Make-Up, (although it's nice to see "with-it" humour, I doubt whether many of the general public will get the tie-up between James Bond and this product)'.[18] One could assume that the television advertisement was specifically aimed at a female audience, as with the Courtelle print advertisement aimed at men. However, Pond's aimed to appeal to both sexes: women are to want to wear the lipstick, and men are to want to buy it for their partner. Similar to that of the Courtelle campaign, as well as the Dannimac raincoat promoted as part of the 'James Bond Look' in *Style Weekly*, the Angel Face lipstick is not explicitly linked to the James Bond novels or films: there was only one colour numbered 007 in the range, and no female character was assigned to the lipstick colour. It could, of course, be posited that although Pond's realized the commercial potential of linking their Angel Face cosmetic brand with James Bond, they did not receive the relevant permission to use the Bond name in the advertisement, as with Courtaulds: note, for example, that it does not reference Fleming, the publishers of the James Bond novels Jonathan Cape Limited, nor Eon Productions. However, Courtelle's print advertisement did acknowledge Fleming and Jonathan Cape Limited.

Nonetheless, the style of Bond-branded fashion products would change with the release of *Goldfinger*, and the 'James Bond'/'007' label would become more explicit in the marketing of such items launched after the success of the film, provided that permission was obtained from the relevant companies. This came once Eon Productions became shrewder towards the lucrative opportunities that such marketing could achieve. Fleming suggested such possibilities to Saltzman in late 1961 on the basis of an unnamed brand, possibly Smirnoff, contacting the author for permission to use James Bond in its marketing:

> Incidentally, I expect you will be getting similar approaches from other branded products used by James Bond. I don't know what your policy in this matter will be, but I personally find that the use of branded names in my stories helps the verisimilitude, so long as the products are quality products. Admittedly one is giving free publicity to these people. But I don't think it matters so long as their products are in fact really good.[19]

Post-*Goldfinger*, the brand tie-ins and merchandising began to be produced in earnest, particularly in Britain, America, France and Japan. On how the rights to market Bond-branded products and merchandise were obtained, Llew Gardner explained that:

Fleming sold a fifty-one per cent share in his merchandising firm Glidrose [Productions Limited] to the City [of London] firm of Booker Bros., headed by his old friend Jack Campbell, for £100,000 [. . .] Robert Fenn who acted as Fleming's film agent now acts as agent for the merchandising business and in turn employs an extensive network of Bondsmen. These are nine promoters, fifteen paid agents and seventeen lawyers hard at it throughout the world exploiting the Bond business and at the same time making sure nobody does any pirating.[20]

In Britain, licences to market Bond-branded items could be obtained from Mervyn Brodie Associates, named after the 42-year-old South African businessman who set the company up.

Brodie was born in Cape Town and 'came to London four years ago as managing director of a South African fruit-canning concern.'[21] On leaving the organization, Brodie created his merchandising business in partnership with fellow South African, Jack Cowper, leading to 'a glimpse of the fantastic rewards to be won from exploiting "character merchandising" [that] came when the partners obtained certain rights to licensed tie-ups with The Beatles'. This led to the pair realizing the potential of the James Bond name: 'We sat down and threw names around [. . .] We thought of Elizabeth Taylor and other names. And then we thought of Bond, and he seemed to us to have the most international flavour.' On the international potential of the James Bond brand, Brodie explained to Maurice Moss: 'His films are publicised all over the world while being made. By the time they are released, they are known everywhere – so look at the money a manufacturer saves on advertising.'[22] Brodie and Cowper 'persuaded the two companies who own the rights to the Fleming books [Glidrose and Booker Bros.] and United Artists [. . .] to go along in return for a share of the royalties', with the Bond market in Britain 'estimated at £5,000,000 – for Bond shoes, ties, shirts, coats, suits, vodka – and anything else that a cold-eyed, deadly elegant, woman-overwhelming secret agent might use' in 1965.[23] Brodie boasted on his ingenuity for selling the rights to manufacture Bond merchandise: 'I suppose I could retire to the south of France now and sit on a beach for the next fifteen years. It is quite impossible to put a figure on this business.'

'If you don't give him 007 . . . I will': The 'Bondanza' in America and Japan

'James Bond 007' branded marketing ventures in America and Japan that arose during 1965 proved to be very lucrative, with Moniot noting 'it soon became apparent that the James Bond phenomenon was much more than a passing fad

[. . .] The resulting marketing phenomenon has been called the "Bondanza" and describes a European-American buying spree unrivalled since Davy Crockett and his coonskin cap.'[24] Tornabuoni explained that the reason behind the popularity of Bond in America was because: 'In many American journals Bond is spoken of not as a fictitious character but as a real person. The Bond style has become a new approach to masculine fashion as it has for a more virile manner of treating women,' citing unattributed sources such as: 'it has increased by forty per cent the sale of [Bond's] favourite brand of champagne, Taittinger, and by thirty per cent the importation of his favourite vodka.'[25] In terms of fashion, Tornabuoni noted that: 'The present most appreciated by men for Christmas 1964 was the diplomatic satchel [attaché briefcase]. Macy's [the New York department store] sold them in hundreds.'

As reported in the *Coventry Evening Telegraph* in 1965, the James Bond name 'helps to sell a variety of articles, from after-shave lotion to jigsaw puzzles. Firms using either "007" or "James Bond" on their products are doing about £14,000,000 [nearly $40 million] worth of business annually and the vogue has just started.'[26] To obtain permission to market Bond-branded items, businesses had to apply to the Licencing Corporation of America, who held the rights to exploitation of all Fleming properties and the permission to use the name 'James Bond 007'. The biggest American manufacturing concern was the Colgate-Palmolive Corporation: 'In January [1965] it started selling in Kansas City and Syracuse an "007" line of toilet articles for men. The experiment was such a success that the goods are to go into shops all over the country in June.' In terms of fashion and clothing, the article notes:

> Soon, there will also be James Bond or 007 jewellery, watches, luggage and men's suits . . . there are James Bond pullovers, T-shirts, pyjamas for men and women, slacks – and the inevitable trench-coat in authentic British style. Gimmick addicts can even buy shoes with false heels (for hiding plans). One pyjama firm has even come up with a special line for children – named 003½.

Specifically, men's and women's '007' shoes were manufactured by Endicott Johnson and '007' raincoats by Spatz Brothers. For women, Tornabuoni explained that the fashion magazine *Harper's Bazaar* 'rejoiced in his [Bond's] frivolous influence: the woman of 1965 was to have her legs completely golden by means of gilded lace stockings.'[27] The Bond influence also reached to fashion advertisements, for example: 'High-class fashion photographs often had disquieting espionage backgrounds, sophisticated models were surrounded by spy-type apparel. Even the advertisement for a brand of gloves consisted of a girl with a black mask over her eyes, and a raincoat with military epaulets from which emerged half a score of gloved hands, menacingly holding a Beretta .25, 007's favourite gun.'[28] The popularity of the licensed Bond-branded products in America led to some firms attempting to capitalize unofficially on the 'Goldfinger effect', termed by *Variety* as 'bondknapping', in which firms would use the name and symbol 'identified in the Bond novels', of which 'the most frequent "bondknappers" have been manufacturers of T-shirts and sweatshirts'.[29] Other unauthorized uses of the Bond name included 'manufacturers of toys (a gun), underwear (a *brassière* and girdle combination labelled "007 – an eye-opener"), liquor (a gin-based 007 drink) and cosmetics (007 Products)'.

Similarly to America, the Bond brand was also popular in Japan, with *Variety* explaining that after the release of *Goldfinger* in Tokyo during April 1965, the film 'smashed a lot of all-time box-office records [. . .] various lines of Bond merchandise, from undergarments and neckties to candy, have been doing a brisk biz here along with the character's trade-marked attaché cases, cuff buttons and cigarette lighters'.[30] It was reported at the same time in the *Daily Sketch* that the Japanese were also interested in purchasing Anthony Sinclair tailored suits similar to those worn by Connery in the films, confirming that the tailor had 'received enquiries' as to his services.[31] Natalie Watson recalls that a client of Sinclair's, Douglas Kendrick, 'wanted to tie him up with a Japanese firm, but Kendrick explained at the start that this would be a very long process and in the end it came to nothing'. In 1966, the *New York Times* reported that the Bond films released in Japan 'have created such an exciting boom that one movie critic wrote: "The Japanese people have been caught up in the Bond whirlwind"'.[32] The 'boom' led to Japan's 'two biggest manufacturers of rayon and other synthetic textiles', Toyo Rayon and Teijin, to produce a 'Bond-look' topcoat and 'other commodities' in the spring of 1965, including shirts, mufflers and synthetic textiles. A spokesperson for Toyo Rayon claimed to the *New York Times* that the company supplied the domestic market with 50,000 topcoats, 125,000 pairs of socks and 20,000 shirts: 'We have embarked upon the sale of the Bond-look merchandise as a means of developing a new market for our company's products among young men.' Interestingly, the *New York Times* also noted that not only were the young men of Japan interested in the 'James Bond look', but also the 'traditionally conservative older man because of what a manufacturer called its "orthodox British style"'.

'Kinky outfits à la Pussy Galore': Galeries Lafayette and 'Bond-Britannia' in France

The large Paris department store, Galeries Lafayette, was particularly successful at marketing Bond-branded fashion and accessories when it launched a 'Bond Boutique' to coincide with the French release of *Goldfinger* in February 1965. One of the reasons behind the desire in France to cash in on the 'Bond phenomenon' towards the end of 1964 and early 1965 was due to the more general rise of

'Anglomania' at the end of 1963. Tornabuoni noted: 'The epidemic of "Bonditis" that has invaded France with more vigour than veneration since the Fifties is of a recent origin and has an interesting history.'[33] Bernard Kaplan wittily noted at the time:

> If Charles de Gaulle really does feel like Joan of Arc nowadays, it's forgivable. The dastardly English are staging an invasion of France that makes the Hundred Years War look like a charade put on for the later convenience of Shakespeare [...] Anglomania is sweeping the country as never before. Everything British, from Welsh rarebit to deerstalker caps, is in fashion.[34]

Explaining that it was in fashion and clothing that 'the English influence is exercising its greatest magnetism', Kaplan noted that it was in

> men's fashions where Britain's grip really shows. This is all the more remarkable since nothing has been more contrasting between the two nations until recently than how Englishmen and Frenchmen garb themselves [...] even off-the-peg costumes exude a faint whiff of Savile Row, or attempt to. The French have gone overboard on blazers (complete with English club crests), regimental ties and, at long last acknowledging that the Paris climate differs in only the slightest particulars from London's, tightly rolled umbrellas.

Nathalie Pernikoff revealed that in 1964 Mervyn Brodie Associates 'have tied up with Service de Méthode [the advertising agency] for promotion of the clothes and accessories worn by Sean Connery in *Goldfinger*. Boussac [Christian Dior] are said to be interested, and a right-bank store [Galeries Lafayette] is expected to have a whole "007 floor" next March to coincide with the launching of the film.'[35] Specifically, Boussac 'invaded the market' with James Bond waterproofs, shirts, pyjamas and dressing gowns, 'all ear-marked with the magic sign 007.'[36] Furthermore, the *Daily Telegraph* reported that '14 French manufacturers have obtained licences to use the 007 label', with Bond-branded items to go on sale in 3,500 shops across France.[37] Other merchandise included: 'The tailor Bayard advertised suits à la James Bond complete with waistcoats. Bally advertised the Bond moccasin and the Bond black shoe for evening wear.'[38]

Andrew Mulligan reported in March 1965 that the fashion pages in French newspapers referred to Bond as 'the Don Juan' of that year, and that 'shock waves from the Bond cult have found their way into fashion stores'.[39] The French lifestyle magazine *Elle* made James Bond its 'masculine hero' and suggested to its readers that they should imitate his women, proposing for the summer that they should wear 'a bikini with a leather belt like that of Ursula Andress in *Dr. No*, an evening dress with a silver *lamé* waistcoat and complete outfits in leather like those of Pussy Galore in *Goldfinger*.'[40] Mulligan explained that Galeries Lafayette created a special 'Bond Boutique'; its archive contains material that evidences this early form of marketing and brand promotion involving the fashions on display that focus on the 007 label, including the press launch (Figure 3.1) and arrival of one of the three Aston Martin DB5 cars used in *Goldfinger*. The report on the cocktail party held to launch the Bond Boutique translates that 'for the first time, the style "James Bond" was launched, intending to make men dynamic, sporty and elegant', and:

> On Friday 19 February at 18.30, a cocktail party met for the occasion of the inauguration of the 'James Bond' Boutique, including members of the executive board, writers, journalists, cameramen and photographers [...] Suits, trench coats, shoes, many items marked with the label 007; not forgetting accessories: key-chains, cufflinks (3000 of them were sold in eight days in Paris) and the famous practical and stylish attaché briefcase. For the first time a car [one of the Aston Martin DB5's used in *Goldfinger*] was presented to the first floor of the store. Put in place before closing time, she climbed the stairs with ease with the staircase covered in boards for the occasion. It is the original car (despite its perfectly sober appearance) as the driver proved by running the different gadgets born from the imagination of Ian Fleming one by one: Puncher blades [...] bulletproof armour plates, numerous interchangeable bumpers, taillights, etc. But no one wanted to end the demonstration by trying the ejector seat. Other objects used in the filming of the first two James Bond films were also present. In the background the original soundtrack [from *Goldfinger*] was played.[41]

The Bond Boutique sold trench-coats 'with 007 printed silk lining' at $80, handkerchiefs with a gold border, 007 cufflinks at $5, a $30 black attaché case, and Bond-style shirts.[42] *The Miami News* noted that 'Shoppers in the Galeries Lafayette [...] receive a letter signed with the name of the secret agent' when purchasing clothing and merchandise from the Bond Boutique.[43]

For the women, Mulligan described that Galeries Lafayette urged that they 'become fit for James Bond'. The clothing range available included 'futuristic rainwear' and golden lingerie, and a sales girl was quoted as stating 'golden sleeveless pullovers at £2 each are the bestsellers'. The *Daily Telegraph* explained that 'there are kinky outfits à la Pussy Galore for the girls, with gold underwear, 007 *negligées* and Secret Agent baby doll nighties'.[44] Tornabuoni believed:

> The ladies too have not been neglected: the manufacturer of female underwear Margarett has produced girdles, vests, shorts, night-shirts of gold lace, and presented them with a photograph of the gilded nude girl in *Goldfinger* [Shirley Eaton] exhorting women 'to be dressed in gold like her' [...] Even brands of lipstick are now advertised with such phrases as 'a good Bond for the lips'.[45]

FIGURE 3.1 The cocktail party launching Galeries Lafayette's Bond Boutique.

Although Galeries Lafayette managed to successfully take advantage of the popularity of Bond after the release of *Goldfinger*, this was not experienced by other smaller French manufacturers and retailers at the time, many of whom closed following attempts to sell 007 branded items.[46]

'From Burton's with Love': British '007 James Bond' merchandise

Although it was apparent that the marketing of Bond-branded products was successful in America, Japan and at Galeries Lafayette in Paris, the marketing of similar products in Britain was not. On the face of it, this would appear surprising: however, by analysing the context behind the different British marketing campaigns, it can be understood why, when focusing on a case study of Montague Burton, the multiple tailoring firm. The context behind why Montague Burton were interested in obtaining a licence to market Bond-branded clothing in 1965 was in part due to British fashion forecasts as early as 1963 that:

Bold chested, bold shouldered, slim legged and stiff fronted. This is how the fashion-conscious British man will emerge next spring [...] Mr. F. C. Vernon [chief designer for Montague Burton] said British men still tended to be individuals where clothes were concerned – ninety per cent of the suits made by his company were to measure. Teenagers have been responsible for the big revolution in the way the British male dressed himself. They were more clothes conscious than their parents were and prepared to spend more. Mr. R. Jones [continental stylist for Montague Burton] said: 'The trouble is that they quickly follow a craze. There has been an avalanche of Beatle suits. Where do we go from here?'[47]

Montague Burton's answer to Jones's question as to which 'craze' young men might want to follow next came towards the end of 1964 following the release of *Goldfinger*, with Lionel Jacobsen, the firm's chairman, announcing that 'talks were well advanced for Burton to buy the right to market clothes under the 007 James Bond brand name'.[48] As noted by the *Evening Standard*, Montague Burton 'is reaching into its shoulder-holster to whip out a weapon to beat its competitors [...] What a glamorous label this could give to Burton clothes. Maybe they'll change their slogan [from "Burton Unbeatable"] to "Bond Unbeatable".[49] Most news reports reacted positively to this announcement; however, some were more cautious in suggesting that Montague Burton's venture would be successful, with the *Irish Press* believing:

There have been signs recently that Burton's is aware of the need for a more dynamic approach [...] Negotiations are well advanced for the acquisition of rights to sell under the '007 James Bond' brand name. Bond has been the model of the smart young men and if Burton's manages to produce a range of clothes to suit this group, it might have hit on a substantial winner.[50]

However, the report warned that:

But it is possible that Burton will have to pitch its sights higher than it has up to now. The 'Bond' image has gone down particularly well with the better off young man, the sort of person that has not previously been attracted to the MB label. If he can be, Burton's will do well! Bond himself would not have been seen dead in Burton's. Will the Bondsmen?

Style Weekly observed that: 'James Bond has come to symbolise a sort of slick, opulent and dangerous way of life to the man in the street. The use of the Bond image could give Burton's a bigger slice of the younger man market and provide them with a valuable weapon in the growing battle for sales among the multiple tailors.'[51] Separately, the shoe company Norvic was already producing a range of

007 shoes. As Anthea Hall observed: 'The success of the latest James Bond film *Goldfinger* [...] has resulted in some interesting fashion side-lights, among them 007 shoes by Norvic, which are styled in the James Bond tradition.'[52] Hall described the shoes as being 'the 007 zebra skin shoe for men, which retails at £6.10s., and for women the "Pussy Galore" style in velour suede at 79s.11d'. This would lead to the satirical *Punch* magazine publishing Eric Busgin's cartoon of a heterosexual couple sitting at a dining table with the caption: 'Do you mind if we sit this one out, darling? My new James Bond 007 shoes are killing me.'[53]

By March 1965 it was widely reported that Montague Burton had signed a deal with Mervyn Brodie Associates to market suits under the '007 James Bond' label.[54] Later in the year, *Style Weekly* reported: 'The cost of a James Bond licence has been estimated at anything between £1,000 and £20,000 down payment, plus substantial royalties. The initial cost to a large firm like Burton's would obviously be considerable.'[55] As well as this, 'a regular commission working out in the region of five per cent on the wholesale selling price' was also reported to be part of the deal.[56] Montague Burton employed Sinclair as a style consultant to assist in designing the range. Nick Davies wrote: 'They call it the 007 look [...] the look of well-tailored, masculine elegance as portrayed by actor Sean Connery. But soon that look will be available to ALL the men in Britain.'[57] Davies explained that Montague Burton had initially obtained exclusive marketing rights for '007 raincoats, sports jackets and slacks', which were to go on sale in '150 selected branches early next month'. On the cost of Bond suits, Davies noted that 'by autumn at the latest, would-be-Bonds will be able to order any of the suit styles seen in Connery's films – at prices from £15.15.s', and on interviewing Sinclair, the tailor explained: 'There will be no gimmicks. The clothes will simply be very elegant. [Although] there will be no room for shoulder-holsters.'

The context behind the hiring of Sinclair was due to the hiring of Savile Row tailors to work for other multiple tailoring firms, the most prominent and successful of which was Hardy Amies for Hepworth's. As Robert Head questioned in 1963: 'Why does Hepworth's profits soar year after year? Answer: The Hardy Amies genius. Since the master of Savile Row started two years ago to design Hepworth's suits at under 25 guineas, their "British Line" has had a huge success.'[58] The partnership was beneficial to both Amies and Hepworth's, as the multiple tailor's 'profits zipped £64,000 last year to a best-ever £886,000', and for Amies: 'In addition to the immense free advertising Hepworth's have given his own business, he collects a handsome – but unpublished – fee, plus a cut from every British Line suit that Hepworth's sell'. In *Tailor & Cutter*'s editorial in April 1965, John Taylor noted that the hiring of Sinclair would 'bring the scent of gun-smoke and Savile Row (via his James Bond range) to Burton's'.[59] Taylor believed that the reason underlying the hiring of bespoke tailors by multiple tailors was 'the change in men's attitude towards their clothes which has come about over the last ten years [is] an interesting sociological point to appreciate. That clothes can now be sold on an "elegance" principle rather than on a "Good English-worsted-wears-like-Iron" principle is a direct result of the affluent society and the Welfare State.' On his contribution to the '007 James Bond' range for Montague Burton, Sinclair is quoted by the *Sunday Citizen* as saying:

> They are trying to smarten up the average man [...] and he certainly could do with it. They are trying to get rid of things like those awful English sports jackets [...] Bond has taste. He is a dream character for most men. Wouldn't everyone like to have the birds fighting over them, and be able to tell a bartender how to make cocktails?[60]

Reporting that Sinclair had 'been paid a large sum of money' to act as Montague Burton's style consultant, the article explained: 'For the first step on the road to Bondism, you can get a Bond suit from the clothing chain for about 15 guineas,' and compares this with the quality of Sinclair's bespoke tailored suits, 'he will make the genuine article for 70 guineas – the same price as the film company paid. "The suits," [Sinclair] says, "would, of course, look exactly the same . . . for the first day".'

Men's Wear explained that the raincoats and jackets would retail at £9.9s., and the slacks at £4.19s.6d: 'Made from a Terelene/cotton mixture, the raincoat is double-breasted with four buttons. It comes with a buckle belt. The slacks have wishbone bottoms, flaps over the slanted pockets and a belt. The single-breasted, three-button jacket has an outside ticket pocket and a flap over the breast pocket.'[61] To assist in marketing the '007 James Bond' range of raincoats, jackets and slacks, *Television Mail* reported that Montague Burton 'will use thirty-second spots on London (R, ATV), Tyne Tees, and STV from April 4 for several weeks'.[62] Not everyone appeared impressed with the television advertisements. Relating the Bond-branded clothing to the 'similar gimmick' of the Davy Crockett hats, toy pistols and 'every childish commodity' of his childhood, Patrick Stoddart stated:

> Well, I for one want nothing to do with this copying. I like to think that the clothes I wear owe nothing to any screen hero, and that my tastes are my own. I won't be told that 'this year you will be wearing double-breasted jackets,' or that if I don't pretend to be James Bond I will be an outcast.[63]

At the same time that Montague Burton were attempting to garner interest in their '007 James Bond' range, *Style Weekly* reported in August that the London-based tie company James Fisher had reached an agreement with Mervyn Brodic Associates to market exclusively '007 James Bond' ties, retailing at one guinea, to coincide with the release of *Thunderball*, which at the time was believed to be in the autumn of 1965: 'Eighteen ties are in the new collection [...] and include plain slubs, stripes and block stripes, all-over patterns and single motifs. Various polyester fabrics are used [...] and all the ties have the James Bond signature in the lining. Considerable emphasis is on blue with about a third of the range using shades of this colour.'[64] At the same time, *Men's Wear* noted that James Fisher were also marketing James Bond cufflinks at 35 shillings 'in round presentation boxes', with two different styles including 'the "007" symbol etched in black on stainless steel', and 'bullet-shaped, gold plated links cast in authentic 24. Bullet mould'.[65]

An executive decision by Montague Burton was made to discontinue the '007 James Bond' clothing range in November 1965 before the release of *Thunderball*. On the cancelling of the range, Montague Burton released the statement: 'Our market research has proved that it would not be a success [...] People may be image-conscious, but buying clothes is an extremely personal business. We found that the young people, although they may like Bond, do not want to dress like him, and middle-aged men don't want a coat that has pockets for hand grenades.'[66] The *Daily Sketch* was the first to report the end of the range, wittily stating: 'Secret agent James Bond has flopped – for the first time in his high-powered life of blondes, Bentleys and Berettas. Britain's men do NOT want to look like him, no matter how often they see his films or read the 007 books.'[67] The *Daily Mirror* wryly observed: 'Every red-blooded Englishman is supposed to identify himself with James Bond. But not, apparently, if he buys his clothes from Burton's [...] Quite a revelation about a good many Englishmen. One in three buys his clothes from Burton's.'[68] The *Evening Standard* followed, analysing the issue with the clothing as being:

> Many people in the trade are not surprised to hear this. Image conscious though people may be, they argue that buying clothes is a complex business. It's alright trying to entice people into the shop with novel window displays, but once inside they will want to try on the clothes. And if they don't flatter the figure no amount of 'secret service' advertising will do the trick.[69]

The *Evening Standard* explained: 'The trade generally thinks that the advertising was good – the TV ads, they reckon, were "superb". But they feel that the project wasn't backed up by the right sort of merchandising.' The window displays were also perceived to not be particularly good, and 'according to one top tailor, the styles [of the clothes] "were not quite right"', with the *Evening Standard* concluding: 'Good display, it seems, is a vital part of the mass tailoring business. No one can hope to sell clothes – especially sports clothes – just on a 007 label.' *Men's Wear* concurred with this view, believing that the promotion had not been 'handled properly', and acknowledged the necessity of dual-gendered marketing in this type of advertising campaign:

> Burton's technique, and the technique of every other 007 licensee to our knowledge, has been merely to use the Bond name as a label on otherwise ordinary merchandise and Bond-type situations to add drama to their advertising. Surely a better technique would be to apply the name only to

authentic Bond-type merchandise, the sort of garment and accessory that readers of Bond books and filmgoers can recognise as the real thing, and to use this as a basis for hinting to the potential customer that the Bond image will confer some of the Bond suaveness, polish, poise and masculinity on him. Or her boyfriend.[70]

Although Montague Burton had ceased the manufacture of Bond-branded outerwear, Jacobsen confirmed to the *Financial Times* that Sinclair would be retained as a style consultant by the multiple tailor, declaring 'the terms of Mr. Anthony Sinclair's appointment [. . .] had in no way been affected by the company's decision to discontinue the "James Bond" range of men's outerwear. Mr. Sinclair's appointment had been made because of his high reputation as a designer generally, rather than his specific connection with "007"'.[71] In the event, Watson believes that Sinclair's association with Montague Burton didn't 'last much longer than a season or two'.

On the news of Montague Burton's 'killing off' of the '007 James Bond' range, *Style Weekly* analysed the other Bond-branded fashion tie-ins, noting 'firms still handling 007 menswear merchandise reported that they were pleased with the results so far', and that Mervyn Brodie Associates had announced 'that new licenses for James Bond shirts, underwear and socks are shortly to be announced'.[72] The article reported that James Fisher had also experienced disappointing sales for its '007 James Bond' ties, cufflinks and tie-tacks, believing the problem to be that there had been no film release. However, Norman Ruffett, managing director for James Fisher, remained optimistic: 'The delay of the premiere [of *Thunderball*] is a blow, of course, but with all the pre-publicity for the film, I think we'll sell a lot as Christmas presents. We are building stocks and I'm convinced that come Christmas we'll have them cleared entirely'.[73] By way of comparison, *Style Weekly* noted that Norvic, who launched the '007 James Bond' shoes after the release of *Goldfinger* in 1964, had been successful, with the company's representative, Bill Giddings, stating that he was 'still very enthusiastic' about the 007 mark, which has a 'very high-priced image', and noted that the shoes 'sold out rapidly' when it coincided with the release of *Goldfinger*. Indeed, following the numerous reports that Montague Burton had cancelled the '007 James Bond' range, and the speculation as to why, Mervyn Brodie Associates evidently believed that damage limitation was necessary, with a spokesman for the company quoted in *Men's Wear* claiming 'that they had received "numerous applications" from clothing manufacturers wishing to take over the outer clothing rights to the "007" merchandising operation [. . .] "The other licensees in the menswear field are more than delighted with the results of their 007 operations. Business for all of them has been very good".'[74] Certainly, some brands were not deterred by the failure of Montague Burton to market their '007 James Bond' range, with Morley marketing '007 Underwear for Men' early in 1966 after the release of *Thunderball* in December 1965, and the range was advertised in the film's pressbook. Similar to Montague Burton, the 007-branded underwear for men did not improve Morley's fortunes, and by the end of 1967 it was reported that the company had been acquired by Coultaulds: 'for the past two years Morley, who manufacture hosiery, underwear and knitwear, have made trading losses and paid no dividends' to their shareholders.[75]

Furthermore, it appears that Montague Burton did not work hard enough to inspire interest in their '007 James Bond' range. As noted by the press at the time, the company would have needed to either market the range to appeal to a more youthful audience, which was not their main market, or target the middle-aged consumer, their key audience. Prior to the launch of the '007 James Bond' brand in April 1965, Montague Burton had released details in January of a 600 store-wide survey it conducted into the purchasing habits of its customers. 12,000 of its customer's wives were interviewed and each asked twenty questions. The results revealed that 70 per cent of women believed their husbands were 'not adventurous in their choice of suits', and 53 per cent 'came straight to the point and said "they stuck to the same old style"'.[76] The survey indicated that 42 per cent of men 'buy one new suit a year', and that 27 per cent owned three suits: 'Of these suits, two are worn regularly according to 38 per cent of the women interviewed.' The most popular colour was grey, followed by blue, bronze, brown and lovat (pale green). The survey results demonstrate that the majority of Montague Burton's customers were unlikely to be interested in the somewhat gimmicky '007 James Bond' outerwear, and would instead remain buying the style of clothing they were used to. As noted by Stoddard in his negative review of the television advertisements: 'my style is my own.' The range also appeared to fail with the younger market, possibly because the marketing did not particularly appeal to that target group.

It is also important to note that the success of the American and Japanese brands, as well as Galeries Lafayette in France, in capitalizing on the success of *Goldfinger* and the rise of the 'Bond phenomenon' was in part due to the launch of the '007 James Bond' branded clothing and accessories being promoted shortly after the release of the film in these countries, whereas the Montague Burton 'James Bond 007' branded items were released in April 1965, seven months after *Goldfinger*'s release in the UK, and eight months prior to the release of *Thunderball*. As reported by Gardner early in 1966: 'High in the major league of character merchandising is the James Bond cult. In the past year many manufacturers in many countries have paid over £250,000 in licence fees on goods ranging from 007 cologne to 007 underpants and including a spectacular variety of toys.'[77] Explaining that 'so far 102 licenses have been issued', Gardner noted: 'Fleming's hero is licensed to kill – these are licenses to make money: a lot [...] Bond has gone down well everywhere (in France the smart girl wears a 007 bra) but nowhere better than in America. "Business there is fantastic, quite fantastic," says [Robert] Fenn [agent to Booker Bros.].'[78] The success of which was summed up by Keith Shackleton, of AP Films Merchandising, quoted in Gardner's article: 'The art of merchandising is to be in at the beginning today and to have the foresight to exploit it tomorrow.' Advice, perhaps, that Montague Burton should have heeded before cancelling their own '007 James Bond' range. Arguably, the type of fashion promoted after the release of *Goldfinger* worked as a forerunner to future marketing campaigns for the Bond film series, although this type of strategy would not be employed directly by Eon Productions until the end of the decade with the release of *On Her Majesty's Secret Service*.

Notes

1 Tornabuoni, 'A popular phenomenon', 19; Drew Moniot, 'James Bond and America in the Sixties: An Investigation of the Formula Film in Popular Culture', *Journal of the University Film Association* 28, no. 3 (1976), 26; Tony Bennett and Janet Woollacott, *Bond and Beyond: The Political Career of a Popular Hero* (Basingstoke and London: Macmillan Education Limited, 1987), 19.

2 Bennett and Woollacott, 15.

3 John Pearson, *The Life of Ian Fleming* (London: Jonathan Cape Limited, 1966), 304.

4 Bennett and Woollacott, 33.

5 Ibid., 36.

6 Alexis Albion offers a comprehensive analysis of the global historical moment of Bond in the mid-1960s, and why the secret agent's commercial formula of 'blood, bikinis and Bollinger' was so popular in her essay 'Wanting to be James Bond', published in Edward P. Comentale, Stephen Watt and Skip Willman (eds), *Ian Fleming & James Bond: The cultural politics of 007* (Bloomington: Indiana University Press, 2005), 202–24.

7 Fleming to Michael Howard, 5 December 1960, published in Fergus Fleming, *The Man with the Golden Typewriter*, 248.

8 Fleming to Howard, 'Saturday [April 1961]', published in Fergus Fleming, 266.

9 Iris Keenan, 'For the Smart Man', *Newcastle Evening Chronicle*, 5 May 1961, 6.

10 Joyce McKinnell, 'Do You Women Prefer Bonds?', *Liverpool Echo*, 15 July 1961, 4.

11 Fleming to Howard, 16 August 1961, published in Fergus Fleming, 290.

12 Fleur Cowles, 'Renaissance of the British Girl', *The Sunday Times Colour Section*, 4 March 1962, 8–12.

13 'Rainwear's Dramatic Look', *Style Weekly*, 22 November 1962, 10–11.

14 Fleming, *The Man with the Golden Gun* (1965; London: Penguin Books, 2009), 10.

15 'Mondays New Comers', *Television Mail*, 17 May 1963, 21.

16 *Pond's Angel Face Lipstick*, TV advertisement, directed by Guy Hamilton (UK: Eyeline, 1963), www.hatads.org.uk/catalogue/record/09fccb60-98da-431a-a21f-5352d78ac0cf/ (accessed 28 December 2018).

17 'Production View', *Television Mail*, 17 May 1963, 18.

18 Ibid., 19.

19 Fleming to Saltzman, 7 December 1961, published in Fergus Fleming, 258.

20 Llew Gardner, 'The Early Birds: Or how to make money out of James Bond and the Daleks', *Tatler*, 29 January 1966, 14.

21 West Yorkshire Archive Service (WYAS), WYL1951/183/11: 'The James Bond Cult: Licensed to kill – in terms of money', *Johannesburg Star*, 1 March 1965.

22 Ibid.: Maurice Moss, '*Modesty Blaise* could boost British fashion', *Drapery and Fashion Weekly*, 15 January 1965.

23 Ibid.: The James Bond Cult.

24 Moniot, 25.

25 Tournabuoni, 18.

26 '"007" Tag works wonders as sales gimmick in U.S.', *Coventry Evening Telegraph*, 12 April 1965, 10.

27 Tournabuoni, 19.

28 Ibid.

29 'Bondknappers Steal 007 Symbols For Sweat Shirts, Bras, Girdles et al', *Variety*, 9 June 1965, 13.

30 '*Goldfinger* hits new heights in Japan', *Variety*, 21 April 1965, 26.

31 WYAS, WYL1951/183/11: 'Let Bond's tailor dress you at 15 guineas', *Daily Sketch*, 25 March 1965.

32 'Move over, Mr. Moto, for Agent 007', *New York Times*, 24 January 1966, 39.

33 Tornabuoni, 19.

34 WYAS, WYL1951/183/9: Bernard Kaplan, 'Wave of Anglomania Sweeps La Belle France', *Montreal Star*, 12 December 1963.

35 WYAS, WYL1951/183/10: Nathalie Pernikoff, 'Young Bloods rebel against the too-casual look', *Style for Men Weekly*, 26 November 1964.

36 Tornabuoni, 20.

37 'Golden Touch', *Daily Telegraph*, 1 March 1965.

38 Tornabuoni, 20.

39 Andrew Mulligan, 'A France fit for 007s to live in', *Observer*, 27 February 1965.

40 Tornabuoni, 19.

41 Archive Galeries Lafayette: 'James Bond', *Lafayette nous voici: Magazine do personnel des Galeries Lafayette*, April 1965, no. 29, 27.

42 Moniot, 26.

43 'A James Bond to frill you', *Miami News*, 24 February 1965, 15.

44 Golden Touch.

45 Tornabuoni, 20.

46 With thanks to Kevin Bertrand Collette, author of *James Bond: Le dossier secret* (Paris: De Rocher, 2012), who informed the author of this.

47 WYAS, WYL1951/183/10: 'Boldness is the key to 1964 men's styles', *Yorkshire Evening Post*, 18 November 1963.

48 Ibid.: 'Burtons planning James Bond 007 tag', *Yorkshire Evening Post*, 10 December 1964.

49 Ibid.: 'Montague Burton is Patching Up Payout', *Evening Standard*, 10 December 1964.

50 Ibid.: 'Burton's Result Good but Unexciting', *Irish Press*, 11 December 1964.

51 'Burton – James Bond?', *Style Weekly*, 10 December 1964, 1.

52 Anthea Hall, 'For the James Bond fan', *Newcastle Journal*, 17 November 1964, 4.

53 WYAS, WYL1951/183/10: Eric Busgin's cartoon published in *Punch* and reproduced in *London Weekly*, 19 November 1965.

54 'City Snipes', *Daily Mirror*, 23 March 1965, 19.

55 'Burton's customer's reject Bond image', *Style Weekly*, 18 November 1965, 3.

56 '*Danger Man* in deal', *Style Weekly*, 8 April 1965, 16.

57 Nick Davies, 'An 007 suit – But there's no holster', *Daily Mirror*, 25 March 1965, 2.

58 WYAS, WYL1951/183/9: Robert Head, 'How to "Cut" a Big Profit', *Daily Mirror*, 30 October 1963.

59 John Taylor, 'Looking ahead?', *Tailor & Cutter*, 9 April 1965, 479.

60 WYAS, WYL1951/183/11: 'Bond, says his tailor, has taste', *Sunday Citizen*, 8 April 1964.

61 'Big TV Drive for Burton's "007" Range', *Men's Wear*, 3 April 1965, 13.

62 'For the record: New campaigns', *Television Mail*, 2 April 1965, 6.

63 WYAS, WYL1951/183/11: Patrick Stoddard, 'Our Taste is Our Own!', *Watford Observer*, 30 April 1965.

64 '007 aids new range', *Style Weekly*, 5 August 1965, 8.

65 'Gift Bar Ideas', *Men's Wear*, 14 August 1965, 22–23.

66 WYAS, WYL1951/183/12: 'Bond goes for a Burton' *Daily Sketch*, 1 November 1965.

67 Ibid.

68 'The inside page: Bond Image', *Daily Mirror*, 11 November 1965, 15.

69 WYAS, WYL1951/183/12: 'Montague Burton kills off that certain image', *Evening Standard*, 10 November 1965.

70 Ibid.: 'Misfire?', *Men's Wear*, 20 November 1965.

71 'Burton keeps "007" Designer', *Financial Times*, 11 November 1965, 19.

72 'Burton's customer's reject Bond image', *Style Weekly*, 18 November 1965, 3.

73 Ibid.

74 '"Many" bid for Bond rights', *Men's Wear*, 20 November 1965.

75 'Courtaulds acquire Morley', *Style Weekly*, 7 December 1967, 1.

76 'Most men ask wife's advice on clothes says Burton survey', *Daily Mirror*, 7 January 1965, 12.

77 Gardner, 14.

78 Ibid., 15.

4 'COMING OUT OF BURTON'S SHORT OF CREDIT': GEORGE LAZENBY (1969)

After Connery hung up his Anthony Sinclair suits for the first time after *You Only Live Twice*, Saltzman and Broccoli turned their attention to who should be cast in the role of Bond in *On Her Majesty's Secret Service*. They also needed to find a new director as Lewis Gilbert had declined the offer. Peter Hunt was both the producers' and United Artists' choice, having worked as an editor on the Eon Productions Bond films since *Dr. No* and as a second unit director on *You Only Live Twice*. A meeting was held between Hunt and the producers to discuss the casting of Bond, and it was questioned whether to 'play' around by choosing an actor to reflect modern culture. Ultimately, it was decided that 'another Sean Connery type' should be cast.[1] As Broccoli put it, the actor 'had to be British, personable and built to fit the Fleming blueprint. Above all, he had to have all the elements of strong box-office potential [...] Harry and I interviewed several possibilities.'[2] These included Michael Billington and Adam West ('Batman'). Over 400 actors were reportedly considered for the role, with *Life* claiming that Ian Richardson, Robert Campbell, Anthony Rogers and Hans de Vries had been seriously considered.[3]

Casting and costuming the new Bond

In the event, it was George Lazenby, an Australian model famous in the UK for the *Big Fry* chocolate advertisements (1967–68), and possessing no formal acting training, who was eventually cast as Bond. With hindsight, Broccoli argued that Lazenby had been on his radar three years prior to his casting in the role, when both were having their hair cut in Kurt's barber shop situated in the basement of the Dorchester hotel in Mayfair, London: 'I looked across to the next chair and saw this handsome character with a strong jaw, great physique and a lot of self-assurance. I remembered thinking what a great Bond he would make.'[4] According to Lazenby, he had deliberately targeted the barber shop, knowing that Broccoli was a regular customer, as was Connery. Prior to attempting to be cast as Bond, Kurt revealed to Lazenby during a hair-cut, which Lazenby requested be 'cut like James Bond', that Sinclair was Connery's tailor. On visiting the tailor, who could not provide Lazenby with a bespoke suit immediately, Lazenby was offered a suit tailored for Connery that had not been collected.

The following day, Lazenby bypassed the casting call and entered the office of David Lovell, the film's casting director, telling Lovell: 'I heard you're looking for James Bond.' Impressed by Lazenby's confidence and looks, Lovell telephoned Saltzman, telling him: 'There's a guy here that really looks the part,' to which Saltzman demanded that he bring Lazenby over to his offices. Fabricating a back story of his non-existent acting career to Lovell, on being asked by Saltzman to repeat it Lazenby allegedly told the producer: 'I just told him, let him tell you.'[5] Meeting with Hunt the next day, Lazenby admitted to the director that he had lied to Lovell, with Hunt suitably impressed: 'What? And you say you can't act? You've fooled two of the most ruthless men I've met in my life. Stick to your story and I'll make you the next James Bond.'[6] Saltzman, however, was not, and complained: 'Get him out of here. He's a "clothes-peg". We'll be the laughing stock of the whole industry if we hire a male model.'[7] However, Broccoli agreed with Hunt: 'The infallible litmus test was to parade him in front of the office secretaries. Their eyes lit up as he swung past their desks and through to our office. Six-foot-two-inches tall – the same height as Connery – he was a hundred-and-eighty-six-pounder who knew how to walk tall and put himself over.'[8] According to consistent reports, it was the fight test sequences that ensured Lazenby was cast in the role, and on viewing the footage United Artists agreed. Owing to Broccoli's and Lazenby's initial connection in Kurt's, it was appropriate that Lazenby was announced to the press as being the next Bond at the Dorchester on 7 October 1968. Lazenby was subsequently photographed for his pre-publicity stills wearing the Sinclair suit that he had purchased to convince the producers and director of his suitability for Bond. Leaning against a lamppost situated on the Thames opposite Big Ben, the suit is cut in the typical Sinclair style with the jacket possessing natural shoulders and roped sleeve-heads, a full chest and gently suppressed waist. The trousers have tapered legs and plain hems.

In the film, Lazenby has the most costume changes of any actor to play the role of Bond in one film: a total of twenty costumes, of which fifteen are tailored items. In order, the outfits include: a ruffled-front dress shirt and black dinner suit trousers, an ivory suit with pink shirt (the first ivory suit to be worn by Bond in the Eon Productions franchise), a black dinner suit with white ruffled dress shirt, a terrycloth bathrobe, a brown golf outfit with orange polo-neck jumper, a navy three-piece herringbone suit with a six-button waistcoat, a houndstooth tweed hacking jacket with a beige silk shirt including a stock tie and beige jodhpurs, a sky blue suit, a Prince of Wales glen plaid check suit, a double-breasted navy blazer and medium-grey flannel trousers, a navy three-quarter length overcoat, a navy chalk stripe three-piece suit with seven-button waistcoat, a Victorian-inspired Inverness overcoat in rust brown tweed over a brown tweed suit, Scottish regalia including a kilt, a light brown cardigan with white shirt and brown tweed trousers, a blue Willy Bognor ski suit, a stolen plaid wool ski jacket, a blue 'action suit' including a large anorak and matching salopettes, and a three-piece lounge suit with black jacket, dove-grey waistcoat and trousers and a white shirt.

In a similar approach to that of Terence Young, Hunt also decided to employ his personal tailor to help create Lazenby's Bond image. The suits, as well as the navy overcoat and rust-brown Inverness coat, were tailored by Dimitrov 'Dimi' Major, whose firm, D. Major Bespoke Tailors Ltd., was based on Dawes Lane, London. Major also tailored the three-piece suit and wedding attire for Marc-Ange Draco (Gabriele Ferzetti), and the Astrakhan fur-trimmed overcoat worn by Blofeld (Telly Savalas) in the film. Major was trained in the art of tailoring by his father, similarly to Sinclair, before being employed by Bernard Weatherill on Savile Row. He started his own tailoring business in 1959. During the early years, Major co-worked with Douglas Hayward, who would later open his own tailoring firm, based in Mount Street in 1968. Hayward would come to tailor Roger Moore's suits for his James Bond films in the 1980s. During the period when Major and Hayward collaborated, the firm on Dawes Lane was known as 'Major Hayward'. In April 1966, Sheila Fitzjones wrote an article on key London-based tailors in *Tatler* magazine, and named the firm as being 'the "in" tailors of the moment':

[Major Hayward] have so much work at the moment that they asked for their address to be left out as they feel that anyone who really wants to come to them will make the effort to track them down! Satisfied customers include such familiar names as Vidal Sassoon, James Fox, Michael Caine, Tony Curtis, Kirk Douglas. Made suits for Terence Stamp for film *Modesty Blaise* [1966] and for Peter Sellers for film *Casino Royale* [1967].[9]

At this time, a 'Major Hayward' two-piece suit cost from 45 guineas, trousers from 12 guineas, and Fitzjones stated that the tailoring style was a '[mixture] of classic tailoring with Savile Row workmanship and modern styling'.

On being interviewed by Spaiser, Andrew Major outlined his father's approach to tailoring and suit structure: 'My father always aimed for an elegant shaped cut, with soft shoulders and a medium-weight canvas for the coat [jacket] and a slim but not over-fitted line to the trousers. The emphasis has always been on a classic look with a nod to the fashion of the day, without adopting the often fleeting extremes of style.'[10] Spaiser explains that Lazenby's suits are all tailored similarly:

they all have a 'classic English cut' with a few acknowledgements towards men's fashion in the late 1960s, specifically a short jacket length and narrow straight-legged trousers.[11] The jackets have soft shoulders, natural sleeve-heads and narrow lapels. They have a full chest and suppressed waist to accentuate Lazenby's figure and have either slanted or straight pockets with flaps, and the bottom of the jackets are normally tailored with a flared skirt and single or double vents. The Prince of Wales glen check suit differs slightly in that its jacket also includes a slanted hacking pocket. The trousers have an extended waist and Daks tops, as with Connery's Sinclair-tailored suit trousers. They are medium rise, with narrow, straight legs and a plain, slanted hem. The pleated trouser variation includes double-forward pleats and cuffed hems. Major was to say on tailoring suits for Lazenby's physique: 'The boy was very difficult to dress, very broad shoulders and slim body, but if he stands right he looks immaculate in my suits.'[12]

The rust-brown, single-breasted Inverness coat disguise, worn by Lazenby when posing as Sir Hilary Bray in order to infiltrate Blofeld's lair on Piz Gloria, is tailored with natural shoulders, a Prussian collar, straight jetted pockets and set-in sleeves (Figure 4.1). It is fastened with four horn buttons. The Inverness coat, often made of herringbone or tweed fabric, was a Victorian heavy-duty overcoat. It became synonymous with Sherlock Holmes after the fictional character was depicted as wearing one in Sidney Paget's illustrations. In Fleming's novel, Bond is described at London Airport in disguise wearing a 'bowler hat, rolled umbrella, neatly folded *Times* and all', all the while feeling 'faintly ridiculous'.[13] The script directly references Fleming, similarly writing: 'Bond emerges from train carrying a battered suitcase, a bulky briefcase, and an umbrella. He wears a heavy overcoat, tweed suit, and a bowler. Curved pipe clamped between his teeth, he peers over rims of pince-nez.'[14] It is perhaps the mention of a 'heavy overcoat' and 'curved

FIGURE 4.1 George Lazenby dressed in a 'Sherlock Holmes' disguise in *On Her Majesty's Secret Service*. Directed by Peter Hunt © Eon Productions/United Artists 1969. All rights reserved.

pipe' in the script, but in the film it was decided to offer a visually humorous reference in costuming the undercover Bond as Holmes.

The Highland regalia worn by Bond as Bray was sourced from Scott Adie Ltd. The Black Watch tartan, also termed as 'Government Sett', was chosen owing to Bray's character having a military background in the novel, serving in the British Army at the Rhine. Created in 1739, the black, green and blue tartan is not affiliated with any clan, so it would not lead to any etiquette issues when Bond wears it in disguise. Following Lazenby's fitting for his jabot and kilt, a tailor at Scott Adie claimed: 'He looks most splendidly Scottish, as he is very tall and has an athletic figure he couldn't be better suited to a kilt.'[15] The boots for the costume were sourced from John Lobb. For the ski suit, designed by Willy Bognor, the colour blue was chosen by Hunt who had an ulterior motive, according to Charles Helfenstein. Apparently, it was because the shade of blue used for the suit matched the blue screen process, meaning that Hunt had to film all ski scenes on location and shortcuts could not be taken by filming the scenes back in the studio should something go wrong.

As argued by Nick Sullivan, Lazenby's wardrobe began to 'show signs of wider lapels and more fashionable use of colour [...] streetwise Lazenby was clearly a different animal from Connery and the notion of the wardrobe consisting only of the classic essentials was already fading, pointing the way to the playboy image of Roger Moore's Bond.'[16] Spaiser concurs, opining: 'Lazenby started with the Connery Bond template but expanded and modernised it. Lazenby's suits did not have the traditional Savile Row look of Connery's suits, but they still looked unquestionably English. Compared to Connery's Anthony Sinclair suits, Lazenby's suits from Dimi Major were cut in a more fashion forward manner.'[17] Sinclair's suits, of course, were 'West End' tailored, rather than 'Savile Row' tailored, as were Major's, although Major had trained in Savile Row. Roger Moore believed that Major 'came up with a rather timeless three-piece suit for the London scenes, featuring wider lapels and pocket flaps, and more fashionable brighter styles for overseas settings. It was a marked departure. Bond was now fitted in a much wider-styled wardrobe, and that gave a feeling of a slightly more casual 007 for the late Sixties.'[18]

Costuming the remaining cast

According to the unit lists and schedules for the film, the wardrobe team in Switzerland included Jackie Cummins as the wardrobe supervisor, John Brady as the wardrobe master and wardrobe assistants Janet Dodson and Jimmy Smith.[19] Marjory Cornelius, the film's costume designer (referred to by Hunt as 'my dress designer'), was employed on the production prior to shooting, however given the indication on the unit list, it is likely that Cornelius remained designing and sourcing the costumes in the UK while the other members of the wardrobe unit attended Switzerland with 'thirty boxes of costumes'.[20]

Cornelius was a personal friend of Hunt: her limited experience included designing Dinah Sheridan and Kay Kendall's costumes for *Genevieve* (1953), which was directed by her husband Henry Cornelius, and the dresses for the theatre play *First Edition* (1954). The production 'kept Cornelius busy' according to Hunt, and the designer had to create thirteen distinct costume concepts for Diana Rigg's character, Tracy di Vincenzo, Bond's love interest and future wife.[21] The 'unlucky' thirteenth costume that appears in the film was, ironically, Tracy's wedding dress. Cornelius physically attended the studio shooting at Pinewood and the Portuguese locations later in the film's production, along with the same wardrobe team as listed for Switzerland.[22] Cornelius's agency is most prominent in her designs for Tracy's costume pieces on display in the film, namely the 'mermaid' Emilio Pucci-inspired dress, the Portuguese riding outfit and the wedding dress. Cornelius is also likely to have designed the white evening gown worn by Tracy in the casino, the Chanel-inspired woollen suit, the light brown ice-skating dress, and the black shift tunic and trousers with a silver fox and black rabbit fur trim hood and sleeves inspired by Rigg's performance as Mrs. Emma Peel in *The Avengers*. The remaining outfits include the hotel dressing gown also worn by Bond, three shift dresses and a pink suit worn in the 'romantic montage' sequence, and a stylized chocolate brown ski outfit created by Willy Bognor. Rigg and Saltzman's wife, Jacqueline, attended Paris fashion shows in order to garner inspiration for Tracy's wardrobe in the film, and this would lead to the sourcing of many of Tracy's costumes for *On Her Majesty's Secret Service*, including the full-length mink fur coat and Jacoli hat that was purchased from Harold J. Rubin based in New York. Other items were sourced from costumier Bermans and Nathans.

At the beginning of Fleming's novel, when Bond saves Tracy's life, he describes the latter as a 'lithe golden figure in the white one-piece bathing suit'.[23] In the script, the costume has been adapted for context, and is described: 'She wears a simple but obviously top-couturièred evening dress.'[24] Thus, Cornelius interpreted the script indication to design the 'mermaid' gown, worn by Tracy in the opening scenes in the film (Plate 4). The designer took direct inspiration from the Italian fashion designer Emilio Pucci, who became famous during the 1960s for his use of innovative textiles and prints in his couture-tailored gowns. In 1964, Valarie Lawford celebrated Pucci as being 'a visionary' and 'an artist with an architect's sense of proportion'.[25] Lawford outlined that the 'Pucci look' was determined by 'the print snowed under by sequins', and the colours were inspired by African designs, Chinese embroideries, Indian fabrics and cathedral stained glass. Cornelius's design consists of a scalloped full-length gown made from dyed sea green silk with gold, blue and pink sequins stitched into a paisley pattern on the body. It has a deep sweetheart neckline and a split to the upper thigh at the front. The trumpet sleeves are cut in a wide Tudor-style. Alongside Pucci, the gown also acknowledges the forthcoming 1970s quasi-hippy fashions. Tracy's low-heeled sandals are dyed in the same sea green as the gown and have a painted gold motif. Hunt later said of the dress that it was 'really lovely; full of sequins [. . .] it was so beautiful on that scale. It's the sort of thing you walk into the sea with.'[26]

The second outfit that Tracy wears is in the casino of the Hotel Palácio Estoril. In the novel, Fleming describes her attire as 'some kind of plain white dress', which is adapted in the script to read: 'She wears a low-cut sleeveless white evening gown.'[27] In the film, Tracy wears a white floor-length, dupioni silk evening gown, structured in a column shape. The shoulders, deep plunging neckline and back yolk are structured with a shawl panel that includes hand-stitched white seed pearls that are corded in drapes and individually knotted together to form scallop shapes. Visible beneath the neckline of the gown is the centre-front gore of Tracy's *brassière*, also embroidered with crystals and seed pearls. The *brassière* can be viewed on fuller display in the scenes that follow in Tracy's bedroom. The front of the gown includes a slit cut to the thigh, revealing an underskirt panel made with white silk and appliquéd Chantilly lace, embroidered with silver and blue threads and seed pearls. The back has a hidden zip fastening. On Bond entering Tracy's hotel bedroom, she wears a short, thigh-length terrycloth dressing gown, knotted at the waist with a matching belt. It is white with a windowpane pattern of navy double lines. As an extra design feature, there are thicker lines framed around the shawl collar and the cuffs of the sleeves.

Tracy is next viewed in her distinctive Portuguese riding outfit (Figure 4.2), designed by Cornelius, that is worn to her father's birthday party. The only direction offered by the script is that Tracy and Olympe (Virginia North), Draco's mistress, wear 'riding habits', and therefore Cornelius obtained her inspiration from the historic Portuguese costume.[28] The fitted black jacket is cut in the style of a bolero, with no collar. It is waist-length with long sleeves. The white cotton blouse underneath has a wide, high-band and close-fitting collar made from a cotton

FIGURE 4.2 Tracy di Vincenzo's 'Portuguese riding outfit'. *On Her Majesty's Secret Service* directed by Peter Hunt © Eon Productions/United Artists 1969. All rights reserved.

Portuguese lace border with a symmetrical floral pattern. The lace is repeated down the centre placket of the blouse. The same lace is also used to form unfastened cuffs that are visible beneath the jacket sleeves. The black culottes are calf-length and wide-legged, worn with knee-length black leather boots. The culottes have a black velvet motif in the shape of vine leaves appliquéd on to the bottom of the outside leg, as per Cornelius's design.[29] Tracy wears a red silk cummerbund around her waist and black leather gloves on her hands. The bolero hat, similar to a Fedora, is designed in direct reference to the historic Portuguese riding outfit. It is made of black woollen felt and has a flat crown with a wide brim. It does not include a ribbon. As an accessory, Tracy has a black leather riding crop that was prominent in the publicity stills taken for the film's promotional campaign.

Following the 'romantic montage' sequence, the script directs that Tracy is dressed in a 'chic ensemble' seated between Bond and Draco who wear business suits in the back of Draco's Daimler.[30] The costume includes a waist-length jacket designed by Cornelius that takes inspiration from Chanel. It is made from a Harris tweed fabric with a white base and mustard yellow and gold square checks. The jacket has a rolled band collar and Roman shoulders with roped sleeve-heads. It includes a side-front closing with a hidden fastening, and the long, fitted sleeves of the jacket have turned-up cuffs fastened with one button covered in the same fabric. Underneath the jacket, Tracy wears a gold silk blouse, of which only the collar and cuffs are visible. The gauntlet cuffs are long and include six fabric-covered buttons, and the Ascot collar of the blouse is a long wide band with the two ends brought to the front and looped over each other with pointed ends. It is pinned to the side of the jacket with a gold brooch. Tracy wears a cloche hat, made from the same suit fabric, which has a turned-up brim and a gold ribbon band. The cloche hat, shaped like a bell, was a popular Art Deco fashion item introduced in the 1920s that received a second vogue in the 1960s. In the 1920s a hat ribbon with a pointed arrow was worn on a cloche hat to symbolize that a woman was single but had already given her heart to someone. Although the hat ribbon on Tracy's is plain, Cornelius may well have been inspired to indicate this message through the blouse collar instead, given its shape.

For Tracy's light brown ice-skating outfit, Cornelius chose to go against both the description in the novel and the script. In the novel, Fleming writes: 'From right across the rink, a girl in a short black skating-skirt topped by a shocking pink fur-lined parka, sped like an arrow across the ice to a crash-stop in front of Bond,' and this is copied in the script.[31] Instead, the dress is a low-waisted A-line mini dress, of which the bodice is fitted and the skirt is cut with a full, wide and flaring hem, with pleats stitched symmetrically at the front, sides and back. It is fastened with a front zip and has a high-necked and wide, pointed collar. The long sleeves are fitted, and the centre-front bib, the collar and cuffs include a gold quilted fabric. Tracy's ice skates are made from patent leather, and she wears a head band in her hair that were selected to match the colour of the dress and dark brown leather gloves.

Tracy's wedding outfit was prominently featured in the film's promotional campaign, and departs significantly from the description offered in both the novel and the script. Fleming wrote that Tracy wore a 'light-grey Tyroler outfit with the traditional dark-green trimmings and stag's horn buttons', with a 'saucy mountaineer's hat with its gay chamois beard cockade'.[32] The *Tyroler* dress, also referred to as a *dirndl*, is a German-Swiss folk costume, generally regarded as traditional dress for women based in the Alps. This was changed for the script owing to Bond and Tracy getting married in Portugal rather than Germany. In the script, it simply notes that Tracy is dressed in a 'wedding dress and veil', which is more in keeping with Bond's nightmare experienced in the novel, with Tracy described as being dressed in 'oyster satin', 'loaded with jewels', and a 'diamond tiara that glittered gorgeously' in her hair.[33] Instead, Cornelius designed an all-in-one trouser suit made from white guipure lace shaped in oversized daisy flowerheads, with smaller daisies and seed pearls appliquéd on to the fabric. It is sleeveless, with a scalloped, low-cut *décolleté* neckline and the wide trousers are straight-cut. Instead of a veil, Tracy wears a detachable, full-length wedding coat made from diaphanous ivory chiffon, which is formed of three tiers of different lengths and has long angel sleeves. Tracy wears white leather ankle boots with a low heel. In terms of Tracy's hairstyle in the film, it is similar to the description of Bond's nightmare in the novel, with Fleming writing 'her golden hair had been piled up grandly into one of those fancy arrangements you see in smart hairdressers' advertisements'.[34] In the film, Tracy wears silk flowers in her hair, which are similar in shape to the white flowers that grow on *cornus kouza* (dogwood) trees. The costume ensemble is designed by Cornelius to reference and combine different elements of Tracy's previous outfits together, including the sleeves of the 'mermaid' gown, the colour and seed pearls of the evening gown worn in the casino, the legs of the Portuguese riding outfit, and the overall floral theme evident throughout the design of the film.

Regarding the significant floral theme of *On Her Majesty's Secret Service*, Hunt specified that he wanted 'flowers, flowers, flowers' throughout the design, and carnations are prevalent throughout. Red carnations are situated in Bond's hotel suite in the Hotel Palácio Estoril, and following their night together, Tracy leaves a red carnation on her dressing gown for Bond to find (Plate 5). Draco wears a red carnation in the buttonhole of his suit when Bond first meets him. In the wedding scenes at the end of the film, there are a mix of red, pink and white carnations, with Tracy peeling the petals off of a white carnation before her assassination. According to consistent interpretations regarding different carnation colours, light red represents 'admiration', dark red 'deep love', white 'pure love and good luck' and pink 'remembrance of deceased'. Therefore, the use of red and white carnations at the first and last meeting of Bond and Tracy represents the journey of their relationship from 'deep' to 'pure' love, as well as the white carnation that Tracy peels being tragi-ironic.

Tracy's wedding ring was created by Charles de Temple, who had created the flamboyant gold finger ring for Honor Blackman to wear at the premiere of *Goldfinger*. Two versions of the wedding ring were made for the film. In Fleming's novel, Tracy's engagement ring is described as 'a baroque ring in white gold with two diamond hands clasped. It was graceful and simple', whereas the ring produced for the film is typical of de Temple's exaggerated style.[35] It is a bi-coloured open work gold band, composed of letters spelling the phrase 'we have all the time in the world' around the exterior and interior, and was described by Sheila Black in the *Financial Times* as 'a marvellous thing of lines and waves and cavities, rather reminiscent of the Swiss mountains where the Bond's honeymooned'.[36] It was made in size K to fit Rigg's finger. Following the film's release, de Temple made an alternate cast of the ring reading 'all the love in the world' to sell or give to his clients, as well as fifty licenced reproductions in silver and gold. According to the *Financial Times*, the reproductions cost 'about £55' each, and were sold at Jean Renét based in Old Bond Street, London.[37]

Savalas's Blofeld is also more fashionably dressed than previous actors to play the character in the Eon Productions Bond films, in keeping with the rest of the cast's stylish costumes. Described in the script as 'an impressive and strongly-built man in his early fifties who is removing a white overall', little of Blofeld's costume is mentioned in the script.[38] In the film, Blofeld is mainly dressed in various shades of brown, with the exception of a burgundy red single-breasted silk waistcoat. It is cut in an unusual style, namely a deep scoop neckline of which the lapels are cut with an inverted notch. There is a gold filigree chain fastened across the inverted notches, and the waistcoat is fastened with five silver-plated buttons. Over the waistcoat, Blofeld wears a fitted dark brown jacket with a Nehru collar that includes distinctive red stitching around the two jetted pockets on the upper chest. The jacket has Roman shoulders and roped sleeve-heads. It has a fastening of five large and decorative mother-of-pearl buttons. Major tailored the light brown herringbone wool overcoat worn by Blofeld in the scenes that follow. It is knee-length and double-breasted, with a six-button fastening. The collar and large lapels are trimmed with Astrakhan fur, as is Blofeld's hat, and the coat has large slanted and flapped pockets.

Unlike the previous Bond films, in *On Her Majesty's Secret Service*, Moneypenny (Lois Maxwell) is also fashionably dressed, with Cornelius providing the character with two stylish costume concepts. Hunt later boasted of Maxwell's performance: 'I think, mainly because I had her dressed very well, Lois Maxwell was better in this film as Moneypenny than she was in any of the others.'[39] Owing to her outfit worn as a guest at Bond's wedding, as well as a *brassière* created especially for Maxwell, the actress's costume fittings were more elaborate than usual. In the script, it described her character as 'chic' and 'impeccable'.[40] For Moneypenny's first scene based in the offices of the Secret Service, she wears a princess-shaped, knee-length dress, made from a yellow and black houndstooth plaid check on a white wool fabric base. Therefore, it creates an illusion of being a jacket, especially given the fitted seams, a deep plunge neckline and square lapels. It is fastened at the waist with a fitted belt of matching fabric. Underneath the dress neckline, a fitted white silk polo-necked top can be viewed, emphasized by a three-tiered filigree gold chain necklace. For the wedding scene, Moneypenny wears a knee-length, A-line aqua blue dress with a straight camisole neckline. Over the dress, she wears a stylized princess cut, three-quarter length jacket in a matching colour. It is open cut, and has slim, shawl collar lapels, two hidden slanted hacking pockets, and a four large cloth-covered button detail stitched either side of the waist opening. The fitted sleeves have double-layer turn up cuffs. Both the lapels and the under layer of the cuffs have a distinctive elongated teardrop patterning in pink, blue, yellow, and green on a navy background. The matching hat has a wide brim and repeats the teardrop fabric on its underbrim. On her lapel, Moneypenny wears an insect-shaped brooch that has ruby eyes, with a turquoise stone body and gold wings set with diamonds.

Marketing

On Her Majesty's Secret Service had the most directly fashion-focused marketing campaign of any of the Bond films to date. Unusually, it was aimed at the female market, which is something that Eon Productions had not previously targeted. As part of the film's pre-publicity campaign, *Ladies Home Journal* advertised a glossy two-page spread including images of the 'Angels of Death' actresses dressed in variations of *Vogue* pattern 7313 alongside Lazenby in his Scottish Highland regalia and Savalas in his burgundy waistcoat. The photographs were taken by Howell Conant on the set of the Piz Gloria lounge. In the advertisement, Nora O'Leary, the patterns editor, states: 'Hold on for the newest James Bond sizzler [. . .] As you'd expect, the movie offers the usual bevy of international beauties, and here they are: eight girls in black and white fashions made from only one great pattern.'[41] According to the description in the *Vogue Pattern Book*, 7313 is a: 'Straight dress in evening or street length, has jewel neckline; with or without banding. Full-length sleeves or sleeveless. Overblouse with full-length sleeves has V-neckline. Pleated skirt, or yoke, and slightly flared pants with waistbands. Recommended for border prints, Cut on crossgrain. No allowance for matching plaid or stripes.'[42] *Ladies Home Journal* mainly dressed the actresses in the 'overblouse' and 'slightly flared pants [trousers]' variation of the pattern, except for two who wore the 'straight dress'. The different patterns were made from the following fabrics: Sylvana Henriques ('Jamaican Girl') in 'see-through lace' from Samuel Ehrman, Catherine Schell (Nancy) in Abraham's 'cotton cloque print', Mona Chong ('Chinese Girl') in 'a dress of flower-striped S. Edwards Ban-Lon', Zaheera ('Indian Girl') in 'paisley silk surah (Chardon Marche)', Angela Scoular (Ruby) in 'giant houndstooth Ban-Lon', Joanna Lumley ('English Girl') in 'Lawrence and Klauber bonded *crêpe*', Dani Sheridan ('American Girl') in 'a basic black silk dress of *crêpe* with ostrich boa', and Ingrit Back ('German Girl') in 'heavily embroidered linen-y Record Lace fabric'.[43]

The film's press book mainly focuses on Tracy's wedding attire, and specifically promotes the ring and the dress. For the ring, reproduced by Arts Galore, it states: 'The fabulous wedding ring [...] has been reproduced and will be on sale throughout the country. The ring is inscribed "All The Time In The World". In an attractive ring case, this will retail at around 10s.0d. Tie up with window displays, point of sale displays etc. etc. for maximum impact.'[44] The wedding dress was reproduced by Berkertex Brides and sold at a recommended retail price of 50 guineas, which was to be on sale at Berkertex boutiques nationally. Given the price, the dress is a rather cheap-looking and poorly constructed version of Cornelius's design, made from white satin including a very heavy floral lace overlay. It is floor-length and A-Line in shape, with a high-rolled band neckline, straight bodice and long lace sleeves. The press book points out that 'there are many ways the dress could be linked with the film', and explains that 'at the London premiere we had an attractive model arrive at the cinema wearing the dress, which resulted in a picture in the *Evening Standard*'.[45] *Kinematograph Weekly* suggested that for fashion-based promotion: 'What about a Swiss reception for the opening with girls in national costume? Apart from the many Swiss products marketed the local sports shop could offer a tie-in with ski wear', and 'contact all traders who have something to do with weddings. They could include: florists, bakers, photographers, jewellers, caterers, stationers (invitation cards) car hire firms and wine merchants', before making specific mention of the Berkertex wedding dress: 'Contact with the local fashion house could bring a display.'[46]

The dress formed part of a competition prize, along with a trousseau of Berkertex clothes and a 'jet flight honeymoon' to Portugal, run by the *Daily Mail* in February 1970. Misleadingly claiming that the Berkertex version was 'a seam-for-seam copy of the exquisite wedding dress', the competition was to find 'Mrs. 007', and asked for women to enter by sending a full-length and recent photograph of themselves and explain in twenty-five words why they believed that they were 'the perfect match for James Bond'.[47] In March, 'slim, pretty brunette', Mrs. Vivienne Downes, aged 23, was announced as the competition winner: 'It's an absolute godsend. I didn't believe it at first, and when I did, I just cried', Downes explained, presumably not because she had just seen the Berkertex version of Tracy's wedding dress.[48] Having already married, Downes thought of the dress: 'I'm sure it will be suitable for parties.' Though she may well have rethought this, given that Downes had not yet had the opportunity to view the film: 'I am a great James Bond fan, and since the film is being shown in Cardiff this week, I'll certainly be going to see it.' Perhaps it was for the best that the *Daily Mail* rewarded Downes the dress before she had a chance to view the film. As Helfenstein wittily put it: 'Neither item [the ring nor the dress] sold well as women evidently weren't that interested in emulating a bride murdered before her honeymoon.'[49]

Reception

The critical reception for *On Her Majesty's Secret Service* was mixed, and on Lazenby's performance it was especially so. Alexander Walker was sympathetic, writing that the actor's voice 'is more suave than sexy-sinister. But he could pass for the other fellow's twin on the shady side of the casino [...] Lazenby wins in fighting his way alone into a skin-fit shirt.'[50] Charles Champlin concurred with Walker's view, comparing both actors: 'It's ironic that Sean Connery, having seen James Bond through the thinly two-dimensional days, should not be around for the new, higher interest Bond. But George Lazenby handles it very nicely.'[51] Michael Kostelnuk believed:

> The predicted demise of the James Bond series after the departure of Sean Connery from the title role, may be a bit premature. [The film] turns out to be as good as the best Connery-Bond and far better than *You Only Live Twice* [...] Lazenby looks far more like the way I envisioned the fictional Bond: a shallower, efficient professional who would kill for an Establishment in which he didn't really believe.[52]

Richard Schmeiszl was probably the most enthusiastic towards Lazenby's performance, however this is likely because he was writing for the Australian *Melbourne Truth*, with Schmeiszl exclaiming: 'Lazenby shows a knack and talent that surpasses even that of the legend of the first Bond, Sean Connery. Lazenby does an excellent job, he has the suave good looks that are perfect for the part [...] Lazenby proves himself a winner in all ways.'[53] However, many critics were unimpressed with Lazenby, often lamenting the loss of Connery. Ian Christie simply stated: 'I don't believe for a moment that this chap George Lazenby is James Bond. I know, and you know that 007 is Sean Connery [...] this new fellow is clearly an imposter.'[54] 'P.D.Z.' directly referenced fashion on reviewing *On Her Majesty's Secret Service*, writing that the film

> carries the slightly faded air of a chic coat two years out of style [...] This Fleming offering, for all its slick elegance, stands trapped between eras, neither new nor old, only imitative [...] George Lazenby, a top male model from Australia, whose open, characterless face and eyes as blank as roulette chips reflect a mind that has never had a thought.[55]

Perhaps the most damning verdict, especially in relation to tailoring, was provided courtesy of Derek Malcolm. The critic annihilated Lazenby's performance:

The general level of everything is quite good as it ever was, except, as I say, the aforementioned Mr. Lazenby, who looks like a Willerby Brothers clothes peg and acts as if he's just come out of Burtons short on credit. It is reported that he just as soon go back to lorry driving and I share his sentiments exactly.[56]

This particular review led to an alleged brief and relatively friendly 'tailoring war' between Sinclair and Major. Following Malcolm's review published in the *Guardian*, Sinclair, or possibly someone on behalf of the tailor, wrote to the editor of *Today's Cinema* to complain:

Since the release of the film *On Her Majesty's Secret Service*, I have found myself increasingly the target of those corner-eyed surveillances generally directed at the central figure in the Amplex advertisements [. . .] Veiled references by well-wishers, and denouncements by film critics, however, finally brought home to me the suspicion that because I made the suits for Sean Connery in the other Bond epics, I am being identified with the sartorial projection of the current James; and quite wrongly. I didn't make <u>all</u> the double-breasted attractions in the early Bond productions (unhappily) – but I would like to put on record that I didn't even make the single-breasted ones in the current picture.[57]

This letter caused an investigation by 'Observer' of the *Financial Times*, who claimed: 'If you think film stars are temperamental, wait until you meet their tailors [. . .] George Lazenby might not go down as the easiest star United Artists has handled, but now the saga of his suits takes the limelight.'[58] On being questioned why Sinclair did not tailor Lazenby's suits for the film, Sinclair became 'unusually reticent, or rather does not utter many printable terms', and the article suggests that: 'Clearly there was a disagreement, as they say. So United Artists went elsewhere.' On being informed as to what Sinclair said regarding the suits, Major replied that the former was 'very cheeky indeed', and explained to 'Observer' that 'I think everyone was very pleased' with the suits he produced for the film.

There was not only an alleged dispute between the two tailors, but a rather larger one simmering between Lazenby and the producers. Following reports that Lazenby had been arrogant on set and upset various members of the cast and crew with his behaviour, the press began to pick up on the tension caused by Lazenby who had been steadfastly refusing to make another Bond film. Due to this, it was Rigg who was sent on the film's official promotional tour in America rather than Lazenby. During the production, Lazenby, who had received $50,000 for the role and was due to receive $75,000 and a percentage to make a second Bond film, believed that he was not being paid his dues, especially when compared to Connery's salary for *You Only Live Twice*. Ronan O'Rahilly, the founder of the pirate radio station Radio Caroline, had become Lazenby's advisor after the latter's casting in the role, and forcefully advised the actor that he should be part of the new youth culture movement rather than stick with Bond.[59] Saltzman reportedly offered Lazenby £1 million to make another Bond film 'anywhere in the world', and following Lazenby's refusal, Arnold and David Picker, executives at United Artists, attempted to persuade him by hosting a meeting at their offices, telling him: 'See all these books here. They're all books that we own that we can make into movies. You can take your pick of anyone of these books and do one in-between each James Bond film.'[60] Again, Lazenby refused, and the actor allegedly donated 'three suitcases full' of his clothing from *On Her Majesty's Secret Service* to the Salvation Army. One final attempt was made, this time by Broccoli. Lazenby simply told the producer: 'No Cubby. I'm out of here.'[61] Thus, the search for another new Bond began.

Notes

1 Broccoli with Zec, *When the Snow Melts*, 177.

2 Ibid., 216.

3 '400 candidates: Which man would you pick as the new James Bond?', *Life*, 11 October 1968.

4 Broccoli with Zec, 216.

5 Matthew Field and Ajay Chowdhury, *Some Kind of Hero: The Remarkable Story of the James Bond Films* (Stroud: The History Press, 2015), 180.

6 Ibid.

7 Ibid.

8 Broccoli with Zec, 216.

9 Sheila Fitzjones, 'Suit yourself', *Tatler*, 2 April 1966, 40.

10 Spaiser, 'Dimi Major bespoke tailors: *OHMSS* style', *The Suits of James Bond*, 20 April 2015, www.bondsuits.com/d-major-bespoke-tailors-ohmss-style/ (accessed 15 June 2020).

11 Spaiser, 'Basted for Bond: Examining George Lazenby's Dimi Major clothes', *The Suits of James Bond*, 28 July 2015, www.bondsuits.com/basted-for-bond-examining-george-lazenbys-dimi-major-clothes/ (accessed 15 June 2020).

12 Observer, 'Temperamentally unsuited', *Financial Times*, 14 January 1970, 18.

13 Fleming, *On Her Majesty's Secret Service* (1963; London: Penguin Books, 2009), 94.

14 Richard Maibaum, *On Her Majesty's Secret Service*, shooting script, 5 September 1968, Sc.223.

15 Charles Helfenstein, *The Making of On Her Majesty's Secret Service* (USA: Spies LLC, 2009), 68.

16 Sullivan, *Dressed to Kill*, 138.

17 Spaiser, 'Lazenby and Moore style: Breaking away from Connery', *The Suits of James Bond*, 10 June 2019, www.bondsuits.com/lazenby-and-moore-style-breaking-away-from-connery/ (accessed 21 June 2020).

18 Roger Moore with Gareth Owen, *Bond on Bond: The ultimate book on over 50 years of 007* (London: Michael O'Mara Books Limited, 2015), 123.

19 BFI, Brinley Jones Collection, BRJ/9/1: Schedule 'A' 1st unit personnel.

20 Helfenstein, 68

21 'Audio commentary featuring Peter Hunt, the cast and crew', *On Her Majesty's Secret Service*, DVD, directed by Peter Hunt (1969; MGM Home Entertainment, 1999).

22 BFI, Robin McDonnell Collection, MCD/54/1: Unit list for location in Portugal, April 1969.

23 Fleming, 7.

24 Maibaum, Sc. 15.

25 Valentine Lawford, 'Pucci the magnificent', *Vogue*, 15 March 1964, 157.

26 'Audio commentary featuring Peter Hunt, the cast and crew'.

27 Fleming, 29; Maibaum, Sc. 58.

28 Maibaum, Sc. 101.

29 Helfenstein, 177.

30 Maibaum, Sc. 108.

31 Fleming, 208; Maibaum, Sc. 399d.

32 Fleming, 312.

33 Maibaum, Sc. 584; Fleming: 226.

34 Fleming, 226.

35 Ibid., 306.

36 Sheila Black, '007's message decoded in Bond Street', *Financial Times*, 7 March 1970, 7.

37 Ibid.

38 Maibaum, Sc. 275.

39 'Audio commentary featuring Peter Hunt, the cast and crew'.

40 Maibaum, Sc. 8.

41 Nora O'Leary, 'Preview: James Bond's girls in journal patterns', *Ladies Home Journal*, April 1969, 107.

42 British Library (P.P.8007r): *Vogue Pattern Book*, April 1969, 4193.

43 O'Leary.

44 BFI, PBM-40115: *On Her Majesty's Secret Service* press book, 1969.

45 Ibid.

46 Mr. Showman, 'Try travel angle on *OHMSS*: Weddings and records, cars and banks could help too!', *Kinematograph Weekly*, 31 January 1970, 23.

47 'Win Mrs. James Bond's wedding dress', *Daily Mail*, 3 February 1970, 19.

48 Pamela Fox, 'Here she is, our Mrs. 007!', *Daily Mail*, 3 March 1970, 26.

49 Helfenstein, 223.

50 Alexander Walker, 'Review', *Evening Standard*, 18 December 1969.

51 Charles Camplin, 'Lazenby bows as the new James Bond', *Los Angeles Times*, 18 December 1969, D1.

52 Michael Kostelnuk, 'On Her Majesty's Secret Service', *Winnipeg Free Press*, 19 December 1969, 33.

53 Richard Schmeiszl, 'On Her Majesty's Secret Service', *Melbourne Truth*, 27 December 1969.

54 Ian Christie, 'Entertainment', *Daily Express*, 16 December 1969, 13.

55 P.D.Z., 'On Her Majesty's Secret Service', *Newsweek*, December 1969.

56 Derek Malcolm, 'Off-the-peg Bond', *Guardian*, 16 December 1969, 8.

57 Letter to the editor, published in *Today's Cinema*, 9 January 1970, 10. Natalie Watson argues that the letter is not written in the style and tone of Anthony Sinclair. It should be noted that although Sinclair made the majority of Connery's suits between *Dr. No* and *You Only Live Twice*, Bermans and Nathans made a small amount of the suits, to which the letter refers.

58 Observer, 'Temperamentally unsuited'.

59 Field and Chowdhury, 193.

60 Ibid., 195.

61 Ibid., 194.

5 'PROVIDED THE COLLARS AND THE CUFFS MATCH': SEAN CONNERY (1971)

Beginning with *Diamonds Are Forever*, James Chapman has argued that the Bond films of the 1970s 'are transitional in that they offered various strategies by which the Bond series attempted to reinvent itself and keep apace with changing popular tastes at a time when many critics were saying loudly that in style and outlook it belonged to the 1960s'.[1] To do this, *Diamonds Are Forever* lends its plot more to that of *Goldfinger* than Fleming's novel, and according to Chapman, the departure from the novel was because '*Goldfinger* was the film which had firmly established the Bond formula and which had marked the series' breakthrough in the American market'. Therefore, Broccoli and Saltzman employed Guy Hamilton, the director of *Goldfinger*, to direct *Diamonds Are Forever*, and Tom Mankiewicz, new to the Bond franchise, to write the script. Once drafted, Richard Maibaum was employed to assist Mankiewicz with the script's revisions. Chapman has argued that *Diamonds Are Forever* exemplifies a 'camp aesthetic', much more so than the previous Bond films released before it, and makes a point of foregrounding ostentation and excess by focusing on visual spectacle as opposed to narrative development.[2] The term 'camp' is difficult to define, but it is generally understood as ostentatious, exaggerated, affected and theatrical behaviour. Charles Gray's performance as Blofeld, the inclusion of two explicitly and exaggeratedly homosexual henchmen, Mr. Wint (Bruce Glover) and Mr. Kidd (Putter Smith), and the ironic glitz and glamour encapsulated by use of the Las Vegas location are exemplars of this in *Diamonds Are Forever*. The 'camp aesthetic' is especially evident in the exaggerated and playful costumes worn by the lead characters in the film and how this influences individual performance, as can be understood by the analysis offered throughout this chapter.

Having once again started another world-wide search to cast Bond, different actors were brought to the attention of Broccoli and Saltzman. Burt Reynolds, an

American film star who had 'a big following, particularly among women', was briefly considered and discarded on the basis that he was 'not British'.[3] The requirement of a Bond being played by a British actor was subsequently dropped by the producers following weeks of interviews with Broccoli revealing:

> We couldn't find a British actor, known or unknown, exciting enough to handle a character who had now become a cult hero. [...] If we were forced to use an American, however, he would still have to have the stamp and style of a British Secret Agent. We needed a good actor, but without the star label, which would have worked against the creating of a new Bond.[4]

It was following this decision that John Gavin, an American actor who had previously been cast in *Spartacus* (1960) and *Psycho* (1960), was signed to play Bond on the basis that: 'He was tall, a good athlete and a fine actor. He performed well in some action tests we made.'[5]

United Artists, however, had a different agenda to the producers, and were concerned that three different actors cast in the role of Bond would be highly damaging to the franchise and the box-office takings. Therefore, David Picker was in serious conversation with Connery over him returning to resume the Bond role, with Picker explaining: 'We had to get Sean back. [...] The only way I could get him back was to make a series of conditions that would enable him to do the film on the terms that he felt comfortable with.'[6] The terms were generous, with Connery offered a salary of $1.25 million and 12.5 per cent of the profits for *Diamonds Are Forever*. Furthermore, United Artists were willing to allow Connery two film projects of his choice.[7] As well as this, Connery's contract stipulated that the film production must be completed within eighteen weeks, and if the production was to run over schedule, the actor was to receive an extra $145,000 for every additional week.[8] It was for this reason that *Diamonds Are Forever* was the first, perhaps only, Eon Productions Bond film that was completed within the schedule. Certainly, Connery's camp and 'Cheshire-Cat-who-got-the-cream' performance in *Diamonds Are Forever* belies the tone in the final scenes of *On Her Majesty's Secret Service*, and was subsequently reviewed: 'Bond himself doesn't appear to have been remotely affected by the brutal slaying of the only woman he truly loved, apart from the fact that he looks like he's tried to find happiness at the bottom of a freezer full of Pukka Pies.'[9]

Re-styling Sean Connery as James Bond

With Connery's return, Anthony Sinclair was re-employed to tailor Bond's suits. Sinclair's suits are similar to the ones he produced for Connery's previous Bond films, albeit of a larger cut due to a Connery 'who was now packing flab as well as a Walther PPK'.[10] Nick Sullivan also argues that Bond's *Diamonds Are Forever* wardrobe 'shows a return to the restraint of the earlier films, although styles had changed in the nine years since *Dr. No* note the Windsor knot, no pocket handkerchief and the widening of the pocket flaps and lapels'.[11] Furthermore, Connery's wardrobe represents the fashion of the early 1970s in the creative choice of tie colour. Of Connery's tailored outfits in *Diamonds Are Forever*, Bond wears five lounge suits, two sports jackets, one blazer and three dinner suits, nearly as many as Lazenby in *On Her Majesty's Secret Service*, and more than Connery had worn in his previous Bond films. Spaiser explains that compared with the suits designed for *Dr. No*, which included a draped chest, the suits in *Diamonds Are Forever* make use of a much cleaner-cut chest.[12] As with the Sinclair suits designed for *From Russia With Love* through to *You Only Live Twice*, the jacket button is positioned at a low stance on Connery's suits in *Diamonds Are Forever*, however this works to make Connery's physique appear more athletic on screen as opposed to emphasizing his V-shaped torso. The jackets in this film also include much deeper vents in the back – around twelve inches in length – and this is another technique to make Connery appear slimmer on screen. The majority of costumes worn by Bond in the *Diamonds Are Forever* work to contribute to the overall camp aesthetic of the film.

On Connery's dinner suits, Hamilton believed that: 'I always think Sean looks so elegant in black with the white shirt. That's why he looks good in a dinner jacket.'[13] Both the ivory and black dinner jackets are, in different ways, reflective of the previous incarnations of the ivory dinner jacket worn by Connery in *Goldfinger*. The ivory dinner jacket appears during the casino scenes in the film. The script directs: '[Bond] is impeccably dressed: white dinner jacket, red carnation, every hair in place – four cuts better looking than anything in the casino. Camera follows as he walks through, drawing appreciative glances from many, especially the women.'[14] Connery wears the jacket with a pleated white shirt from Turnbull & Asser, a black satin bowtie and a pair of midnight blue trousers with a darted front and a matching satin stripe down the outside legs. Although he does not wear a red carnation with this outfit as directed in the script, he wears one in his buttonhole with the black dinner jacket later in the film. This dinner jacket is made of black wool with decorative lapels and pocket flaps of black and claret-patterned satin. It is lined in blood-red, blue and brown patterned art silk. This suit is one of the more flamboyant pieces reflective of early 1970s fashion than the other, more restrained, suits worn in the film. This is evident in the use of wide lapels inclusive of a silk burgundy facing and the slanted pockets with flaps, which dinner jackets of the 1960s did not usually have. Spaiser points out that this is the first Bond film to include a cummerbund with a dinner jacket, and in *Diamonds Are Forever* it is used as a plot device: it is used as a harness when Bond breaks in to Willard Whyte's apartment in Las Vegas.[15] This device is repeated in Timothy Dalton's costume for

Licence to Kill. The final dinner jacket in the film, worn by Bond when he and Tiffany Case (Jill St John) are on a cruise ship, is made from dark navy velvet and is similar to a velvet smoking jacket, albeit that Bond is wearing his before dinner. The velvet dinner jacket is made in a similar style to that of the other Anthony Sinclair jackets worn by Bond in *Diamonds Are Forever*, however it has a shawl collar as opposed to lapels. Unlike the typical dress shirt which Bond normally wears with a dinner jacket, in this scene he wears a pale blue shirt without the pleated fronts, the collar of which is fastened with a thistle-shaped black bowtie.

Other pieces of Connery's wardrobe designed for *Diamonds Are Forever* that are reflective of the look and style established in his previous Bond films include the light grey mohair suit (*Dr. No*), as well as the navy blazer with dark grey flannel trousers and a light blue cotton shirt (*Dr. No* and *Thunderball*), and a light-weight suit made from a Prince of Wales glen check fabric (*Goldfinger*). Other costumes include a herringbone tweed 'half-Norfolk' sports jacket with a three-button fastening, a belted back and large flapped hip pockets. The jacket is worn over a black shirt and with black plain front trousers with a plain hem. Later in the film, Bond wears another half-Norfolk jacket, this time in a tweed fabric woven with tan, black and red threads. Further emphasizing the period, Bond wears a tan-coloured polo-neck jumper underneath this jacket, and brown twill trousers with a darted front, frogmouth pockets and plain hems. In London, Bond wears a dark grey flannel suit, of which the jacket has wide lapels, beneath which Bond wears a cream shirt and amethyst-coloured grenadine silk tie. On rescuing Whyte, Bond wears a cream suit made of Irish linen, with a matching-coloured shirt and a distinctive, short 1970s-style pink satin tie. Bond also briefly wears an 'Air Force' blue single-breasted lounge suit, an unusual colour choice for Bond's suits. It also differs from other Sinclair suits in that it has peaked lapels which are normally included on double-breasted suits.

Styling character for a camp aesthetic

Tiffany's costumes in the film differ greatly from Fleming's novel in keeping with the script's direction, however they do reflect the character's expensive taste which has been adapted from the book. In the novel, Bond meets a 'half-naked' Tiffany, 'sitting astride a chair in front of the dressing table', dressed in black *brassière* and 'tight' black lace knickers before she dresses

> to go out except for her hat, a small black affair that swung from her free hand. She wore a smart black tailor-made over a deep olive green shirt buttoned at the neck, golden-tan nylons and black square-toed crocodile shoes that looked very expensive. There was a slim gold wristwatch on a black strap at one wrist [later revealed to be Cartier] and a heavy gold chain bracelet at the other. One large

baguette-cut diamond flared on the third finger of her right hand and a flat pearl earring in twisted gold showed on her right ear where the heavy pale gold hair fell away from it.[16]

In an earlier draft of the script written by Mankiewicz prior to Jill St John's casting, Tiffany is introduced wearing a brunette wig when she disappears 'nude' from the living room in her apartment in reference to the novel. She then wears a blonde wig, leading to Bond quipping: 'Weren't you a brunette when I came in?', followed by a red wig as she passes Bond his drink with ice after dusting it for fingerprints in her bedroom, with Bond noting: 'I don't care for redheads, terrible tempers', before returning to the bedroom and subsequently revealing to Bond that her natural hair is platinum, causing Bond to state: 'Now that colour suits you. A little brittle and hard like the crust on a pie.'[17] After the red-haired St John was confirmed as being cast on 3 March 1971, the later script places the coloured wigs in the order that would be viewed in the film – platinum blonde, brunette and red – to reflect St John's natural hair colour. The wigs were provided by St John who had a line of wig creations being sold in America at the time. It was following the release of *Diamonds Are Forever* that St John went on a 'wig promotion tour' to Texas department stores, and explained that the red wig would 'just sell out at once'.[18] The scene also dictated the costumes that were designed for St John, and both actors' lines are deliberately written to pun costume and jewellery in these scenes. Italics are the author's emphasis to specify Mankiewicz's costume direction evident in the script:

38. CLOSE ON GIRL – BOND'S POV
Shapely, *nude*, blonde girl disappears from living room.

[…] 40. INT. BEDROOM – DAY
As lush as the living room, with four poster bed. The girl is now in *black panties, fastens black bra behind her*. She stands in front of vanity table on which we see a multitude of bottles, jars, hairsprays, etc.

> GIRL
> (calling out)
> There is no Mr. Case. The T is for Tiffany.

> BOND's VOICE
> Tiffany Case. Definitely distinctive.

> TIFFANY (o.s.)
> I was born there. On the first floor while my mother was looking for a wedding ring.

> BOND
> I'm glad for your sake it wasn't Van Cleef and Arpels.

41. INT. LIVING ROOM – DAY

> **BOND**
> Weren't you blonde when I came in?

> **TIFFANY**
> Could be.

> **BOND**
> I tend to notice little things like that – whether a girl's a blonde or brunette.

> **TIFFANY**
> And which do you prefer.

> **BOND**
> Provided the collars and cuffs match. . .

43. INT. LIVING ROOM – DAY

Tiffany enters through another door dressed in *something short and see-through*.

> **BOND**
> That's quite a nice little nothing you're almost wearing. I approve.

> **TIFFANY**
> I don't dress for the hired help. Let's see your passport, Franks.

44. BACK TO SCENE

> **TIFFANY**
> (closing passport)
> Occupation – Transport Consultant. That's a little cute isn't it?
> (hands it back to Bond)
> I'll finish dressing.

> **BOND**
> (the perfect gentleman)
> Please don't on my account.

51. BACK TO LIVING ROOM

Tiffany reappears, wearing *a chic cocktail dress*. Her hair is now red.[19]

On the employment of the 'extravagant costume designer' Donfeld, credited in the film as 'Don Feld', to design St John's costumes, Joyce Haber believed that: 'The costumer and the locations seem eminently suitable for a playgirl like Jill.'[20]

Donfeld, who became a costume designer in the early 1960s, was the second highest paid freelance designer in Hollywood by 1970 after Irene Sharaff. Compared to a Hollywood studio costume designer's salary at the time, ranging from between $450 to $750 a week, Donfeld commanded $1,000 a week and more.[21] Donfeld was very outspoken on the way he approached costume designing, explaining that on actresses' views relating to their costumes:

> As I want her to feel good in her clothes I take this into consideration [if they are self-conscious about anything] but the actress should never inflict her opinion on the designer. Costumes must move and flow in harmony with the sets, scripts and character to be enacted. To achieve this is a designer's job … not that of the actress.[22]

Considering that St John had been 'on leave from her task of picking out fashions for Interstate Stores' after being cast as Tiffany, Donfeld and St John appeared to get along well with one another, with St John saying on reflection that they 'had lots of fun with the costumes, some of which I still have. I still have the bikini I wore on the oil rig.'[23]

It was decided by Donfeld that instead of a 'black bra and panties', Tiffany would be dressed in a nude-coloured *brassière* with diamanté detailing on the cups, and this is likely due to Tiffany needing to appear nude on Bond entering her apartment. His costume concept of a sheer black *négligée* was designed to interpret 'something short and see-through'. The design for this costume, one of four that survive with each painted in a medium of watercolour and gouache, is typical of Donfeld's unique and distinctive renderings, including a sketchy, stylized and elongated female form. In this design it is evident that Donfeld was heavily influenced by Yves Saint Laurent's dress designed for the 1968 'Rive Gauche' ready-to-wear label, and this is consistent with the designer's belief that for contemporary films he would dress an actress in costumes influenced by fashions evident two years prior to his design concepts. The range was the most emblematic example of the sheer look at this time, namely a floor-length, shapeless, kaftan dress with long sleeves, made from transparent chiffon and a belt made of ostrich feathers. Demonstrating that the costume had been designed after the wig revisions in the script, Donfeld's concept includes Tiffany wearing a long brown curly wig. The *négligée* has a low V-shaped plunging neckline cut to the navel. It flares out slightly from the one-button fastening, and includes a wide black band made from satin-silk around the hem, which is cut to the upper thigh. The long, flowing angel sleeves also include a matching band around the cuffs, in an ironic interpretation of Bond's line that is delivered to Tiffany: 'Provided that the collars and cuffs match.' Both bands at the hem and cuffs are trimmed at the top edge with gold beads. For the 'chic cocktail dress', Tiffany is costumed in a floor-length silk jersey gown. The bodice has long fitted sleeves and a plunging neckline with latticed corset lacing placed at the bottom. The bodice is gathered at the waist with a black and gold glitter band. The skirt of the gown is gathered and bias-cut to emphasize the hips. With the gown, Tiffany wears a choker necklace made of black onyx stones with a heart-shaped pendant and tassel detail that drops between her sternum.

Later, Tiffany wears a long jersey cotton A-line maxi dress that has a black bodice and a purple skirt. This costume begins the two-toned colour scheme evident in the rest of Tiffany's costumes throughout the film that are reflective of her split allegiance between Bond and Blofeld. The dress has a distinctive red halter-neck with piping detail across the neckline and under the bust, and the skirt is gathered and bias cut to allow the garment to skim the curves of the body. This costume, with its colour and piping detail, is referenced later in the film on Blofeld's oil rig. In those scenes, Tiffany begins by wearing a plain purple bikini with spaghetti straps and ribbon bows tied between the bikini cups and on either side of the low-cut briefs. Tiffany is told by Blofeld to 'put something on over that bikini first, my dear. I've come too far to have the aim of my crew affected by the sight of a pretty body', and this leads to Tiffany wearing a 'little top to her outfit', as directed in the script, which was interpreted by Donfeld as a short purple and red harlequin-style wrap top with long fitted sleeves that exposes the midriff (Plate 6). On the left, the bodice is red with a purple sleeve, and on the right, it is purple with a red sleeve. It has alternate black and white piping detail on the neckline that crosses over and is tied between the midriff as well as the sleeves. With both of these outfits, Tiffany wears low-heeled clear plastic shoes.

Of Tiffany's other outfits, three are reflective of the fashionable quasi-hippy trend that developed over the 1970s, including her costume on the flight from Amsterdam to Las Vegas, and the costume worn at Circus Circus. On the flight, Tiffany wears a full-length sheepskin coat that is dyed purple with a short fur trim. It is fitted to the waistline flaring out to the hem line, and is double-breasted with a wide, high-stand collar, has flapped pockets and a deep vent at the back. Underneath the coat, Tiffany wears a fitted orange jersey knit jumper with a scoop neckline and short purple hot pants that match the shade of the coat. The hot pants are fastened with a matching purple belt on her hips to contrast with the orange jumper. Tiffany wears an orange and purple patterned chiffon headscarf wrapped in her hair that particularly evokes 1970s fashions. Tiffany's costume for Circus Circus is a three-piece jersey trouser suit including an ivory jacket with a brown and ivory trim across the waist, flared sleeves and a small high-stand collar attached to a V-neckline. It is worn with a pair of matching flared ivory trousers and a corresponding peach-coloured knitted jersey polo-neck fastened with a front zip with brown and ivory collar and cuffs. This relates back to Bond's previous quip. In the final scenes with Bond aboard the cruise ship, the script directs that Tiffany be dressed 'in long robe covering nightie'.[24] Donfeld interpreted this costume to emphasize harlequin patterning and, as with Tracy's wedding dress in *On Her Majesty's Secret Service*, it works to combine all of the different costumes worn by Tiffany throughout the film. Tiffany's costume is made from ivory and pale pink sheer silk, which forms a heavily draped dressing gown with plunge neckline and full, pleated harem trousers that are gathered at the waist and are hemmed with fitted cuffs at the ankle. The full-length gown has long angel sleeves that are fitted to the elbow before widely flaring out to the hem edge. It is ruched at the waist with pale purple silk and cream and pink ribbon ties.

For Charles Gray's performance as Blofeld, he was advised by Mankiewicz to play the character 'like Hedda Hopper, the notorious gossip columnist', in keeping with the camp style of the film's script.[25] As with the return of Connery and his Sinclair-tailored suits, we also see a return of Blofeld wearing the Mao suit costume in *Diamonds Are Forever* (Figure 5.1) that was favoured by Donald Pleasence's Blofeld in *You Only Live Twice*. However, unlike *You Only Live Twice* when the Mao suit worked as a visual signifier of SPECTRE's support for the Peoples Republic of China, the Mao suit is not reflective of the film's plot in *Diamonds Are Forever*. For Gray's Blofeld, the suit is similarly cut to that of Pleasence's, however with a key difference: Gray's include four pockets instead of two. This is ironic, given the nature of what the pockets represent on the Chinese version of the suit, namely the 'Four Cardinal Principles': propriety, justice, honesty and shame, and the opposite of what Blofeld's character represents in the Bond films. The Mao suit has important role within the film's plot. In this film, Blofeld attempts to deceive Bond by creating lookalikes of himself through plastic surgery. In the 'Blofeld reveal' scene, Bond breaks into Whyte's apartment to confront him about the diamond smuggling, and instead meets two 'identical' Blofelds, who have stolen Whyte's identity. In the ensuing drama, Bond kicks Blofeld's cat towards the Blofeld that he believes to be the original and shoots him, only to find that he mistakenly kills the doppelgänger instead. This is discovered when the cat with a diamond-studded collar enters the room:

299. ANGLE ON THE OTHER DOOR
Appearing through a crack in another door – another white cat – this one with a gleaming diamond choker.

300. WIDER ANGLE
The cat runs across the room, jumps in Blofeld #1's lap. BLOFELD pulls the gun, smiles at BOND.

BLOFELD
Right idea Mr. Bond.

BOND
(glum)
Wrong pussy.[26]

To allow viewers to be able to differentiate between the two Blofeld's during this scene, their Mao suits differ slightly in colour. The 'real' Blofeld (#1) wears a grey version, and the 'fake' Blofeld (#2) a brown khaki version. Interestingly, in the other

FIGURE 5.1 Ernst Stavro Blofeld's Mao suit in *Diamonds Are Forever*. Directed by Guy Hamilton © Eon Productions/United Artists 1971.

scenes which involve Blofeld in this film, he is wearing the brown khaki version of this suit.

Neither Blofeld nor his cat escape the influence of the camp aesthetic in *Diamonds Are Forever*. The cat gets treated to a diamond studded collar, and both play a key role in Maurice Binder's title credits, as well as in the scene outlined above. When Blofeld escapes from the Whyte House Casino, he is costumed in drag, inclusive of a blonde wig, large sunglasses and a variety of cheap costume jewellery. Whether the wig was one of those provided by St John remains unknown. When Tiffany is abducted by Blofeld, a close-up of the latter's face is shown in full, and is painted with ludicrous looking make-up including bright red lipstick, garish blue eyeshadow and thick mascara. Other than the need to disguise himself in order to escape the casino, there is no reason for Blofeld to dress in drag, other than for humour and the camp aesthetic. The script directs: 'A LARGE, HUSKY-LOOKING WOMAN in fur coat with veil makes her way in wobbly shoes towards hotel front door. In her arms she holds a large white cat.'[27] Although pure conjecture, one might speculate that Gray's performance as a cross-dressing Blofeld may have led to his casting in his next film role, 'The Criminologist', in *The Rocky Horror Picture Show* (1975).

In the early version of the script, the secondary character Plenty O'Toole (Lana Wood) is described as 'a Hugh Hefner dream-come-true with a sweet face, towering over the other ladies like a colossus'.[28] The 'colossus' description was dropped in later script revisions following the casting of Wood who was five-foot-two-inches tall. Due to her height, the actress had to stand on a wooden box in the casino scenes when standing next to Connery, and in the bedroom scene between the pair, she was provided with extremely high-heeled shoes in order to reduce their height difference. The shoes, made from purple satin dyed to match her gown, have three-inch court heels and have silver-coloured soles. In the script, and particularly in the film, the only real purpose of Plenty's character is to briefly wear an evening gown in the casino before Bond strips it off of her in his hotel room, and to gift Bond with lines such as:

O'Toole   Hi, I'm Plenty.

Bond   But of course.

O'Toole   Plenty O'Toole.

Bond   Named after your father perhaps?

Soon afterwards, Plenty is found murdered after being mistaken for Tiffany. Of the four scenes she appears in the script, two are cut from the film: when she dines with Bond after their gambling at the craps table and when she sneaks back to Bond's room after being thrown in the pool and steals Tiffany's address from the latter's handbag. Owing to these scenes being cut, the film emphasizes the perception of Plenty's character being merely a *Carry On*-style creation dreamt up by Mankiewicz, who recommended Wood's casting, especially as she has no purpose in the film other than wanting to opportunistically sleep with the 'highest bidder' in terms of casino earnings, and her wanting revenge on Tiffany for replacing her in Bond's bed. Her costumes, too, were sourced with the main purpose of foregrounding her cleavage to assist in emphasizing jokes about the size of her breasts. The purple silk-jersey evening gown is sleeveless, and has a plunging V-shaped neckline. It is high-waisted, cut in an empire line and is floor-length. The bias-cut skirt of the gown is gathered underneath the waistband in order to flow over the hips. The back, which is cut in a symmetrical V-shape similar to that of the neckline, is fastened with a zip as directed in the script to allow for ease of removal by Bond. To further emphasize her cleavage, Plenty wears an elaborate and chunky gold-plated brass 'Shandelle' choker necklace created by Monet, inclusive of chain link detailing ending in a pendant and tassels placed between her sternum. Once undressed in Bond's hotel room, she is seen wearing pink floral lace full-cut briefs with silver tassels at the waistband.

On her death, Plenty is wearing a sexualized version of Ophelia's dress as depicted in John Everett Millais' painting *Ophelia* (1851–52), which is made all the more poignant given that she has been tied to a concrete slab using a peach-coloured chiffon scarf with white polka dots to give the illusion of a painful death by drowning. The sheer white silk and chiffon diaphanous dress is cut in a similar style to that of the purple evening gown with a plunging neckline, however the skirt is two-tiered and is cut above the knee. It is cinched at the waist with a sage green silk belt with a four silk-covered button detail at the centre, and has long, full set-in sleeves that is gathered at the shoulder cap and wrist, with the cuffs gathered and tied together with blue ribbon. Plenty is wearing the same necklace as worn in the casino, and wears white leather shoes with a court heel and an ankle strap.

For the homosexual henchmen, Mr. Wint and Mr. Kidd, the characters' sexuality in the film was present in Fleming's novel, with Leiter informing Bond that Kidd: 'Probably shacks up with Wint. Some of these homos make the worst killers.'[29] Furthermore, their sexuality is alluded to in the form of dress in Fleming's novel, with one key component always missing from their outfits. Wint is described as 'a big, fattish guy' clothed in: 'Black trousers. Brown shirt with white stripes. No coat or tie. Black shoes, neat, expensive [...] no wristwatch,' and Kidd: 'He was smaller than the other one and thinner. Wearing dark trousers and a grey shirt with no tie.'[30]

This is similar to how they are costumed in the film. In Mankiewicz's script, both Wint and Kidd's sexuality is more explicit, and they are initially described as: 'Though not particularly muscular or athletic, WINT and KIDD look highly sinister,' and 'WINT is older and pudgier than KIDD. They watch the [scorpion] fight with a strange, gleeful absorption.'[31] Mankiewicz describes them as 'primping' and 'giggling' to each other throughout the script and includes various moments of hand-holding between the pair, for example in South Africa and Amsterdam: 'WINT holds black tin box, takes KIDD's hand. They walk off slowly through the burning wreckage,' and: 'KIDD takes WINT's hand. They stroll leisurely off the bridge.'[32] When tracking Bond and Tiffany on the flight from Amsterdam to Las Vegas, in the early version of the script Kidd remarks to Wint: 'They're both on board. And I must say, Miss Case seems quite attractive,' to which Wint, described as 'shocked', replies: 'Mr. Kidd! Really...'[33] In the revised script and film, Wint's line is omitted and Kidd says instead: 'Miss Case seems quite attractive... [Wint looks at him curiously] For a lady.'[34] The Whyte House Casino scenes in the script offer more explicit commentary on Wint and Kidd's sexual preferences, for example when watching Shady Tree's (Leonard Barr) show:

111. LINCOLN LOUNGE – NIGHT – CLOSE ON SHADY TREE
[...] CAMERA PULLS BACK to reveal the lounge audience, most enjoying themselves. Two unamused faces sit down front – WINT and KIDD [...] WINT nudges KIDD, gestures off to one side. They look appreciatively:

112. CLOSE ON THE DRUMMER – WINT AND KIDD'S POV
A cherubic young drummer with wavy blonde hair as he hits the rimshots which signal Tree's jokes.

113. BACK TO WINT AND KIDD

WINT
Isn't he beautiful?[35]

This scene, as well as the hand holding and giggling between Wint and Kidd was mostly omitted from the film as well, although the black humour and the pair's twisted application of proverbs remain. The 'primping' description in the script influenced Glover's performance as Wint: the actor regularly sprayed himself with cologne throughout the film, an act that in turn informed the film's final scenes. Reflecting on Wint and Kidd, Mankiewicz believed that: 'It was a very risky kind of deal, the relationship between Mr. Wint and Mr. Kidd [. . .] They were clearly "two gentlemen who kept company with each other." Even though they're vicious, they're funny vicious.'[36] Regarding their homosexuality, Mankiewicz admitted that 'today, one would not be able to get away with that'.

The costume interpretation for the pair reflects the script and supports the actors' performance of their individual characters, and they are often dressed in fashions more directly reflective of the early 1970s than that of Bond, who admittedly has his fair share. The script, the actor's performance and their different costumes work to present the pair as comically clichéd homosexuals, and this is indicative of how homosexual men were portrayed in cinema produced at the time. Often, Kidd's homosexuality is emphasized more in his costume than that of Wint's, whereas Wint's homosexuality is more acute in his effeminate performance and use of cologne as a prop. This is likely due to Smith being a musician with little acting experience. In their first scenes in South Africa, Wint is dressed in a grey herringbone tweed jacket with wide notched lapels, under which he wears a white shirt with a long-pointed collar and a wide black knitted tie. The jacket is worn with light grey chinos. Kidd is dressed in a khaki safari suit, the jacket of which has a camp collar, a black-buttoned front, four patch pockets and buttoned cuffs. It is fastened with a matching belt around the waist. The shirt worn underneath is made of a paler shade of khaki than the jacket, and he wears a knitted black tie. On visiting Mrs. Whistler, Wint and Kidd are dressed similarly although there are subtle differences between their costumes and the ways that the characters wear them (Figure 5.2). They are both dressed in two-piece tan-coloured suits, of which

FIGURE 5.2 Exaggerated suit styles worn by Mr. Wint and Mr. Kidd. *Diamonds Are Forever* directed by Guy Hamilton © Eon Productions/United Artists 1971. All rights reserved.

the jackets are single-breasted with notched lapels, albeit Wint's are wider than Kidd's. Both have one-button fastenings, which are unusual in this style of suit, and Wint wears his fastened whereas Kidd's is unfastened. Both men's suits have cuffs that are fastened with four buttons. Under the suit jackets, Wint wears a white cotton shirt with a pointed collar and a brown silk tie, and Kidd wears a pale blue cotton shirt, again with a pointed collar, and a silk tie that is colourfully patterned in red and yellow. It is in this scene that Wint is first seen spraying himself with cologne.

On the Skinny Bridge in Amsterdam, Wint and Kidd are dressed in two-piece suits, however this time each suit is reflective of the different character's personality in contrast to one another. Wint wears a single-breasted, grey tweed herringbone suit with distinctive wide mauve checks. The jacket has a natural shoulder, and includes wide notched lapels, two flapped hacking pockets and a ticket pocket, and a two-button fastening. The white shirt has a narrow collar and is worn with a dusky pink-coloured silk tie. Comparatively, Kidd wears a dark grey pinstripe suit, the jacket also having natural shoulders, and a two-button fastening, however Kidd only wears the top button fastened unlike Wint. The jacket only includes two flapped pockets although the pointed cut of the flaps is unique and they are fastened with a brass button. Kidd wears a pale blue shirt with pointed collar and a silk tie that is alternately coloured in pale blue and navy diagonal stripes. Kidd wears a French beret in the same colour shade as his shirt. During the flight, in the crematorium and in the casino, Wint and Kidd wear exaggerated costumes that work to emphasize their sexuality, particularly in the case of Kidd. Wint is dressed in a two-piece navy suit, with wide notched lapels, a two-button fastening and two slanted hacking pockets with flaps. With the suit, he wears a white and ecru-coloured striped shirt and a navy silk tie with pale blue paisley patterning. Kidd wears a burgundy three-piece suit made of serge that includes red and blue chalk stripes. The jacket has peaked lapels, a two-button fastening and two large flapped pockets. It has double vents at the rear. Underneath the jacket and waistcoat Kidd wears a white shirt with a pointed collar and a colourful blue and burgundy paisley patterned silk tie.

Critical reception

Although the trade papers were less enthusiastic about *Diamonds Are Forever*, with 'Whit' writing for *Variety* that Broccoli and Saltzman 'have reached the point where a sustained story means little in prepping an 007 picture', and the *Independent Film Journal* believed that the film was 'a disappointment', the majority of critics in the UK and the USA offered positive reviews of the film, with most relieved at Connery's return to the Bond role.[37] In Britain, Patrick Gibbs referred to Lazenby as 'A.N. Other' and believed that 'it was very good' to see Connery back, albeit that he 'appears to have added to his waistline since he first appeared in the role in 1962, and perhaps to grin less readily than he did. Still, for a combination of elegance and energy he would be difficult to beat.'[38] Donald Zec, as with Gibbs, picked up on the 'slightly over-caloried shape of Sean Connery' and although: 'The excruciatingly implausibility of this picture stands out a mile, so does its success.'[39] Similarly, John Russell Taylor declared that Connery 'is the only proper screen James Bond [...] if a little heavier than yore in the role, is still undoubtedly, irreplaceably Bond', however the critic admitted that the film 'is not exactly tops in the Bond film canon, but it is more than enjoyable enough [...] Essentially, of course, it is a manifestation of the greater British tattiness – schoolboy fantasies of sex (mainly in outrageous double-entendre) and violence, villains out of 1950s B-features and saucy seductresses out of a Purley formation dance-team.'[40] Margaret Hinxman praised *Diamonds Are Forever*, arguing that the film 'comes close to being the ideal Bond film', and: 'Goodness, how we missed [Connery] last time!'[41] Madeleine Harmsworth agreed with Hinxman in that 'this is the best Bond of the lot', with Connery 'thankfully back in the role he created', and Gavin Millar concurred that Connery 'makes a welcome return'.[42] Similarly, Cecil Wilson believed: 'It's so nice to see [Connery] back where he belongs – back in the role of sex, skulduggery and dry Martini ace James Bond.'[43] In America, Charles Camplin was relieved that: 'After that one embarrassing interlude with a counterfeit Bond whose name is already lost to memory', the film was 'a smashing good entertainment with nothing on its mind except entertainment', and Vincent Canby believed that 'nothing becomes [Connery] as much as the character he wanted to leave'.[44]

On the secondary characters, St John was praised for her performance as Tiffany, often described as 'pretty', and Gibbs believed that the character is 'pleasantly cool and decorative', and her costumes demonstrated that she 'certainly knows what dresses show off her going points'. Wilson concurred, writing that the character was 'cool and sizzing', Russell Taylor felt that St John was 'funny as the main feminine interest', Camplin liked St John's 'nice, broad comedic style', and the *Independent Film Journal* noted that the character was an 'alluring Dragon Lady'. Hinxman believed that both St John and Wood were 'stylish', and Millar wryly noted that St John's 'sparsely clad bottom play a large part in the fandango' in reference to her bikini. For Gray's Blofeld, Gibbs felt that the 'impassive' actor worked as 'a good foil to the volatile Bond', and Hinxman described Gray as 'fondling his cats and leering suavely'.

On Glover's and Smith's portrayal of Wint and Kidd, there is a difference in the description of their homosexuality between the UK and American press. In the UK, critics would often find creative ways of doing this, for example Hinxman referred to the pair as 'a couple of fey grown-up kiddies' who are 'satisfyingly eery', the word 'fey' having long been used to describe effeminate homosexual men. Similarly, Zec described Wint and Kidd as 'the two main "heavies" are a couple of precious, perfumed gents who are not so much henchmen as consenting adults', believing that 'while the late Ian Fleming may be laughing in to his celestial Martini, the late Humphrey Bogart will be quietly throwing up'. Derek Malcolm was one of the few British critics to directly refer to the henchmen as 'queer killers' and noted that they were played for laughs.[45] In America, both Camplin and Canby were more explicit, with the former referring to Wint and Kidd as 'camp killers', and the latter 'two gentle gunmen, who are fond of their jobs (and in love with each other)'.

Peter Schjeldahl made the clearest statement of the pair's sexuality in a mainstream newspaper, writing that Wint and Kidd are 'a winsome pair of homosexual killers, so charming they practically steal the show [...] these fey killers are, by all odds, the least sinister villains in any Bond movie, and one can only conclude that their seaminess (earning them one of the most atrocious ends in movie history) is to be inferred from the fact they are homosexual'.[46] In the gay press, John Marvin wrote in 1973 that that along with boasting 'a pair of gangsters who were homosexual lovers', Blofeld in *Diamonds Are Forever* 'is apparently meant to be a little bit sweet as he slinks about the set with his pet cradled in his arms', arguing that in the early 1970s, the 'clearly defined' homosexual characters fall into 'two equally demeaning stereotypes – the effeminate bitchy queen, or the vicious brutal sadist'.[47] James van Maanen later wrote in 1975 that Wint and Kidd were 'depicted with a strange blend of the brutal, sadistic and the screamingly fey', and complained that compared to Lotte Lenya's portrayal of a lesbian Rosa Klebb, 'who was the very model of butch tact' in *From Russia With Love*, the henchmen were merely 'screaming mimis'.[48] *Gay News* would review the film when it was released on ITV at Christmas in 1978: 'Two homosexual characters Mr. Wint and Mr. Kidd find themselves tipped into the hetero machismo Bondage world as baddies, what else? All ends "happily" for Bond fans in the last scene when gay Mr. Kidd goes up in a puff of smoke.'[49]

Notes

1 Chapman, *Licence to Thrill*, 149.

2 Ibid., 133.

3 Broccoli with Zec, *When the Snow Melts*, 221.

4 Ibid.

5 Ibid.

6 Field and Chowdhury, *Some Kind of Hero*, 201.

7 Connery only made one film as per his agreement with United Artists, *The Offence* (1972).

8 John Cork and Bruce Scivalli, *The James Bond Legacy* (London: Boxtree, 2002), 131.

9 Neil Alcock, 'BlogalongBond: *Diamonds Are Forever*: Blofeld blows it again', *The Incredible Suit*, 27 July 2011, http://theincrediblesuit.blogspot.com/2011/07/blogalongabond-diamonds-are-forever.html (accessed 20 June 2020).

10 Alexander Walker, *National Heroes: British cinema in the Seventies and Eighties* (London: Orion, 2005), 57.

11 Sullivan, *Dressed to Kill*, 133.

12 Spaiser, 'Comparison: Grey suits in *Dr. No* and *Diamonds Are Forever*', *The Suits of James Bond*, 27 May 2014, www.bondsuits.com/comparison-grey-suits-in-dr-no-and-diamonds-are-forever/ (accessed 21 June 2020).

13 'Commentary', *Diamonds Are Forever*, DVD, directed by Guy Hamilton (1971; UK and USA: MGM Home Entertainment 2000).

14 BFI, S6502: Tom Mankiewicz and Richard Maibaum, *Diamonds Are Forever*, revised draft screenplay, 13 April 1971, 32.

15 Spaiser, 'A flamboyant black dinner suit in *Diamonds Are Forever*', *The Suits of James Bond*, 12 January 2013, www.bondsuits.com/flamboyant-black-dinner-suit-diamonds-are-forever/ (accessed 21 June 2020).

16 Fleming, *Diamonds Are Forever* (1956; London: Penguin Books, 2009), 42.

17 Mankiewicz, *Diamonds Are Forever*, revised draft screenplay, 24 February 1971, 12–15.

18 Joyce Haber, 'Jill heads up wig promotion tour', *Los Angeles Times*, 11 July 1972, G10.

19 BFI, S6502: 13–16.

20 Haber, 'Jill will join Sean in new Bond film', *Los Angeles Times*, 4 March 1971, E10.

21 Haber, 'Costume designer gives stars a dressing down', *Los Angeles Times*, 19 April 1970.

22 Julie Byrne, 'Fashion – don't open till '68', *Los Angeles Times*, 16 October 1966, D4.

23 Field and Chowdhury, 208.

24 Mankiewicz, 119.

25 Laurent Bouzereau, *The Art of Bond: From storyboard to screen, the creative process*, (London: Boxtree, 2006), 167.

26 Mankiewicz, 79.

27 Ibid., 91.

28 Ibid., 32.

29 Fleming, 146. Fleming uses the word 'homo' as a pejorative term referring to homosexual men.

30 Ibid., 145.

31 Mankiewicz, 4.

32 Ibid., 7, 11.

33 Ibid., 21.

34 BFI, S6502: 22.

35 Mankiewicz, 31.

36 'Commentary'.

37 'Whit', '*Diamonds Are Forever*', *Variety*, 15 December 1971, 14; '*Diamonds Are Forever*', *Independent Film Journal*, 23 December 1971, 25.

38 Patrick Gibbs, 'Bond is back as his old Connery self', *Daily Telegraph*, 30 December 1971, 7.

39 Donald Zec, 'Bond is forever', *Daily Mirror*, 30 December 1971, 12.

40 John Russell Taylor, '1971: A vintage year for the cinema', *The Times*, 31 December 1971, 7.

41 Margaret Hinxman, 'Tom and Jimmy', *Sunday Telegraph*, 2 January 1972, 16.

42 Madeleine Harmsworth, 'Vintage Bond, well bottled', *Sunday Mirror*, 2 January 1972, 27; Gavin Millar, 'US war Bond', *Listener*, 13 January 1972, 29.

43 Cecil Wilson, 'It's that man again, causing chaos in all the best places', *Daily Mail*, 30 December 1971, 22.

44 Charles Camplin, '*Diamonds*: The Bond that binds', *Los Angeles Times*, 16 December 1971, G1; Vincent Canby, 'A benign Bond: 007 stars in *Diamonds Are Forever*', *New York Times*, 18 December 1971, 34.

45 Derek Malcolm, 'Bond is forever', *Guardian*, 30 December 1971, 8.

46 Peter Schjeldahl, 'Bond is back – and *Diamonds* got him', *New York Times*, 26 December 1971, D15.

47 John Marvin, 'The gay villains', *Queen's Quarterly* 5, no. 4 (August 1973), 17.

48 James van Maanen, 'Deviant sex in the movies: Villains, villains and more villains', *After Dark: The Magazine of Entertainment*, March 1975, 44.

49 'Burn', *Gay News*, 14 December 1978–10 January 1979, 9.

6 'LICENCE TO FRILL': ROGER MOORE (1973–75)

Diamonds Are Forever had been a box-office success and, as Connery had finally hung up his Anthony Sinclair-tailored suits for the last time, Broccoli and Saltzman again had to consider who would be the next Bond. This time Broccoli was insistent that Roger Moore would be ideal: 'He looked more the public-school drop-out, the socially well-connected gent, than did the more coarse-grained Sean Connery.'[1] However, Saltzman and United Artists were not quite as enthusiastic. By this time, Moore was an established television star, having played Simon Templar in *The Saint* (1962–69) and Lord Brett Sinclair in *The Persuaders!* (1971–72). Saltzman was concerned that Moore was already established, and this went against the former principle of hiring a relatively unknown actor. Furthermore, United Artists feared that Moore might not be appropriate for a role established by Connery and suggested that 'an American actor with a big name' should be considered instead. However, due to Broccoli's uncompromising stance, Saltzman and United Artists eventually agreed to cast Moore in the role. To begin with, Moore was offered a three-film contract with the option for more: he would subsequently make seven Bond films in total, beginning with *Live and Let Die*.

Out of all the actors to be cast in the role of Bond, Moore was the most fashion-conscious, and demonstrated a genuine interest in the menswear industry beyond modelling knitwear prior to his acting career. This is evident in his Bond films, in that he would have three different tailors providing his suits – Cyril Castle (1973–75), Angelo Vitucci (1977–80) and Douglas Hayward (1980–85) – and Frank Foster made the majority of Moore's shirts. Moore's interest in fashion is particularly evident in the credit he was afforded in *The Persuaders!*: 'Lord Sinclair's clothes designed by Roger Moore' accompanied by a copy of Moore's signature in large print. This was for two reasons: the first being Moore's insistence that his tailor at the time, Castle, make his suits for the series, and because of his involvement with the Bradford-based worsted textile manufacturing firm, Pearson and Foster Ltd., which provided the cloth for his suits.

In 1967, Patricia Rushton arranged a meeting between Moore and David Wilkinson, the managing director of Pearson and Foster, to discuss the possibility of the actor contributing to marketing menswear fabrics on behalf of the company. It was agreed that Moore would make a 'significant' contribution to the designing and marketing of a 'Roger Moore Collection', rather than his name merely being attached as a 'gimmick' or a 'labelling operation'.[2] Initially, Moore was to travel three or four weeks a year to various parts of the world in order to promote the company. The employment of Moore coincided with a major change of policy at the textile firm, including the investment in new design facilities and the factory being re-equipped with a Sulzer weaving plant.[3] In a letter from Wilkinson to his staff regarding the 'Roger Moore Collection', he explained that there would be a considerable 'prestige and sales advantage' to Pearson and Foster's customers who wanted to purchase fabrics produced by the collection for two key reasons: first, what the company termed 'Identification Syndrome' and second, the promise that 'each year between filming seasons, Mr. Moore will make overseas tours in connection with The Roger Moore Collection'.[4] As Wilkinson explained:

> It is established that people in all income groups form positive groups in relation to persons seen through the TV media. It is clear that the character played by Mr. Moore [Simon Templar] is sympathetic and excellent for the requirements of our various activities in Menswear and accessories. The part harmonises with Mr. Moore's real-life interests in men's wear to an even greater extent than his role in *The Saint* series.[5]

The success of Moore's involvement with the firm became apparent almost immediately, with the *Financial Times* reporting that the company was 'now securely back in profit'.[6] At the Annual General Meeting on 17 July 1969, the chairman told shareholders: 'We have been delighted by the interest shown in the business by Mr. Moore and his real contribution to aiding our growing business with overseas markets. Recently Mr. Moore returned from a world tour which he undertook specifically for the purpose of gaining first-hand knowledge of the markets.' Furthermore, the *Financial Times* outlined that Moore's contribution had assisted in turning a £78,901 loss into a £73,064 pre-tax profit.[7] In August 1969, Moore attended a promotional tour on behalf of Pearson and Foster in Australia as the department store, Anthony Squires, had negotiated the publicity as part of their offer to purchase 200 pieces of cloth from the firm.[8] The agreed publicity also consisted of six presentation books with patterns and 'glossy photos' of the actor in his various different film and television roles and a 'suggestion Mr. Moore will do a five-minute film at Elstree [Studios], or produce a 20 second TV commercial to promote stores around Australia'.[9]

Wilkinson believed that: 'Roger was ideal because he genuinely enjoyed the whole scene and had great interest in designing and clothes, with a background of art and able to draw his own designs.'[10] Due to Moore's enthusiasm for fashion and design, Wilkinson soon arranged for the actor to become involved in designing a collection of Terylene clothing as part of the 'Roger Moore Collection', noting in a company proposal that Moore 'has to be extremely fashion conscious and [is] always on the lookout for new ideas in men's clothing for his screen roles', translating 'fashion ideas in his own style'.[11] Furthermore, Wilkinson invited Moore to become a member of Pearson and Foster's Board of Directors in 1970. This was agreed in a three-year contract, whereby the actor would be paid £5,000 per annum from July 1971 and gifted £500 worth of ordinary shares.[12] *Style Weekly* reported in early 1970 that the 'intrepid Mr. Moore' will have 'an even more active integrated part', explaining that as well as Australia, Moore had also visited America and had been 'drumming up business more generally'.[13]

After Moore's appointment to the board, one of the events he attended was the British Menswear Guild conference on 10 October 1970. Liz Gill reported that Moore had been loaned from Pearson and Foster in order to promote the Guild, of which Pearson and Foster were indirectly connected through providing cloth to some of its members. The firm arranged for Moore to attend the conference via its private plane, a four-seater Cessna.[14] The actor was specifically employed to promote the 'Windsor look' fashion, made famous by Edward, Prince of Wales in 1924. On Moore's 'modified' suit depicting the 'Windsor look', naturally made from Pearson and Foster cloth, Gill believed that he looked 'prosperous and dashing', and was popular with delegates. Moore later recalled of his work for Pearson and Foster:

I turned up to board meetings, attended some Menswear Guild conferences and generally lent my name to the company and took an interest in textiles and fabrics, in exchange for a rather nice remuneration. It was all rather fascinating, and I much enjoyed my visits to Bradford Mill. Consequent to my involvement, the company offered to outfit me for any films and TV shows. I took them up on it for *The Persuaders!*, and made a few comments about the type of clothes I thought Brett Sinclair would wear. That secured me the credit.[15]

Unfortunately for Pearson and Foster, Moore's initially positive connection with the firm did not assist them in the long term. The *Financial Times* reported in October 1970 that Pearson and Foster had appointed receivers following heavy losses after the company 'had tried to do the right thing by investing in the most modern and productive plant working on four shifts and trading up into more specialised markets, accompanied by some extrovert (for Yorkshire) marketing activities with a twin-engined aircraft and Mr. Roger ("The Saint") Moore'.[16] This led to Pearson and Foster running 'disastrously short of working capital and the levels of sales needed to sustain its new machines and heavy central overheads was never achieved'. As Sinclair McKay later quipped, the 'Roger range': 'Tragically [...]

never materialised, thus depriving the world of a range of powder-blue safari suits and flared drip-dry action trousers.'[17]

Live and Let Die (1973)

Broccoli and Saltzman employed Tom Mankiewicz to write the script of *Live and Let Die*, and the shooting script was completed by 2 October 1972, before principal photography began in New Orleans on 13 October. Mankiewicz updated Fleming's novel *Live and Let Die*, and included the characters of Mr. Big and Solitaire, as well as its plot that centred on a criminal operation of smuggling. The character of Dr Kananga (Yaphet Kotto) was also introduced, who is later revealed in the film to be the dual character of Kananga/Mr. Big. On Moore, Broccoli and Saltzman were keen for the actor to adopt the 'Bond image':

> His TV image was too glossy and soft-centred compared with the virile dynamite we had in Sean's Bond. Essentially, we had to bury the Saint and all that lightweight giggling of *The Persuaders!*. Apart from cosmetic stuff like cutting his hair, getting rid of that naughty-boy smile and the one raised eyebrow, and making him altogether leaner and tougher, we had to make Roger believe that he was 007.[18]

Although Broccoli and Saltzman were keen for Moore to 'drop' his previous television image, Moore demanded that Castle make his suits for *Live and Let Die*, arguing that Castle would provide Bond with 'a more contemporary look for the 1970s. Lots of modern colours, sports jackets and trousers became the new norm. The designs were fashionable, yet also elegant and comfortable.'[19] Unlike Connery and Lazenby, Moore was afforded his own agency when it came to the suits he wore.

On his approach to tailoring, Castle believed that: 'A good suit is like a car. It has to be serviced. If it is not properly looked after it becomes a shapeless mess.'[20] Castle made a name for himself as a tailor to the rich and famous, having been awarded the *Tailor & Cutter* award for 'Best Dressed Star' in 1954. *Tailor & Cutter* reported that Castle, alongside his brother Claude, had originally been based in Sackville Street before moving to 42 Conduit Street, and their clients included 'some of the top professional men in the film world.'[21] Other celebrity clients besides Moore included Terry-Thomas, Richard Todd, Lee Mortimer and Terence Stamp. Prince Rainier of Monaco 'was so impressed' by Castle's suits that he 'deserted the Italian who usually dresses him' in 1963.[22] The suits that Castle tailored for Rainier would take 'three to four days to complete', with David Morton noting that Castle's clients 'almost all prefer light-weight materials, and it's unusual for him to make a three-piece suit'.[23] On the cut of Castle's suits, Morton explained that the tailor

tends towards narrower lapels on a lounge suit with a moderately suppressed waist and natural shoulders with a minimum of padding. Trousers are almost all made with plain bottoms, and narrow raising on the side seams. Plain fronted, pleat-less trousers are asked for more and more. I am glad to hear that Cyril Castle shares my boredom with shawl collars on dinner jackets.

It was reported by Christopher Ward that for the duration of *The Saint*, Castle produced more than 200 suits that were individually priced at 70 guineas, due to the amount of action sequences that the actor and stuntmen were involved in.[24] Ward also noted that at the time, Moore owned 'something like 60 suits of his own, all of them very smart, very expensive, and very square'. Moore offered his thoughts on male sartorial style to Ward:

I don't believe in these pretty clothes that men are wearing now. Men who say 'I must have this because it is the trend,' are like girls with dreadful legs who wear mini-skirts. Every man needs a minimum of three suits: A grey suit for daytime wear, a black suit for evening and social occasions and a lightweight for summer and warm weather.

By 1975, it was reported that the price of a two-piece, made-to-measure Castle suit had risen to £250, and a bespoke 'grey cashmere suit embroidered with a gold jet stripe' made for Frank Sinatra cost £300, and this would have made the costume budget for Moore's early Bond films more expensive.[25] Unlike the alleged 'tailoring war' between Sinclair and Major in 1970, there was no such issue arising between Sinclair and Castle. As Natalie Watson explains:

When Roger Moore took over, he naturally wanted his tailor to make the suits, and so the baton was passed to Cyril Castle. He and Anthony Sinclair were very good friends and Cyril Castle had the graciousness to chat with my father about it. My father told him: 'I've had a fair crack of the whip, now it's your turn.'

Spaiser explains that Moore's Castle suits created for both *Live and Let Die* and *The Man with the Golden Gun* had jackets that were structured with straight, narrow shoulders with light padding and gently roped sleeve-heads. The single-breasted variation had medium-wide lapels, a two-button fastening, and was cut with a lean or full chest and a suppressed waist. The pockets would either be straight or slanted 'hacking' pockets with flaps. The skirt of the jacket flared out slightly, as did the cuff of the sleeve.[26] Castle would tailor the double-breasted jacket with wide peaked lapels, a full chest and six buttons. Both the dinner jacket and the blazer made for *The Man with the Golden Gun* were also double-breasted with wide, peak lapels and a full chest, however they differ from the other jackets in that they have stronger roped sleeve-heads. Moore's dinner jacket also included six mother-of-pearl buttons as well as slanted jetted pockets and a cocktail cuff.[27] This particular jacket cuff was one of Castle's particular signatures that he included on some of his tailored suits, which Jeremy Hackett noted: 'This stylish affectation has its roots in military uniforms and was made fashionable in the late 1950s and early 1960s by the smart tailors of the time.'[28] In *Live and Let Die*, Moore wore trousers with Daks top adjusters which were high-rise with front darts, slightly flared legs and a plain hem.

In Mankiewicz's script, it could be presumed that he affords Moore a scene that emphasizes the actor's love of fashion and knowledge of tailoring:

291. INT. ROYAL ORLEANS HOTEL SUIT [*sic*]. DAY
CAMERA PANS with TWO WAITERS wheeling a table with Southern fried chicken into the suite. PICKS UP BOND in front of a mirror, TWO TAILORS fussing around him as he tries on a jacket. The chair behind is piled high with shirts and accessories. An exasperated LEITER talks on the phone. BOND glances over at him as TAILOR holds up a particularly bilious tie.

> BOND
> (to tailor)
> That's a bit flashy . . .
> just the other four please.

[. . .] He takes off jacket, hands it to TAILOR.

> BOND
> Don't forget the double vents. You
> can bring the rest round this
> afternoon.

TAILOR'S bow, leave.[29]

However, this scene is actually an adaption of Fleming's novel, when Bond is visited by a tailor when staying at the St Regis Hotel in New York: 'The afternoon before he had had to submit to a certain amount of Americanisation at the hands of the FBI. A tailor had come and measured him for two single-breasted suits in dark blue light-weight worsted (Bond had firmly refused anything more dashing) and a haberdasher had brought chilly white nylon shirts with long points to the collars.'[30] In the film, the dialogue is switched around: 'That's fine. Don't forget the double vents,' and: 'That's a little frantic. I'll keep the other three.' In the scene, Bond wears a partially basted chocolate brown suit jacket which, when he takes it off, has a patterned art silk lining in burgundy and blue. As a visual reference and a tailoring joke, the 'Cyril A. Castle' label is also visible, which would not normally be included until the suit was complete, as with the lining. The jacket has padded shoulders and roped sleeve-heads, as well as two slanted pockets with flaps. It is marked to include a two-button fastening. A single vent has been included for irony, and to emphasize Bond's request about the double vents. Another costume quip is included earlier in the film during Moore's first scenes that is not a reference to the novel: the magnetic watch that can be used for a variety of things, not least unzipping dresses. The script outlines:

27. CLOSE ON GIRL'S BACK AND ZIPPER
BOND'S hand passes close to the zipper top – <u>without touching it</u>. The top suddenly <u>snaps straight out</u>. Holding his hand some distance from her back, he lowers it, <u>unzipping her dress</u>.

28. CLOSE ON THE TWO OF THEM
The GIRL moans as the zipper is heard sliding down.

GIRL

Such a delicate touch.

BOND

Sheer magnetism.[31]

In *Live and Let Die*, Moore's tailored outfits included a navy double-breasted Chesterfield coat, underneath which Bond wears a navy worsted flannel suit; a light grey suit made from tropical wool, worn with a cream-coloured shirt that includes a spread collar and a plain burgundy tie; a beige tropical wool suit with a cotton white and brown butcher stripe shirt, which Bond wears after hang-gliding, appearing to transform from wearing the navy worsted flannel suit into the beige tropical wool suit that is achieved through cod clothing; a tan sports jacket made from a basketweave that Bond wears with dark brown woollen trousers and an ecru-coloured shirt fastened with a patterned brown silk tie and crocodile-skin shoes; and a double-breasted dark grey suit made from dupioni silk, worn with a cream shirt and a grey silk tie with red motif. The navy Chesterfield overcoat (Figure 6.1) is particularly fine and is celebrated by many Bond fans as one of Moore's most stylishly tailored outfits. This is also true of tailors: on being asked what his favourite item worn by Moore's Bond was, Del Smith replied that it was this one. The coat is double breasted, with a black velvet collar and wide peaked lapels. Three-quarters in length, it has a six-button fastening, flapped patch pockets on both hips, Castle's signature cocktail cuff and a deep back vent. The tie worn with this outfit is made of navy silk and has white and red diagonal stripes. It has been identified by Spaiser and Christopher Laverty as being a Royal Navy regimental tie, in keeping with Bond's history as a Commander of the Royal Navy and also enhances Bond's Britishness while visiting New York given its Union Jack colouring.[32]

FIGURE 6.1 James Bond's stylish navy Chesterfield overcoat. *Live and Let Die* directed by Guy Hamilton © Eon Productions/United Artists 1973. All rights reserved.

In *Live and Let Die*, Bond also wears three dressing gowns. The first is labelled 'Washington Tremlett Ltd., 41 Conduit Street, London', made from woven lemon-yellow cotton and monogrammed with 'J.B' in burgundy silk on the breast pocket. It has burgundy piping on the three-quarter length sleeves and a shawl collar. Given that this creation was sourced from the bespoke tailor based next door to Castle, it is likely that either he or Moore recommended them. The next dressing gown Bond wears is made from a luxurious dark blue crushed velvet fabric with a shawl collar and matching belt. The fabric is embossed with a paisley pattern. The last dressing gown worn by Bond is made from a white terrycloth flannel and has a blue and red windowpane checked pattern. It was sourced from Sulka, who had previously provided Miss Taro's sheer silk dressing gown in *Dr. No*. Unlike Connery, who managed two films before making his first fashion faux pas in *Goldfinger* with the towelling jumpsuit, Moore manages to get one in early in *Live and Let Die*: the casual light blue denim jacket with matching denim trousers, and a white mesh vest beneath the jacket, which would be worn later by Rosie Carver (Gloria Hendry) as dictated in the script. The jacket has a spread collar, a four-button fastening and two flapped patch pockets on the chest that are fastened with a button. The trousers are flared and fastened with a white leather belt.

Julie Harris was employed as the costume designer for *Live and Let Die*. Prior to working in costume, Harris worked for a court dressmaker, assisting in the creation of the white evening gowns to be worn by debutantes before her employment with the costumier Nathans, prior to its takeover by Bermans. After this, Harris was hired as Elizabeth Haffenden's assistant at Gainsborough Pictures. On her employment at Gainsborough, Harris worked as the solo costume designer on *Holiday Camp*

(1947) before working for the Rank Organisation as its lead costume designer. Due to Harris' work as a debutante dress designer and subsequent work on Gainsborough's costume films, Harris 'developed a specialism in elegant modern dress', according to Sue Harper, and was 'particularly expert at predicting the staying power of new fashions', who 'valued tonal coherence', cooperating with designers working on other aspects of a film.[33] Colour was Harris' particular speciality, writing for the *Girl Film and Television Annual* in 1975: 'The moral is that it's not what you wear, but the way you wear it [...] *colour* is the thing of paramount importance.'[34] Following her work for Rank, Harris decided to become a freelance costume designer. It was during the 1960s that Harris became particularly noticed for her creative, intelligent and inventive costume designs, especially for her work on *A Hard Day's Night* (1964), *Help!* (1965) and *Casino Royale* (1967). This was recognized when Harris won the Academy Award for Best Costume Design – Black-and-White in 1966 for her work on *Darling* (1965), and received a British Academy Film Award for Best Costume Design – Colour for *The Wrong Box* (1966) the following year.[35]

On her approach to designing costumes, Harris explained that in order of importance her 'fundamental priorities' were: 'the script, the character, the director's requirements, the actor's likes and dislikes, the art director's opinion, the action', lamenting that 'last of all [...] comes what the [costume] designer would like.'[36] Explaining that her first task was to read the script, Harris would make 'a breakdown of the number of costume changes, and what kind of clothes are needed. Then it's discussed with the director and producer. And probably the artistic director too ... Then, probably, you make the sketches.'[37] *The Times* revealed that each of Harris's design sketches took 'around an hour' to complete, 'and is an exquisite vignette of the person she is designing for'.[38] Harris believed that her role 'was never dull', and that as well as the women's costumes: 'I also do all the men's things [...] then there are the extras to be dressed [...] Some clothes we buy, some are made. It depends on the budget that can be anywhere from £500 to £5,000 according to a particular film.'[39] Addressing changing styles, Harris noted: 'I never follow high fashion, even if the character is supposed to be a rich, fashionable woman, because styles date so quickly', and that for contemporary clothes, the designer considered the length of skirt hems to be the 'greatest problem'.[40]

Due to her background in women's fashion and costume, Harris much preferred designing clothes for women than men, noting: 'Men can be as – if not more – difficult as the ladies. Once they've accepted style and colour, you've still got to find ties, cufflinks, shirts that will please them – and without their being with you.'[41] Harris particularly 'enjoyed' working on *Live and Let Die* because 'money was no object'.[42] Given that Harris preferred to design period costume and work on the female wardrobe, this is likely another reason that she enjoyed her work on *Live and Let Die* owing to Solitaire's (Jane Seymour) costumes which allowed her to be creative; they notably adopt a quasi-ethnic and period quality, as demonstrated by her designs. Along with Harris, other members of the wardrobe team included

Laurel Staffell (wardrobe supervisor), John Hilling, (wardrobe master), Joanna Wright (wardrobe mistress), and Colin Wilson (wardrobe assistant).

Harris dressed the dual character of Kananga and Mr. Big in a variety of distinctive and vibrant suits that reflect his character as being a business owner and dictator of San Monique. In the script he is referred to by Bond as a 'foreign prime minister' and by Harold Strutter of the CIA as a 'two-bit island diplomat'.[43] Other than this, there is little description of Kananga or his costumes, and therefore Harris's interpretation would have been based upon discussions held with Hamilton and Syd Cain, the art director, as to what the character should be dressed in. Kotto first met Moore when trying on a new suit for the film: 'I walked over to him and I said: "How do you like this new suit Julie just made for me?" He looked at the suit and looked at me and said, "Marvellous sense of humour she has, doesn't she"?'[44] On Harris's sense of humour, Harper argues that the designer 'always had an excellent sense of how far fashion parody could be pushed', and that her previous work on *A Hard Day's Night, Help!* and *Casino Royale* was witty.[45] An example of Harris's humour includes Ursula Andress's pink evening gown embellished with feathers and made from chiffon and silk for *Casino Royale*, that was designed to start off pale pink and end up deep pink over the duration of a lengthy scene between Andress and Peter Sellers. This joke was subsequently lost in the editing of the film.

Kananga is dressed in coloured fabrics that reflect his surroundings, a particular quality and signature of Harris's designs. In order, Kananga wears a midnight blue jacket with waistcoat and medium-grey trousers, a tan suit, a suit with purple and grey patterning, a white blazer and a pair of grey trousers, and a midnight blue suit. A recurring motif that appears in the majority of Kananga's costumes is the colour themes of red and orange, reflective of his irate and controlling nature. In terms of Harris's visual humour, the suits have been deliberately cut to accentuate the flamboyance of Kananga's villainous character, and this is particularly emphasized in the purple and white two-piece suits, as well as Mr. Big's 'American gangster' trench coat. Spaiser believes that at least three of Kananga's suits have been sourced from Castle, and given the tailoring style this is likely, albeit everything about Kananga's suits is more exaggerated than Bond's.[46]

Kananga's distinctive purple and grey double-breasted suit, made from silk, has wide peaked lapels. It has six buttons, two slanted hip pockets with flaps and deep double vents. The length of the coat has been deliberately cut long. The jacket has softly padded, straight shoulders, a clean chest and a suppressed waist with a flared skirt. It includes a flared cuff on the sleeves, as with Moore's, albeit more exaggerated. Underneath the jacket, Kananga wears a pink shirt with a deep point collar that is a recurring feature in all of the shirts worn by the character. It is fastened with a tie made from a purple silk base with pink diamond patterning, working to complement the grey diamond chain-link patterning evident on the suit fabric. Kananga wears a matching purple silk pocket square placed in the jetted breast pocket of the jacket. The ostentatious colour tone is reflective of Kananga's character in relation to power, spirituality, cruelty and arrogance, and is selected to contrast with and emphasize the set design which is bathed in red.

The most unusual costume worn by Kananga in *Live and Let Die* is a white blazer that has been tailored to reflect the dual personality between Kananga and Mr. Big that assists in Kotto's performance (Figure 6.2). The script briefly indicates that Kananga/Mr. Big is 'dressed in wild clothes'.[47] This blazer is likely to have been tailored by Castle given its similarities to the purple jacket including the flared cuffs and skirt. Besides this, the cut of the blazer is very unlike the tailor's normal style and is extraordinarily flamboyant. This is deliberate, so as to highlight the dual personality of the character. The blazer is made from a triaxial weave to give it a diamond patterning on the body. A triaxial weave is an unusual choice for a suit fabric and is normally used in upholstery projects. It is constructed from three yarns running in different angles and a porous structure that creates a cane-like patterning. The blazer has rounded, wide notched lapels with quilled piping on the edges for definition. The blazer noticeably differs from Kananga's other suits in the shoulders, which in this suit have been tailored in a Cifonelli style. The plain pale grey trousers are fitted with a flat front and flare out toward the hem. Beneath the jacket, Kananga wears a tie-dyed red and orange shirt with an exaggerated point collar as well as a pair of white gloves.

In Kananga's final scenes, he breaks away from flamboyant colour and instead wears a navy jacket that differs from the previous style of his others. It is similar in colour to Bond's Chesterfield overcoat. However, the suit is more in keeping with a military style that recalls previous Bond villains, namely Dr. No in his Nehru jacket and Blofeld in his Mao suit. Kananga's jacket has a Balmacaan collar with a unique

FIGURE 6.2 Kananga's distinctive triaxial-weave suit. *Live and Let Die* directed by Guy Hamilton © Eon Productions/United Artists 1973. All rights reserved.

and distinctive small notch cut into the lapel frame. It has four patch pockets placed symmetrically between the chest and hips, double vents and is fastened with five fabric-covered buttons. The matching, fitted trousers have single pleats and are slightly flared. With the suit, Kananga wears a white silk cravat and white shirt, though this is not often visible in the film.

As Mr. Big, Kotto's costume is more in keeping with the characterization of an American gangster, and interpreted by Harris to be more reflective of the other African-Americans situated in Harlem and New Orleans in *Live and Let Die*. Unlike Kananga, Mr. Big is afforded the following description in the script: 'He is a truly frightening specimen – bearded, with wild Afro hair, dark glasses, enormous features, an ugly scar running down one cheek.'[48] This description was changed for the film, and Kananga instead wears a latex mask over his face that slightly distorts his features and an Afro wig. Mr. Big wears a stylized and extravagant long suede trench coat dyed in a dark tan brown. It is double-breasted, with a wide Ulster collar with notched lapels and six gold-plated, widely spaced buttons. Belted at the waist, it has epaulettes on the shoulders that are fastened with a single gold-plated button and wrist straps on the sleeve cuffs. From the back, the trench coat has a stitched-down yoke, is structured from four panels and has a deep back vent. Deliberately cut to be too small to fasten correctly, the Nehru-style dark brown velour shirt can be viewed beneath the coat, accompanied by matching-coloured trousers. Mr. Big wears matching brown leather gloves and a chunky gold chain around his neck.

In terms of *Live and Let Die*'s female characters, Mankiewicz originally intended for Solitaire to be Black and Rosie Carver to be white. In Fleming's novel, Solitaire is white, however in keeping with the inspiration taken from blaxploitation films to write the script, Mankiewicz wrote the part of Solitaire with Diana Ross in mind. After David Picker refused, Solitaire and Rosie were switched, with Jane Seymour cast in the role of Solitaire and Gloria Hendry as Rosie Carver. Two of Harris's costume sketches for Solitaire can be viewed in the special collections at the BFI.[49] The first design, 'suggested' for the 'Harlem sequence', is a gown with a colour scheme of purple, magenta, turquoise and gold, and is formed by a collage of mixed media with two layers of paper, demonstrating Harris's creative approach to depth and eye for colour. The first layer includes three fabric panels made from sari silk that have been glued to the paper. The top and bottom fabric panels have a horizontal blue and purple striped patterning, and the middle panel has a vertically striped pattern; the first stripe a red base with yellow polka dots, the alternate stripe a turquoise base with gold swirls in boxes, and in between the two stripes the fabric includes a dice-shaped pattern in red with alternate turquoise and yellow dots. A white chiffon fabric that includes a sparkling gold filigree pattern in diamond shapes has been fastened over the three fabric panels. For the second layer, Harris sketched Solitaire's figure in pencil, ink and watercolour on tracing paper, a technique that the designer was trained to do by Haffenden. The body is cut to reveal the fabric on the first layer underneath and has another sari silk fabric glued onto the second layer to depict a long shawl. This fabric has a purple base, with a magenta floral pattern including dark blue pistils at the centre and an overlay of swirling white spots. The gown's design has a sleeveless halter-neck with a plunging neckline in a burgundy colour that is painted in watercolour, and its shape forms an empire-line dress, with the skirt flaring outwards to the hem.

Harris noted on the sketch: 'Bolero dress and shawl in various patterned materials [. . .] Solitaire to wear "affro" [sic] wig'.[50] Although this design was created after the casting of Seymour, given that her skin is painted white, her Afro wig may well have been included to connect the character to Mr. Big, who is described in the script as wearing one too. Harris has also painted exaggerated eyelashes onto her interpretation of Seymour's face to accentuate the hair and ethic style of her costume. The design provides a very clear example of the different agencies involved in the realization of an individual costume. The rendering has been completely reimagined for the Harlem scenes in the film by the maker of the costume, likely due to the overarching red colour scheme in the scenes involving Mr. Big/Kananga, as well as the style and the cut of the dress. In the film, Solitaire wears a modest high-necked, full-sleeved and long gown reminiscent of the traditional Turkish *kaftan* (Plate 7). It is made from crushed velvet in a ruby red colour, and the rounded 'jewel' neckline is embellished with long silver teardrop pendants with the front bib and back yolk of the fitted bodice inclusive of silver embroidery and sequin detailing. The sleeves are fitted to the elbow before they flare out to the cuffs in a kaleidoscope of colours including purple, gold and red; the cuffs are also embroidered in silver thread in a pattern similar to the bodice. The gown is fastened with a hidden zip at the back, and the A-line skirt flares out to the floor. A matching red velvet cloak is worn in the previous scene.

The other surviving costume sketch for *Live and Let Die*, titled 'Alternative for "lying on the floor" sequence if a <u>front view</u>', reflects the quasi-hippy and bohemian trend of the 1970s.[51] This design is made from one layer unlike the other costume design and has no fabric swatch attached to it, however Harris notes that it is to be made from '*crêpe* in bright colour with "tie-dye" pattern on trouser skirt which would be very full'. It is rendered in the medium of pencil and watercolour, and the costume is a vibrant orange jumpsuit that includes two spaghetti straps that leads to a plunging neckline cut to the waist which has lacing detail in the centre. The waist is seamed with the trousers fitted over the hips and flowing out palazzo style to a very wide flared hem as dictated in Harris's notes. To demonstrate the tie-dye effect, Harris has painted white and yellow watercolour swirls over the trouser legs. Next to the painted design, Harris has included a separate uncoloured pencil sketch to suggest an alternative, noting 'could have full sleeves if more covered up look required'.[52] The pencil sketch suggests a similar costume shape, but the spaghetti straps have been replaced with sleeves that are long, full and set-in, with the fullness of the fabric held at the wrist by a cuff. It appears that the sleeve is gathered at the top cap as well as the wrist according to the sketch. Unlike the previous sketch for the Harlem scene, this costume rendering appears similar to the costume realized for the film. The cut and shape are similar to that of Harris's design, however it differs in that it is made from a solidly coloured scarlet red silk jersey fabric with no tie-dye patterning, most likely due to it being in keeping with the colour scheme of the set. The straps of the trouser suit are wider and form into a curved scoop neckline that is cut to just below the bust rather than the waist. As an interpretation of Harris's design, the maker has included three fabric bars between the lower base of the neckline rather than laces, thus appearing more stylized. The maker also chose to go with Harris's sleeveless version of the design.

Solitaire's costumes begin to change following sexual intercourse with Bond, becoming plainer and more Westernized in cut and style. They are reminiscent of the more conservatively dressed 'Bond girls' from the 1960s films, including Tatiana Romanova in *From Russia With Love* and Tilly Masterson in *Goldfinger*. The illusion to Tatiana is particularly highlighted at the end of the film when Solitaire wears a blue chiffon nightgown with matching nightdress, albeit it is darker in colour with circular sleeves. After her 'sexual awakening', Solitaire wears the first of two shirts created by Frank Foster. The tunic blouse is made from an orange linen-cotton blend and has a Balmacaan collar that can be either worn open or closed. When worn open, it forms notched lapels, as Solitaire's does in *Live and Let Die*. It has fitted sleeves with gauntlet cuffs, two side vents, a straight hem, and is fastened with small mother-of-pearl buttons. With the blouse, Solitaire wears a long gold filigree chain necklace, and white linen trousers with flared hems.

As an irony, the final ethnic costume that Solitaire wears reflects her sexual awakening, and is cut as an empire-line, floor-length gown. It is made from a *lamé* silk that has a red base and a pattern of yellow and purple that includes a variety of emblems: butterflies, stars, leaves and flowers. The plunging neckline, framed with gold lace that includes a red ribbon centre appliquéd on to it, is cut underneath the bust, and has a gold butterfly and tassel motif placed at the centre. The gown has a natural shoulder and a fitted shoulder cap cut to the elbow with the same lacing appliquéd to the sleeve band along with a fringe of small red tassels. From there, a yellow chiffon with orange patterning has been stitched underneath the cap and is gathered to create a puffed sleeve that finishes in a shirred ribbed cuff made from gold silk at Solitaire's wrist. This sleeve is cut in a lantern style. The A-line skirt is cut from the high-waist seam and flares out to the ground, as with the character's other similar dresses.

Solitaire's final costume was designed to reflect that the character is to be part of a sacrificial ritual, and is understood to be Harris's favourite costume in the film. It is a white chiffon and silk empire-line dress, designed to enhance Solitaire's 'damsel in distress' look. The dress has a *décolleté* neckline that is cut in a deep scoop and finishes in a V shape that ends in between her sternum and includes a white silk piping for emphasis. The short chiffon circular sleeves are slashed in order to drape on either side of the Solitaire's shoulders. The bodice is fitted and includes ruched and gathered detailing over the bust to the waist, of which the hem is covered with a white chiffon sash that is knotted at the back. The skirt is made from chiffon panels that have been cut on the bias to accentuate drape and create a delicate and ethereal illusion, which is emphasized from creating two slits from hem to thigh on both sides. The hem is calf-length at the front and lengthens towards the rear in order to create a short V-shaped train. Both this dress and the red jumpsuit present the viewer with a visual irony, as they work to eroticize the character by being virginal and carnal at the same time.

Rosie Carver's costumes are more Westernized than that of Solitaire's, and include a white dress, a colourful wrap dress and a bikini, which are more in keeping with previous 'Bond girl' costumes. Rosie first wears a white, structured halter-neck dress made from a silk jersey fabric. It has a plunging neckline and cloverleaf notched lapels with rounded corners. The panelled bodice is cinched at the waist with a matching belt that is fastened with a circular gold-plated clasp. The skirt is cut in an A-line and hemmed at the knee, and two large patch pockets are stitched on either side of the hips. The dress is fastened at the front with a zip. Rosie also wears an Afro wig with the costume, which is similar to Harris's sketch for Solitaire's 'bolero dress'. Rosie is then costumed in a wrap dress made from a *crêpe* silk with a button fastening down the front. It has a wide point collar with fitted sleeves that are hemmed above the elbow, and is cinched at the waist with a sashed belt of matching fabric. It is knee-length, and the fabric colour base is jade green and includes a purple and white tie-dye pattern on the top of right-hand sleeve that continues to flow in a spiral serpentine pattern around the body of the dress. In terms of its colour scheme and fabric, Rosie's dress is reflective of Harris's costume sketch for Solitaire's 'bolero dress', as with the Afro wig. Beneath the dress, Rosie wears a vibrant and colourful string bikini. The bikini top has a halter-neck fastened with yellow piping that is continued between the sternum. The left cup is made from a magenta fabric with an abstract print of hearts and lines forming a waved line pattern in red and blue which continues over on the right cup that has a white fabric base with an orange and blue patterning. The briefs, that are tied with piping bows on both sides of the hips, have a yellow base with a similar patterning. Overall, the ensemble is cut to offer a continuous patterning of waves and heart shapes, in a similar style to that of the wrap dress.

The reception for *Live and Let Die* was mixed. Unlike Lazenby, critics welcomed Roger Moore, although they could not resist comparing him to Connery. For example, Margaret Hinxman quipped that: 'After watching one non-actor, George Lazenby, and now a very pleasing actor, Roger Moore, attempting to fill 007's shoes,' Hinxman believed Moore played a 'suave and resourceful 007'.[53] Dilys Powell concurred, writing that Moore was 'alright' and, referencing his style, 'the elegance (for Mr. Moore always looks like a proper English gent) acquires a touch of irony; it will do [. . .] he's not yet quite a 007 but he is a pretty good 008'.[54] Some specifically referenced Moore's sartorial style in *Live and Let Die*, with Felix Barker pointing out: 'In the new figure of Roger Moore in *Live and Let Die*, 007 is a very natty dresser. Investigating the murder of three British agents, he follows a clue to a smoky Harlem nightclub inconspicuous in a Savile Row overcoat, Trumper [Dennis Price] haircut and club tie,' and notes that Bond's armoury is reduced to a watch 'which can deflect bullets and comes in useful for unzipping women's dresses'.[55] John Russell Taylor argued that Moore's Bond 'is by now almost as period a figure as Bulldog Drummond, with his little antique snobberies of drink and dress', and that: 'It's as if Moore, and probably the producers too, decided that Bond's licence to kill should be extended to a licence to frill'.[56] Perhaps the best comparison between Connery and Moore in terms of their sartorial differences came from Alexander Walker: 'Roger brings [*Live and Let Die*] a fashion-plate distinction while Sean lent [his Bond films] a saturnine rakishness. I wouldn't say there's a whit to choose between which man can fight his way more ruthlessly into a dress shirt. Both are virile specimens, in their respective ways'.[57]

The Man with the Golden Gun (1974)

After the success of *Live and Let Die*, United Artists were keen to begin production on the next instalment of the Bond franchise immediately. Pre-production work for *The Man with the Golden Gun* based on Fleming's novel began in the summer of 1973. Principal photography started in April 1974, and was filmed at Pinewood and on location in Thailand and Hong Kong. The wardrobe team for the film included Elsa Fennell as the wardrobe supervisor, returning after *Diamonds Are Forever*, Tiny Nicholls as the wardrobe master, and Colin Wilson and Evelyn Gibbs as the wardrobe assistants. There is no evidence to suggest that a costume designer was employed on the production.

In order of appearance, Bond's costumes in *The Man with the Golden Gun* include:

1   A double-breasted suit in medium-grey fabric including a chalk stripe, with a white shirt and red silk tie.

2   A single-breasted suit in marine blue, with a pale blue shirt and a deep red satin tie.

3   A double-breasted, navy blazer with a hopsack weave, worn twice in the film, firstly with a shirt that includes blue and white dress stripes fastened with a pale blue satin-silk tie and a pair of dark navy trousers, and secondly with a white cotton shirt, a regimental tie with blue and white stripes and cream linen trousers.

4   A cream safari jacket and brown silk trousers.

5   A single-breasted light grey silk suit with a white shirt and navy tie.

6 A dark olive pinstriped suit worn with a twill-weave cotton shirt that has tan and white dress stripes, fastened with an olive tie made of shantung silk.

7 A cream slim-fitted shirt made from *crêpe de chine* with a short hem and a wide open-cut collar, worn with flared cream linen trousers.

8 A double-breasted ivory dinner jacket made from dupioni silk with black trousers and a cream *crêpe de chine* dress shirt with a pleated front and mother-of-pearl buttons, fastened with a silk black bowtie.

9 A cotton judo outfit.

10 A charcoal herringbone suit with a white cotton voile shirt that includes a thin ticking stripe in light grey fastened with a black satin-silk tie.

11 A sage green cotton safari shirt and cream linen trousers.

12 An on-trend single-breasted sports jacket made from grey, red and black plaid checks, worn with black high-waisted trousers and an ecru-coloured shirt fastened with a black woven silk tie. Neil Norman recognizes the pattern on the suit as a 'Texas check'.[58]

13 The black jacket taken from the two-piece suit worn by Scaramanga's mannequin of Bond.

The art silk linings of some of Bond's suits in this film are occasionally visible and appear very on-trend. The marine blue suit lining has a burgundy base with a printed blue circular geometrical pattern, the light grey silk suit has a lining made from a white base and an indigo blue paisley pattern, and the charcoal herringbone suit has a claret-coloured lining with a similar geometric pattern to the marine blue suit. It is in *The Man with the Golden Gun* that Moore wears the first of his distinctive safari jackets and shirts in a Bond film, however it should be noted that Moore previously wore a navy safari suit for some promotional shots for *Live and Let Die* that was not worn in the film. Although a fashionable trend in the 1970s, Nick Sullivan explained that Moore's

> appearance may now seem extravagant, but Moore does no more in his films than Connery did in his, merely reflecting the tastes of his time. Even Moore's flared trousers and safari jackets fall far short of the overblown looks available to men in the Seventies. His wardrobe is a simple, understated version of the prevailing and often outrageous trends in menswear.[59]

The safari suits and shirts would later become synonymous with the dated look of Moore's Bond films, with many fans and critics making light of them in hindsight. For example, Stuart Heritage argued that 'James Bond actually died long ago, when Roger Moore strapped himself into his first male girdle and started wheezing around in a safari suit.'[60]

For the cream safari jacket, tailored in silk and structured in a similar way to Moore's other single-breasted suits, it follows the traditional look of safari suits and includes epaulettes on the shoulders, four flapped patch pockets with inverted box pleats that are fastened with one button, a four-button fastening and one rear vent. Notably, the safari jacket includes the stylish addition of contrasting brown stitching around the different elements of the suit, for example the epaulettes, collar and pocket flaps, to emphasize these details. The jacket also differs from typical safari jackets in that they would normally have an open collar, but Moore's version includes a stylized wide and pointed Balmacaan-style lapel instead. The sage green cotton safari shirt was produced by the Hong Kong-based tailor Jimmy Chen. As with the safari jacket, it includes four inverted box pleat patch pockets, epaulettes, and a four-button fastening made from pearlescent buttons, however is more in keeping with traditional safari menswear in that it has a wide, pointed open collar. It is fitted by the inclusion of a belt stitched on to the back.

In the novel, the explicitly homosexual Scaramanga is described in his Secret Service file as being six-foot-five-feet, 'slim and fit', with a 'gaunt, sombre face' that has 'light brown eyes', and 'reddish' hair with 'long sideburns'.[61] Excepting the hair, Christopher Lee fits Fleming's physical description of Scaramanga well, although the script and film omits the homosexual characterization. In Fleming's *The Man with the Golden Gun*, Scaramanga has a 'cat-like menace', with large shoulders and a narrow waist, and wearing 'a well-cut, single-breasted tan suit and "co-respondent" shoes in brown and white. Instead of a tie, he wore a high-stock in white silk secured by a gold pin in the shape of a miniature pistol.'[62]

In the script, Scaramanga is described in the opening scenes as wearing 'golden trunks' as he emerges from the sea, which is a direct reference to the novel.[63] In the film, the swimming trunks are not golden, but instead pale khaki in colour, suggesting they were a somewhat hurried costume purchase. Following this, Scaramanga dresses in a navy catsuit and white sport shoes that fits with Fleming's description of the character, in order to assassinate Rodney, an American gangster that attempts to outshoot him in Scaramanga's 'fun house'. The catsuit is made of a velour fabric and includes white piping detail stitched down the shoulders, sleeves, body and outside leg. Scaramanga then wears a black suit, which is single-breasted and has a slim cut, with flared cuffs on the sleeves and double vents.

Scaramanga is mainly costumed in an off-white suit throughout the film prior to Bond arriving on his island. This outfit is described in the film as: 'a white linen suit, black tie, *crêpe* soled loafers, and a lot of jewellery. All gold.'[64] Two versions of this suit were made for Lee by Bermans and Nathans, with both being made from polyester. One version had a single-breasted jacket with a three-button fastening made from a mother-of-pearl effect. Tailored with an open Balmacaan collar, the Neapolitan shoulder is lightly padded with a slight shirring on the sleeve cap. The coat of the suit is slim-fitting with a lean chest and slightly suppressed waist so as to emphasize Lee's tall athletic figure. The jacket's sleeves include plain cuffs and the body has two slanted flapped hip pockets. According to a Bonhams auction listing, the suit has a white satin-effect lining and is labelled 'CHRISTOPHER LEE SUIT 1 6581 MAN WITH GOLDEN GUN'.[65] The trousers, which were auctioned separately, were made from a cream-coloured wool (colour 6721).[66] The legs have a narrow leg, a darted front and plain hems. The second version of the suit jacket was a double-breasted blazer. The fabric used for the lining was the same as the single-breasted jacket, however the label indicates that the blazer fabric was made from polyester in slightly different colour shade of '6581' rather than '6271'.[67] The blazer includes a four-button fastening made from gold-plated buttons with a mother-of-pearl-effect centre. It has wide notch lapels that are distinctively cut, and straight, wide shoulders with roped sleeve-heads. The blazer is cut with a full chest and suppressed waist, and includes a Barchetta welt breast pocket and two flapped slanted hip pockets. The cuffs on the blazer sleeves are flared. It was decided in the film that Scaramanga would only wear the single-breasted version, presumably to ensure continuity and consistency.

With the suits, Scaramanga wears white shirts made by Frank Foster with a spread collar and square double cuffs that are fastened with gold cufflinks, the left one forming the trigger of Scaramanga's golden gun. They are worn with a black knitted silk tie. As explained by Matthew Field and Ajay Chowdhury, the jewellers Colibri are credited in the film for producing the different elements of the gun, however their creation was 'unstable and did not have the required look', and thus a different jeweller, J. Rose, was quickly enlisted to create the gun.[68] At the end of the film, Scaramanga wears a pale blue tropical outfit made from a lightweight cotton fabric. It was created for Lee by Thai tailor 'Harry'. The shirt has short sleeves with epaulettes on the shoulder. It is cut loose, intended to drape over Lee's frame. It has a high point collar and a five-button fastening made with off-white buttons. The waist is suppressed due to it having a gathered half-belt stitched at the back, and it is cut with a straight hem. It has three patch pockets with box pleats; one is placed on the left breast and includes a separate, narrow pocket for the pen that forms part of the golden gun, and two on either side of the hips. The back of the shirt has a horizontal yoke and an inverted centre seam that is cut into a vent. The trousers, which are made from a slightly darker shade of blue and appear to be made from a heavier cotton, have single pleats and a slight flaring towards the plain hem.

The character of Mary Goodnight (Britt Ekland) was established in Fleming's novel *On Her Majesty's Secret Service* and included in *You Only Live Twice*. In *The Man with the Golden Gun*, Fleming expanded Goodnight's role to assist Bond in his mission. The script updates Goodnight's characterization, however in keeping with 1970s 'Bond girls', appears as a simpler, vacuous and less resourceful woman, which is in part reflected by her costume. Bond also treats her in a more derogative way in the script than in the novel, with Bond 'sourly' exclaiming to her when she arrives late: 'You're a great help, Goodnight,' and later, after she manages to get herself locked in the trunk of Scaramanga's car, Bond describes her as a 'silly cow', although this line in the script is omitted in the film.[69] The script first describes Goodnight in her gold-coloured MGB sports car: 'At the wheel is an attractive, chicly-dressed girl in her middle-twenties.'[70] Little can be seen of Goodnight's full outfit, which is presumably a dress, in the film, however it is sleeveless and has notched lapels, and is made from a silk fabric that includes a geometrically squared 'brick path' pattern in jade green, white and navy. With the dress Goodnight wears a headscarf of matching fabric over her hair.

When Goodnight meets Bond for dinner at the Oriental Hotel in Bangkok, the script references Fleming's novel. In the novel, Goodnight asks Bond what she should wear to dinner, to which he replies: 'Something that's tight in all the right places. Not too many buttons.'[71] Goodnight is later described as being perfumed in Chanel No. 5 and dressed in

> a single string of pearls and a one-piece, short-skirted frock in the colour of a pink gin with a lot of bitters in it – the orangey-pink of the inside of a conch shell. It was all tight against the bosom and the hips. She smiled at [Bond's] scrutiny. 'The buttons are down the back. This is standard uniform for a tropical Station.'[72]

Bond replies: 'I can just see Q Branch dreaming it up. I suppose one of the pearls has a death pill in it,' to which Goodnight flirtatiously quips: 'Of course. But I can't remember which. I'll just have to swallow the whole string.'[73] The script adapts this for the Bangkok scene in the film:

318. ARCADE
[…] GOODNIGHT seated at a table. She looks particularly pretty. […]

BOND
I approve.

GOODNIGHT
You do?

BOND
Not the champagne. Your frock. Tight
in all the right places. Not too many
buttons.

GOODNIGHT
Standard uniform in south east Asia.
(she takes another sip)
The buttons are down the back.

BOND
Designed by Q no doubt. One of them's
a suicide pill, I suppose.

GOODNIGHT
(smiling)
No, but the bottom one has a homer
in it.[74]

The 'frock' is interpreted as a backless aqua blue floor-length gown made from silk. It has a gathered halter-neck and a deep sweetheart neckline, as well as being gathered at the under-bust seam to create a ruching detail and emphasize an empire-line shape. A fabric-covered button detail has been stitched at the bottom of the neckline between the sternum, likely to reference Bond's comment about buttons, although it is ironically fastened at the back with a zip. The skirt of the gown is circular and cut on the bias to create a fit-and-flare silhouette that flows around the body as Goodnight strides away from Bond. With the gown, Goodnight wears a silver chained princess necklace with a sapphire and silver pendant cut in an oval shape.

In Bond's hotel suite, Goodnight is described as wearing 'a diaphanous short nightgown' in the script, which is interpreted as a chiffon baby-doll nightdress. It has plaited spaghetti straps with a camisole neckline that has a banded leaf detail. The fabric has a pale blue base with aquamarine tie-dye patterning. It is cut micro-length above the thigh and the chiffon is cut in a circular pattern that flows from the neckline that sits just above Goodnight's chest. In the final scenes of the film, Goodnight is costumed in a bikini as indicated in the script, which also features in the film's promotional photography. The bikini top is cut in the shape of a 'bullet' *brassière*, and has string bikini briefs tied at both hips. It is made from a Lycra material that includes a camouflage style in purple, blue, white and green colours, of which the patterning seamlessly repeats over the top and briefs. In the script, Bond admires Goodnight stating 'what a marvellous tan', however the film is more in keeping with Bond's patronizing tone towards the character: 'Aren't we a little overdressed, Goodnight?'[75] In the script and film, Scaramanga replies to Bond: 'I like a girl in a bikini – no concealed weapons.' Ekland reflected on the difficulty of performing in such a costume: 'You're very vulnerable when you're half naked. I could feel [the heat of the explosion] and I freaked out. I threw myself on the floor. And you see Roger dragging me up and that was real.'[76]

Andrea Anders (Maud Adams) is a curious addition to the bad 'Bond girl' trope of the films. Her character is not included in Fleming's novel, and in some ways Andrea's characterization is more reflective of Pussy Galore in *Goldfinger* and Tiffany Case in *Diamonds Are Forever* than that of Fiona Volpe in *Thunderball*, Helga Brandt in *You Only Live Twice*, and Rosie Carver in *Live and Let Die*. In *The Man with the Golden Gun*, Andrea is the mistress of Scaramanga, but although she works on his behalf and is sent to collect his order of golden bullets, she sends the British Secret Service one of the bullets with '007' etched on the casing in the hope that Bond will be sent to kill Scaramanga. As she states to Bond: 'You don't walk out on Scaramanga. There's no place where he wouldn't find me. I'm chained to him as long as he lives.' Therefore, Andrea is ideologically positioned as being against, rather than for, Scaramanga, and her death in the film seems an unnecessary cruelty, particularly as Andrea believes that she has to have sexual intercourse with Bond as well as obtain the Solex Agitator in order for Bond to kill Scaramanga on her behalf. However, the audience have already been made aware that Bond intends to kill the latter if necessary, regardless, and thus Andrea is positioned as merely a means to an end for Bond to obtain the Solex Agitator. Indeed, on Bond discovering her death at the Bangkok Stadium the following day, he does not appear to be particularly affected by it, and is more interested on the whereabouts of the Solex Agitator which is emphasized when he rifles through her handbag in order to try and find it.

Andrea's costumes in *The Man with the Golden Gun* are reflective of her ambiguous allegiance that is split between Bond and Scaramanga; this is enhanced by her costumes that are alternately black and white. Andrea first appears at the beginning of the film lounging on Scaramanga's private beach. She wears a halter-necked one-piece swimsuit that differs from the description in the script that suggests the character wear a bikini.[77] The piped neck of the swimsuit is crossed over the collarbone and it has a contoured and fitted top half to avoid the inclusion of a constructed shelf *brassière*. The gusset is cut high over Adam's thighs to emphasize her legs and willowy figure; Adams being five-foot-nine-inches tall. This swimsuit would be worn by Adams in the promotional photographs for the film. In the Macau casino, Andrea wears a two-piece white suit, likely made from a silk-linen blend. The peplum jacket has a wide, spread collar and bouffant sleeves that are gathered at the shoulder and the winged cuffs. The back of the jacket as two inverted pleats known as a princess seam. It is belted at the waist to emphasize Adams's silhouette, and the jacket is worn with a knee-length semi-circular skirt. The necklace worn by Andrea in this scene was auctioned by Christie's and was described as: 'An oriental carved malachite pendant of fruit and foliage design, with a diamond set floral mount, suspended by a continuous yellow metal link chain.'[78]

During the scene between Bond and Andrea in her hotel suite, she wears a white terrycloth towelling robe as dictated by the script. It has a shawl collar that is emphasized by Bond when he seizes it to threaten her, and is fastened by a matching belt and has a ribbed cuff detail and two patch pockets. When she arrives at Bond's suite in order to seduce him, Andrea wears a black silk evening gown that, as with the swimsuit, has a halter-neck. It has a plunging neckline, with a smocking detail gathered at the back, and is floor-length with an A-line skirt gathered at the hips and cut on the bias. In Andrea's final scene at the Bangkok Stadium, she is dressed in white once again. Though little of the costume can be viewed due to the juxtaposition of the camera angles, Andrea wears a wide-brimmed straw hat and a silk-linen suit jacket that has slim notched lapels. A bullet wound above her breast is visible, unlike in the script that indicates that 'there is a bullet hole in the front of her dress'.[79] The 'Andrea Anders' character type would be revisited later in the Bond franchise in the form of Lupe Lamora (Talisa Soto) in *Licence to Kill*. The reception for *The Man with the Golden Gun*, as with *Live and Let Die*, was mixed. Due to various reasons, there was a three-year wait before the next Bond film, *The Spy Who Loved Me*, would be released. During this break, changes were made towards the costuming of the Bond films, most specifically in relation to who would tailor Moore's suits.

Notes

1 Broccoli with Zec, *When the Snow Melts*, 227.

2 Alan Davidson, 'There's Moore than meets the eye? Roger Moore's fashion world as a real *Persuader!*', *RogerMoore.com*, 2005, www.roger-moore.com/old/Roger/pages/exclusive.htm (accessed 30 June 2020).

3 Hugh O'Neill, 'Fashion favours Yorkshire', *Financial Times*, 21 August 1970, 10.

4 Letter from the managing directors' office to staff at Pearson and Foster, n.d., quoted in Davidson.

5 Ibid.

6 'Pearson and Foster (Bradford) Ltd', *Financial Times*, 24 June 1969, 29.

7 'Saint helps turn loss into £73,000 profit', *Financial Times*, 24 June 1968, 19.

8 Davidson.

9 Ibid.

10 Ibid.

11 Ibid.

12 Excerpts of the contractual agreement between Moore can be viewed here: www.roger-moore.com/old/Roger/pages/exclusive.htm (accessed 30 June 2020).

13 'The Saint on board', *Style Weekly*, 12 February 1970, 4.

14 Liz Gill, 'Dashing Saint puts on the style for Amsterdam', *Bradford Telegraph and Argus*, 12 October 1970, 13.

15 Roger Moore with Gareth Owen, *My Word Is My Bond*, 165.

16 'Shrinking in order to expand', *Financial Times*, 19 October 1970, 29.

17 Sinclair McKay, 'Wearing well', *Daily Telegraph*, 22 July 1998, 23.

18 Broccoli with Zec, 229, 230.

19 Moore with Owen, *Bond on Bond*, 123.

20 'What the experts say', *The Times*, 14 March 1969.

21 'Tailors of the stage, screen and radio', *Tailor & Cutter*, 4 September 1964, 1294.

22 'On people', *Daily Mail*, 18 April 1963, 4.

23 David Morton, 'Man's world: Take three', *Tatler*, 13 February 1966, 52.

24 Christopher Ward, 'The Saint makes a sartorial sortie', *Daily Mirror*, 3 August 1968, 7.

25 Tom Merrin, 'Holding hands at midday', *Daily Mirror*, 16 May 1975, 72; Nigel Dempster, 'Jet set', *Daily Mail*, 18 December 1975.

26 Spaiser, 'Basted for Bond: Examining Cyril Castle', *The Suits of James Bond*, 9 July 2015, www.bondsuits.com/basted-for-bond-examining-cyril-castle/ (accessed 30 June 2020).

27 Ibid.

28 Jeremy Hackett, 'Men's style Jeremy Hackett is Mr. Classic', *Independent on Sunday*, 12 June 2005, 151.

29 Tom Mankiewicz, *Live and Let Die*, shooting script, 2 October 1972, 65, 66.

30 Fleming, *Live and Let Die* (1954; London: Penguin Books, 2009), 26.

31 Mankiewicz, 8–9.

32 Spaiser, 'Navy in New York: A Chesterfield coat and navy suit in *Live and Let Die*', *The Suits of James Bond*, 23 December 2010, www.bondsuits.com/navy-in-new-york/ (accessed 6 July 2020).

33 Harper, *Women in British Cinema*, 215.

34 Harris, 'Fashion is what you make it', *Girl Film and Television Annual* 1 (1975), 109.

35 For a close analysis of Harris's work on *Darling*, see Melanie Williams' article 'The girl you don't see: Julie Harris and the costume designer in British cinema', *Feminist Media Histories* 2, no. 2 (2016), 71–106.

36 Ernestine Carter, 'Flicker fashion', *The Sunday Times*, 3 September 1966, 23.

37 Anne Hooper, 'So you want to be a movie fashion designer?', *Photoplay*, September 1966, 61.

38 'Women behind the scenes of success', *The Times*, 19 July 1967, 9.

39 Felicity Green, 'Actresses, unlike other women, get a chance to see themselves from the back view . . .', *Daily Mirror*, 11 May 1966, 9.

40 Shirley Flack, 'How she sees the stars . . .', *Daily Mail*, 12 November 1959, 6; Carter, 1966.

41 Carter.

42 'Julie Harris', *Daily Telegraph*, 1 June 2015, 27.

43 Mankiewicz, revised 30 January 1973, 24.

44 With many thanks to Matthew Field for bringing this anecdote to the author's attention, which was published in Field and Chowdhury (eds), 'Remembering Roger Moore', *MI6 Confidential Special Publication*, May 2018, 7.

45 Harper, 216.

46 Spaiser, 'Dr Kananga: The purple suit', *The Suits of James Bond*, 31 July 2013, www.bondsuits.com/dr-kananga-the-purple-suit/ (accessed 6 July 2020).

47 Mankiewicz, revised 8 January 1973, 70.

48 Ibid., 21.

49 They have been reproduced in Simmonds, *Bond by Design*, 126, 127.

50 BFI, Julie Harris Collection, PD-14766: *Live and Let Die*, Solitaire, '20', n.d.

51 Ibid.: *Live and Let Die*, Solitaire, '6', n.d.

52 Ibid.

53 Margaret Hinxman, 'Full house', *Sunday Telegraph*, 8 July 1973, 18.

54 Dilys Powell, 'Bond stunts back into business', *The Sunday Times*, 8 July 1973, 39.

55 Felix Barker, 'Obviously – this Bond is no secret agent', *Evening News*, 5 July 1973.

56 John Russell Taylor, 'Live and Let Die', *The Times*, 6 July 1973.

57 Alexander Walker, 'Live and Let Die', *Evening Standard*, 5 July 1973.

58 Norman, *Dressed to Kill*, 120.

59 Sullivan, *Dressed to Kill*, 142.

60 Stuart Heritage, 'Is James Bond past his sell-by date?', *Guardian*, 5 July 2010, www.theguardian.com/film/filmblog/2010/jul/05/james-bond-past-sell-by?CMP=share_btn_fb (accessed 11 July 2020).

61 Fleming, *The Man with the Golden Gun*, 30.

62 Ibid., 66.

63 Ibid., 87.

64 Richard Maibaum, *The Man with the Golden Gun*, first draft screenplay, 7 January 1974, 34.

65 Bonhams, 'Lot 194: Christopher Lee from *The Man with the Golden Gun*, 1974', *The Angels Star Collection of Film and TV Costumes*, 6 March 2007, www.bonhams.com/auctions/15337/lot/194/?category=list&length=364&page=1 (accessed 10 July 2020).

66 Bonhams, 'Lot 109: Christopher Lee from *The Man with the Golden Gun*, 1974', *Entertainment Memorabilia including items from the Angels Collection of Television & Film Costumes*, 16 June 2009, www.bonhams.com/auctions/16808/lot/109/ (accessed 10 July 2020).

67 The Prop Gallery, 'James Bond: *The Man with the Golden Gun*', n.d., www.thepropgallery.com/francisco-scaramanga-costume (accessed 10 July 2020).

68 Field and Chowdhury, 260.

69 Maibaum, 27, 97.

70 Ibid., 27.

71 Fleming, *The Man with the Golden Gun*, 47.

72 Ibid., 51.

73 Ibid.

74 Maibaum, 75, 76.

75 Ibid., 118.

76 Britt Ekland interviewed by Marion d'Abo, *Bond Girls Are Forever*, documentary (USA: Sony Pictures Home Entertainment, 2006).

77 Maibaum, 1.

78 Christie's, 'Lot 271: *The Man with the Golden Gun*', *Film and Entertainment*, 12 December 2001, www.christies.com/lotfinder/lot/the-man-with-the-golden-gun-1974-3839538-details.aspx?from=searchresults&intObjectID=3839538 (accessed 10 July 2020).

79 Maibaum, 88.

7 BREAKING HIS TAILOR'S HEART: ROGER MOORE (1976–80)

Following the release of *The Man with the Golden Gun*, the tensions that had steadily risen over time between Broccoli and Saltzman finally came to a head, and Broccoli was left the sole owner of Eon Productions and the producer of the Bond films in a joint agreement with United Artists. It was due to this that the production of *The Spy Who Loved Me* was delayed. Hamilton was originally intended to be the director, however due to the delay Hamilton left after agreeing to direct *Superman* (1978), although he would later be replaced for that film by Richard Donner. Other directors were briefly considered before Lewis Gilbert, who had directed *You Only Live Twice*, agreed to direct the film. Principal photography for *The Spy Who Loved Me* eventually began in September 1976.

Moore had since become a UK tax exile, and therefore he requested that his Italian tailor, Angelo Vitucci of Angelo Roma, make his suits for *The Spy Who Loved Me* and *Moonraker* so as to avoid visiting London for fittings.[1] It is the first time in the Eon Productions franchise that Bond wears an Italian-tailored suit. The employment of Vitucci for *The Spy Who Loved Me* and *Moonraker* did not cause much consternation among critics and British tailors as it subsequently would do on the employment of Brioni to tailor Pierce Brosnan's suits in *GoldenEye*. Vitucci had formally been employed in 1952 by Nazareno Fonticoli and Gaetano Savini, the founders of Brioni, as a male model and a member of the marketing team. Vitucci continued to work for the firm during the 1950s. In 1963, Vitucci decided to leave Brioni and create his own fashion atelier, Angelo Roma. Alan Flusser writes that Vitucci had 'flare and finesse' with his 'slim-fitted, hand-styled' suits, and achieved 'instant success' from his premises that were based 'around the corner' from Brioni.[2] Flusser explains: 'Compared to the Brioni house style, Angelo's shoulders are slightly wider and more sloped, but resolutely self-conscious.' Clients included Frank Sinatra, Tony Curtis and Telly Savalas, as well as many from the

Middle East, and Vitucci negotiated licences to sell his suits in England, the United States and Japan. The tailor was also later employed by the British retailer Marks & Spencer as a menswear consultant in 1970. By 1996, the cost of a bespoke two-piece suit ranged between $1,800 and $2,500 and would take around three to four weeks to make.

In terms of suit stylings for film during the middle of this decade, Neil Norman argues that

> suits started to appear ridiculous: wide lapels, flared trousers and unsuitable materials all connived to destroy the credibility of the wearer. Heroes looked more like rock stars in civvies. Bond fever was cooling slightly, Roger Moore was getting older [...] The suit was no longer sexy attire for a hero [...] The concept of the suited hero performing deeds of derring do in a crumple-free, crease-resistant suit was outmoded. It was no longer the mark of the stylish individual hero but of either the corporate yes-man or the undercover yob.[3]

This is a slightly unfair argument in relation to Moore's Vitucci suits, especially as Vitucci ensured that they were highly fashionable and in keeping with trends of the mid to late 1970s. In a more balanced argument, Sullivan explains: 'The fashion business [...] tends to look on the Seventies as "the decade that style forgot", preferring if anything to parody it, conveniently forgetting that the decade's greatest fashion excesses went hand in hand with the growth of fashion itself and the far wider accessibility of fashionable clothing.'[4] As Spaiser points out, Vitucci's suits encompass the 'bold 1970s look' that 'are beautifully cut in the Roman style with straight shoulders and an elegant clean cut. For *The Spy Who Loved Me*, Vitucci widened the already wide lapels that Moore previously wore [...] and he also widened the flared trouser legs for an updated look.'[5] The single-breasted jackets have a lean chest and suppressed waist, and normally have a two-button fastening, a welt pocket, two slanted hip pockets with flaps, four cuff buttons and double vents. The high-rise trousers have a flat front and a slanted hem. The single-breasted blazer in *The Spy Who Loved Me* has a similar structure to that of the single-breasted suit jacket, but differs in that it has a two-button fastening with silver metal buttons and a ticket pocket. The safari sports jacket has wide lapels with a fish-mouth notch and swelled edges, a flapped breast pocket and two flapped patch pockets. It has buckled straps on the cuffs and a single vent at the rear, in keeping with safari jackets of the period. Spaiser argues that the sports jacket has an 'unusual cut': 'The front of a jacket is typically cut away and thus curved below the button at the waist. On this jacket, the edges of the foreparts are straight and only have a small curve at the corner. They edges are, however, slightly angled apart for a more dynamic look than a straight front would provide.'[6] Bond's distinctive midnight blue double-breasted dinner jacket has wide peaked lapels with a satin facing, six matching fabric-covered buttons, three cuff buttons, two jetted hip pockets and no vent. As with *Live and Let Die* and *The Man with the Golden Gun*, Moore's Frank Foster shirts have a wide and pointed collar, however in *The Spy Who Loved Me* and *Moonraker* the cuffs are cut in a 'Lapidus' style, so-called after Ted Lapidus. This cuff type is cut in a square barrel shape and includes an extended button tab to fasten it.

Ronald Paterson, the Scottish-born fashion designer who was once referred to as 'the couturier's Sean Connery' on a trip to America in 1964 due to his dark and handsome looks, was employed on *The Spy Who Loved Me* as the costume designer, although he is credited in the film as a 'fashion consultant'.[7] Some of his costume concept sketches survive that were produced for *The Spy Who Loved Me* and have been published by Eon Productions, including designs for Bond's costume in the 'Arabian Nights' sequences and Anya Amasova/Agent Triple X's (Barbara Bach) Russian military uniform.[8] Paterson was recognized for his clothes that were 'flattering and colourful, and often presented in unpredictable ways'.[9] Paterson was also renowned for his 'skilful handling' of heavy-weight fabrics such as tweed.[10] His mentor, Elsa Schiaparelli, introduced him to the Paris couture scene. On finding work with Madame Alix Grès at her haute couture fashion house, Paterson learnt to model dresses directly on a mannequin without a paper pattern and with the minimum of cutting, a technique that he would apply to his own later work that would lead him to be celebrated as 'a master of draping silk jersey'.[11] It was during the 1960s that Paterson came to design costumes for theatre and television, and produced designs for female leads including Isabel Dean and reportedly Honor Blackman for *The Avengers*.[12] In another Bond connection, Paterson also designed patterns for *Vogue's* 'Couturier Design' range, including pattern 1391, produced in 1964, which was modelled by Tania Mallet who played Tilly Masterson in *Goldfinger*. Rosemary Burrows is credited as the film's wardrobe supervisor, however no other members of the wardrobe team are credited in *The Spy Who Loved Me* as they had been in previous Bond films, which was particularly unusual by this time.

The Spy Who Loved Me (1977)

Bond wears a total of ten outfits in *The Spy Who Loved Me*, far less than in *Live and Let Die* and *The Man with the Golden Gun*. Bond's costumes include a distinctive banana yellow ski suit made by Willy Bognor, worn with a red knitted ski hat, goggles with black lenses and a yellow frame, a red leather backpack and red ski boots. Following the credits, Bond wears a Royal Navy Commander's dress uniform and later a Royal Navy greatcoat over the top of the uniform in these scenes, both made from dark navy wool. Both items were likely tailored by Bermans and Nathans. *The Spy Who Loved Me* is the only film during Moore's tenure as Bond that he would wear this uniform. Similar to Connery's uniform worn in *You Only Live Twice*, Moore's is cut in traditional English military style, with straight shoulders, roped sleeve-heads, a clean chest and a suppressed waist. The jacket is double-breasted, has wide peaked lapels, and includes an eight-button fastening with gilt buttons including a crown and anchor motif. Two campaign ribbons are worn over the breast. Underneath the jacket, Bond wears a white shirt and a black silk tie. The greatcoat is cut in the traditional English military style from Melton cloth, and is double-breasted, including ten gilt buttons, two of which are covered by the collar, also with crown and anchor motifs as with the dress jacket. It has a wide Napoleon collar. Bond's Commander rank insignia is stitched on the epaulettes in gold embroidery. There are two flapped hip pockets, and the rear of the greatcoat has a belted back and a deep single vent. Bond's white peaked cap has a gilt Royal Navy badge and a single row of gold oak leaves on the black peak.

In Egypt, Bond first wears traditional Arab dress when riding a camel through an Egyptian desert to meet with his acquaintance, Sheikh Hosein (Edward de Souza). Paterson designed Bond's costume for the 'Arabian Nights' sequence as directed in the script: 'In a CLOSE SHOT we see that the rider of the first camel is BOND, in full "Lawrence of Arabia" garb.'[13] The costume design, as with Paterson's other sketches, is minimalist and lightly sketched, formed in pencil and ink in line drawings that adopt a rather staccato fashion, similar to his fashion designs. The sketches are painted in watercolour. Paterson notes on the design: 'Bond: All white classic with plastron front, fastens on side neck and down edge of plastron,' and described the plastron as: 'Irregular [. . .] very fine embroidery stitch in white.'[14] In the film, Bond wears a white *ghutrah* headscarf with a black *agal* rope cord knotted to fasten the *thagiyah* skullcap worn underneath the *ghutrah*. The *dishdasha* robe, a long, fitted tunic which has a two-button fastening on the band collar and is stitched to have a buttonhole on the sleeve cuff for *kabak* (cufflink) fastenings, is white, although the plastron differs from Paterson's design. A plastron is an ornamental front that consists of a colourful material made from lace or embroidery. The plastron on Bond's *dishdasha* is embroidered with alternate tan, dark brown, black and cream stitches to form a rectangular shape with intermittently spaced bands. The *dishdasha* is accompanied by long *sirwal* trousers. Over the *dishdasha*, Bond wears an open *bisht* cloak made from a beige silk. The *bisht* is often worn 'for prestige by royals or important figures and on special occasions'.[15]

After Bond arrives in Cairo, he is dressed in a tan safari jacket that is worn with stone-coloured trousers and a blue and white cotton toile shirt, fastened with a silk tie that has diagonal stripes in shades of blue, white and red. In the script, Bond is described in these scenes as wearing 'a beautifully-cut lightweight suit picking his way through the burnouses'.[16] It was during these scenes that the script originally included the traditional tailoring quip during Bond's fight with Sandor on the roof of Aziz Fekkesh's apartment:

PLATE 1 Honey Ryder's famous entrance wearing the ivory cotton bikini and webbing belt. *Dr. No* directed by Terence Young © Eon Productions/United Artists 1962.

PLATE 2 The *Goldfinger* golf game costumes. Directed by Guy Hamilton © Eon Productions/United Artists 1964.

PLATE 3 Gendered double standards between James Bond and Fiona Volpe reflected in costume. *Thunderball* directed by Terence Young © Eon Productions/United Artists 1965. All rights reserved.

PLATE 4 Tracy di Vincenzo's 'mermaid' gown inspired by Emilio Pucci. *On Her Majesty's Secret Service* directed by Peter Hunt © Eon Productions/United Artists 1969. All rights reserved.

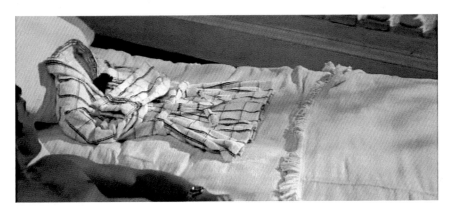

PLATE 5 Example of the carnation theme prevalent throughout *On Her Majesty's Secret Service*. Directed by Peter Hunt © Eon Productions/United Artists 1969. All rights reserved.

PLATE 6 Harlequin two-tone colour scheme on Tiffany Case's two-piece bikini. *Diamonds Are Forever* directed by Guy Hamilton © Eon Productions/United Artists 1971. All rights reserved.

PLATE 7 Solitaire's ethnic gown, adapted from Julie Harris's 'bolero dress' costume sketch as it appears in the film. *Live and Let Die* directed by Guy Hamilton © Eon Productions/United Artists 1973.

PLATE 8 Hugo Drax's tunic and trouser combination. *Moonraker* directed by Lewis Gilbert © Eon Productions/United Artists 1979.

PLATE 9 May Day's Ascot costume with signature cowl and distinctive hat. *A View to a Kill* directed by John Glen © Eon Productions/MGM/United Artists 1985. All rights reserved.

PLATE 10 'Costume 4', Kara Milovy's opera dress realized by Lawrence Easden. *The Living Daylights* directed by John Glen © Eon Productions/MGM/United Artists 1987. All rights reserved.

PLATE 11 Franz Sanchez's 'manly' pink *Miami Vice*-style shirt. *Licence to Kill* directed by John Glen © Eon Productions/MGM/United Artists 1989. All rights reserved.

PLATE 12 Lupe Lamora's Oscar de la Renta evening gown in 'Nancy Reagan red'. *Licence to Kill* directed by John Glen © Eon Productions/MGM/United Artists 1989. All rights reserved.

PLATE 13 Paris Carver's Ocimar Versolato 'fashion statement' gown. *Tomorrow Never Dies* directed by Roger Spottiswoode © Eon Productions/MGM 1997. All rights reserved.

PLATE 14 James Bond's and M's oppositional monochromatic costumes. *Quantum of Solace* directed by Marc Forster © Eon Productions/MGM/Columbia Pictures 2008. All rights reserved.

PLATE 15 Sévérine standing next to Amedeo Modigliani's *Woman with a Fan* (1919). *Skyfall* directed by Sam Mendes © Eon Productions/MGM/Columbia Pictures 2012.

PLATE 16 James Bond's Tom Ford 'Windsor' dinner suit reminiscent of *Goldfinger*. *Spectre* directed by Sam Mendes © Eon Productions/MGM/Columbia Pictures 2015.

48D. EXT. FLAT ROOF APARTMENT BUILDING CAIRO. DAY

BOND crouches on the roof above him, reaches down and grasps the sleeve of SANDOR's jacket. [Bond questions where Fekkesh is] SANDOR's fingers slip from the guttering. Now he is held only by BOND's grasp of his sleeve. He looks up at BOND imploringly. The sleeve starts to rip away from the jacket at the shoulder.

> BOND
> Your life's hanging by a thread. Come on – where is he?

> SANDOR
> (gasping)
> Pyramids . . . the Pyramids.

The sleeve rips away from the jacket and SANDOR, with a scream of fear, falls into space. Bond looks at the empty sleeve he is still holding, then with a shrug he tosses it over the edge of the roof.

> BOND
> <u>Not</u> a tailor I'd recommend.[17]

This tailoring quip, which is also a reference to Alfred Hitchcock's *Saboteur* (1942), was omitted from the film. In the Mujaba Club, Bond is described as wearing a 'tuxedo' in the script.[18] With the midnight blue dinner suit, of which the trousers have a satin waistband and a braided ribbon trim on the outside seam, Bond wears a white dress shirt with a plain front and mother-of-pearl buttons, which is fastened with a wide satin-silk bowtie (Figure 7.1). This is later loosened after Bond and Anya's fight with Jaws (Richard Kiel) in which Bond appears particularly dishevelled, an unusual look for Moore's portrayal.

Aboard the train to Sardinia, Bond wears a tan-coloured dupioni silk suit. Bond initially wears it with a wide-striped shirt of cream and light brown that has a wide pointed collar, and is fastened with a satin-silk tie with diagonal stripes in light and dark brown and cream-coloured shades. On alighting from the train, Bond wears the same suit and tie with a white monochrome shirt, which works for continuity after his previous shirt becomes bloodied and ripped during a fight with Jaws. On visiting Karl Stromberg's (Curt Jürgens) lair, Atlantis, Bond wears a single-breasted dark navy blazer with white gaberdine trousers. Underneath the jacket, Bond wears a cream silk shirt with alternately spaced dress stripes and a dark blue shantung silk tie. Bond is seen in his shared hotel room with Anya wearing a black casual outfit, consisting of a knitted V-neck jumper that is worn over a black sheer silk shirt and black flat front trousers. During the battle scenes at the end of *The Spy Who Loved Me*, Bond wears what is termed as 'Naval battledress', a style that was developed in 1943 during World War II and has since become defunct. Bond's version includes a waist-length jacket made from a dark navy serge fabric with notched lapels and a three-button fastening made from similar buttons to his earlier naval costumes. The two patch pockets placed over the chest have inverted box pleats and flapped pockets that are fastened with one button. The shoulder epaulettes include gold embroidery woven in a Commander's insignia. Underneath the jacket, Bond wears a navy knitted polo-neck jumper. The trousers are made from the same fabric as the jacket, and are long-rise with a darted front and straight leg.

Anya wears nearly as many costumes as Bond in *The Spy Who Loved Me*, and this is a reflection of how they are positioned as one another's opposite number in the Secret Service and the KGB. Anya is first costumed in the film wearing a stylized Russian military uniform, in keeping with her being a Major in the Soviet Army. Paterson's costume design and the realized costume is similar in structure and cut, although, as Meg Simmonds notes, it differs slightly in that: 'On film, Anya wears a Russian *Papaha* hat, normally reserved for generals or high-ranking officers.'[19] The skirt suit is made from a fine twill weave in khaki green. The jacket includes a Mandarin collar with rectangular red felt fabric appliquéd on to it and a gold-plated button with a hammer and sickle motif fastened on either side. The natural shoulders are fitted, and include red felt epaulettes with sparkling gold ribbon detail with one gold metal star to symbolize Anya's rank. The jacket has fitted sleeves and turn-up cuffs, is fastened with five gold buttons that have the same details as the collar and epaulette buttons, and has been tailored to have a suppressed waist and a flared skirt to accentuate Bach's figure. Two patch pockets are stitched onto the hips, and have curved, pointed flaps. The A-line skirt that is worn underneath the jacket is cut to flare out towards the hem and includes a straight centre-front seam. Anya wears knee-high brown leather boots with the outfit. This suit, as with Bond's military attire, was likely created by Bermans and Nathans.

In the Mujaba Club, the script directs that Anya 'is looking extravagantly feminine in a beautiful, low-cut evening dress'.[20] Thus, Paterson chose to costume Anya in her most glamorous attire for *The Spy Who Loved Me* in these scenes, namely a backless midnight blue, floor-length silk gown that includes a fitted bodice and a skirt that has been cut on the bias in order to widely flare out towards the hem to create a fit-and-flare silhouette (Figure 7.1). The creation of the gown has been attributed to Baroness Franka Stael Von Holstein, a Zagreb-born designer who worked for Norman Hartnell before establishing her dress label Franka, based at Dover Street in London.[21] The gown has a plunging *décolleté* neckline and a cross-strap back that is adorned with translucent Swarovski crystals that continue over the bodice. The skirt of the gown is structured though asymmetric panels that have a slit cut from thigh to floor on either side of the hips. Anya's jewellery matches the Swarovski crystal embellishment on the gown, and the earrings, necklace and bracelet are coloured in black and clear diamante crystals. *Quantum of Solace* would later pay homage to the image of the dishevelled Bond and Anya walking across the desert in their evening clothes.

FIGURE 7.1 James Bond's and Anya Amasova's evening wear. *The Spy Who Loved Me* directed by Lewis Gilbert © Eon Productions/United Artists 1977. All rights reserved.

When Bond and Anya report to the combined base of MI6 and the KGB, Anya wears the first of two off-white sheath silk wrap dresses. This is reflective of Paterson's 'Nassau' ensemble created for his spring collection in 1964 that included a wrap-around skirt, inspired in part by his mentor Schiaparelli's development of the wrap dress in the 1930s. Anya's A-line wrap dress is hemmed below the knee and is fastened asymmetrically with a four-button fastening, covered in matching fabric. It has a stand-up, rounded and open-cut collar, and the short sleeves are gathered at the cap and have a plain hem. There are no pockets included on the dress, and it is structured at the back by having a gathered horizontal back yoke in order to create a fitted bodice. The waist is accentuated by the inclusion of a slim sash made from matching fabric. After wearing a similar wrap dress on the train bound for Sardinia, Anya changes into a floor-length pale pink nightgown made of silk. It includes spaghetti straps and has a low-cut scoop neckline. The nightgown is cut on the bias in an empire-line, and in an allusion to the previously worn midnight blue evening gown, the nightdress has a slit cut from thigh to floor on the left side. The colour has been selected to complement Bond's attire in this scene in order to visually demonstrate both their mutual collaboration as well as their progressing relationship. In the script, it suggests that Anya wears a 'chiffon nightgown' in this scene, however the nightgown was made from sheer silk instead, and this is perhaps due to the role the fabric would take later in the scene when it is suggested that the hem could be used as a bandage for Bond's wounds.[22]

On arrival in Sardinia, Anya has changed her outfit and wears a knitted jersey top in blue with a pencil skirt in a slightly lighter shade of blue that works to provide a sheath silhouette. It is tightly fitted, and reminiscent of Paterson's hobble skirt shape that the designer developed in the mid-1950s in order to tailor and direct the 'Paterson walk'. In contrast to the blue shades of Anya's costume, the waist is cinched with a red patent leather belt that is fastened with a square silver buckle. On Anya discovering that Bond was directly involved in the death of her lover, Sergei Barsov (Michael Billington), the character wears a khaki-coloured shear silk dress, that works to foreground 1970s fashions. The colour is reflective of her allegiance to the KGB and Russia rather than to Bond in this scene. The dress is cut in a kaftan shape and has a gathered and tucked wide scoop neckline with a small key-hole cut above the chest that creates ruching over the bust. It has a natural, gathered waistline, accentuated by a thin sash belt of matching fabric. The skirt flows out towards the floor. Its loose and wide-cut angel sleeves are gathered from the cap and flare out to the cuff, and the dress is gathered at the waist seam in order to emphasize the flare of the skirt. In the final scenes of the film, Anya wears a deep ruby red silk gown that has been provided by Stromberg. It has an unusual cut so as to enhance Bach's figure, particularly her chest. Effectively, it is a floor-length, maxi-gown that exposes most of Anya's midriff. The revealing top half has been cut in the shape of a halter-necked *brassière* bikini top. The straps are crossed over the chest, and the top is fastened with a hook-and-eye fastener at the back. The front fabric panel that connects the bikini top to the skirt is linked to the centre-front frame in between the cups. A slim-fitted, A-line skirt that has been cut on the bias is attached to this panel and scoops behind the back, fastened with a zip. Anya wears two gauntlet-shaped cuffs on her wrists that are made from matching-coloured silk fabric.

The film's villain, Stromberg, wears a rather eccentric array of similar and monochromatic clothes in the film that are the same cut and shape. Generally, they take the form of an unstructured tunic made from heavy shantung silk, in keeping with the assumed foreignness of previous Bond villains, although they do not adopt specific elements of the Nehru or Mao suits favoured by Dr. No and Blofeld. On Bond meeting Stromberg for the first time, the latter wears a deep burgundy tunic that has a V-neck collar and no visible front or back fastening nor any back vents. The tunic is cut with a horizontal front yoke and has a natural shoulder with long sleeves and slightly flared plain cuffs. It has a straight, plain hem at the bottom. The trousers, made from a matching fabric, have a flat front and plain hems. Underneath the tunic, Stromberg wears a black silk shirt with a stand-up ruched polo-neck collar. Around his neck, Stromberg wears a long thin black cord with a yellowing shark tooth pendant, reflecting his passion for the ocean and its various aquatic species. On Stromberg's super tanker, *Liparus*, he again wears a matching tunic and trousers combination, this time made from dark grey shantung silk fabric, although this version includes subtle differences. It has a wide pointed spread collar with inverted notches and a visibly wide placket that includes a two-button fastening which Stromberg wears unfastened in the film. As with the previous outfit, the tunic has natural shoulders and loose-fitting sleeves, however in this version they are gathered from the cap and at the ribbed cuffs. This tunic has two short slits cut on either side of the hips. Stromberg wears a pale grey silk cravat around his neck, and the trousers have single pleats with plain hems.

Stromberg's briefly wears a two-piece suit at the end of the film, possibly made from a gabardine wool, in mid-brown. The jacket has natural shoulders, as with Stromberg's other outfits, roped sleeve-heads and narrow notched lapels. Underneath the jacket Stromberg wears a white shirt with a pointed spread collar, fastened with a distinctive silk cravat made from red silk with a white paisley pattern detail.

In *The Spy Who Loved Me*, the assigned bad 'Bond girl' Naomi (Caroline Munro) is not particularly prominent in relation to the film's narrative or plot, however she wears a distinctive costume in her small amount of screen time. In Stromberg's lair, the script describes Naomi as being 'beautiful, dark [and] typically Grecian, wearing diaphanous white robes swathed about her'.[23] Instead, the character wears a backless cream-coloured trouser suit with tan brown leather knee-high heeled boots. The outfit is sleeveless and includes wide notched lapels on the fitted bodice, cut with a plunging neckline to the waist to accentuate Naomi's cleavage. The legs of the all-in-one suit are voluminous and are hemmed to below the knee with turn-up cuffs. Naomi's waist is accentuated by a wide brown leather belt that matches the colour of her boots. It includes a unique gold buckle fastening stylized in the shape of a goldfish: the symbol of the Stromberg Shipping Line. This motif is repeated on the pair of brown leather gauntlet cuffs that Naomi wears on her wrists. It is possible that the inclusion of the separate wrist cuffs worn by Naomi here suggests that the ruby red silk gown that Stromberg dresses Anya in at the end of the film may well have been designed to indicate that it has been taken from Naomi's wardrobe.

Moonraker (1979)

Originally, the film that was due to follow *The Spy Who Loved Me* was *For Your Eyes Only*, however owing to the popularity of *Star Wars* (1977), *Close Encounters of the Third Kind* (1977) and the science-fiction boom of the late 1970s, Broccoli decided to adapt *Moonraker* instead, given the title reflecting a science-fiction theme; as Broccoli noted: 'Putting James Bond in orbit brought Ian Fleming into the space age.'[24] Broccoli, as with Moore, had since left the UK due to increasing levels of taxation for higher earners, and Lewis Gilbert, the director, had a disinclination to work in the UK. Thus, it was decided to film at the Epinay Studios and Billancourt Studios in Paris, and was made as an Anglo-French co-production under the 1965–79 agreement.[25] Principal photography commenced on 11 August 1978 and was completed mid-February 1979. The film was budgeted at $34 million (£17.7 million).

As with many members employed as *Moonraker*'s production crew, the wardrobe department was French. Jacques Fonteray was employed as the costume designer, along with Colette Baudot as the wardrobe mistress and Jean Zay as the wardrobe master. On meeting the French film director, Marcel Carné, Fonteray designed the costumes for *Les Tricheurs* (*The Cheats*), released 1958. What began as a way to subsidize his career as a painter would develop into a full-time role, and henceforth Fonteray would work on many theatre productions and films throughout the 1960s until the early 1990s. Notable French film credits included *The King of Hearts* (1966), *Barbarella* (1967), and *Boulevard du Rhum* (1970). As argued by Elizabeth Castaldo Lundèn, Fonteray's background in painting and sculpting informed his approach to designing costumes, including 'the interplay of materials, and his way of working with the fabrics, which resembled sculpting'.[26] Castaldo Lundèn explains Fonteray's process behind his costume concepts:

> Unlike most trained costume designers, Fonteray conceived his sketches as paintings, giving them full backgrounds frequently – but not exclusively – in dark colours that resemble his work as a painter. To develop a design, he prepared several drafts before arriving at the desired image, giving them numbers to keep track [of] the latest versions. [...] When taking on a project, he initially read the script, collected documents about the period 'to its own style', drew several sketches, met with the director to get [their] vision of the film and the personalities of each character, and finally embarked on preparing sketches to show the director.[27]

Castaldo Lundèn explains that with *Barbarella*, the science-fiction genre afforded the designer the opportunity to showcase his artistic background. The 1964 'moon girl' collection designed by André Courrèges and Paco Rabanne's debut collection '12 Unwearable Dresses in Contemporary Materials' created from aluminium, chain-link metal and Rhodoid plastic in 1966 would in part inspire Fonteray's designs for *Barbarella*, and this film would come to influence the designer's approach to *Moonraker*.

In the film, Bond first appears on a private jet wearing a blue double-breasted blazer, a white polo-necked jumper with a ribbed collar, and khaki chino trousers that, as with the character's other trousers in the film, flare out towards the hem. The blazer has notched lapels, natural padded shoulders with roped sleeve-heads, a four-button fastening made from gilt metal and double vents. The jackets worn in the film are all similar in structure, and are cut with a clean chest and suppressed waist, as with *The Spy Who Loved Me*. Following the title credits, Bond wears a three-piece suit, which is the first time that Moore wears one playing Bond. It is navy with a very closely spaced and narrow pinstripe. The jacket has wide notched lapels, a Barchetta curved welt pocket on the breast, two patch pockets with flaps on either side of the hips, a two-button fastening and double vents. There are three buttons fastened onto the sleeve cuff, which is a typical embellishment on the majority of Bond's jackets in the film. Underneath the jacket and waistcoat, Bond wears a white silk *crêpe de chine* shirt with a long point collar, a design included on all of Bond's shirts for *Moonraker* except the safari shirt. It is fastened with a satin-silk tie with a silver colour base and diagonal navy stripes with alternative pin dot pattern.

The first of Fonteray's costume designs available to view in the Cinémathèque Française is Bond's third outfit in the film, worn on his arrival at Los Angeles Airport and at Château Drax between scenes 26–75. Each of Fonteray's costume concepts created for Bond directly respond to the scene numbers in the script. In keeping with Fonteray's approach to his sketches, this design is labelled number 3: the third version of the design. The sketch includes a facial template for Moore that Fonterey uses throughout all of his designs, and Bond's silhouette is defined in black pastel drawn on the point. A recurring feature of Fonteray's *Moonraker* designs is that the background includes broad strokes made from rubbing the pastel on its side running across the centre of the page. Colour is added to the pastel sketch of the costume through the medium of gouache. Bond in this concept wears a navy blazer with light grey trousers. From the pastel detailing, the jacket has wide peaked lapels, a khaki-coloured puffed pocket square in the breast pocket, two flapped patch pockets on the hip, a two-button fastening and three buttons on the sleeve cuff. The shirt underneath the jacket is white and includes thin blue dress stripes, and is fastened with a dark grey tie. Bond holds a tan-coloured attaché briefcase in his left hand.[28] In the film, Bond wears a single-breasted blue blazer, lighter in colour than in the design, though retains the silver metal buttons and pockets. With the blazer, Bond wears a pale blue cotton shirt that is fastened with a striped satin-silk tie in navy, red, white and beige colours. Bond wears stone-coloured chino trousers made from a cavalry twill weave.

During the evening at Château Drax, the script directs that Bond 'is wearing his usual prowling kit – black polo-neck pullover, black slacks, black rubber shoes'.[29] Bond's black 'prowling outfit' was interpreted slightly differently in the final film, in that he wears a knitted silk jersey shirt with a pointed spread collar that is fastened with a zip down the chest rather than a 'polo-neck pullover'. There is a patch pocket stitched over the breast, and turn-up cuffs on the sleeve of the shirt. Bond wears black worsted wool trousers that have a slight flare in the leg, which is fastened at the waist with a black leather belt that includes a brass squared full buckle. Bond later wears the 'prowling outfit' on infiltrating Sir Hugo Drax's (Michael Lonsdale) hidden laboratory in Venice.

During the pigeon shooting sequence on Drax's estate, Bond is described as wearing a 'well-tailored tweed suit'.[30] For this scene, Fonteray designed a costume concept titled 'Chasse' (hunt), of which this design is numbered as version five and directly corresponds to scenes 84–91 in the script.[31] Fonteray has written 'vests, tweed Plus Anglais → [more English]' to indicate the design inspiration and tailoring of Bond's costume in these scenes.[32] Sketched on a light brown piece of paper, the pastel background of the design includes heavy brown hatching with black spirals layered and blended over the top behind Bond's trouser legs. An on-point line in black pastel is drawn to emphasize the ground behind in between the trouser hem and the shoe. The sketch depicts a single-breasted jacket with structured shoulders and roped sleeve-heads. The jacket has wide notched lapels, a welt pocket with a dark brown puffed pocket square, and a two-button fastening. The body of the jacket includes pastel colours in varied tones, depicting a light grey base with light and dark brown patches blended over the top. The shirt worn underneath the jacket has a black pastel base and a dark brown collar with a fine gold stripe detail. The tie is sketched with a white and silver base, and diagonal dark grey stripes. The trousers are painted in a light brown gouache with dark brown hatching blended over the thighs and outside seam for emphasis.

Fonteray has sketched two ink line drawings to the left-hand side of the design to emphasize certain tailored elements of the jacket. The first sketch depicts the back of the jacket and includes the word 'double' scribbled next to it with an arrow pointing towards the skirt of the jacket to note the type of vents it should be tailored with. The second sketch, drawn below the first, provides a silhouette of the front of the jacket, and emphasizes the notched collar, the pocket square and the flapped patch pocket on the hip. On the jacket sleeve, Fonteray has sketched a curved line over the elbow to possibly indicate pads, and two buttons on the cuff. In the realized costume, Bond wears a suit made from heavy Donegal tweed in light brown. The elbow patches have been interpreted in brown suede. It differs from Fonteray's design in that the sleeves have a four-button cuff, and the body of the jacket includes a slanted, flapped ticket pocket above the right hip pocket. There is no pocket square included in the flapped breast pocket, and the shirt worn underneath the jacket is white with a narrow point collar that is fastened with a brown knitted silk tie instead.

On arriving at St Mark's Square, Bond wears a grey silk dupioni suit. Underneath the jacket, Bond wears a white *crêpe de chine* silk shirt with a large pointed collar, fastened with a dark navy satin-silk tie that includes a red oval pattern with a white pin dot centre. Bond then wears the same blue blazer worn on his arrival in Los Angeles, albeit with a different shirt made from a cream fabric that is fastened with a satin-silk tie detailed in a similar way to striped ottoman fabric in olive, magenta and purple stripes interwoven with pink ovals. In Rio de Janeiro, the script describes the character as being 'smartly dressed, a carnation in his lapel'.[33] Fonteray followed this description in his interpretation presented in the costume concept.[34] The background of the design includes blue pastel hatching that has been blended to represent the blue sky on Bond leaving the aircraft. As with the previous design, Fonteray has drawn a point-line in black pastel to represent the pavement between the hem of Bond's trousers and his shoes. The costume design depicts a two-piece double-breasted suit, coloured with a combination of white pastel blended with shades of silver and light grey gouache. The jacket has wide peaked lapels, slanted shoulders with roped sleeve-heads, a welt pocket with a folded pocket square and a blue flower in the lapel buttonhole, two jetted hip pockets and a four-button fastening painted in silver gouache. The suit trousers are sketched with single-forward pleats. The shirt worn underneath the jacket is white and fastened with a tie shaded with pastel that has a silver base with black and white stripes. To accentuate the colour scheme of the design, Fonteray has included diagonal hatching in white pastel over the suit trousers that extends over the silhouette of Bond's figure and continues to the background. In *Moonraker*, the costume is very different to that of Fonteray's original costume concept, and is realized as a cream two-piece single-breasted suit in keeping with Vitucci's tailoring style. There is no carnation or flower in the lapel buttonhole, and the jacket is fastened with one mother-of-pearl button. Bond's shirt in these scenes is made from light brown and is worn open-necked without a tie unlike in the design. There is a pocket square tucked into the welt pocket as with the design, however it is made of the same fabric as the shirt and is therefore light brown. Bond carries the brown leather attaché briefcase that was previously depicted on Fonteray's design for Bond's arrival in Los Angeles.

After checking in to the Pelerina Hotel, Bond dresses in a dinner suit as directed in the script.[35] In the costume concept created by Fonteray, the background is one of the most vivid of the designer's sketches for Bond, and includes a blended black and grey background in the mixed medium of pastel and gouache, with a black hatched pastel overlay and broad strokes of ecru pastel towards the centre.[36] It is the seventh version of Fonteray's design, and the silhouette wears a single-breasted dinner suit with a black gouache base and white pastel to accentuate the notched lapels, perhaps to denote a satin facing. The jacket has similar shoulders to Fonteray's other renderings. It has a welt breast pocket with a folded pocket square depicted in blue pastel, and there is a red carnation in the buttonhole. There is a white button detail on the sleeve cuffs of the jacket. Underneath the jacket, Bond wears a high-collared white shirt with a pleat emphasis, fastened with a black bowtie painted in gouache. The cuffs of the shirt are just visible beneath the sleeve. The trousers match the colour of the jacket, and include a darker black line of on-point pastel down the outside leg to donate a satin seam, which is emphasized by diagonal hatches in white pastel that overlay the black gouache.

The Vitucci suit in the final film is cut in the same way as the dinner suit in *The Spy Who Loved Me*. The white dress shirt has a pleated placket with mother-of-pearl buttons and cocktail cuffs, and is fastened with a satin-silk black bowtie as with Fonteray's design. Unlike Fonteray's design, Bond does not wear a carnation in his buttonhole, nor a pocket square. Bond continues to wear the dinner suit the following morning, and the bowtie has been removed with the shirt collar placed over the jacket's lapels to make the character appear more dishevelled. After Bond and Dr Holly Goodhead (Lois Chiles) manage to escape from Jaws, the script includes the obligatory tailoring jest:

237. EXT. GRASSY SLOPE. LOWER CABLE CAR STATION. DAY

After a moment [Holly] sees that BOND is sitting three or four feet away, his head bowed, a hand held to the torn lapel of his tattered dinner jacket, as if he is feeling for a broken rib. He winces as if in pain [...]

> HOLLY
> James – have you broken something?

Bond looks at his lapel.

> BOND
> Only my tailor's heart.[37]

Bond subsequently travels to a monastery in Pampas, and the film adopts Western genre motifs from *The Magnificent Seven* (1960), including a direct reference to the film by using its 'swelling music' as denoted in the script, with 'three gauchos' riding on horseback towards the monastery, the middle of which is Bond. The script describes the scene that follows: 'It is high noon. The street is deserted. Along the street come BOND and the two GAUCHOS. They ride towards a monastery which abuts on the street.'[38] Based on the script's direction, Bond is thus appropriately attired in a long square-cut woollen *poncho* that is woven with a tan base including different shades of brown with a beige tasselled fringe detail, influenced by Clint Eastwood's attire in the *Dollars* trilogy. Underneath the *poncho*, Bond likely wears a brown and white plaid-checked *chiripa*, in keeping with the theme of the costume, adorned with a dark brown silk neckerchief around his neck. The outfit includes accordion pleated trousers, termed *bombachas*, that are gathered at the ankles and worn beneath brown leather riding boots. Bond wears a wide brimmed Andalusian *sombrero* made from dyed black woven straw with a high pointed and flat crown, and includes a thin black leather strap knotted underneath the chin.

On being sent to the Amazon river, the script directs that Bond wear 'a safari suit'.[39] In Fonteray's costume concept titled 'Saharienne B', the number 10 written on it denotes the number of versions that the designer sketched before the realized costume was completed.[40] The background of the design, sketched on light brown paper, includes blended crosshatching in blue and white pastel above the left shoulder of Bond's silhouette, and white on-the-side broad pastel strokes behind Bond. Black and blue on-the-point lines have been sketched horizontally behind the knee and at the trouser hem, with blue hatching blended into the paper in between the lines. The safari suit is depicted in a white gouache base with white pastel strokes on the left shoulder, the two patch pockets on the hip and the trousers for emphasis. The shirt has notched lapels, epaulettes and short sleeves. Forteray has sketched two inverted box pleat patch pockets with pointed flaps that are fastened with a button over the breast in black pastel. It is belted at the waist. The trousers have single pleats and a turn-up cuff. Bond is sketched wearing a black strap on the left wrist, possibly denoting a watch. Fonteray notes on the concept 'Manches longuers', suggesting that there is the option to have long sleeves, which the realized costume includes.[41] In the film, Bond's safari costume consists of a matching shirt and trouser combination, made from a pale khaki green cotton drill fabric, and therefore more in keeping with the jungle surroundings. However, it includes certain parts of the design elements as indicated in Fonteray's concept, though not a belt. The shirt has a wide rounded point spread collar, and the sleeves have wide turn-up cuffs with a one-button fastening.

In the script, it is noted that the technicians based in Drax's pyramid are 'dressed uniformly', and Fonteray interpreted a costume concept of a functional yellow jumpsuit suitable for the subsequent scenes set in space, which Bond wears in order to infiltrate Drax's space station.[42] The background of the design includes pastel in black and white crosshatching. The male silhouette is depicted as wearing a black and yellow jumpsuit, painted in gouache, of which the body includes a high rounded stand-away collar, with wide shoulders and a curved front yoke in black. The shoulders include yellow epaulettes with a silver fastening. The black fabric is painted as continuing down the outside seam of the voluminous sleeves that end in a fitted black cuff. A large circular Drax Industries logo is included in the centre of the chest. The body and legs of the jumpsuit are painted yellow, and it is fastened at the waist with a matching yellow belt. Yellow ankle boots are fastened over the trouser legs. In the realized costume, created by Bermans and Nathans, the jumpsuit is created from a mustard yellow cotton with no black front yoke, however the rest of the design is similar to how Fonteray envisaged in his concept. The jumpsuit has a thin silver collar, and the shoulders include silver shoulder straps with a quilted yellow fabric overlay. The Moonraker logo is situated over the left breast rather than in the centre. The waist is belted with a matching leather belt that includes silver piping around the edges, of which Bond's belt also include two utility boxes situated on the front. There are silver zip fastenings that run down the torso and forearms, as well as black zip fastenings on the bottom of the outside leg seam. There are two cargo pockets situated at the front of the trouser hem and two similar pockets placed above the knee on the outside leg. All pockets include two silver popper fastenings. The hems of the trouser legs are cuffed and are similarly fastened to the pockets. The jumpsuit is worn with yellow leather gloves and yellow boots with white soles. It is worth noting that in the posters designed for *Moonraker* by Daniel Goozee, Bond is depicted as wearing a silver foil spacesuit rather than the yellow version designed for the final film.

The novel's villain, Sir Hugo Drax, was updated in the film from being a Nazi who created a nuclear rocket in order to destroy London to a megalomaniac billionaire who owns Drax Industries and is employed by NASA to create space shuttles. Bond meets Drax for the first time in the latter's château, 'seated at a grand piano, playing a Chopin Nocturne'.[43] Drax is dressed in a tailored navy serge two-piece suit, of which the jacket has a clean chest and is close fitted. It is cut in a similar shape to a Mao jacket but has distinctive and more Westernized details. It has a straight, Neapolitan shoulder that is wide, padded and includes a roped sleeve-head, the sleeve cap including a slight notched gathering. The jacket has a narrow and extremely pointed collar, and no back vent. There is a straight flapped patch pocket stitched over the left breast, and two matching pockets placed on either side of the hips. The jacket is fastened with two buttons that are hidden underneath a placket.

During the pigeon shooting sequence, the script describes Drax as being 'dressed a little over-correctly in a knickerbocker suit and soft hat'.[44] This is reminiscent of Auric Goldfinger's exaggerated outfit worn during his golf competition against Bond in *Goldfinger*. Instead of wearing tweed and knickerbockers, in the film Drax wears a distinctive two-tone double-breasted suit made from dupioni silk, over which he wears a brown wool Inverness coat with a spread collar. The jacket of the suit has wide notched lapels in navy, that directly contrasts with the light grey fabric that forms the body of the jacket and trousers. The navy fabric is repeated on the turn-up cuffs on the jacket sleeve. It is fastened with six tagua nut buttons. Underneath the jacket, Drax wears a chocolate brown silk shirt with a gold gilt tie pin. Drax's outfit is completed with a black velvet Tyrolean hat with a Gamsbart fur plume sourced from a chamois and a black grosgrain ribbon band.

Later, the script makes direct reference to Fleming's novel and directs that Drax be dressed in a smoking jacket, which is plum-coloured and later worn with 'a brown satin tie and yellow shirt' in the novel.[45] However, in keeping with the opulent surroundings of the set, the wardrobe team elected to costume Drax in a three-piece suit made from black flannel with grey chalk stripe detail, which instead references what the character wears in Blades, the fictional London-based gentleman's club, which would also be referenced in *Die Another Day*.[46] Drax's double-breasted suit jacket in the film has straight natural shoulders with roped sleeve-heads, and is cut with a clean chest and a fitted waist. It has peaked lapels and two jetted hip pockets, a six-button fastening and has double vents at the rear. The suit trousers are tailored with wide straight legs. Underneath the jacket, Drax wears a white silk shirt with a point collar and French cuffs that are fastened with square onyx and gold cufflinks, and the shirt is fastened with a black knitted silk tie.

At the end of the film, Drax wears a similar tunic and trouser combination (Plate 8) to that of his first outfit. This jacket is made from a beige dupioni silk that is fastened with four gold-plated buttons underneath a hidden placket. It has two straight flapped patch pockets placed on either side of the hip. The collar is cut to be narrow and extremely pointed and the jacket has no back vent. Drax wears a white cotton shirt underneath the tunic jacket that has a square French cuff. The trousers are made from a dark brown wool and have a plain front. During these scenes, Drax explains to Bond that the fictional *Orchidae Nigra* (Black Orchid) has pollen which causes sterility in men. Therefore, it is made implicit in *Moonraker* that Drax is sexually impotent. This is in keeping with both Drax's Nazism, in which he seeks to create a master race of 'perfect physical specimens' although he is not included in the procreation process, and the portrayal of the majority of the villains in Fleming's novels who, with the exception of Emilio Largo, are depicted as physically grotesque and are either homosexual, asexual or impotent.

The character of Galatea 'Gala' Brand was renamed Dr Holly Goodhead for the dubious reason of affording Moore a suitable pun, and updated to be an American CIA agent. Bond first meets Holly at Drax's château; in the script she is described as 'slim' and 'very beautiful, with a cool, self-confident face. She wears a zip-fronted tunic like a jump suit.'[47] Holly's costume in the film has been interpreted differently, with her wearing a functional off-white cotton dress that has a tube silhouette and is hemmed at the knee. The front of the dress has a notched T-shape lapel, with a wider top collar and narrow lapel under the gorge line; the slim-cut shoulders have epaulettes, with turn-up cuffs on set-in sleeves that are gathered at the sleeve cap. There is a patch pocket placed over the breast with a one-button fastening and two open patch pockets placed on either side of the hips. A sashed belt cinched at the waist is made from the same fabric of the dress and is knotted in a bow at the centre-front. The dress is fastened with buttons from the chest to above the hem to create a kick pleat opening at the bottom. The back of the dress has a horizontal yoke across the shoulder, and an inverted centre seam. The waist seam includes pleats to allow for drape in the straight-cut A-line skirt.

In Venice, Holly wears a coffee-coloured silk chiffon A-line dress cut in a barrel silhouette that is hemmed at the knee. The fabric is alternately woven with a silk and satin silver *lamé* and has a printed pattern including black and white pin dots. The bodice includes a round collar made from black velvet with a black ribbon pussy-bow detail and is cut in a similar shape to a blouse, fastened at the front with four black buttons. It has slim bouffant sleeves, gathered at the sleeve cap and tapered at the square cuffs, made from black velvet as with the collar. The dress has a natural waist, and the skirt fits over the hips and includes box pleats flaring out to the hem. The hem includes a pleated frill made from similar fabric with alternative horizontal stripes. The dress is cinched at the waist with a black velvet belt. The gown was sourced from Givenchy in Paris.

In her hotel room, Holly is described in the script as 'looking ethereal in a long flimsy nightgown and a filmy wrap'.[48] The realized costume is interpreted differently, and instead Holly wears a white sheer silk evening gown (Figure 7.2) that is reminiscent of Marilyn Monroe's white dress in *The Seven Year Itch* (1955) in terms of cut and structure, although the skirt of Holly's gown is not pleated as Monroe's is, and it is floor-length with a train at the rear. The backless gown has a fit-and-flare silhouette, and is sleeveless with a halter-neck fastening that is gathered at the neckline seam to provide a ruched detail over the bust and enhance Holly's

FIGURE 7.2 Holly Goodhead's white silk gown inspired by Marilyn Monroe in *The Seven Year Itch* (1955). *Moonraker* directed by Lewis Gilbert © Eon Productions/United Artists 1979. All rights reserved.

shoulders and collarbone. The bodice has a plunge neckline that is seamed under the bust with four darts and is waisted with a self-belt panel. The skirt of the gown is made from bias-cut panels with two side seams stitched on either side of the hips, and the gown is fastened with a zip at the rear of the skirt. Holly's costume does not include a wrap shawl. It is during these scenes that Bond discovers that Holly works as an agent on behalf of the CIA through her gendered gadgets, including a Christian Dior perfume that works as a flamethrower; 'a trifle overpowering, your scent?' Bond questions on trying it. In Rio de Janeiro, Holly wears a black sheer silk jumpsuit that has a plunging V-neck, full-length fitted sleeves with turn-up mitered cuffs, a waist seam with slight gathers to accentuate her hips and ankle-length fitted trouser legs. It is cinched at the waist with a black patent leather belt that includes a black square buckle. Holly's ankle is emphasized by the wearing of black patent leather d'Orsay-heeled shoes. This costume would appear in some of the promotional shots with Chiles wearing a black chiffon diaphanous overcoat over the jumpsuit.

Notes

1   In *Bond on Bond*, Moore incorrectly attributes Angelo Litricio as tailoring his suits for *The Spy Who Loved Me* and *Moonraker*, 124.

2   Alan Flusser, *Style and the Man: How and where to buy fine men's clothes* (New York: Harper Collins, 1996), 346.

3   Norman, *Dressed to Kill*, 107.

4   Sullivan, *Dressed to Kill*, 141.

5   Spaiser, 'Poll: Which tailor dressed Roger Moore best?', *The Suits of James Bond*, 3 January 2017, www.bondsuits.com/poll-tailor-dressed-roger-moore-best/ (accessed 12 July 2020).

6   Spaiser, 'Tan cotton safari sports coat in *The Spy Who Loved Me*', *The Suits of James Bond*, 8 July 2011, www.bondsuits.com/tan-cotton-sports-coat-spy-who-loved-me/ (accessed 13 July 2020).

7   Serena Sinclair, 'Now, off-the-peg Paterson', *Daily Telegraph*, 19 October 1964, 15.

8   See Cosgrave, Hemming and McConnon, *Designing 007*, and Simmonds, *Bond by Design*.

9   'Ronald Paterson', *The Times*, 17 July 1993, 19.

10 Victoria and Albert Museum, n.d., http://collections.vam.ac.uk/item/O83747/ skirt-suit-paterson-ronald-inglis/ (accessed 12 July 2020).

11 'Ronald Paterson'.

12 'Ronald Paterson', *Daily Telegraph*, 15 July 1993, 23.

13 BFI, S4498: Christopher Wood, *The Spy Who Loved Me*, revised final shooting script, 23 August 1976, 17.

14 Cosgrave, Hemming and McConnon, 104.

15 Matthew Priest, 'The kandora explained', *Esquire* (Middle East), 22 February 2016, www.esquireme.com/culture/kandora-explained (accessed 13 July 2020).

16 BFI, S4498: 25.

17 Ibid., 29.

18 Ibid., 35, 38.

19 Simmonds, 153.

20 BFI, S4498: 35.

21 Ella Alexander, 'The name's Bond', *Vogue*, 6 July 2012, www.vogue.co.uk/gallery/ designing-007-james-bond-exhibition-preview-barbican (accessed 14 July 2020).

22 BFI, S4498: 60.

23 Ibid., 19.

24 Broccoli with Zec, *When the Snow Melts*, 254.

25 For further details regarding the coproduction treaty, see Justin Smith, 'Une entente cordiale? A brief history of the Anglo-French film coproduction agreement, 1965–1979', in Lucy Mazdon and Catherine Wheatley (eds) *Je T'Aime . . . Mon Non Plus: Franco-British Cinematic Relations* (New York and Oxford: Berghahn Books, 2010).

26 Elizabeth Castaldo Lundèn, '*Barbarella*'s wardrobe: Exploring Jacques Fonteray's intergalactic runway', *Film Fashion & Consumption* 5, no. 2 (2016): 194.

27 Ibid.

28 Cinémathèque Française (CF), D039-017: Jacques Fonteray, 'Los Angeles Airport [s.d.] [Costume Model]', n.d.

29 Christopher Wood, *Moonraker*, draft screenplay, 19 May 1978, revised 29 August 1978 – pink, 25.

30 Ibid., revised 29 August 1978 – salmon, 29.

31 CF, D039-020: Fonteray, 'Chasse [s.d.] [Costume Model]', n.d.

32 Ibid.

33 Wood, revised 20 June 1978, 61.

34 CF, D039-015: Fonteray, 'Arrival in Rio [s.d.] [Costume Model]', n.d.

35 Wood, revised 19 May 1978, 65.

36 CF, D039-019: Fonteray, 'Black smoking [s.d.] [Costume Model]', n.d.

37 Wood, revised 1 August 1978 – blue, 75A.

38 Ibid., revised 20 June 1978, 95.

39 Ibid., revised 3 August 1978 – blue, 98.

40 CF, D039-016: Fonteray, 'Saharienne B [s.d.] [Costume Model], n.d.

41 Ibid.

42 CF, D039-018: Fonteray, '[*Moonraker*], [s.d.], [Costume Model], n.d.

43 Wood, revised 1 August 1978 – blue, 15.

44 Ibid., revised 29 August 1979 – salmon, 29.

45 Fleming, *Moonraker*, (1955; London: Penguin Books, 2005), 123, 197.

46 Ibid., 48.

47 Wood, revised 20 June 1978, 18.

48 Ibid., revised 15 August 1978 – blue, 51.

8 'YOU CAN ALWAYS SPOT A HAYWARD': ROGER MOORE (1980–85)

For Roger Moore's 1980s Bond films, he recommended another of his personal tailors, Douglas Hayward, to create his suits. Hayward made Moore's suits for his last three Bond films: *For Your Eyes Only*, *Octopussy* and *A View to a Kill*. Moore and Hayward came to develop a close friendship, and Moore was later quoted in Hayward's obituary: 'Doug was among the five best tailors in London – though I have no idea who the other four were. For me he was the one and only tailor.'[1] Hayward's daughter, Polly Westmacott-Hayward, explained that the pair 'were very close, my father knew Roger Moore before he was famous and he helped him out by making him look good for auditions and things like that'.[2] Glenys Roberts, Hayward's former wife, outlines how Hayward, 'the funniest man I ever met', began his career:

> When he was at school, Hayward decided that he wasn't going to do a blue-collar job: he didn't want to get his hands dirty. His mother worked in a bullet factory during World War II and his father used to clean the boilers at the BBC. He didn't want to do that, he wanted a clean job, so he decided to become a tailor.[3]

Hayward was initially employed by the firm Montague Burton in Shepherd's Bush. Roberts reveals that due to Hayward's working-class accent it was requested that he work in the back room of the shop and 'work on his act'. It was during his time at Burton's that Hayward met some of his future clients, including Peter Sellers and possibly Richard Burton, due to their working at the BBC Television Theatre in 1953. Hayward also obtained some contacts through Melissa Stribling, the sister of his first wife Diana, who was married to the film director Basil Dearden. After leaving Burton's and working as 'the front of house man' for tailor Robbie Stanford,

Hayward met Dimi Major who was employed by Stanford as an out-worker. They went on to form a '50/50 tailoring partnership', and Del Smith explains that 'Hayward was the personality; a great networker who could get the clients, and Major was the craftsman who made everything in the workshop.' On leaving the partnership to form his own bespoke tailoring firm in 1967, Hayward briefly worked from Frank Foster's workshop in Pall Mall, during which time he would arrange to visit clients personally. Roberts recalls that 'because he couldn't invite customers [to the Pall Mall workshop] he did it all out of the back of his Mini. He just went to see the clients; he was offering a service that I don't think anyone else was doing.' He subsequently purchased premises based at 95 Mount Street, so as to 'avoid the military mentality' of Savile Row, and the tailor remained based there until his death in 2008.

Much loved by both staff and clients alike for his humour and easy-going approach to life, Smith outlines what it was like to work for Hayward:

> You only had two jobs to do if you wanted to get along well with him: firstly, you needed to turn up on time, and secondly, you needed to complete your work to a high standard. Hayward liked to control what was happening in his workshop: ensuring that all of his suits maintained a high quality of workmanship was really important to him.

Hayward employed a small staff: two cutters, an alteration tailor, a seamstress, a trouser maker, and would outsource a waistcoat maker if required. On process, Westmacott-Hayward explains that Hayward would always measure clients and cut the pattern, before the small team would work on creating the suit, noting that the tailor 'was a perfectionist in terms of details'. Smith believes that what is particularly impressive about Hayward's approach was how the tailor came to network and develop relationships with so many 'known' people including stars, businessmen, politicians and peers, leading to Savile Row questioning 'who *is* this guy?' Besides Burton, Moore and Sellers, Hayward's notable clientele included, but was not limited to, John Barry, Tony Bennett, Michael Caine, Terry Donovan, Clint Eastwood, John Gielgud, Rex Harrison, John Le Carré, John Osborne, Michael Parkinson, Harold Pinter, Terence Stamp and Tommy Steele. Hayward's female clients included Faye Dunaway, Mia Farrow, Jean Shrimpton and Sharon Tate. The photographer Terry O' Neill famously referred to Hayward as '"the buddha of Mount Street". You wouldn't believe the number of people who go to him for advice. He's probably the best-loved man in London.'[4] Hayward himself admitted: 'I suppose women talk to their hairdresser and men talk to their tailor. If you give them the chance all their worries will come flying out.'[5]

On the style and cut of a Hayward suit, Roberts explained that the tailor was heavily influenced by Italian suit styles that he was introduced to by Maria Letitzia, the wife of Ken Adam, who 'took him to Italy and really showed him how the

Italians made clothes. At the time, Italian tailors were perceived as inferior by the British, but he learned a lot about style and he incorporated the Italian, slightly more relaxed, romantic look into his suits,' and also made use of Italian suit fabrics. Smith concurs, noting that in terms of structure, Hayward

> *really* knew how to put a jacket together. His suits were British with an Italian influence, and they were more relaxed than the more militant Savile Row style. They were very distinctive. In terms of the outward appearance of a Hayward suit, the jackets would include soft shoulders with a structured line, not so much of a roped sleeve-head. Because of the shoulders, this gives the Hayward suit a softer, more elegant silhouette. The jackets always had a side vent and three or four-button cuffs. One of his signatures was to include frogmouth, or 'drop-cross', pockets in the trousers. There were also internal parts of the suit that would be signature Hayward that can't be seen.

In comparison to a Savile Row jacket, which typically included a longer collar and a slanted gorge-line, Smith explains that a Hayward jacket 'had a higher notch and square gorge-line', and that the buttons would be placed three-quarter inches lower than the natural waistline and have a slim arm for sleeves. Post-1970, the suits became slimmer in cut. Hayward told Dylan Jones:

> The basics of a suit you don't mess about with: single-breasted, with two or three buttons, side vents, straight jacket pockets with flaps (no one has waistcoats any more, thank God). You make it simple and you make it well. There's no great secret to it, you bring your taste to it and, of course, the way you actually cut the suit. Tailoring is the same everywhere, it's just how you interpret the rules [...] I've always thought that if you line up ten of my suits, no one should be able to tell who the tailor is, except me. If you go to Anderson & Sheppard, or Huntsman, or any Savile Row tailor, you can tell them from thirty yards. They are very elegant, beautifully made, but they have a particular style.[6]

Jones believed that Hayward's suits were '"striking" regardless of their intended anonymity', and as Moore put it: 'You can always spot a Hayward.'[7] Another distinctive element of a Hayward suit was that they were tailored with lightweight cloth, as Smith explains: 'During the 1960s, the average weight for a suit would be fourteen ounces, and a more lightweight suit would be eleven or twelve ounces.' Smith reveals that Hayward particularly 'loved using tweeds', and that Herringbone tweed was one of the most popular choices with clients in particular. Owing to this, James Coburn referred to Hayward as 'the Rodin of tweed'.[8] A two-piece bespoke Hayward suit would cost around £250 towards the end of the 1960s, £700 in the mid-1980s, and by the late 1990s, £2,750. By way of comparison, a Savile Row two-piece suit in the late 1990s would cost on average £3,500.[9]

Hayward was commissioned to tailor suits for film based on his personal friendships with actors, who would recommend that Hayward tailor their suits to the producer and/or director. Hayward's previous credits for suits he produced for film include Laurence Harvey in *The Spy with a Cold Nose* (1966), Stamp in *Modesty Blaise* (1966) of which Hayward appeared in a cameo role, Noël Coward in *Boom!* (1968), Stephen Boyd in *Assignment K* (1968) and Caine in *The Italian Job* (1969). Hayward was named as the costume designer for *The Reckoning* (1970) and credited as costuming the men for *Dominique* (1980). On process, Smith explains that between the 1960s and mid-1980s an actor and director for a film would arrive at the tailor's premises to discuss what was needed, including for which scenes and what different types of climate the suits would be worn in. The contemporary process differs in that the tailoring firm will need to go through various layers of stylists and production assistants before meeting the actor: 'it used to be "Come and see my tailor", now it's more like the stylist telling the actor "You're wearing this"'. On the timescales for tailoring a bespoke suit, one could be made in three to four days, provided that time was dedicated to it, 'but, as it is, a suit takes about six weeks to complete', and Hayward and his team could only feasibly produce up to fifteen bespoke suits per week, especially owing to the tailor needing to 'see everything that comes out under my name. People want my stamp, so I have to make sure that I'm there.'[10]

As Moore was already a personal client and friend of Hayward's, Smith believes that it would have been easier to tailor the suits for Moore's Bond films as Hayward knew the colours that suited the actor's skin tone. It is likely that there would have been a three-week turnaround to produce the suits for Moore's Bond films, including around two to three copies of each suit for Moore and around twelve for the stuntmen. Hayward would have worked closely with the wardrobe department during this period in order to communicate about the design details for the film. Smith explains that it would not have been possible for Hayward to work continuously on tailoring suits for film, owing to the timescale and number of items needed to be produced, however there were certain times of the year when it would be quieter in terms of his personal clients' needs, particularly in October/ November and January/February. Between 1960 and 1985, Smith notes that tailors would instantly recognize where a suit had been sourced from and who tailored it, and thus it was really important to the tailor that the quality of the suit was 'perfect' owing to concerns that other members of the tailoring community would be critically assessing it. Hayward's principle towards tailoring Moore's Bond suits was

> keep them as classic as possible, as I believe people will be watching Bond films in twenty years' time [. . .] keep noticeable details, such as turn-back cuffs, to a minimum. Fred Astaire could walk down the street today in a suit that was made for him in the 1930s and look fabulous. I have always borne that in mind

when making clothes for films and I don't think I have ever done work for a film I am now embarrassed by.[11]

Spaiser has analysed the individual components of the different suits that Hayward tailored for Moore in his 1980s Bond films. Beyond the signature structure outlined by Smith, the single-breasted jacket consistently included medium lapels, a moderately full-cut chest, a suppressed waist, straight pockets with flaps, three cuff buttons and double vents.[12]

Regarding Hayward's legacy, Roberts argues: 'He revolutionised British tailoring, which was very stuffy,' and owing to the combined British and Italian influences evident in his suits, Hayward 'added something to British tailoring that that wasn't there before: I think that a lot of his success was due to that, because he could make everyone look very romantic with it. That's what tailoring is all about: correcting your faults and making you look fantastic!' Westmacott-Hayward concurs, and explains that this, combined with his sense of humour, enabled his clients to leave with confidence and created life-long friendships. Hayward was also involved with establishing Ralph Lauren's 'Purple Label' in 1995, who was another personal client and friend who often gifted Hayward with various teddy bear toys, however Hayward requested that he not be directly credited for the range. David Bailey, the celebrated fashion photographer, quipped that 'his suits might be the most distinctive sartorial event since Mr. Levi invented jeans'.[13] Le Carré acknowledged Hayward as being the inspiration behind the lead character, Harry Pendel, in his novel *The Tailor of Panama* (1996) which, as Westmacott-Hayward wittily explained: 'On the grounds that you hear all sorts of things whilst you're measuring someone's inner leg, it's the perfect spy scenario.' Furthermore, many of Hayward's later staff would go onto develop their careers working for tailors based on Savile Row, as with Smith who went on to work for Kilgour and is due to set up his own tailoring firm. Smith continues to tailor his suits with soft, structured shoulders, and thus Hayward's legacy has filtered into the tailoring of Savile Row suits today, something that Hayward himself would doubtless find deeply ironic, given that he was turned away from Savile Row firms owing to his Cockney accent on starting out as a tailor.

For Your Eyes Only (1981)

The plot of *For Your Eyes Only* draws upon two of Fleming's short stories that were published as a collection in 1960: the story of the same name and 'Risico'. John Glen, who had formerly worked as the editor for the Bond films *On Her Majesty's Secret Service*, *The Spy Who Loved Me* and *Moonraker* was hired as the film's director. Principal photography commenced on 15 September 1980 with a budget of $28 million (£11.6 million).

Hayward tailored four suits and one blazer for Bond in *For Your Eyes Only*. Bringing a more traditional look for a Bond of the 1980s minus the wide lapels and flared trousers, Bond first wears a charcoal three-piece suit on visiting the grave of his wife Tracy. The waistcoat, as with the others produced by Hayward for Moore, has a six-button fastening and four welt pockets. Underneath the jacket and waistcoat, Bond wears a particularly vibrant shirt that is made from a blue and white striped cotton with a white pointed and high spread collar and white double-button mitered cuffs. The majority of Bond's Frank Foster shirts made in this decade all have similar details. A charcoal silk tie is worn to complement the suit fabric. The trousers are flat-fronted with wide straight legs, and are fastened with a leather belt. At the Secret Service headquarters in London, Bond wears his second three-piece suit, this time tailored from navy worsted flannel with light grey chalk stripes. The jacket has a two rather than a three-button fastening. In these scenes, the frogmouth pocket on the trousers, one of Hayward's signatures, can be viewed. Underneath the jacket and waistcoat, Bond wears a pale blue cotton shirt and a satin-silk navy tie with alternate thick gold and thin pale pink diagonal stripes.

Bond's next suit is made from a pale grey lightweight flannel fabric which Hayward particularly favoured. It is worn with a cream-coloured cotton shirt fastened with a light grey silk tie. In Corfu, Bond wears the first of his double-breasted jackets tailored by Hayward. It is a navy blazer with six brass buttons, worn with beige chinos likely made from gaberdine, and a pale blue unfastened shirt. The blazer differs from the previous suit jackets in that it has peaked lapels, and is cut slightly wider. Spaiser believes that it is likely made from a worsted wool serge fabric.[14] At the casino, Bond wears a black dinner suit. The jacket has a notched lapel, and is fastened with one button. Unusually, the button, as well as the three buttons included on the sleeve of the jacket, are not fabric-covered but rather made of black horn. The trousers include a high waistband made from silk, that doubles as a cummerbund. This is a signature of Hayward's dinner suit trousers that would be included in *Octopussy* and *A View to a Kill*. The white shirt worn beneath the jacket is made from a cotton fabric with tonal stripes, and has a pleated front placket with a mother-of-pearl button fastening, and square French cuffs that are fastened with rectangular gold and mother-of-pearl cufflinks. The shirt collar is fastened with a black satin bowtie. Bond's final suit in *For Your Eyes Only* is made from a light brown gaberdine. The shirt is made from a light blue cotton and is fastened with a cotton tie woven with blue and grey threads in a delicate waved *piqué* weave.

Elizabeth Waller was employed as the film's costume designer, and Tiny Nicholls and Marina Drecker were hired as the wardrobe master and the wardrobe mistress respectively. Waller worked in repertory theatre before being employed by the BBC as a 'designer of period and modern dress', and was one of its forty-nine full-time staff designers until 1980.[15] The most notable production that Waller worked on was *Elizabeth R* (1971), of which she received an Emmy Award for 'Outstanding

Achievement in Costume Design' and a Royal Television Society/Pye Award for 'Best Costume Design' in 1972. With the advent of colour television on the BBC from 1967, costume changed from being a technical department to a creative one, and thus for *Elizabeth R* it was agreed that Waller receive 'the lion's share' of the design budget allocation.[16]

Waller's experience of working within the more significant budget afforded to *Elizabeth R* set her in good stead for designing costumes for *For Your Eyes Only*. This film was intended to 'bring Bond back to earth' following his previous adventure into space with *Moonraker*, and therefore Moore appears wearing more casual clothing than in his previous Bond films, including in two towelling dressing gowns, a blue Willy Bognor ski suit, a blue wetsuit, a yellow diving suit, and a khaki green blouson jacket, drawn in with a tightly fitted waist that has elasticated ribbed detail. This detail is repeated on the set-in sleeve cuffs. The jacket differs slightly in that a blouson would normally include a pointed spread collar, however Bond's has a deep rounded neckline with no collar. It has a horizontal front and back yoke and is fastened at the front with a zip. Beneath the jacket, Bond wears a short-sleeved cotton shirt in a light beige colour, with a wide pointed spread collar worn unfastened. The shirt is fastened with mother-of-pearl buttons, and includes short sleeves that end with slim turn-back cuffs, a U-line open patch pocket over the breast, and a horizontal back yoke. The light brown linen trousers are cut in the same way as Bond's suit trousers. This is the first of many blouson jackets that Moore would come to wear in his last three Bond films. At the end of the film, Bond wears a costume similar to what is described in the script: 'in climbing gear, boots, woollen socks, nylon cougale, gloves, etc'.[17] In the film, Bond wears a dark blue quilted nylon gilet jacket that is sleeveless, and fastened at the front with a zip. Suede navy patches have been appliquéd onto each shoulder, and two rounded pockets are placed at the centre-front on either side of the zip fastening, as well as two patch pockets on the hips and a game pouch at the rear. Beneath the gilet, Bond wears a chunky two-tone grey jumper knitted from Shetland wool with a rounded neck, and a dark blue shirt with a wide pointed spread collar. Bond wears black ribbed corduroy trousers with the outfit.

Both Aril Kristatos (Julian Glover) and Milos Columbo (Topol), are adapted from Fleming's short story 'Risico'. Kristatos is described in the script as 'a charming, expansive, international business executive in his middle fifties'.[18] To reflect this, Kristatos wears a stylized maxi-length grey trench coat with dark brown fur, likely mink, on the wide notched lapels and collar in his first scene. It has the typical elements of a trench coat; however, this version differs slightly in that it has set-in sleeves and has a scalloped western yoke stitched above a centre-back seam. Beneath the coat, Kristatos wears colours that hint of his allegiance to Soviet Russia, namely an olive green double-breasted blazer with six gold buttons and a red polo-neck jumper.

During the casino scenes, Kristatos wears a double-breasted black dinner suit. The jacket has satin-faced peaked lapels and soft, natural shoulders. It has six cloth-covered buttons, two jetted pockets placed on either side of the hips, and no back vent. Underneath the jacket Kristatos wears a white shirt with mother-of-pearl buttons and a spread collar that is fastened with a black satin bowtie. By way of comparison, Columbo is referred to in the script as being: 'a tanned, well-groomed, well-tailored man in his middle fifties. Ruggedly handsome, he looks as though he had a zest for life, an ironical sense of humour, and undeniable authority.'[19] Thus, Columbo is dressed in a black three-piece dinner suit, of which the jacket has natural shoulders with roped sleeve-heads, satin-silk faced peaked lapels and a one-button fastening. Unusually, it has two slanted flapped patch pockets on the hips which also include a satin-silk facing. The skirt of the jacket has double vents. Colombo's low-cut and scooped waistcoat is made of black silk, and is worn with a white shirt with a pleated placket that is fastened with smoked mother-of-pearl buttons. A black silk bowtie is fastened at the spread collar. The shirt has French square double cuffs that are fastened with circular gold cufflinks that have a dark blue background and a white dove motif in the centre.

Columbo later wears a double-breasted blazer made from navy wool that was tailored by Robbie Stanford. The blazer has straight shoulders and roped sleeve-heads, narrow peaked lapels, and is fastened with four brass buttons that include a crown and anchor motif. It has one open patch pocket over the left breast, and two straight open patch pockets on each hip. The sleeves include a two-button fastening, and the skirt of the jacket has double vents. The blazer is lined with blue art silk. Columbo wears the same shirt as he did in the casino, and the outfit is worn with cream gaberdine trousers with a flat front that are fastened with a slim white leather belt. This outfit has been selected in part to demonstrate Columbo's personality and his allegiance towards Bond in these scenes after they have both been double-crossed by Kristatos.

The lead 'Bond girl', Melina Havelock (Carole Bouquet), is based on Fleming's character, Judy Havelock, in his short story *For Your Eyes Only*. Her character and costume are described:

> The girl looked like a beautiful unkempt dryad in ragged shirt and trousers. The shirt and trousers were olive green, crumpled and splashed with mud and stains and torn in places [. . .] She looked like a beautiful dangerous customer who knew wild country and forests and was not afraid of them. She would walk alone through life and have little use for civilisation.[20]

Carrying a bow and arrow, a weapon that would be changed to a crossbow in the film, Bond notes that the character is a combination of 'good hard English stock spiced with the hard peppers of a tropical childhood. Dangerous mixture.'[21] This would be adopted in the script description of the character: 'She is a shapely twenty-seven-year-old brunette wearing travel clothes. A briskly poised competent marine archaeologist, half-Greek, half-English, she reflects her ancestry, warmth overlaid with reserve.'[22] Melina's costumes have been selected to be tasteful and expensive looking, to reflect her class as the daughter of Sir Timothy Havelock and work as a mantle to shroud her passionate Grecian nature that lies beneath.

On attempting to avenge the death of her parents, the script suggests that Melina be dressed in 'camouflage', and the character is dressed in her key costume that consists of a dark brown khaki safari jacket with matching trousers (Figure 8.1). The jacket has natural shoulders and roped sleeve-heads, and a spread collar that is worn unfastened. Unlike typical safari jackets, it differs in that it has no epaulettes on the shoulder. It has straight-cut sleeves with a one-button fastening on the plain cuff, and is cinched at the waist with a belt. Four flapped patch pockets are placed symmetrically over the chest and hips, and have inverted box pleats and a one-button fastening. It is fastened with a zip. With the costume, Melina wears a feminine bucket hat with a wide, down-sloping brim, a black grosgrain ribbon and a mesh face veil made from embroidered black silk tulle that appears to be a stylized version of a mosquito net face covering. This is designed to emphasize the shot in which Melina takes off her hat to reveal her long brunette hair as it cascades down her back. At the end of the film, Melina wears a variant of this costume: a padded brown suede jacket that has dark brown leather strips appliquéd over the seams on the shoulders, sleeves and side panels. The long sleeves are cut off a dropped shoulder, banded at the cap and cuffs with a matching leather strip, and the jacket is fastened at the front with a zip and includes two large open patch pockets on the hips. Underneath the jacket, Melina wears a hooded, cowl-necked caramel-coloured jumper knitted in a chunky rib stitch, and a pair of dark chocolate brown trousers made from crushed velvet. Over the trouser hem, Melina wears dark brown suede boots to match the jacket.

FIGURE 8.1 Melina Havelock's camouflage outfit. *For Your Eyes Only* directed by John Glen © Eon Productions/United Artists 1981. All rights reserved.

Raemonde Rahvis was credited in the film with providing the 'wardrobe for Miss Bouquet and Miss Harris': in reality this entailed realizing the dresses worn by Melina and Countess Lisl von Schlaf (Cassandra Harris) in the casino scenes, and Melina's midi-length mink fur opera coat. At the age of 78, *For Your Eyes Only* was the last film production the fashion designer would work on. Until the mid-1970s, Rahvis worked as part of a two-woman team with her sister, Dora, after setting up Rahvis Gowns in 1929. The sisters' first involvement with film came in the year that they first opened their premises, when Betty Compson wore a Rahvis wedding dress to star in Victor Saville's *Woman to Woman* (1929). Known as 'the London Schiaparelli's', the sisters would successfully transition between designing dresses and gowns for fashion and for film, and they came to work on over 40 films.[23] Melina's coat has large notched lapels, wide shoulders and long angel sleeves. Two large slanted jetted pockets are included on the hips, and the coat has a flared skirt and a deep back vent. It has a silver art silk lining, and is fastened with buttons hidden by a centre-front placket. Underneath the coat, Melina wears a maroon polo-neck jumper, white fitted trousers with slim-cut legs, as well as leather gloves and knee-high leather boots that have both been selected to match the colour of the jumper.

Little can be viewed of Melina's Rahvis gown in the casino scenes, although it was used prominently in promotional shots. It is a floor-length, low-backed gown made from a deep red silk. The bodice has spaghetti straps and a fitted wrap-over bodice with a plunge neckline. It is stitched with vertical darts to create a ruched detail over the bust. The natural waistline seam is covered with a wide matching silk band, and the circular skirt, cut on the bias, is gathered underneath the waist band so as to emphasize a fit-and-flare silhouette. In contrast, Lisl, who is described in the script as 'a willowy beauty in her early thirties, elegantly gowned and coiffed', wears a sari-inspired floor-length Rahvis gown made of silk, with an overskirt panel in pale blue and an underskirt in a darker shade of blue.[24] The sleeveless maxi-cut gown is asymmetrical and cut with an off-the-shoulder neckline. The neckline includes a ribbon trim made with white and navy sequins appliquéd in alternate stripes with an intricate crossed key-hole patterning made from a mixture of blue and clear Swarovski crystals in the centre. The trim is repeated on the hem of the overskirt. In keeping with the Rahvis sisters' signature use of chiffon in their gown designs, a pale blue chiffon angel sleeve panel is attached at the back of the shoulder. The over-panel has a slanted asymmetric hem, and the under panel is cut full-length and straight.

Unlike Melina and Lisl, the character of Bibi Dahl (Lynn-Holly Johnson) appears particularly out of place in the film, especially as she is afforded little narrative agency or character development in the script. Her apparent purpose is to demonstrate that Bond has to draw the line somewhere in employing his 'the things I do for England' approach in having sexual relations with women. According to Johnson, it was Michael G. Wilson who wanted 'to create a character who antagonised Bond'.[25] In the script, Bibi is described as being 'seventeen, apple-cheeked, pretty, well-developed, wholesomely girlish'.[26] Bibi's limited agency becomes particularly evident when considering the small amount of information that she provides Bond, namely that Erich Kriegler (John Wyman) is an East German defector, which could have easily been obtained elsewhere.

The character's main scene involves breaking into Bond's hotel suite, taking a shower, attempting to kiss Bond and affording the latter patronising lines such as 'Now get dressed – and I'll buy you an ice cream,' and 'All I can say is don't grow up anymore. I don't think the opposite sex could survive it.' Bibi's costumes, too, are limited to either ice skating training outfits or Willy Bognor ski attire, and this enhances the character's lack of development and little purpose. According to Johnson, cast in the role owing to her being a professional skater, she:

> Always had costume dresses made by somebody who only did skating competition dresses. In London they took me to [Bermans and Nathans] a place who had never done a skating dress. It's particular because the skirt has to flow in a particular way and I remember thinking this is not going to work, these people have never done a skating dress. But they made a beautiful dress and I still have it.[27]

The dress that Johnson refers to is the ice-skating dress that Bibi wears in her first scenes. The costume is formed of a pale blue elasticated spandex Lycra leotard with silver spangled detail, cut with a high rounded neck and fitted sleeves. It includes oval-shaped blue and clear crystals stitched into a spray pattern over the neck and chest. It has a chiffon mesh drop micro-skirt cut in the shape of short fins and stitched over either side of the hips finishing in a low V-cut at the centre-front and back. It is notable that this variant of 'Bond girl' has not appeared in subsequent films.

Octopussy (1983)

It was decided early in production that *Octopussy*, the title of which was borrowed from Fleming's short story, would be partially filmed in Udaipur, India and at Checkpoint Charlie in West Berlin, Germany, with a budget of $27.5 million (£15.8 million). Principal photography began on 16 August 1982. Although not directly adapting Fleming's *Octopussy*, in which Bond is sent to Jamaica to obtain the confession of Major Dexter Smythe, the script included the character of Octopussy (Maud Adams), revealed in the film to be the daughter of Dexter Smythe, and therefore the short story forms the film's back story. The film does, however, adapt the Sotheby's auction described in another of Fleming's short stories, 'The Property of a Lady'.

Emma Porteous was employed as the film's costume designer and the first in this role to work on consecutive Bond films. Tiny Nicholls returned as the wardrobe master, and the majority of the costumes for the Indian and circus scenes were produced by Bermans and Nathans. Porteous first worked as a sketch artist for a Paris-based couturier for ten years before being employed as costume designer at ATV and subsequently Rediffusion (later London Weekend Television). While working for LWT, Porteous was asked whether she would like to work as a freelance costume designer for the film *Performance* (1970).[28] As Sue Harper observes, Porteous's work in the 1970s was 'both economical and stylish', and her designs for *Swallows and Amazons* (1974) and *The Lady Vanishes* (1979) were 'marvels of succinctness'.[29] It is on being employed on larger budget films, including *The Island of Dr Moreau* (1977) and *Clash of the Titans* (1982), that Porteous was afforded greater autonomy and creative agency in her costume concepts, which could 'permit daring and ground-breaking designs', explains Harper.[30] This is indeed true of her work on the Bond films, with Porteous reflecting: 'You probably get more of an outlet on a Bond film. You can really go to town. They're modern, but you can be really wild.'[31]

On the general process that Porteous adopted to design costumes, the designer drew heavily upon her experience on working in television, and explained that she began breaking down the script to gather ideas and would then meet with the set designer to discuss them, after which she would go away to draft sketches. Once the initial concepts had been completed, Porteous would then show them to the producer and director for further discussion. On what influenced her designs beyond the script direction and discussion with relevant personnel, Porteous explained: 'You always have influences – things one has seen in the theatre, or one's favourite designers, so it's always in the back of your mind but you don't confess to anything.'[32] Porteous was also keen to stress that her finalized designs were very much a collaborative effort between herself and the hair and make-up designers working together for a unified look: 'When I did my designs, I tried to do the make-up and hair with them, so that made it much easier. It's very difficult to design just the clothes in isolation, but the other designers had their own ideas and we all contributed together.'[33] In particular, Porteous's designs possess a keen eye for colour and detail, similar to Julie Harris's for *Live and Let Die*. Unlike other designers' sketchier, whimsical and lyrical concepts, for example Mendleson's and Fonteray's designs, Porteous's are exacting with the rounded and cheerfully coloured gouache brushstrokes conveying types of fabric and patterning contained within a pencil line sketch of the character's silhouette. The minutia of fabric detail included in Porteous's designs works to offer a clear direction for the costume maker so as to replicate the realized costumes to a particular specification. Another of Porteous's signatures on her designs is to create a frame for the figure's silhouette by consistently writing the film title and costume name in the top right-hand corner of the paper which is connected to a right-angle pencil line that ends at the opposite bottom left-hand corner, underneath which Porteous signs her name.

Porteous has explained how different it was to design costumes for a Bond film: 'Doing a James Bond film, which has such a reputation for elegance and glamour, everyone's beautiful and without a crease, does mean that you approach it in a different way; it's a whole new area to work in. [*Octopussy*] was an unbelievably happy film, there was no trouble in it.'[34] The designer spent between twelve and fourteen weeks preparing for the film. Part of Porteous's inspiration behind her *Octopussy* designs came from buying 'many marvellous books on India', and attending 'lots' of exhibitions, including one held at the Victoria and Albert Museum, and another at the Commonwealth Institute at Kensington. On Moore, Porteous believed that he 'looks the perfect English gentleman', and although Hayward tailored his suits, the designer assisted in the fabric selection, explaining 'it's a question of picking beautiful fabrics and putting him in them. He's a good clothes-horse, the least trouble of anyone.'

Many revisions were made to the script prior to and during the commencement of filming, and it is likely that these revisions accommodated many of the realized film costumes. For example, in the script's opening scene it offers clear direction as to Bond's 'cod costume' outfit that changes from 'a tweed hacking jacket over a turtleneck sweater, tan riding breeches, butcher boots, riding gloves, and a horsey cloth cheese-cutter cap' into a Latin American officer's uniform. This involves both the cap and jacket being turned inside-out to create an officer's cap and tunic, which is 'replete with insignia, several rows of medal ribbons and leather belt with holstered revolver attached'.[35] The sweater is to be 'pulled away' to reveal a 'shirt collar with neatly made tie and colonel insignia on the collar wings'.[36] In the film, Bond wears a yellow turtleneck sweater, underneath which is a beige cotton shirt with pointed collar fastened with a black satin-silk tie. The shirt has epaulettes fastened on the shoulder with one brass button, and two patch pockets on the breast with box pleats and scalloped pointed flaps that are also fastened with one button. The dark olive green trousers have a flat front and are fastened with a brown leather belt. The bizarrely described 'horsey cloth' cheese-cutter cap was made from the same fabric as the jacket. When Bond switches the brown herringbone tweed jacket inside-out, the officer's tunic is made from an olive green cotton drill fabric and has a four-button fastening down the centre-front made from black horn. It has four patch pockets on the breast and hips, all with scalloped flaps fastened with one button as with the shirt. The breast pockets include box pleats and the hip pockets inverted pleats. There are epaulettes on the shoulders and the jacket has a wide, spread Balmacaan collar, and a square turn-up cuff on the sleeve with a one-button fastening.

Bond next wears a dark grey serge three-piece suit with a light blue chalk stripe during the Sotheby's auction scene. Underneath the jacket and waistcoat, Bond wears a pale blue cotton shirt that is fastened with a maroon red silk tie. On arriving in Delhi, India, Bond is described in the script as wearing 'a well-cut tropical suit'.[37] In the film, this consists of a tan brown suit made from gaberdine. Underneath the jacket, Bond wears a white shirt that is fastened with a slim silk tie made from a darker tan brown base with contrasting thin diagonal stripes in light tan brown. When taking part in a game of backgammon against Kamal Khan (Louis Jourdan) in India, Bond is 'smartly dressed in white jacket'.[38] In the film, the linen ivory dinner jacket in is worn with black trousers and a white shirt with mother-of-pearl buttons on a plain placket that is fastened with a black satin bowtie. The jacket has peaked lapels, a Barchetta curved welt pocket, a one-button fastening and jetted pockets. The shirt includes square French cuffs that are fastened with rectangular onyx cufflinks.

During a chase through the streets of Udaipur on a three-wheeled auto-rickshaw ('Tuk Tuk'), the breast of Bond's dinner jacket is pierced with a knife blade, as noted in the script: '[Bond] Pulling open jacket. Point of blade has cut through his breast pocket and embedded itself in a wad of bills filling inner pocket of jacket. He pulls knife out, throws knife and bills away'.[39] The dinner jacket is subsequently repaired in Q's workshop, which is not directly alluded to in the script. On returning to his hotel wearing the repaired dinner suit, Bond later wears a padded, calf-length dressing gown made from cotton that has a powder blue base with diagonal pinstripe in alternate red and yellow colours after having sexual intercourse with Magda (Kristina Wayborn). The sleeves have mitered turn-back cuffs, which have dark blue piping on the edges that is included on the shawl collar and the breast pocket.

After being imprisoned in Khan's fortress, a 'house boy' enters Bond's room with Gobinda (Kabir Bedi) to return a 'freshly pressed black jacket and black trousers'.[40] This implies that Bond was due to wear a dark dinner suit as the white dinner jacket had not been repaired by Q Branch and Bond had to change his outfit. The potential continuity error is overcome by including a shot of the wardrobe in which Bond finds that the clothes from his hotel suite have been transferred. Rather than being black, the realized suit is made from a wool and mohair blend fabric in midnight blue. The jacket includes satin-faced notched lapels and a one-button fastening that is cloth-covered. Underneath the jacket, Bond wears a white shirt that has a pleated placket with mother-of-pearl buttons which is fastened by a black silk bowtie.

After dinner with Khan and Magda, Bond changes into his safari-shirt jacket, created by Frank Foster, in order to escape Khan's fortress. Made from a pale green cotton fabric, the jacket has a notched pointed spread collar that is worn unfastened, shoulder epaulettes, a flared skirt, four patch pockets with inverted box pleats that have pointed flaps fastened with one button, a four-button fastening down the centre, and mitered cuffs on the sleeves. The buttons are made from an olive-coloured horn. The jacket differs from typical safari suits and shirts in that it is not belted. The back of the jacket has a western yoke, one centre-back seam, and deep double vents.

In West Berlin, Bond wears his last suit in the film, namely a dark charcoal grey suit. A white shirt that is fastened with a navy silk tie with yellow polka dots is worn underneath the jacket. It is during the train scenes that Bond discovers the plan to place a bomb in the cannon at the circus that is travelling to the US air base. To go undercover, he changes into Mischka's (David Meyer) 'Twin 1' red tunic, black leather jacket and knife belt. The design for the identical twins' costumes forms part of the collection of Porteous's costume designs held by the BFI.[41] In the script, the costume is described as 'a loose Russian blouse with bell sleeves and Cossack pants tucked into boots. Around his waist is a belt of throwing knives'.[42] The costumes made by Kortach closely conform to Porteous's design, and includes a wine-coloured polyester tunic with a high, rounded Mandarin collar that is fastened with three matching buttons on an asymmetric placket. The tunic has full set-in sleeves fastened with a gauntlet cuff. A wide black leather belt detailed with studs is worn fastened around the waist. Over the tunic, the twins wear an unfastened black leather jacket that is cut to the waist and includes a zipper-teeth detail down either side of the opening. The wide, loose-fitting, black trousers are worn with the hems tapered by black knee-high patent leather boots. This costume is worn until Bond infiltrates the circus and changes into a clown costume, in order to diffuse the bomb. It is described in the script as 'a clown with a grotesquely painted face, red bulb of a nose, orange wig, bowler hat, checkered [sic] vest, baggy pants, and a floppy coat with balloons attached to it'.[43] In the final scenes of Octopussy, Bond wears a navy blouson jacket in the fight sequence based at Khan's fortress, which includes a wide, unfastened spread collar, a front zip fastening, and four pockets: two welt pockets on either side of the chest and two patch pockets with flaps that are fastened with one button. The navy trousers have a flat front, and underneath the jacket, Bond wears a white shirt with a spread collar.

Khan was originally described in an early version of the script as 'a striking figure in his wine-coloured turban and forked beard', however the character was later altered to be more Western after the casting of Jourdan.[44] Instead, the character is described in a later script as 'a striking figure, immaculately dressed in Western clothes. In his early forties, darkly handsome and self-possessed, his body is lithe and athletic,' and depending on where the scenes are set, Khan's costumes alternate between Western and Middle-Eastern in terms of influence and style.[45] Due to this, Khan wears a navy two-piece suit at Sotheby's auction house. The jacket has slim notched lapels and straight, wide and padded shoulders with roped sleeve-heads. Details include a Barchetta welt pocket with a white silk pointed pocket square, a one-button fastening, jetted hip pockets and no back vent. Beneath the jacket, Khan wears a white shirt with a pointed collar that is fastened with a navy silk tie. During the backgammon game, Khan wears the first of his Nehru-style jackets that directly contrasts with Bond's dinner suit. This version is made from a midnight blue shantung silk with a light blue paisley pattern etched on the coat. It has white piping detail on the collar and cuffs to create the illusion of a shirt being worn underneath the jacket. It is fastened with buttons beneath a hidden placket, of which Khan only fastens the button under the neck, leaving the rest of the jacket open underneath. Beneath the jacket, Khan wears a black crew-necked shift silk jersey. The black silk trousers are similar to Bond's in that they include a high waist to suggest a cummerbund.

Following this, Khan wears a Western two-piece suit made from a beige herringbone silk that has a slight shadow stripe which has a similar cut and structure to his navy suit. Underneath the jacket, Khan wears a dark brown silk shirt with a spread collar and mother-of-pearl buttons. The sleeves have French square double cuffs that are fastened with circular gold-plated cufflinks with a mother-of-pearl centre. During the dinner scenes at his fortress, Khan reflects Bond in that he wears a midnight blue dinner suit in order to work as a mirror between the two characters unlike the backgammon game. There are, however, subtle differences, including that Khan's dinner jacket has natural shoulders and roped sleeve-heads, satin-faced peaked lapels, jetted hip pockets and a single vent. Underneath the jacket, Khan wears a white shirt with a pointed collar that has mother-of-pearl buttons and a pleated placket, which is fastened with a black silk bowtie. The character also dresses similarly to Bond in the scenes that follow, albeit in a dark olive green linen safari shirt-jacket. The details on the jacket include straight shoulders and roped sleeve-heads, pointed notched lapels and four pockets. The sleeves have a mitered square French turn-up cuff, and the shirt-jacket is belted, with an olive green button fastening down the centre. Khan wears the outfit with a beige safari hat made of cloth. During the two circus scenes, Khan dressed in a single-breasted grey tweed blazer with a one-button fastening made of black horn. Underneath the blazer, Khan wears a blue shirt with a pointed collar that is fastened with a navy silk tie, and dark charcoal grey gaberdine trousers. On returning to India, Khan has changed into another of his Nehru suits, this version made from shantung woven silk, the tunic of which is fastened with buttons that are hidden beneath an asymmetrical placket. It has natural shoulders with roped sleeve-heads, a high and rounded Mandarin collar, a welt pocket, a clean chest and double vents. The trousers are made from matching material.

Gobinda is initially described in the script as 'a tall imposing Sikh in Indian suit and turban'.[46] Instead, the character wears a Western-influenced pale brown two-piece suit, of which the jacket has a long coat cut with lean shoulders and a suppressed waist, and soft natural shoulders with roped sleeve-heads to accentuate Bedi's tall, slim physique. His costumes often mirror that of Khan's. The jacket details include notched lapels, a two-button fastening, jetted hip pockets, and four cuff buttons on the sleeve. Underneath the jacket, Gobinda wears a white shirt with a pointed collar that is fastened with a striped silk tie. A red turban is worn by Gobinda due to the character's assigned religion. Del Singh, at the time a 19-year-old based in Peterborough, was called by 'someone asking if I was a Sikh, and if I wore a turban. I didn't know if it was a wind up [...] but I asked what relevance it was if I was a Sikh. They said they were from Eon Studios filming the next James Bond film in the area, and they needed some help.'[47] Unsure whether someone was jesting with him, Singh and his brother were asked to attend the Marriott hotel near where *Octopussy* was due to be shot at the Nene Valley Railway. On entering the assigned hotel suite, the Singhs realized that the request was genuine:

> Kabir Bedi, who was playing the villain came over. He said he did not normally wear a turban and needed to know how to do it. They showed us the turban they had from when they were filming in India, and said it kept coming off. We had brought a proper one – my school turban, and we showed them that. Ours was so much bigger – theirs looked like a bath towel.

It was explained to the Singhs that they would be needed on set to tie Bedi's turban every day and were offered £50 each for the job. Eon Productions also purchased 'three or four' of Del Singh's school turbans.

During the backgammon game, Gobinda wears the first of his Eastern-influenced costumes, namely a Mao tunic jacket with a long-cut coat made from ecru-coloured *crêpe*-weave silk. With the tunic, Gobinda wears dark brown gaberdine trousers that have a flat front and a plum-coloured turban. During the dinner scenes hosted at Khan's fortress, Gobinda wears another version of the Mao costume, albeit the tunic is made from a pale grey silk with matching trousers. The tunic has a low, rounded Mandarin collar, two welt pockets on both sides of the chest, a six-button fastening, a flared skirt, and no vent. A white turban is worn with the costume. In West Berlin, Gobinda wears a dark grey two-piece suit with a double shadow stripe. Underneath the jacket, Gobinda wears a white shirt that is fastened with a light grey silk tie, and a blue turban completes the costume. On returning to India, Gobinda has changed into a brown shantung silk Nehru suit, with a six-button fastening, of which the tunic has a lean chest and suppressed waist, and no vent. The character wears a garnet-coloured turban.

Octopussy, the lead 'Bond girl', is first viewed wearing one of her main costumes in the film: a floor-length, unlined, sheer satin-silk ivory dressing gown. It has a customized orange and blue octopus on the back, designed by Maciek Piotrowski which was hand-painted by a local Udaipur artist straight onto the plain silk. It is cut on the bias, and has dropped, full-length kimono sleeves, a wrap front, and a plain ivory satin sash belt worn knotted at the waist. The skirt of the dressing gown has two long slits from thigh to hem on either side of the hips. After Bond infiltrates her palace, Octopussy wears her other main costume: a pale blue two-piece sari made from sheer silk with a silver beaded filigree detail, of which the skirt has a wide silver hem. The matching blue chiffon scarf includes a sprayed silver edge in a scallop pattern, repeated from the hem of the skirt. This costume is worn for the obligatory 'ideological conversion' scene between Bond and Octopussy, similar to the scene between Bond and Pussy Galore in *Goldfinger*, and is worn in the final scenes of the film on-board the prop plane which Bond rescues her from.

Magda is the secondary 'Bond girl' in the film, yet is unusually afforded more screen time than Octopussy and is therefore dressed in more costumes. Magda is described in the script as 'a strikingly beautiful Swedish girl in her middle twenties, fashionably dressed'.[48] For the Sotheby's scenes, Magda wears a khaki green fitted peplum jacket that has straight, wide padded shoulders with gathers stitched across the seam and dropped long Gigot sleeves ending in a turned-up gauntlet cuff. It has peaked lapels faced with a paler green-grey satin fabric that is repeated on the sleeve cuffs. It is belted at the waist, with gathered pleats flaring out below the jacket's waist seam. Underneath the jacket, Magda wears a cowl-necked sheer-silk blouse made from the same fabric as the lapels and cuffs, which is fastened with three fabric-covered buttons stitched to an asymmetric placket. The jacket and blouse are paired with an A-line skirt made from the same fabric as the body of the jacket, and is hemmed at mid-calf. Her costume was likely sourced from Harrods.[49] During the backgammon game, Magda is costumed, as per the script description, as 'chicly dressed'.[50] This is translated into a long, fitted gown with a gold silk under-panel including an appliquéd, intertwined black floral lace overlay and black French seam detail. The gold under-panel has a sweetheart neckline and is strapless, and the black lace overlay has a rounded horseshoe neckline and long, set-in, dropped lace sleeves that are gathered and frilled at the cuff. The bodice of gown includes a loose rectangular cape that is attached at the shoulder seam, and the waist is cinched with an elasticated black belt that includes a gold-plated butterfly. The gold underskirt is knee-length with the black lace overlay hemmed underneath to create the illusion of a train at the back.

During her first dinner with Bond, Magda wears a Westernized two-piece sari made from a mauve-coloured brocade silk created by Bermans and Nathans, underneath which she wears a purple silk bikini. The sari top is sleeveless with a sweetheart neckline and is cut underneath the bust with an elasticated hem, fastened with two hook-and-eye clasps at the front between the centre-front frame. The skirt, made from the same brocade silk with a chiffon overlay, is fitted and has silver sparkle detailing and a patterned silver hem. The chiffon shawl is wrapped over the hips and continues over Magda's shoulders; it also includes a silver key-hole patterning on the hem. Magda later uses the chiffon shawl to escape from Bond's hotel suite: Magda ties the 'tail' of the sari to the top balcony railing before she 'flips forward over the top rail'.[51] The sari unravels to reveal the bikini worn beneath as Magda reaches the ground. Porteous explained that she visited Southall in London, 'the most incredible place' to source fabrics for the Indian costumes: 'I found all my Indian jewellery there, wonderful silks and things.'[52] Porteous particularly enjoyed designing the Indian costumes: 'I can't tell you what fun it's been, everywhere there is cleavage and legs to show off, and Indian fabrics are just wonderful.' While she had fun dressing the supporting cast in brocade bikinis, both

Adams and Wayborn had to get used to performing in saris, though 'once they got the hang of it they seemed to enjoy themselves'.[53]

Porteous notes on her design for Magda's circus costume that it is a 'black sequin tail-coat, "diamante" waistcoat, + band on black silk top hat. Diamante bow-tie'.[54] On both sides of the tailcoat, Porteous has painted a white floral fastening at the base of the notched lapels. Both the shawl-lapelled waistcoat that is fastened with buttons and the bowtie are painted in a textured white gouache to depict diamante crystals, and the hatband is painted to appear as though a string of pearls. Underneath the waistcoat, Magda is depicted as wearing a black leotard and black fishnet stockings. Porteous explained that, as with the Indian costumes, she very much enjoyed the scope allowed to be creative for the circus scenes, which 'was unbelievable' and 'great fun' to do.[55] For inspiration, Porteous visited a circus that was held at Chessington Zoo along with Broccoli and other members of the crew.

A View to a Kill (1985)

The title of Moore's final Bond film was borrowed from the title of Fleming's short story 'From A View to a Kill', however it did not use any elements of the author's work. Glen returned to direct *A View to a Kill*, and principal photography started on 1 August 1984, budgeted at $30 million (£23 million). Renate Wienert was employed as the wardrobe supervisor. Unlike previous Bond films, with Bermans and Nathans employed to realize the bulk of the costumes, C & G Costumers were employed instead. The since-dissolved company went onto work with Porteous to realize the costumes for *Aliens* (1986).

During the pre-title sequence, Bond wears a white hooded ski suit designed by Willy Bognor including matching jacket, trousers and gloves for camouflage among the snow. On Bond's return to London, he wears a three-piece charcoal grey mohair suit, named in the script as a 'business suit'.[56] Underneath the jacket, Bond wears a matching waistcoat over a shirt with a white collar and pink and white dress stripes on the body, fastened with a red satin-silk tie. On being told by M (Robert Brown) 'you have exactly thirty-five minutes to get properly dressed, Double-O-Seven' for Ascot, Bond changes into a mid-grey herringbone morning suit, consisting of tailcoat, waistcoat and trousers. The tailcoat has natural shoulders with roped sleeve-heads and peaked lapels. Bond wears a white shirt underneath the waistcoat and a satin-silk tie that has a grey and white diamond pattern formed in a harlequin check. A light grey felt top hat with a black grosgrain ribbon is worn with the suit, as are a pair of grey gloves, and Bond wears a white carnation in the lapel buttonhole. On visiting Paris, Bond wears a midnight blue worsted dinner suit, underneath which he wears a white shirt that is fastened with a black silk bowtie. The jacket is double-breasted with black, satin-faced peaked lapels.

When Bond poses as James St-John Smith (pronounced 'Smythe'), he wears a light grey single-breasted twill-weave blazer and dark grey gaberdine trousers. It is tailored in a more exaggerated style to reflect that Bond is undercover. The blazer has natural padded shoulders with strong roped sleeve-heads and a notched lapel with distinctive stitching around the edges. Underneath the jacket, Bond wears a pale blue shirt with mitered gauntlet cuffs and a pointed spread collar, fastened with a black satin-silk tie that has Argyle tartan stripes in red and white. Later, Bond wears an ivory silk dinner jacket with black trousers. The jacket has notched lapels, a welt pocket, jetted hip pockets and double vents. It is fastened with one button and there are three buttons on the sleeve cuffs, all of which are made from brown horn. The white shirt has a pleated placket with mother-of-pearl buttons, fastened with a black silk bowtie.

On infiltrating Max Zorin's (Christopher Walken) laboratory, Bond wears a midnight blue velour tracksuit with matching jacket and trousers that were sourced from FILA. The jacket has a white piping trim on the stand-away crew collar at the neck, two welted hip pockets, the neckline darts, outside sleeve seam, shoulder dart and armhole seam. The following morning, Bond wears a single-breasted dark blue blazer with light grey gaberdine trousers. Beneath the blazer, Bond wears a white shirt that is worn unfastened to reveal a burgundy silk cravat. Zorin challenges Bond to a steeplechase, and the latter changes into a brown tweed riding jacket with a natural shoulder and notched lapels. With the jacket, Bond wears an off-white shirt that is fastened with a yellow knitted wool tie, and fitted dark brown jodhpurs with matching leather riding boots. Bond has a brown leather riding crop and a tan brown crushed velvet riding hat.

When in San Francisco, Bond wears a mid-grey suede blouson jacket that is fastened with a centre-front zip and decorated with 'perforated panels' on the front and back of the jacket coat and the inside of the sleeves, and lined with black art silk. The blouson was sourced from Leather Concessionaires, who notably provided Indiana Jones's (Harrison Ford) leather jackets for *Raiders of the Lost Ark* (1981) and *Indiana Jones and the Temple of Doom* (1984). With the jacket, Bond wears loose fitting grey worsted trousers with reverse pleats and a straight leg. After wearing a black wetsuit and a black silk Chinese dressing gown with a shawl collar and a dragon motif embroidered over the right breast, Bond wears a tan gaberdine suit when meeting Stacey Sutton (Tanya Roberts). Beneath the jacket, Bond wears a white shirt that is fastened with a satin-silk tie with a bronze base and diagonal grey and blue combined stripes. During the San Francisco City Hall scenes, Bond is costumed in a brown leather blouson jacket with a rounded Nehru collar and an extended tab button fastening that is worn unfastened. Bond wears a pale blue shirt with a pointed button-down collar that is worn unfastened beneath the jacket, and brown flannel trousers. Bond later switches the leather blouson for a grey Zorin Industries cotton-nylon blend blouson to infiltrate the mine which Bond continues to wear in the final scenes of the film.

Zorin, the film's lead villain, was originally written with David Bowie in mind. As Grace Jones put it, this was because 'they were chasing fashion and looking to reach a wider audience by involving more pop and rock [. . .] they definitely wanted this to be a rock 'n' roll MTV Bond'.[57] Bowie turned the role down, and Walken was subsequently cast. The actor enjoyed working on the production: 'The film was very well made. The sets, the costumes, there was a lot of very good workmanship on those movies'.[58] In the script, Zorin is described as 'tall, slender, impeccably dressed, in his late thirties. Unusually handsome he has one grey eye and one blue eye,' referring to Bowie.[59] Jones believes that Walken was 'styled in the film to be a very Thin White Duke Bowie – lean, mean, blond, and suavely narcissistic'.[60] As part of Zorin's characterization, his costume always includes a silk pocket square in the breast pocket of his jackets. At Ascot, Zorin first wears a charcoal grey morning suit that, as with Bond's, consists of tailcoat, waistcoat and trousers. The tailcoat has slim, straight and padded shoulders with roped sleeve-heads. It includes peaked lapels, and is fastened with one button at the waist seam that emphasizes Walken's physique. Zorin also wears a white carnation in the lapel buttonhole, mirroring Bond. The waistcoat is fastened with six buttons, and the trousers are slim-fitting with a flat front and plain hems. Underneath the waistcoat, Zorin wears a white shirt with a wing-tab collar that is fastened with a mauve-grey woven silk cravat. Zorin wears a light grey felt top hat with black grosgrain ribbon.

At his stud farm, Zorin wears a grey wool blazer with a speckled weave and dark grey gaberdine trousers. The blazer has wide, natural shoulders and roped sleeve-heads, notched lapels and a Barchetta curved welt pocket that holds a puffed navy silk pocket square. It is fastened with two buttons and has a single back vent. Underneath the blazer, Zorin wears a white shirt with a spread collar that is fastened with a silk navy tie that matches the pocket square. During the evening, Zorin wears a black double-breasted dinner suit to contrast with Bond's ivory single-breasted version. The jacket has straight, padded shoulders, satin-faced peak lapels, a welt pocket with a navy silk puffed pocket square, a four-button fastening and double vents. The white shirt worn beneath the jacket is fastened with a black satin bowtie. After wearing a black judo outfit, Zorin wears a light grey silk dupioni single-breasted suit, of which the jacket's coat is cut long, and is slim-fitting with narrow shoulders and a suppressed waist. It has slim notched lapels and a welt pocket with a peaked navy silk pocket square. Zorin wears a pale blue shirt with a button-down spread collar that is fastened with a navy silk tie with alternating diagonal stripes in blue and yellow.

Zorin wears an all-black riding outfit for the steeplechase, of which the jacket is similarly cut to his previous suit in that it has a long coat with slim shoulders and a suppressed waist. It has notched lapels with a high gorge, a welt pocket with a peaked burgundy silk pocket square, a widely spaced three-button fastening set at a high stance, a single vent, and is lined with burgundy art silk. Zorin wears a white shirt with a pointed spread collar fastened with a black satin-silk tie beneath the jacket, and fitted black jodhpurs worn with matching leather riding boots. His riding hat is covered with black crushed velvet. After this, Zorin changes into a dark navy two-piece suit made from silk dupioni. The jacket is single-breasted, with natural soft shoulders and notched lapels, and its breast pocket includes a peaked burgundy silk pocket square. Underneath the jacket, Zorin wears a white shirt with a pointed collar that is fastened with a burgundy silk tie to match the pocket square. Aboard his airship, Zorin wears a mid-grey two-piece suit, including a double-breasted jacket with peaked lapels, wide natural shoulders, with the same pocket square as the previous suit. Beneath the jacket, Zorin wears a beige shirt with white butcher stripes that is fastened with the burgundy tie. In San Francisco City Hall, Zorin wears a light grey dupioni silk two-piece suit. The patch pocket on the breast includes a square-folded maroon silk pocket square. Underneath the jacket, Zorin wears a white shirt with grey shadow stripes and is fastened with a red silk tie. In the final scenes of the film, Zorin wears a navy double-breasted blazer and light grey flannel trousers. Beneath the blazer, Zorin wears a white shirt that is fastened with a satin-silk tie that has a navy base with diagonal light blue stripes.

Stacey Sutton, the good 'Bond girl', first appears at Zorin's stud farm and the script describes her as 'unusually beautiful and smartly dressed in her early thirties'.[61] In these scenes, Sutton wears a cream silk peplum-style jacket and matching trousers. The jacket has natural shoulders with shawl lapels which is worn unfastened. It has full-length sleeves with a padded sleeve cap and plain cuffs fastened with one button. Underneath the jacket, Sutton wears a black Lycra jersey top that is fitted and has a low V-shaped crew neckline. During the evening, Sutton wears a full-length silver silk gown with a rainbow-coloured crimped chiffon overlay. The chiffon overlay is made from the pastel colours of white, lilac and blue, and the bodice has four spaghetti shoulder straps, two on the shoulder and two placed off-shoulder, with a scoop neckline that is ruched over the front and back panels. The gown has a natural waistline that is emphasized by a belt, and the waist seam is pleated to create a chiffon train that gathers towards the back. The fitted silver silk skirt is cut on the bias. On infiltrating San Francisco City Hall with Bond, Sutton wears another white silk peplum jacket with a low V-shaped crew neckline, straight, wide and padded shoulders and set-in angel sleeves that have turn-up cuffs fastened with one gold button. It is seamed at the hip to create a gathered flare, and cinched at the waist with a gold belt. The jacket is paired with a white silk circular A-line skirt that is cut at the bias and hemmed at the knee to create a fit-and-flare silhouette. This outfit would later be worn underneath Stacey's cod costume of Zorin Industry coveralls, however it differs from the script's description of her costume: 'May Day has [Stacey] by the coveralls. Stacey struggles, unzips coveralls and squirms out of them. She is now dressed in the short, lightweight summer dress that she started the evening in. May Day throws the coveralls away in disgust.'[62]

The most distinctive costumes in *A View to a Kill* are afforded to May Day (Grace Jones), the bad 'Bond girl'. Jones developed a passion for crochet and sewing her own wardrobe from an early age, and became inspired by the fashion choices of the Supremes, recreating versions of their style by sewing in her mother's basement, 'using the same Butterick and *Vogue* patterns they would use when they started and had no money. I would cut up old dresses and make new ones from the material.'[63] There are consistent reports that Jones was approached for the role of Octopussy, however according to Jones 'there was some anxiety about having a black woman as a villain. A Bond movie is, for all the appearance of sex and violence, a fundamentally very conservative franchise.'[64] Jones was later offered the part of May Day, and agreed owing to her regret of turning down the role of Zohra in *Blade Runner* (1982). For May Day's costumes, Jones was heavily involved in the design stage of the process, more so than previous women cast in the Bond films:

I knew what I wanted, how I was going to look as a 'Bond girl'. [...] I looked at Disney colours, because I figure being a 'Bond girl' was like being in a cartoon [...] I took in tips I had learned from Issey [Miyake] and Kenzo, and had direct input from one of my other designers who became a friend, Azzadine Alaïa.[65]

Jones particularly praised the Parisian designer's clothes for 'making me look masculine and feminine at the same time'.[66] She also 'tried to create a silhouette for May Day', believing that: 'A silhouette is very important,' a belief shared with Alaïa.[67] Porteous concurs:

All her costumes were extraordinary because she's a very extraordinary woman. A lot of them were based on her own sort of clothes and there is no way in the world you can force her into something she doesn't like because she has very, very strong views on how she should look. So you've got to work very closely with her.[68]

On the realized costumes, Porteous was particularly pleased, believing: 'She was fun, not difficult really. Once you've got Grace into something right she looks amazing.' Jones wanted her costumes to use leather, as Porteous explained: 'She loves tight trousers, leather trousers, suede trousers, and leather and suede jackets.' Due to the action that May Day was involved in, Porteous had to ensure that the clothes would not only look good on Jones, but also work around the stuntmen needing to perform in them, therefore 'you can't always design things which are sleeveless or strapless. You've got to accommodate.'

As a designer, Alaïa was recognized as being particularly 'body conscious' when considering fit and image, with *Vogue* celebrating: 'What he did first – and does better than anybody else – is a special kind of total body-focussed dressing. [...] The key: the fabrics, the built-in shape, the distinctive seaming ... and the extra sizzle he gives everything.'[69] In order to create his innovative clothes, Catherine Patch explained that the designer 'uses cuts and zippers – often curved – instead of darts, folds, pleats and other traditional ways of shaping garments to the body. [...] Alaïa's clothes are unadorned and minimally detailed. He uses no accessories and the lines of his clothes are generally clean and simple.'[70] This approach dominates May Day's costumes. The character first appears in the Ascot scenes wearing a fitted scarlet silk jersey gown with an asymmetric neckline to accentuate Jones's figure (Plate 9). The sleeveless gown is backless, with the pencil skirt hemmed at the knee, and cinched at the waist with a black patent leather belt that includes a flat bow detail at the centre. There is a cowl attached to the neckline of the gown to create a variant of a halter-neck. The cowl is a signature look worn by May Day in the film, and its colour always dictates the colour accent of the character's eyeshadow, with the exception of May Day's final scenes. The most distinctive part of the costume is the hat, which is structured to be a combination of a high-top hat, known as a 'stove pipe', and a fez, made from black satin that includes a floating black tassel on the top and a scarlet knee-length one-tiered veil cut the same length as the gown. The draped veil is split on both sides and worn short at the front. Hanging sleeves are formed within the veil's interior, and May Day wears black patent leather opera gloves with a three-button fastening at the wrist through the arms of the sleeves.

At Zorin's stud farm, May Day wears a maroon purple silk jersey and Lycra body-line gown. In keeping with the previous costume, this floor-length gown is also backless and is cut in a deep scoop to reveal the Jones's spine crevice, and finishes in a small train at the back. Two long fabric strips are stitched onto the back yoke to form a stylish back cowl. The harlequin cowl includes a scarlet lining, and is attached to the shoulder which is padded and cut straight, with long leg of mutton sleeves that have a padded sleeve cap and taper in towards the wrists. In the scenes between May Day and Zorin later that evening, May Day wears a fitted black cotton Lycra leotard, cut small, with a scoop neckline and high-cut thigh. It is worn with matching over-the-elbow arm and knee-high leg warmers, the latter of which are covered with cutaway leather boots with four buckles stitched on the outside seams. May Day later covers her leotard with a stylized mink-coloured thick towelling dressing gown that has wide turn-up cuffs on the flared in-set sleeves, a matching sash belt tied at the waist and a wide shawl collar. It has a cowl hood attached that May Day later wears over her hair. For the first and only time in a Bond film to date, May Day has sexual intercourse with Bond who does not intend to or succeed in ideologically realigning her, but rather to offer a plausible explanation as to why he was not in his suite. During the steeplechase between Bond and Zorin, May Day wears the first of her distinctive leather outfits; a black jacket and a pair of tight-fitting trousers created by Lawrence Easden (Figure 8.2). The jacket has padded shoulders and leg of mutton sleeves, which include silver studs across the puffed sleeve cap and lattice work detail on the back, finishing in gauntlet cuffs. It is fastened with a centre-front zip and has a high, fitted waist that

FIGURE 8.2 May Day's leather outfit produced by Lawrence Easden. *A View to a Kill* directed by John Glen © Eon Productions/MGM/United Artists 1985. All rights reserved.

includes three leather-covered buttons placed asymmetrically for detail. Underneath the jacket, May Day wears a variant of the previous cowls: this version includes a harlequin two-tone chiffon hood made of black and gold.

In Zorin's airship, May Day dresses in one of her few outfits that does not include a hood or cowl: a charcoal grey mohair two-piece suit, including a jacket and a fitted knee-length pencil skirt, that has light grey chalk stripes. The jacket has wide-cut notched lapels, rounded and extremely padded shoulders, loose sleeves that taper towards the wrist with fitted cuffs, and a one-button asymmetric fastening. The jacket has a cinched waist which is structured by a hidden internal belt in order to emphasize an asymmetrically flared skirt. It includes two jetted pockets on the hips. For May Day's final scenes in the film set in Zorin's mines, the character is costumed in a stylized version of the uniform worn by the other employees. May Day wears a duotone cowl attached to a twisted four-knot bolero made from Lycra jersey material in utilitarian slate grey and heather colours. The jacket has padded shoulders and in-set fitted sleeves. Under the jacket, May Day wears a matching fitted shift dress made from silk jersey that is sleeveless as well as backless, with V-shaped backstraps stitched from the shoulder to above the hip. It has a boat neckline and is cinched at the waist with a black leather belt and hemmed at the thigh. With the outfit, May Day wears ruched black leather thigh-high boots.

The critical reception for *A View to a Kill* particularly praised Jones's visual style and costumes. 'Jagr' of *Variety* remarked that: 'Grace Jones is a successful updating of the Jaws-type villain. Jones just oozes '80s style and gets to parade in a number of sensational costumes giving a hard but alluring edge to her character.'[1] Janet Maslin believed that 'Miss Jones doesn't do much with her dialogue, but her startling visual presence is one of the film's bigger assets', with Bill Hagen concurring that 'as is customary, there's no stinting on locations or costumes in a Bond movie, and certainly not in *A View to a Kill*', and that Jones 'is sensuous and wicked in the tradition of Bond's bad girls'.[72] Alan Karp argues that Jones 'really steals the show. An astonishing physical presence [...] it's Jones who's primarily responsible for providing the film with some much needed pizzazz'.[73] Similarly, Sean Usher perceived the character to be the saving grace of *A View to a Kill*, who is 'all teeth and androgynous muscle as the master criminal's hit person'.[74]

Notes

1   'Douglas Hayward', *Daily Telegraph*, 30 April 2008, 21.

2   Polly Westmacott-Hayward, interview with the author, 7 November 2019. All quotations from Westmacott-Hayward that are included in the monograph were taken from this interview.

3   Glenys Roberts, interview with the author, 8 November 2019. All quotations from Roberts that are included in the monograph were taken from this interview.

4   'Douglas Hayward'.

5   Ibid.

6   Dylan Jones, 'Bespoke Buddha', *The Sunday Times*, 19 April 1998, 420.

7   'Douglas Hayward'.

8   Veronica Horwell, 'Doug Hayward: Working class actor to the stars', *Guardian*, 3 May 2008, www.theguardian.com/lifeandstyle/2008/may/03/fashion.mainsection (accessed 23 July 2020).

9   Del Smith.

10 Jones, 420.

11 Moore with Owen, *Bond on Bond*, 125.

12 Spaiser, 'Basted for Bond: Examining Roger Moore's Douglas Hayward clothes', *The Suits of James Bond*, 28 August 2015, www.bondsuits.com/basted-for-bond-examining-roger-moores-douglas-hayward-clothes/ (accessed 23 July 2020).

13 Jones.

14 Spaiser, 'Double-breasted blazer in Corfu in *For Your Eyes Only*', *The Suits of James Bond*, 28 March 2011, www.bondsuits.com/double-breasted-blazer-corfu-for-your-eyes-only/ (accessed 24 July 2020).

15 Winefried Jackson, 'A close shave for Queen Bess', *Sunday Telegraph*, 21 February 1971, 9.

16 Ibid.

17 Richard Maibaum and Michael G. Wilson, *For Your Eyes Only*, screenplay, 12 August 1980, 104.

18 Ibid., 218.

19 Ibid., 65.

20 Fleming, *For Your Eyes Only* (1960; London: Penguin Books, 2009), 75, 76.

21 Ibid., 77, 82.

22 Maibaum and Wilson, 11.

23 'Pierrette's London Causerie', *Illustrated Sporting and Dramatic News*, 10 June 1953, 8.

24 Maibaum and Wilson, 62.

25 Field and Chowdhury, *Some Kind of Hero*, 329.

26 Maibaum and Wilson, 32.

27 Field and Chowdhury, 329.

28 David Richardson, 'Emma Porteous, Costumes: *1999*', *TV Zone*, 'Supervillains Special' (No. 9, June 1993), 9.

29 Harper, *Women in British Cinema*, 218.

30 Ibid.

31 Howard Maxford, 'A stitch in time: A *Starburst* interview with Emma Porteous, *Starburst Yearbook* 26 (1995), 61.

32 Richardson, 13.

33 Ibid., 11.

34 Alan Fox and Stephen Payne, 'It was great fun to do! Part 1: Bond *A View to a Kill* and *Octopussy*', *Starburst* 88 (1985), 18.

35 Richard Maibaum and Michael G. Wilson, *Octopussy*, screenplay, 10 June 1982, 1.

36 Ibid.

37 Ibid., revised 6 August 1982, 30.

38 Ibid., 35.

39 Ibid., 41.

40 Ibid., revised 6 August 1982, 56.

41 BFI, Emma Porteous Collection, SPD-2393408: Emma Porteous, '*Octopussy*: Twins 1 & 2/Knife throwers/Practice costume', 1982.

42 Maibaum and Wilson, 11.

43 Ibid., 11.

44 Field and Chowdhury, 344.

45 Maibaum and Wilson, revised 6 August 1982, 25.

46 Ibid., 28.

47 The Newsroom, 'Del's tribute to Roger Moore after becoming 007's turban tier', *Peterborough Telegraph*, 26 May 2017, www.peterboroughtoday.co.uk/news/dels-tribute-roger-moore-after-becoming-007s-turban-tier-1117910 (accessed 3 August 2020).

48 Maibaum and Wilson, revised 6 August 1982, 24, 25.

49 Prop Store, 'Lot #412 – James Bond: *Octopussy* (1983)', 30 September 2019, https://propstoreauction.com/view-auctions/catalog/id/169/lot/47036/ (accessed 2 August 2020).

50 Maibaum and Wilson, 36.

51 Ibid., revised 13 August 1982, 53.

52 Fox and Payne, 18.

53 Sunil Sethi, '*Octopussy*: James Bond comes to Udaipur', *India Today*, 31 October 1982, www.indiatoday.in/magazine/society-the-arts/films/story/19821031-octopussy-james-bond-comes-to-udaipur-772309-2013-07-31 (accessed 6 August 2020).

54 BFI, SPD-2393408: Emma Porteous, '*Octopussy*: Magda (in circus costume)', 1982.

55 Fox and Payne, 18.

56 Maibaum and Wilson, *A View to a Kill*, first draft screenplay, 20 June 1984, revised 13 July 1984, 8.

57 Grace Jones with Paul Morley, *I'll Never Write my Memoirs* (London and New York: Simon & Schuster, 2015), 273.

58 Field and Chowdhury, 391.

59 Maibaum and Wilson, revised 13 July 1984, 12.

60 Jones with Morley, 275.

61 Maibaum and Wilson, revised 13 July 1984, 36.

62 Ibid., revised 20 July 1984, 129.

63 Jones with Morley, 52.

64 Ibid., 273.

65 Ibid., 276.

66 Lesley Nonkin, 'Talking fashion: Azzedine addicts', *Vogue*, 1 November 1988, 452.

67 Linton Mitchell, 'Grace Jones – an exotic enemy who is really very sweet', *Reading Evening Post*, 24 June 1985, 8.

68 Fox and Payne, 15.

69 'Fashion: Nobody's better . . . the all-shape dressing of Azzedine Alaïa', *Vogue*, 1 March 1985, 490.

70 Catherine Patch, 'Innovative Alaïa clings to tight look', *Toronto Star*, 10 April 1986, C8.

71 'Jagr', '*A View to a Kill*', *Variety*, 22 May 1985, 36.

72 Janet Maslin, 'The Screen: James Bond', *New York Times*, 24 May 1985, C10; Bill Hagen, '*View to a Kill*: Bond no longer grade-A in movie market', *San Diego Union Tribune*, 28 May 1985, C7.

73 Alan Karp, '*A View to a Kill*', *Box Office*, 1 December 1985, 17.

74 Shawn Usher, 'Renewing that trusty licence to thrill', *Daily Mail*, 13 June 1985, 3.

9 LICENCE TO TAILOR REVOKED: TIMOTHY DALTON (1987–89)

In September 1985, Maibaum and Wilson began to work on the script for *The Living Daylights*. It was during this period that Moore announced he would not be returning as Bond. Therefore, Barbara Broccoli, working on *The Living Daylights* as an associate producer, travelled to Australia in order to talent scout potential actors. Lambert Wilson and Sam Neill were subsequently tested, the former being favoured by Cubby Broccoli, the latter the choice of Wilson, Barbara Broccoli and John Glen, who was to direct the film. Pierce Brosnan was seriously considered for the role by the production team, however owing to his contract with NBC over *Remington Steele* (1982–87), he could not be released in time for the production of *The Living Daylights*. It was Dana Broccoli who suggested Timothy Dalton. Dalton proved his appropriateness for the role during his tests, and he was announced as the next Bond on 6 August 1986. The budget for the film was $34 million (£22 million).

The Living Daylights (1987)

Wanting to embody Fleming's characterization of Bond, Dalton desired to move away from Moore's portrayal in order to make the character his own. This included Bond's attire, with Dalton stating: 'His suits were made of serge, quite rightly, because he'd have to fight, run, jump; he had them tailored in Savile Row, but they weren't made from expensive cloth. You got that sense quite powerfully in the early movies; it was only as their scope and size developed that they became, quite suddenly, a fashion parade.'[1] This is not a strictly accurate interpretation of Fleming's Bond besides the character not wearing Savile Row suits: in *Dr. No*, Major Boothroyd states in relation to Bond's .25 Beretta and holster: 'I think we can do better than this, sir,' which Bond associates with 'the sort of voice Bond's first expensive tailor had used'.[2] According to Glen, Dalton's engagement with the costumes began in the very first wardrobe consultation, and 'when Bond wasn't wearing the obligatory tux, [Dalton] wanted a more casual look, perhaps more in keeping with the times', specifically requesting a leather jacket.[3] It is therefore ironic that although Dalton wanted a more 'casual' look for his Bond, the actor would be costumed in three different dinner suits in *The Living Daylights*. However, Dalton stated: 'This Bond may wear a black dinner jacket but he prefers off-the-peg clothes from Bond Street or King's Road', and according to Geoffrey Aquilina Ross, Dalton refused 'to change outfits for every scene as if in a fashion parade, as Moore did'.[4] Emma Porteous, returning as the costume designer for *The Living Daylights*, confirmed: 'Dalton has chosen dark colours and wears only white shirts. If he puts on a tie there is no noticeable pattern. He wants all his clothes cut fashionably big and loose.'[5] Twelve copies of each suit were made for the stuntmen to wear.

For the 'obligatory' dinner suits, all made from black fabric, Dalton wore two that were created by Bermans and Nathans, and one that was tailored by the luxury fashion house Lambert Hofer, based in Austria. The first dinner suit, worn in the scene at the beginning of the film when Bond meets Saunders in a concert hall in Bratislava, Czechoslovakia, was actually created for Dalton to wear in the film *Brenda Starr* (1986), produced immediately before *The Living Daylights*. The Bermans and Nathans label stitched on the jacket collar indicates that it is 'costume 3' for 'Brenda Star [sic]', made in colour '4926'.[6] The jacket has a wide, satin-faced shawl collar, a one-button fastening, jetted pockets and no vent. The trousers include double-reverse pleats and a black silk stripe. The suit is worn with a white dress shirt with narrow pleats and a black satin-silk bowtie. Dalton also wears white clip-on braces, the first Bond to do so in an Eon Productions film. The reason for Dalton wearing a dinner suit created for another film is likely because this scene was changed during the production of the film: in the draft screenplay, Bond meets Saunders in a book store, not a concert hall, and the script directs that Bond is 'dressed as a tourist' as opposed to in evening dress.[7] Because of this, the line delivered by Saunders to Bond on the latter's arrival to the hall, 'You're bloody late. This is a mission, not a fancy-dress ball', offers a double entendre and a sly recognition of the dinner suit having been produced for *Brenda Starr*. The wearing of the *Brenda Starr* dinner suit in the concert hall scene, which is shortly followed by Bond's aborted assassination attempt on Kara Milovy (Maryam d'Abo), necessitated that a cod costume be created: when Dalton uses his jacket to cover his shirt, he appears dressed in all black for the assassination attempt. Bond's second dinner suit in the film, worn to the opera house in Vienna, was made for *The Living Daylights* by Bermans and Nathans. This version is different in that it has satin-trimmed notched lapels and heavily padded shoulders, and the trousers have wide-tapered legs. At the end of the film, Bond very briefly wears the Lambert Hofer dinner suit. It is made of worsted, and is a rare example of Dalton reflecting Moore's

Bond's fashion choices in the wearing of a double-breasted dinner suit: Moore wore four, in *The Man with the Golden Gun*, *The Spy Who Loved Me*, *Moonraker* and *A View to a Kill*. Dalton's Lambert Hofer version is trimmed with black satin lapels, has double vents, flapped hip pockets, and a claret-coloured art silk lining.

The majority of the other suits Dalton wears in *The Living Daylights* were sourced by Porteous from Benjamin Simon and Sons Limited, a wholesale clothiers and men's tailoring firm based in Leeds, which is the only tailoring firm based in the UK outside of London that has been employed to provide Bond's suits in an Eon Productions film. It has been speculated by Nick Sullivan that Dalton's suits were selected from ready-to-wear ranges, in keeping with Dalton's request.[8] If so, an off-the-peg two-piece wool suit from Benjamin Simon would cost around £115 at the time the film was produced. In order of appearance, the Benjamin Simon suits included a black and grey herringbone three-piece suit, a 'gun club' sports jacket with a black, brown, blue and green twill-woven check pattern that is worn with dark brown flannel trousers, and a fawn gaberdine suit. The similarities between these suits in terms of structure are that the jackets all have straight and heavily padded shoulders that extend beyond Dalton's natural shoulder, as well as straight, flapped hip pockets and double vents. The trousers all have double-forward pleats and full tapered legs. The 'Midas touch' of Bond did not work for Benjamin Simon, as it did not with other firms on previous occasions: three years after the release of the film, the company went bankrupt.

Two further suits worn by Dalton were sourced from Ralph Lauren and Paul Smith. The Ralph Lauren three-piece suit is worn by Bond in the first London-based scenes. It is made of worsted navy with a chalk stripe pattern. The jacket has wide shoulders, flapped pockets and double vents, and the trousers have forward pleats and plain-hemmed bottoms. The waistcoat is unusual in that it fastens with seven buttons, which work to complement Dalton's tall and athletic figure. On Bond's return to Bratislava, he wears a medium-grey flannel suit sourced from Paul Smith. The jacket is distinctive in that it is narrow and soft-shouldered unlike Bond's other suits. The suit is worn beneath a full-length, navy cashmere overcoat. Anecdotally, Glen revealed that Dalton wasn't a 'man that liked suits with too many pads in them – he likes something that feels comfortable', and recalled: 'In fact, on a couple of occasions, he was known to rip pads out of suits if you weren't careful, and having just spent £1,000 on a suit, you don't want the pads being pulled out of it.'[9] Glen is likely referring to the Ralph Lauren three-piece suit.

Three of Bond's other costumes in the film are more casual, in keeping with Dalton's request. The black leather jacket was created by Kenzo. It is three-quarters in length, with a concealed zip and button fastening and angled slash zipper pockets on the chest. Underneath the jacket, Bond wears a light beige cloth shirt and a knitted dark grey crew-neck jumper made of Shetland wool. The charcoal grey woollen flannel trousers are narrow with a plain hem. The second casual outfit is worn by Bond in Tangier. It includes a beige blouson with set-in sleeves and slashed side pockets. This is worn with a dark blue knitted shirt and tan-coloured cotton chinos. When Bond dresses in disguise as a Mujahideen soldier in the latter half of the film, he is dressed in a pale grey cotton shirt and pale grey harem-style loose trousers, fastened with a black and grey striped knitted belt. Over the shirt Bond wears a medium brown and suitably scuffed leather waistcoat. He wears a dark grey turban on his head with a distinctive light grey stripe pattern to match the belt. This costume was created by Bermans and Nathans. Black leather ankle combat boots, fastened with laces, are worn by Bond during these scenes. A full close-up of the boots is afforded later in the film when Bond fights Necros (Andreas Wisniewski); the boots become significant when Bond is able to cut the laces in order to let the latter drop to his death.

For the rest of the cast playing the Mujahideen soldiers, the authentic costume items were sourced by Harriet Sandys who owned the London-based shop Out of the Nomads Tent. The collaboration reportedly came about when Sandys was purchasing items in Peshawar in the Khyber Pass, and met a 'young photographer' who explained that Broccoli was 'having issues' with some of the costumes. After returning to London, Sandys was persuaded by Tiny Nicholls to help find appropriate Afghan clothing for the film and was offered a payment of £1,000 for her assistance. The brief was to find items for a band of drug smugglers, a Mujahideen Commander and his 200 men, 100 women and children, forty horses, twenty camels and Kara, the brief for her costume being 'sexy, see-through and easy-to-slip-out-of'.[10] Provided with £12,000 out of the film's costume budget, Sandys, with the help of her contact, Gul Mohammed, a Kabuli rug merchant, sourced costumes for the animals, including *Turkoman* saddle cloths for the horses and *Baluchi* camel headdresses studded with cowrie shells and mother-of-pearl. In the medieval area of Qissa Khwani Bazaar, Peshawar, Sandys sourced the men's black and white striped turbans and a shirt 'richly embroidered with traditional Kandahar *khamak* stitching' (one of three traditional Afghanistan embroidery patterns, the others being *kochi* and *uzbaki*) for Kamran Shah (Art Malik) to wear. For the bulk of the costumes needed for the scenes set in Afghanistan, two local charities were commissioned to produce items of clothing from 1,500 metres of camouflage and sand-coloured cotton.

For the female lead, Kara, Handys sourced a 'flamboyant' *shalwar kameez* of apple green and cherry pink colours, covered in embroidery and made from Japanese polyester.[11] This costume would not be used in the film, and instead Kara would be costumed in a pale blue silk *shalwar kameez* ('costume 8') made by Bermans and Nathans and more in keeping with the colour palette of the set design. The costume included silver and white threads embroidered in a geometric floral pattern on the chest and the sleeves of the tunic, and was worn with a chiffon turquoise scarf.

Along with the *shalwar kameez*, Porteous designed a further eight costumes for Kara. Glen requested to Porteous that the costumes worn by the character needed to be designed with the position of Kara's legs in mind as she was a cellist.[12] Therefore, costumes one, two, five and nine were designed to accommodate this. 'Costume 1' is a boat-necked black dress with a slim bodice, three-quarter length fitted sleeves and a full, pleated A-line skirt. 'Costume 2' is a sheer silk white turtleneck blouse and a long black woollen pleated skirt, which Kara wears mainly under a full-length pale grey trench coat that has wide, notched lapels, padded shoulders, and a long back vent. 'Costume 5' is a full-length dressing gown, described by Porteous on her costume design as being made from 'pale blue/grey silk', and includes a shawl collar in contrasting white silk. The full skirt of the gown has a circular cut so that it provides even drapes flowing out towards the ground, and has a deep slit in the side panel.[13] 'Costume 9' is a long-sleeved, full-length, silk gown in a salmon pink colour. As with 'Costume 1', it is similar in that it has a boat neckline and a full, pleated A-line skirt, but is made of a finer quality of fabric, reflecting Kara's position as a soloist on her world tour.

For 'Costume 3', Kara dresses in a dove cotton ski jacket with detachable sleeves and an imitation fur collar which was sourced from FILA. Underneath, she wears a white polo-neck jumper and black cotton trousers. 'Costume 4' is Kara's most significant in the film, and Porteous took her inspiration directly from the script, in the scenes after Kara and Bond arrive at the Im Palais Schwarzenberg hotel:

357. LOBBY DRESS SHOP. KARA
looks at exquisite evening dress in showcase.

                    BOND
          Like it?

                    KARA
          For a princess or wife of Commissar.

                    BOND
          Let's buy it.

                    KARA
          Don't joke. Who will pay?

                    BOND
          Georgi, of course.

She brightens. They enter shop.[14]

In her costume design, Porteous describes the gown as a: 'Deep blue silk jersey dress [with a] crystal embroidered belt.'[15] The costume was realized by Lawrence Easden who produced May Day's leather outfits in *A View to a Kill*. It has a halter-necked body with a beaded tassel attached to the neck and a matching wrap-around skirt including a waistband of geometric 'Greek-key' patterned beadwork in clear glass and blue beads (Plate 10). Worn over the dress is an 'Opera-style' coat made of midnight blue velvet, of which the cuffs are embroidered with corresponding beadwork to the waistband of the dress, and the body of the coat includes clear glass and blue tasselled beads that are attached with gold arras thread. Another version of Porteous's costume design reads: 'Deep blue silk coat, to match dress – embroidered with tiny crystal tassels'.[16] In the film, the dress appears in a Cartier boutique. This leads to the most glamorous scenes in the film and the likely most expensively costumed: the Vienna opera scene with Kara wearing the dress and Bond in his Bermans and Nathans dinner suit. The scene used 250 extras, all of whom needed to be suitably attired in appropriate evening wear.

For 'Costume 6', Kara is dressed in a stylized crisp white cotton nurse uniform. The collar of the dress has notched lapels, and is cinched at the waist with a thin white leather belt with silver metal clasp. It is fastened down the front with white buttons, and the most distinctive part of the costume is the capped sleeves with an embroidered band with small white appliquéd flowers around the cuff. Kara is posing as a nurse in order to transport Bond's drugged form on to an aircraft bound for Afghanistan. On Bond waking and finding himself on-board the flight, Kara has changed into 'Costume 7'. On the costume design, Porteous writes that it includes a 'line-striped cotton shirt, worn with cotton trousers – boots (to be worn with Afghan costume)'.[17] Directly reflecting the colours of Bond's costume in this scene as opposed to the khaki and green Russian uniforms worn by General Koskov and his henchmen, Kara is visually aligning herself and her empathy towards Bond. The collarless blouse with beige and cream stripes was sourced from Nicole Fahri, and the trousers were created by Lawrence Easden.

The Living Daylights was generally praised by critics, particularly in welcoming Dalton to the role as a younger, fitter Bond than Moore, though few made mention of his sartorial style. Reviewing the film for *Variety*, Pitt believed that 'Timothy Dalton's a class act, [he] registers beautifully on all the key counts of charm, machismo, sensitivity and technique'.[18] On d'Abo, Pitt believed her to be 'acceptable', and 'in a part meant to be something more than that of a window-dressed mannikin, [d'Abo] handles her chores well'. Rita Kempley was one of the few who connected Dalton's Bond with his clothing in 'the snazzy spy thriller', noting: 'Dalton, no waffler, develops the best Bond ever. He's as classy as the trademark tuxedo, as sleek as the Aston Martin,' and believed that 'his granite good looks are shaken, not stirred. Dalton does not play a pompous, mean-spirited Bond like Sean Connery or a prissy, sissy Bond like Roger Moore. Both were as aggressively heterosexual as pubescent *Playboy* subscribers.'[19]

Licence to Kill (1989)

Glen directed *Licence to Kill*, his fifth consecutive Bond film and his last. Inspired by the avenue afforded to him by Dalton's younger, tougher performance as Bond,

Glen wanted to make a film reflective of the more gritty, action-packed offerings of *Lethal Weapon* (1987) and *Die Hard* (1988).[20] Maibaum and Wilson returned to draft the script, and based it on Dalton's approach and style in playing Bond. Although it was the first film in the Eon Productions franchise not to use a Fleming title, its plot does reference *Live and Let Die* and the short story 'The Hildebrand Rarity'. The film was budgeted at $32 million (£17.9 million), and due to pressure to keep the cost of the film down, it was decided to produce *Licence to Kill* abroad.

Porteous was due to return as the costume designer for *Licence to Kill*, however owing to other commitments she was unable to do so. Bob Ringwood was subsequently considered for the role but declined, having decided to work on *Batman* (1989) instead.[21] Thus, Jodie Tillen was employed on the production at the last minute, likely due to her experience of sourcing costumes in America. Tillen began her career as a costumier working for Costumers Local 705, the American equivalent of Bermans and Nathans, and had previously worked as a costume supervisor on *Looking for Mr. Goodbar* (1977), and as a costume designer on the films *Night Shift* (1982) and *No Man's Land* (1987). Tillen had also worked as the costume designer on the pilot series of the NBC American crime drama, *Miami Vice* (1984–89), and it was her approach to costuming this show that would directly influence her costume decisions in *Licence to Kill*. Described by Bettilane Levine as '*the* fashion show of the season', Tillen adopted an unusual colour palette to dress the male leads, Sonny Crockett (Don Johnson) and Rico Tubbs (Philip Michael Thomas).[22] Dressed in the colours of pink, mauve and buttercup yellow, and wearing trousers without belts and shoes without socks, Levine argued that *Miami Vice* possessed 'some of the coolest, flashiest, trendiest men's clothing ever seen on small screens'. Tillen explained to Levine that the style and colour were directly inspired by the Miami location: 'aqua water, sand, lavender, aqua and turquoise buildings. We used that as the show's palette, carrying [it] through to cars and sets.' Tillen argued: 'The show has made it OK for men to enjoy fashion and to wear colour. They're not threatened by it anymore. It doesn't mean you're any less of a man if you wear lavender. It's just a shade. You don't have to be stuck with a grey suit and a white shirt.'

In an interview with Sally Hibben, Tillen explained that being employed on *Licence to Kill* was 'the most thrilling job I've ever done in my life', as well as 'the biggest canvas I've ever had to work on'.[23] Though the script may have been 'tailor-made' for Dalton, Tillen's initial approach towards costuming Bond caused tension. Tillen explained: 'The Bond people have very specific ideas [...] and on occasion they have had to pull the reins in because I was stepping out of line with what Bond is. And what Bond is, is the most important thing. It took a while for me to get my creativity to work within their vision.' Dalton would later complain of her ideas: 'She wanted to put me in *pastels*. Can you imagine? I thought, "No, we can't have that." The clothes say so much about Bond. He's got a naval background, so he needs a strong, simple colour like dark blue [...] I cut the wardrobe down by three-quarters. Bond was never flash or ostentatious.'[24] Tillen was more diplomatic in regards to her and Dalton's disagreement:

> Timothy has a very clear vision of whom he believes the character to be [...] He's a very rough and tumble kind of guy, he likes things to be real, to reflect what has happened to him [...] So we had to make sure we have five or six sets of clothes that are progressively dirtier or sweatier for the appropriate shots.[25]

Tillen also explained that in terms of her interpretation of the script's continuity she was limited in what costumes Bond could wear throughout the film. Revealing her talent for ensuring the costume details were correct, Tillen outlined: 'Bond is caught off-guard, so he's not really prepared for this sort of adventure. He was going to a wedding and just had a couple of outfits in a suitcase, so we were really restricted on reality.'

Due to this, as well as the disagreement between Dalton and herself, Tillen decided to dress Bond in 'a certain classic elegance'. According to Bronwyn Cosgrave, Tillen sourced Bond's suits from Stefano Ricci.[26] However, the available evidence suggests this is unlikely. The Stefano Ricci brand, established in 1972, was neither producing bespoke nor ready-to-wear suits in 1988/1989, but rather luxury ties, shirts and menswear accessories. The first bespoke suits were produced by the company in the mid-1990s.[27] By the time of *Licence to Kill*, the Bond films demanded at least thirty-five copies of each suit due to the action sequences, and therefore: 'A little tailor who's cutting suits from very traditional cloth could never cope with that. It would be far too expensive with production on a small scale,' Cosgrave admitted, apparently without irony.[28] Bond wears the same dinner suit in the two casino sequences and the final scene of the film. Due to this, many copies of the dinner suit would have needed to have been sourced or made, especially due to the action it received, including being drenched in water after Bond leaps into a swimming pool. Therefore, the suit, of unknown provenance, would have likely been sourced from a ready-to-wear range or Costumers Local 705. Spaiser believes that it is possibly made from a wool or cashmere blend, and that the jacket has wide padded shoulders with wide black satin-faced notched lapels and a low gorge. It is unusually fastened with two buttons placed in a low stance. The trousers have double-reverse pleats and a black silk braid down the outside leg.[29] The white shirt has a spread collar and a striped bib with a placket front that includes four onyx studs, the only time in the franchise that Bond has worn such a shirt. The onyx studs are used to mirror the ones that are included on Franz Sanchez's (Robert Davi) dress shirt: Davi explained that he and Dalton had consulted Fleming's *Casino Royale* and discussed that they wanted the hero and villain to mirror each other in terms of character: 'It's a heavyweight title match. Bring Bondian elements to the villain and villainous elements to Bond. You had a shared nuance.'[30] The inclusion of onyx studs on both shirts is a visual embodiment of this.

Bond wears fewer suits in *Licence to Kill* than in *The Living Daylights*, and this is partly due to continuity, more action sequences, and Dalton's personal preference for more casual wear in the role. The film opens with Bond dressed for Felix Leiter's wedding to Della Churchill in a morning suit. The script indicates that Bond and Leiter are 'resplendent in top hats, swallowtail coats and striped trousers, white roses in their buttonholes'.[31] Spaiser explains that the morning suits in *Licence To Kill* were a popular style for American weddings during the 1980s, and given the similarity to the suits in this scene, they are likely to have been bulk hired.[32] Indeed, Tillen outlined that for the extras employed for the wedding scenes, she and Barbara Broccoli went 'on a rapid shopping spree to New York' to buy up 'all the model dresses and samples from the fashion houses, in order to give the scene a glittering feel'.[33] The costumes for the extras have a colour palette of white, pink, silver and blue in this scene, and this enhances the costumes worn by the main cast. For the morning dress, Bond wears a mid-grey coat with peak lapels and a breast pocket, which is traditionally cut with a single button fastening and a waist seam, cutting away to the tails at the back of the coat. The trousers include cashmere stripes in black and grey, and have double-reverse pleats. The dove grey waistcoat is fastened with five shanked metal buttons and has two jetted hip pockets. Underneath the waistcoat, Bond wears a white shirt with a wing collar and a pleated bib, and the dress cravat has grey, black and white stripes. The dove grey felt top hat with a black ribbon band, that works to complement the waistcoat in terms of colour, was sourced from Lock & Co. The outfit includes a white carnation in the buttonhole: a reference to Lazenby's wedding attire in *On Her Majesty's Secret Service*.

The other two suits worn by Bond in *Licence To Kill* include a charcoal lightweight tropical wool suit and a dark blue sharkskin suit. The former is worn by Bond on the way to Pan Air International Airport. The jacket is very 1980s in style, and is full cut with padded, extended shoulders and medium-width notched lapels. It has a low gorge, a two-button fastening set at a low stance, two flapped pockets and no vent. Beneath the jacket, Bond wears a blue shirt with a point collar and the trousers have triple-reverse pleats. The dark blue suit, worn by Bond in the film's climax, is similar to the charcoal suit in cut and style, and is likely to have been sourced from the same menswear outfitter of unknown provenance. Bond wears the suit with a white shirt, also with a point collar. For Bond's casual wear, Tillen sourced items of Bond's clothing from Fred Segal in Los Angeles. The first piece is a navy shirt-jacket which has a large, baggy fit, also reminiscent of 1980s fashions. The jacket is constructed with a yoke at the back, similar to men's shirts, and has a four-button fastening, which Bond wears with a white shirt underneath. The trousers are beige chinos with triple-reverse pleats, fastened with a dark brown leather belt. On Bond's visit to the Barrelhead Bar, he wears the same navy shirt-jacket. This mixing and matching of Bond's costumes is prominent in *Licence To Kill*, emphasizing Tillen's approach towards continuity and in turn offering a more authentic realism in the film. In this scene, Bond wears a blue shirt with a short spread collar and replica mother-of-pearl buttons. The trousers again have triple-reverse pleats, and are made from a dark blue cotton that is slightly lighter than the jacket.

Unlike Dalton, Davi was unable to escape Tillen's *Miami Vice*-influenced agency, with the designer insisting that Sanchez wore pink: 'Robert in real life is a man's man and I wanted to put him in an orchid shirt with grey trousers. This caused some trepidation initially, but he is so male that he looked beautiful,' and, in an apparent aside aimed at Dalton, Tillen praised Davi, who 'made it work for him [. . .] he realised that it was just a colour, it doesn't change who he actually is'.[34] Thus, the *Miami Vice* theme becomes ironically flipped in *Licence to Kill*, with the villain wearing what was at the time synonymous with male heroes clothing. Sullivan has argued that the distinction between the hero and the villain in the 1980s Bond films became less obvious, and it was the villain who adopted the designer brands, 'influenced by the prevailing Hollywood style movies of the day, such as *American Gigolo* (1980), which not only catapulted Richard Gere to fame, but his designer Giorgio Armani too'.[35] This particular approach is clearest in *Licence to Kill*, and Sullivan describes Sanchez as being 'the ideal Medellin/Miami smoothie, dressed down in pastel knits and flowing silk shirts'.

Sanchez is first costumed in a long blue linen jacket with wide, notched lapels. Underneath the jacket he wears a white cotton shirt with an unfastened collar – this would be a recurring motif in Sanchez's costumes, as with Bond's – and onyx stud fastenings. His second costume is a loose-fitting black cotton shirt and grey, high-waisted, woollen trousers with triple-reverse pleats that are fastened with a brown leather belt. He can later be seen wearing black loafers without socks. This would later be a trope of Blofeld's (Christoph Waltz) costumes in *Spectre*. In the first casino scenes, Sanchez is dressed in a luxury silver and grey striped silk shirt, fully fastened with onyx buttons: it is this shirt that later mirrors Bond's attire. Sanchez is then dressed more formally in the scenes that follow, positioned as Bond's opposite. Wearing a dinner suit in a board meeting with his crime syndicate, the costume includes an ivory dinner jacket with wide, padded shoulders that are extended beyond the natural shoulder and a shawl collar. Underneath the jacket Sanchez wears a black silk shirt with white diamond button fastenings. The jacket is paired with black woollen trousers. It is in the scenes that take place at Sanchez's villa that the character wears the pink '*Miami Vice*' shirt (Plate 11). It is large and loose fitting and cut in a similar style to the character's previous attire. Worn open-necked, it has a camp collar and two pockets on the chest. With the shirt, Sanchez wears grey triple-reverse pleat trousers, fastened at the waist with a light grey belt. As with his earlier costume, Sanchez again wears black loafers with no socks.

In *Licence to Kill*, we see the return of the good and bad 'Bond girl' trope, in the form of Pam Bouvier (Carrie Lowell) and Lupe Lamora (Talisa Soto), and their costumes are reflective of such, with Tillen explaining: 'The women are glamorous and beautiful and elegant and classy. But in this film, the two girls are very different.[36] Pam is a former CIA agent and army pilot, who assists Bond in his mission against Sanchez. Hibben noted of her characterization: 'Pam is all-American – she can do anything, she's willing to take chances.' Her surname is a reference to Jackie Kennedy, the wife of former American president, John F. Kennedy, as is her undercover name of 'Ms Kennedy', leading to a quip from Bond that highlights sexuality and gender after he refers to her as 'Miss Kennedy':

Pam   It's *Ms* Kennedy. And why can't you be my 'executive secretary'?

Bond (*laughing*)   We're south of the border. It's a man's world.

Lowell's performance is very much influenced by the tough and resourceful screen heroines appearing in Hollywood cinema of the late 1970s and 1980s, including Ripley (Sigourney Weaver) in *Alien* (1979) and Marion Ravenwood (Karen Allen) in *Raiders of the Lost Ark* (1981). Her costumes accentuate this and are selected to emphasize her tall and statuesque figure. Although the character can be understood as progressive within the Bond films, in that Bond is reliant on her in the film to assist him in a bar fight, for which she has come better prepared, to provide weapons after Bond's have been taken from him, and to fly the plane at the end of the film, Lowell later reflected on her audition:

I remember the [casting] description was 'It's a "Bond girl" . . . but she's different from all the "Bond girls". She's tough and in charge, and when you first meet her, she's out with the guys.' [. . .] I put on my jeans and a pair of cowboy boots, a leather jacket and a T-shirt and went to the audition. They took one look at my costume, this was on a Friday, and said: 'You have to come back on Monday. You can't audition for a Bond film in this costume. You have to wear something tight and sexy.' So I spent the weekend going to really cheesy contemporary-casual stores and I found this pink *lamé* zip-up halter-neck dress that sort of zipped all the way up and it was really fitted and it probably cost $9.99. And that's what I wore to the audition on Monday. They loved it.[37]

As per Lowell's audition dress, the majority of Pam's costumes would include halter-necks, although Tillen argued: 'Even when Pam becomes glamorous, there is a function to the glamour that still has a lean and close style.'[38]

On Bond meeting Pam in the Barrelhead Bar, she wears an all-black costume that includes a fitted black sleeveless gilet that is trimmed with black leather armholes and has a front zip fastening, worn over a bullet-proof vest and a cotton camisole top. The costume includes black cotton Lycra leggings and leather calf-high boots. After convincing Bond to let her assist him in his mission, he tells her: 'Well, if you're going to stay and be my executive secretary, you'd better look the part. [. . .] Buy yourself some decent clothes,' and the script offers the direction of her costume in the scene that follows: 'She wears an elegant executive secretary's suit.'[39] The suit worn by Pam in this scene is actually a navy and white silk dress which is designed to appear as though a typical 'power suit' prominent in fashion during the 1980s. It has wide, padded shoulders with roped sleeve-heads and long sleeves. The neckline is cut in a low V-neck, and an illusion of wide, notched lapels is created in white over the navy fabric of the dress. To emphasize the illusion, a white 'seam' runs down the dress from where the lapels meet. The skirt of the dress is hemmed just above the knees. Four large white plastic buttons are stitched length-wise down the dress.

In keeping with the 'glamorous but functional' brief afforded to the character, Tillen designed what later became termed as the 'Rip-Away Hem Dress': a floor-length, halter-necked, backless evening dress with cross-strapped detail at the back and a slit down the left thigh (Figure 9.1). It is dark purple in colour, trimmed with 'beetle-wing' black pearls and including Swarovski crystal bead detailing that necessitated one month of manual workmanship.[40] According to Davi, the design of this dress was inspired by an outfit worn by Soto to her audition for the role of Lupe.[41] Because the character would later need to run in the dress, it had to be multi-layered so that Lowell could remove the bottom hem to shorten it, which was Glen's idea. Tillen and the wardrobe department used trial and error in order to achieve this: first, they attempted to create a detachable seam with Velcro, however this caught and created 'lumps': the seam needed to be invisible to provide a reveal to the audience. Following this, 160 fasteners were tried, but these created a ridge: 'since the dress is made up of faceted beads, the ridge picked up the light.'[42] More ridges were created, making them appear similar to the Swarovski crystal beads. Tillen reflected: 'It was very exciting when it finally worked [. . .] That for me was the most challenging thing – when a director needs something to behave in a certain way and you try and retain the style and keep the integrity of the outfit while it fulfils its function.'[43] The shoes worn with the dress were sourced from Yves Saint Laurent. Lowell later complained of the dress: 'It weighed a ton. At one of my fittings I got zipped into it [and] my skin got caught in the zipper which was excruciatingly painful. They had to cut it off me.'[44] Underneath the dress, Pam wears a lace garter cum leg holster which was specially designed by Tillen to hold the character's .25 Beretta 950.

When assisting Bond in planting money aboard the *Wavekrest*, Pam wears a silver-grey one-piece Lycra swimsuit underneath her Harbour Pilot uniform disguise. It has slim straps, a high-cut thigh and is gathered in the centre bust to accentuate Lowell's athletic figure, and is somewhat reminiscent of Ripley's attire worn in the final scenes of *Alien* when the character wears a cotton vest top and white Lycra bikini briefs, both actresses having similar figures. On piloting the plane towards the end of the film, Pam is dressed in a deep V-necked greige-coloured silk dress that is hemmed just below the knee. It has capped sleeves, a sash belted around the waist with a knot tied in the centre, and is cut on the bias to

FIGURE 9.1 Pam Bouvier's 'Rip Away Hem Dress'. *Licence to Kill* directed by John Glen

allow for a flowing A-line skirt. For her final scenes, Pam wears a floor-length aqua blue satin-silk and chiffon evening gown. It is strapless, with a sweetheart neckline and ruched detailing across the bust, and is cut on the bias in an empire-line, allowing for the pleats to fall to the floor. With the gown, Pam wears a chiffon turquoise shawl.

Lupe is the abused and long-suffering mistress of Sanchez, and in the opening scene the viewer immediately becomes aware of the darkness of their relationship, with Sanchez ordering her lover's heart be cut out before he proceeds to whip her in punishment for her infidelity. On dressing the character, Tillen offered a curious interpretation, which conflicts with Lupe's abuse and her back story as a slum survivor yet addresses the luxurious dress that Sanchez pays for on her behalf: 'Lupe is a woman who has always had a man to take care of her. She has a pampered life and is always perfectly dressed in beautiful, expensive, rich, sensual, luscious clothes.'[45] Lupe is first dressed in a white, spaghetti strapped, low-cut, cotton-blend wrap dress, with ruched gathering at the waist and bust to emphasize her figure. The floaty style of the dress works to highlight her vulnerability to the audience. The scene includes a rare continuity error: as the costume is worn following Lupe's whipping and is white, the back of the dress should include blood spotting; later in the film her unhealed wounds draw Bond's attention. During these scenes, Lupe wears a deep red, three-quarter length wrap-over dressing gown made from sheer silk that includes a contrasting red floral pattern. It has narrow lapels, long wide sleeves, and a distinctive yoke stitched at the back, fastened with a red silk sash. This red colour would be used later in the first casino scene in *Licence to Kill*, evoking a connection between the two costumes in both scenes and reflect Lupe's passionate character.

In the casino scenes, Lupe wears a vibrant floor-length, column-shaped gown sourced by Tillen from Oscar de la Renta and adapted for Soto's figure (Plate 12). The gown's colour, originally referred to by de la Renta as 'fire engine red' became known as 'Nancy Reagan red' after she wore the gown at a fundraising event in 1988. Although the decision to dress Lupe in the same gown was most likely due to Tillen's interpretation of character's brief rather than the fact Reagan wore it, comparing the casino gowns worn by both female characters in these scenes offers an interesting political comparison between the two, especially given the inspiration behind both of Pam's surnames used in the film, and offers commentary on the different and opposing political stances between Pam and Lupe. The gown uses floral re-embroidered lace appliquéd onto the bodice and long, fitted sleeves. It has a plunging V-neck with scallop lace detailing on both the neckline and at the hem of the gown, and distinctively padded leg of mutton shoulders. The shoes were dyed to match the colour of the gown. In terms of jewellery, Lupe wears white diamond earrings in a teardrop shape. Unlike Lowell, Soto enjoyed wearing her evening gown, stating that it was her 'favourite' costume for *Licence To Kill*.[46]

In Sanchez's villa, Lupe is dressed in a white jersey jumpsuit. It is halter-necked, with a sweetheart neckline and a structured bodice. The trousers are reverse-pleated and taper towards the ankle. They have a brocade lace stripe detail appliquéd down each outside leg. Lupe's waist is accentuated through the wearing of a wide white leather belt with a distinctive large circular white plastic buckle. In these scenes, Lupe is reading Seymour M. Hersh's *The Price of Power: Kissinger in the Nixon Whitehouse* (1983). As with the wearing of a dress that Reagan wore at the Whitehouse, the decision to have Lupe read a book that details the faults of the Nixon administration and the relationship between Nixon and Kissinger is an attempt to provide the character with a further dimension and a political outlook.

The critical reception of *Licence to Kill* was mixed. Tillen's costumes influenced by *Miami Vice* obviously made an impression on some critics, with Hal Hinson writing: 'Actually, what Broccoli and his team have created with *Licence to Kill* is a clunkier, squarer, far less stylish episode of *Miami Vice*.'[47] On Dalton, Hinson directly referenced his costume: 'It's time to find a new Bond. This one is tuckered out, spent, his signature tuxedo in sore need of pressing,' and argued that Dalton 'turns Agent 007 into a brooding blue-collar grunt. Who would want to jump into this Bond's shoes?' David Elliott, although liking Dalton's performance who he believed to be 'dark and debonair', felt that Dalton was used in the film 'as little more than a firing pin for an explosion party', and that the film 'is like an overblown, less stylish *Miami Vice* episode'.[48] Pete Brown similarly complained that *Licence to Kill* 'serves up a moody, humourless Bond', and that without a 'compelling' character, the film 'rarely rises above a good episode of *Miami Vice*'.[49] Margaret Walters felt that, in terms of costume, Davi 'is far more stylish than Bond – and yes, sexier', in keeping with the switching of 1980s 'hero' costumes.[50] On the women, Adam Mars-Jones complained of Lowell's character:

> Although in their first scene together she turns out to have a bigger gun than Bond (cue the knowing laughter from a crassly sophisticated audience), she is

soon relegated to role of decorative back-up. Although she has never been mannish in the slightest degree, Bond instructs her to buy some proper clothes. She retaliates by having her hair cut glamorously short, but slides meekly enough into cocktail dresses and the emotions that go with them.[51]

However, Caryn James disagreed, believing that Pam was 'the most playful, modern Bond heroine in years', noting that Pam posing as Bond's secretary is 'a clever way for the writers to preserve, if only for old times' sake, some of Bond's traditional macho chauvinism, and it doesn't prevent Pam from packing a gun in her garter'.[52]

Notes

1 Sheila Johnston, 'A cleaner, harder 007', *Independent*, 16 June 1989, 28.

2 Fleming, *Dr. No*, 23.

3 Field and Chowdhury, *Some Kind of Hero*, 401.

4 Geoffrey Aquilina Ross, 'Dressed to kill', *Illustrated London News*, 30 May 1987, 62, 63.

5 Ibid.

6 Bonhams, 'Lot 77: Timothy Dalton's tuxedo worn in *The Living Daylights*', *Entertainment Media*, 18 June 2008, www.bonhams.com/auctions/15801/lot/77/ (accessed 10 June 2020).

7 Richard Maibaum and Michael G. Wilson, *The Living Daylights*, second draft screenplay, n.d., 10.

8 Sullivan, *Dressed to Kill*, 159.

9 'Commentary', *The Living Daylights*, DVD, directed by John Glen (1987; MGM Home Entertainment, 2000).

10 Serena Allott, 'Dressed to kill: A bazaar look for Bond', *Daily Telegraph*, 3 July 1987.

11 Ibid.

12 'Commentary'.

13 Christie's, 'Lot 461: *The Living Daylights*, 1987', *Pop Culture: Vintage Film Posters and Memoribilia*, 24 June 2009, 69.

14 Maibaum and Wilson, 63.

15 Meg Simmonds, *Designing 007*, 221.

16 Paul Duncan (ed.), *The James Bond Archives*, 389.

17 Simmonds, 220.

18 'Pitt', '*The Living Daylights*', *Variety*, 1 July 1987, 10.

19 Rita Kempley, '*Living Daylights*: Derring-do with a difference', *Washington Post*, 31 July 1987, C1.

20 Field and Chowdhury, 415.

21 Field brought this information to the author's attention.

22 Bettilane Levine, 'Pink is for pussycats – and the tough guy cops on *Miami Vice*', *Los Angeles Times*, 21 June 1985.

23 Sally Hibbin, *The Making of Licence to Kill*, (New York: Salem House, 1989), 63.

24 Moore with Owen, *Bond on Bond*, 128.

25 Hibbin, 62.

26 '50 years of Bond style: Bronwyn Cosgrave interview', *Real Style Network*, n.d., www.realstylenetwork.com/fashion-and-style/2012/10/50-years-of-bond-style-bronwyn-cosgrave-interview/ (accessed 11 June 2020).

27 Personal email correspondence between the author and Alina, an employee of Stefano Ricci Customer Service, with details confirmed by Stefano Ricci's Head Office, 19 June 2020. This information is also confirmed on Stefano Ricci's website: www.stefanoricci.com/us-US-en/Luxury-lifestyle/one-family-story.aspx (accessed 27 October 2020).

28 '50 years of Bond style: Bronwyn Cosgrave interview'.

29 Spaiser, 'Black tie in *Licence to Kill*: Bond breaks the rules', *The Suits of James Bond*, 25 May 2011, www.bondsuits.com/black-tie-in-licence-to-kill/ (accessed 12 June 2020).

30 Field and Chowdhury, 427.

31 BFI, S18050: Wilson and Maibaum, *Licence to Kill*, final draft script, n.d., 1.

32 Spaiser, '1980s style morning dress in *Licence to Kill*', *The Suits of James Bond*, 9 December 2011, www.bondsuits.com/morning-dress-mistake-in-licence-to-kill/ (accessed 12 June 2020).

33 Hibbin, 28.

34 Ibid., 62.

35 Sullivan, 156.

36 Hibbin, 63

37 Maryam d'Abo with John Cork, *Bond Girls Are Forever*, documentary (MGM Home Entertainment, 2006).

38 Hibbin, 63.

39 BFI, S18050: 62.

40 Ella Alexander, 'The name's Bond'.

41 Field and Chowdhury, 427.

42 Hibbin, 63.

43 Ibid.

44 Field and Chowdhury, 427.

45 Hibbin, 63.

46 Ibid., 55.

47 Hal Hinson, '*Licence to Kill*: Bond without the bubbly', *Washington Post*, 14 July 1989, www.washingtonpost.com/wp-srv/style/longterm/movies/videos/licensetokillpg13hinson_a0a94a.htm (accessed 11 June 2020).

48 David Elliott, 'James Bond deserves a better Bond movie than *Licence*', *San Diego Union Tribute*, 13 July 1989, D7.

49 Pete Brown, 'Video view: Home video news and reviews', *Associated Press*, 18 December 1989.

50 Margaret Walters, 'Cinema', *Listener*, 15 June 1989, 31.

51 Adam Mars-Jones, 'Low-tar espionage: *Licence to Kill*', *Independent*, 15 June 1989, 17.

52 Caryn James, 'Dalton as a brooding Bond in *Licence to Kill*', *New York Times*, 15 June 1989, 8.

10 COOL BRIONI: PIERCE BROSNAN (1995–2002)

Following Timothy Dalton's departure from the series, Pierce Brosnan was cast as Bond for *GoldenEye*. The film was reportedly budgeted at £30 million ($50 million). According to Debbie McWilliams, casting director for Eon Productions, she considered ten British actors for Bond as the role was being 'completely re-assessed' after a six-year hiatus caused by legal disputes between Eon Productions, MGM and Pathé Communications.[1] Brosnan, McWilliams asserted, was 'absolutely right for now. He has a great physical presence: extremely handsome and tall with a sexuality on screen. He can deliver humour, action and danger, and there is a special air of mystery about him.' Broccoli explained the decision behind Brosnan's casting: 'We want him [Bond] to be a little more flinty with a little more humour which has to come back. There is hopefully going to be more of a vulnerability within certain areas of him.'[2] Reflecting that Bond had to be moved successfully from the 1980s into the 1990s, Broccoli believed that Brosnan had 'to have a certain bite and edge' to achieve this.

Certainly, there was a 'bite and edge' to the tone in which British journalists sceptically reported on Brosnan's attire, notably a dark Giorgio Armani suit and brown brogue shoes, worn at the official press release to announce his casting as Bond. Susannah Herbert denounced in the *Daily Telegraph*:

> Bond's creator, Ian Fleming, would not have approved of this sartorial solecism. Secret agent 007's sense of style was as celebrated as his skill with fast cars, guns and girls. In *From Russia With Love* he even unmasked a villain posing as an English man after noticing he had a Windsor knot in his tie and drank red wine with fish. [Brosnan] evidently does not share Bond's somewhat self-conscious love of smart labels.[3]

This was to become a consistent complaint made by the press in relation to the costume decisions taken for Bond in *GoldenEye*, reviving the 'tailoring wars' surrounding the Bond films.

GoldenEye (1995)

Lindy Hemming, whose previous costume credits included *The Krays* (1990) and *Four Weddings and a Funeral* (1994), was hired by Eon Productions as the costume designer for *GoldenEye*. Hemming explained her approach to costume design: 'It's about looking at people and trying to understand what they do, why they are wearing what they are, what they are saying by their clothes. Everyone makes judgments using all those subtle signals, whether they be intentional or otherwise.'[4] It was at Hemming's insistence that Brioni, the Italian menswear couture house, credited with tailoring bespoke suits for clients such as Robert Kennedy, Nelson Mandela and HRH Prince of Wales, was offered the contract to tailor Brosnan's suits. Working in collaboration with *GoldenEye*'s director, Martin Campbell, Hemming explained her choice: 'We decided that this Bond would be a man who always wore his suit; most of the time he didn't go looking like he was ready for action, but then things happened to him.'[5] In terms of Brosnan's own input into his character's sartorial choices, Hemming ensured that the actor was 'constantly consulted' about her approach to costuming Bond, stating that they both 'wanted him to look modern, but not trendy like someone in advertising. Although he should have a tailored look, brought up on the Savile Row tradition, his lifestyle has changed [...] Pierce's own demands were that the design had to reflect the lightness of modern man, but still be svelte and smooth.'[6] As with earlier designers, Hemming is also endorsing the inaccurate belief that Bond wears Savile Row suits.

Part of the reason behind Hemming's decision to use Brioni was due to the demands of producing a large number of suits in the short amount of time required for filming units based in different countries working at the same time.[7] Brioni had eighteen master tailors, eighteen second-class tailors, ten women employed for buttonholes, a further ten women to line suit canvasses and a final ten women specializing in trousers, a striking difference between this outfitter and Hayward's firm. Brioni reportedly produced twelve to seventeen versions of each of Brosnan's suits for *GoldenEye*: 'On top of this', Hemming explained, 'we had to hold back spares to replace the damaged clothes and brand-new suits in case Pierce has to reshoot earlier scenes.'[8] Hemming praised the professionalism of Brioni in producing the suits: 'It all arrived immaculately. The insides are light, the material soft and everything looks tailor-made', revealing that Brioni produced made-to-measure rather than bespoke suits for Brosnan's Bond. It is believed that Brosnan had to agree a clause in his contract stipulating that he 'may not wear a tuxedo in any other [non-Bond] film', and this would cause issues for the remake of *The Thomas Crown Affair* (1999).[9]

On the news that Brioni would be tailoring Brosnan in *GoldenEye*, Baz Bamigboye took up the thread originally stitched by Herbert's article in taking umbrage with the lack of Britishness in Bond's attire in the *Daily Mail*: 'He's given up smoking, taking to wearing Italian suits and, when not taking his old Aston

Martin DB5 for a pleasure spin, drives a German car to work.'[10] Mike Ellison took a similarly critical view in the *Guardian*: '[Bond] must be quintessentially British. But a few flaws in the image [have] appeared [...] Take the 41-year-old Brosnan. He is Irish, the first O'007. Bond must look the part in suits pitched somewhere between modern and traditional Savile Row, and these were supplied by Italian designer Brioni.'[11] Ellison was at least relieved that not all fashion choices were foreign, citing that 'at least the pen-hand grenade in the pocket [of the jacket] is a British Parker. And the Bond feet are clad in the finest of leather from Church's of Northampton.' David Lister in the *Independent* also condemned the decision, claiming that Fleming would 'be doing somersaults in his grave. James Bond, the epitome of British sophistication and style, is to wear a nifty Italian suit and drive a German sportscar.'[12] Gordon Arnell, spokesman for Eon Productions, became somewhat exasperated with the criticism from the British press over the design decisions made for *GoldenEye*, replying: 'Look, it's really not worth making an issue over this [...] We commissioned Brioni to make Pierce's suit as a trendier version of Savile Row. Bond is known for high style. And he will be wearing British shoes.'[13] Regardless, Quentin Letts later reported that London-based tailors were 'distinctly peeved' about the costume arrangements, and the 'W1 tailoring establishment greets this hype with the sort of disdain it usually reserves for clip-on braces and ready-made ties.'[14] Hugh Holland, of Bernard Weatherill based on Savile Row, was quoted: 'We make the best made-to-measure suits in the world. In terms of fit, it is a million miles away.' These complaints are, of course, ironic, given that no previous Bond had worn a Savile Row-tailored suit.

Brioni tailored six different types of suit for Brosnan in *GoldenEye*: a charcoal grey three-piece suit with a blue windowpane check, a blue double-breasted blazer fastened with six brass buttons and worn with beige trousers, a Prince of Wales check suit, a cream lightweight suit made from linen with a twill weave, a three-piece black dinner suit and a navy suit. The cream suit was described at auction as being tailored from silk including a 'fine herringbone pattern' with a matching silk lining adorned with the Brioni logo.[15] Brosnan's shirts and ties were sourced from Sulka in the colours of sky blue, ivory and white linen for the shirts, and the ties were made from woven silk that were mostly blue, with some including yellow or red weave details. The Church's shoes included brown brogues, a black leather shoe 'between a brogue and a toe-cap' and black leather evening shoes. For the action sequences, Brosnan wore Timberland boots.

Spaiser has analysed the construction of Brosnan's suits, explaining although there are slight variants between the shape and length, there are similarities across all four of his films. Brosnan's jackets include straight, padded shoulders, roped sleeve-heads, medium lapels and a lean chest with gently suppressed waist.[16] The jackets can have either single or double vents, some have ticket pockets, and the hip pockets alternate between being straight or slanted. For *GoldenEye*, Spaiser explains that Brosnan wears a longer jacket which is fuller in cut, which can include either a two or three-button fastening placed at a lower stance, adapted from Brioni's 'Augusto' range. The double-breasted blazer is fuller-cut with straight pockets and has six brass buttons and double vents to reflect Bond's status as a Commander of the British Navy. In *GoldenEye*, Brosnan wears a six-button waistcoat with two welt pockets to accompany his three-piece suits. The trousers are generally medium high-rise, have double-reverse pleats, tapered legs and turn-up cuffs. Brosnan later reflected how the costumes, and in particular the suits, helped him to get into the character of Bond: 'When Lindy Hemming was describing the cut of Bond's suit – I wasn't quite sure what she was talking about. But then I put it on and the suit really makes you stand up straight.'[17] Hemming designed Brosnan's black combat gear, worn predominantly in the opening scenes in the film. It included a specially designed assault waistcoat with customized pockets for weapons and explosives. Spaiser identifies the jacket underneath the waistcoat as being a modified design of the American M-1965 field jacket (also known as the M65), made of nylon and cotton blend fabric with a zip fastening.[18]

The film's villain, Alec Trevelyan (Sean Bean), was mainly dressed in black multipurpose combat uniforms for *GoldenEye*. Hemming's interpreted Trevelyan as being 'a man of mystery', wanting his costumes to provide a 'sleek and menacing' aura.[19] For his black combat gear, worn as 006, it was Campbell who decided that Bean should be identically dressed to Brosnan's Bond so it would appear that the costume was 'secret agent standard issue'. One of the key costume pieces worn by Trevelyan included a full-length leather overcoat with a mink collar sourced from Mulberry, costing 'well over £2,000', which Hemming was particularly 'pleased' with.[20] Another was the slim-tailored, high-fastened double-breasted charcoal suit tailored by Eddie Kerr ('Mr. Eddie') based in Berwick Street, London, and worn with a slate grey shirt from Donna Karan fastened with a woven black silk Armani tie.

For the 'Bond girls', Natalya Simonova (Isabella Scorupco) and Xenia Onatopp (Famke Janssen), their costumes 'were designed to vividly reflect their contrasting personalities and lifestyles'.[21] To do this, Hemming rejected 'the many super sexy late Seventies Bond-inspired looks on spring's ready-to-wear catwalks', opting instead for 'a style that admirers of early Bond films will already be familiar with', demonstrating her agency and desire to distance herself from the previous costume designers employed on the Bond films.[22] Hemming explained on approaching costuming the good 'Bond girl', Natalya, that 'she has all the modern clothing, most of which is bought [...] there are several outfits'.[23] Natalya's main outfit consisted of a tapestry coat from Kenko with an Afghan lamb fleece on the collar, cuffs and hem, a short grey-coloured angora mix cardigan with mother-of-pearl-effect buttons sourced from French Connection, a lemon-coloured lace blouse, a skirt that switches between either a brown box-pleated mini-skirt from Joseph or a floaty *crêpe* skirt by Ghost, worn over opaque tights and Kurt Geiger lace-up boots. Hemming's approach towards Natalya's 'ordinary' costuming was because the character was a non-wealthy Russian worker, and though her clothes were designer, the ensemble was put together in an 'ordinary' way.[24] Scorupco boasted of her character: 'I'm a modern "Bond girl". You won't catch me running around in high heels and a bikini.'[25]

For Natalya's high-heeled opposite number, Xenia, Hemming explained that Janssen had nine main outfits, mainly black, inspired by the shape and style of the dresses designed by French fashion designers Thierry Mugler and Claude Montana, as well as the British-born designer John Galliano and the Italian brand Prada.[26] The hats worn by Xenia in *GoldenEye* were sourced from milliner Philip Sommerville, and the character's shoes were sourced from Jimmy Choo. According to Sophie Laybourne, Janssen's wardrobe was designed to reflect the 'height of fashion', and 'accentuate her height and give her an aura of mystery and danger'.[27] Hemming explained that with Xenia, she wanted to 'avoid' what she termed a 'feminist crusade': 'I have no objection to "Bond girls" spilling out of their halternecks, oh no, no, no! [...] We were approached by a lot of designers doing plasticy [*sic*] things, but I didn't want the film to be fixed at such a fashion moment. The Eighties Bond films look incredibly dated. The vintage Sean Connery films don't.'[28] This is somewhat ironic, given Hemming's desire to distance the costumes from the 1970s 'Bond girl' look. One of the most distinctive costumes worn by Xenia is for the Monte Carlo casino scene, with a mood board created by Hemming including the note 'Cruella [de Ville] meets Morticia [Addams]'.[29] Made from black *panné* velvet, the gown is floor-length and high-necked with a structured bodice that is seamed to emphasize Janssen's bust. The production notes propose that the dress is reminiscent of the Wicked Queen character in *Snow White* (1937).[30]

Other notable costumes created for Xenia were inspired by the military, and included a Lycra *crêpe* catsuit and an olive green leather uniform with knee-length boots and a peaked cap. For her 'combat' costume worn in the jungle, Hemming dressed Xenia in a Rifat Ozbeck mesh vest with shoulder pads, satin combat trousers 'with back and front fully opening heavy duty zips' made of 'jumbo plastic', and Harley Davidson boots.[31] Laybourne argued that Xenia's costumes 'will be more Nadja Auermann in vixen siren mode' than 'big-haired, busty, Claudia Schiffer babe'. Lisa Armstrong, the associate editor of British *Vogue*, was particularly pleased with Hemming's approach to costuming Janssen: '"Bond girls" were always the epitome of glamour, but recently the girls have looked like sexy slappers. The Eighties films were a fashion catastrophe. You want to see curves, but *elegant* Moneypenny curves: Fifties style glamour still strikes a chord.'[32]

In the script, Moneypenny (Samantha Bond) receives specific costume direction leading to the formulaic costume quip evident in previous films:

107. INT. MI6 HEADQUARTERS. M'S OUTER OFFICE. NIGHT.
MONEYPENNY, hair done up and dressed to thrill in a little black number, stands up from her desk as Bond enters.

108. INT. MI6 HEADQUARTERS. CORRIDOR/FOLLOWING. NIGHT.

Bond and MONEYPENNY, walking. He looks her over, registering surprise.

> BOND
> I've never seen you, after hours, Moneypenny. Lovely.

> MONEYPENNY
> Thank you, James.

> BOND
> Out on some kind of professional assignment?
> Dressing to kill?

> MONEYPENNY
> ... I know you'll find it crushing 007, but I do not sit
> at home every night praying for some kind of
> international incident so I can run down here all
> perfumed up to impress James Bond. I was on a date,
> if you must know.[33]

Based on this, Hemming explained that: 'We wanted a far more sophisticated, up-market look [...] I designed a black dress, with a *crêpe* Empire-line body, a very low neckline and tight black sleeves.'[34] Hemming further noted that owing to the set design: 'Both Moneypenny and M's outfits had to contrast with offices designed in tan, chrome and beige.' Moneypenny's distinctive dress drew praise from critics, with Brenda Polan stating that Moneypenny is 'a beautiful woman in her 30s with an interesting private life, a glamorous wardrobe, and some rather tart responses up her designer sleeve'.[35] Ivan Waterman similarly believed that the character 'is ravishing in a black lace evening dress, she puts Bond down, suggesting that he will have to move his act on ten years to stand any chance in the bedroom'.[36] Rachel Kelly was also impressed: 'Samantha [Bond] is a very different Moneypenny, more Ms than Miss. She dresses in a little black cocktail number specially designed to flatter her handsome shoulders and slim waist. There are no painted nails or tippy-tappy heels.'[37]

For M, the casting of veteran British actress Judi Dench marked an attempt to address the sexism of the Bond film franchise up until *GoldenEye*, as well as to acknowledge Stella Rimington's appointment as Director General of MI5 in 1992. Hemming explained that M 'had to be stylish and sharp and powerful. I put her in a Sonja Rykiel suit. It's a cream, heavy *crêpe*, with pewter buttons and a Mandarin collar, worn with dark brown sheer tights and chocolate brown shoes from Joanna & David.'[38] The most oft-quoted line after the release of *GoldenEye* was delivered by M, accusing Bond of being 'a sexist, misogynist dinosaur, a relic of the Cold War', however not all critics or scholars lauded Eon Productions' new approach to addressing the sexism inherent within the Bond films through a new female M.[39] In Adam Mars-Jones's review of *GoldenEye*, he praises M in an ironic, sexist way through costume: 'Judi Dench gives Stella Rimington a master class in how to be head of the secret service without looking like a power-dressed bunny rabbit.'[40]

Reviews of *GoldenEye* on its release in November 1995 were, on balance, positive, with critics apparently forgiving of Brosnan's Bond for the crime of dressing in Brioni. Waterman praised: 'There is a new face to the hero. But the immaculate cut of the tuxedo and the crack of the Walther PPK pistol are as familiar as Monty Norman's theme tune.' Christopher Tookey believed that although Brosnan lacked the 'rugged virility of Sean Connery', he did have 'the "straight" look of an old-fashioned matinee idol and a self-mocking, public-school Englishness which suits Bond very well, bringing him closer to the sophisticated Old Etonian Fleming had in mind.'[41] Mars-Jones was positive in relation to Brosnan, stating that the actor 'walks lightly and confidently in those bespoke footsteps', and Georgia Brown praised that Brosnan was 'smoother than an unbruised vodka Martini [...] Tailored by Brioni, our newest Bond looks impeccable if a trifle slight.'[42] Not everyone was as impressed, however, with Nigel Andrews complaining: 'We know 007 is a tailor's dummy wired for wise cracks. But Connery and Moore suggested wit and mischief in reserve. Brosnan seems to have signed on at the charm clinic only to come away with a personality by-pass.'[43] Brigit Grant echoed this: 'Brosnan was more of a Milk Tray man who failed to deliver', as did Quentin Curtis: 'Tall and stringy-limbed, Brosnan, in his blazer and slacks, can too much resemble a golf-club Lothario, better suited to the 19th hole tipple than the 11th hour crisis.'[44] Philip French simply put it: 'Brosnan wears a dinner jacket with the confidence of a croupier and smirks a lot.'[45]

Tomorrow Never Dies (1997)

After the box-office success of *GoldenEye*, Roger Spottiswoode was employed to direct *Tomorrow Never Dies*, made for a budget of $80 million (£48 million). Barbara Broccoli and Michael G. Wilson continued to co-produce the Bond films following the death of Cubby Broccoli in 1996. Hemming returned as the costume designer for this film, and was retained by Eon Productions to design the costumes for the rest of Brosnan's Bond films and Daniel Craig's first, *Casino Royale*. Hemming explained that she and Brosnan were happy to continue the connection with Brioni: 'there was no doubt in our minds that we should turn again to Brioni for James Bond's tailored clothing. The suits he wore last time for *GoldenEye* went a long way to re-establishing the character in the public eye.'[46] Spottiswoode, however, gave Hemming a different brief for Bond's suits: 'He wanted this Bond to be more realistic and we were asked to make him more contemporary [...] The pocket handkerchief would have to go.' Consulting with Checcino Fonticoli, Brioni's master tailor, Hemming decided to 'retain the single-breasted, three-button style with slanted ticket pocket, opening cuffs and occasional waistcoat. The trousers were kept comparatively slim, with single pleats and turn-ups.'[47] In the film, Bond wears four items of clothing tailored by Brioni, namely a dark blue 'French' colour three-piece suit made from English cloth; a dark camel-coloured Chesterfield overcoat made from cashmere, described by Hemming as 'very soft and tailored with a long line to around mid-calf and double-breasted'; a three-piece midnight blue dinner suit and a charcoal grey suit.

The three-piece dinner suit is the most distinctive outfit in the film, worn with cufflinks sourced from Dunhill. Spaiser believes that Hemming was inspired by 1930s dinner suits for this piece due to the slightly wider lapels, the strong shoulder – a specific Brioni tailoring style – and a double-breasted waistcoat with shawl lapels. Spaiser suggests that the suit is made from barathea wool.[48] The charcoal grey suit was 'the most damaged outfit of them all and there must [have been] around eighteen suits as a back-up', according to Hemming.[49] Other notable costumes for Brosnan in *Tomorrow Never Dies* included Bond's dark brown leather military jacket. It was also one of Hemming's favourite costumes in the film: 'It is a really lovely leather jacket which I had made. I took an old German Second World War jacket and stole some ideas off it. I made sure that we got some really old, oily leather.' Five copies were made of the jacket, and Brosnan wore it with khaki Army fatigue trousers, a top from Napinock, 'which looks like Jean-Paul Gaultier crossed with ex-naval marine sweater with a zip down the front', and a TSE cashmere polo-neck jumper.

It is in *Tomorrow Never Dies* that Bond wears a full Royal Navy Commander's dress uniform, the first time since Moore in *The Spy Who Loved Me*. It was created by the costumier Angels, which had acquired Bermans and Nathans in 1992. It includes a double-breasted reefer jacket with a high front fastening, brass buttons and braided arms. With the uniform, Bond wears a white shirt and a plain black tie. Spottiswoode and Hemming had a disagreement over Bond's costume for the motorbike action sequence. The designer wanted to dress Bond in 'a suit at this point, in the faintest straw colour in a herringbone Irish linen. [Spottiswoode] said that Bond was discussing arms and weapons with Wai Lin, so did not want them to look as if they were on holiday.'[50] Instead, a compromise was reached, and Bond was dressed in a dark blue denim shirt, Highmark black combat trousers and navy cotton Trax plimsoll trainers.

The villain, Elliot Carver (Jonathan Pryce), was originally named Sir Elliot Harmsway in an early script draft. The name 'Harmsway' is a reference to Alfred Harmsworth, 1st Viscount Northcliffe, a British newspaper and publishing magnate who held vast influence over popular opinion in the Edwardian era. In the script, Harmsway is described as 'a man with an EVIL EUPHORIA – showing off all the charm and charisma that's made him one of the world's most powerful media tycoons'.[51] Later in the script, Harmsway's clothing is also described: 'He pulls on his £2,000 Saville [*sic*] Row suit jacket.'[52] Hemming was also inspired by Robert Maxwell, the late media tycoon, in costuming Carver, explaining: 'He is a minimalist monster and we figured that even though he could wear anything he

FIGURE 10.1 Elliot Carver's Kenzo suit. *Tomorrow Never Dies* directed by Roger Spottiswoode © Eon Productions/MGM 1997. All rights reserved.

wanted, this sort of man would go to a tailor and say: "Give me ten identical suits. I never want to look different." Robert Maxwell did it.'[53] Hemming interpreted Carver's costume differently from the script, and his suits and black leather shoes were sourced from Kenzo's 1997 spring collection (Figure 10.1). Made of black nylon drill fabric, they were selected to reflect elements of Nehru and Mao suits. Beneath the suits, Carver wears a black silk polo-neck shirt designed by Prada. The Kenzo suit jacket was constructed with one chest slash, a six-button fastening and two flapped hip pockets. The interior is lined with a pinstriped black satin. The trousers had side-cinching buckles, a zip fastening and cuffed hems.

The costume worn by Carver's wife, Paris (Teri Hatcher) was designed by Ocimar Versolato, the Italo-Brazilian designer termed 'the engineer' by *Vogue*, who became famous after designing dresses for the fashion house Lanvin, specifically his 'sexy dresses in sheer fabrics with angular cutouts and plunging backs'.[54] Paris's floor-length, jet-black evening gown is embellished with cock-feathers and chiffon caped sleeves, and is shaped with a corseted waist (Plate 13). Hemming said of the design: 'It's a movie star's dress, with a Rita Hayworth look and plenty of curves. Teri [Hatcher] has huge, wonderful breasts – natural, too – and the dress curves up with this pencil body and strange flowers and feathers.'[55] Hemming argues that the gown was 'the most important fashion statement in the film'. With it, Paris wore 'the highest'-heeled black Gucci shoes: 'The only reason [Hatcher] can stand in them is that they have a platform on the front,' explained Hemming. David Morris provided Paris's jewellery; a 25-carat white diamond collar necklace made from platinum, later termed the 'Bond Necklace', and a ring made from a 25-carat sapphire surrounded by white diamonds. Morris had previously worked on the Bond films *Diamonds Are Forever* and *The Man with the Golden Gun* owing to his personal friendships with Moore and Maurice Binder. Hatcher was later derogative of the gown: 'It's a beautiful dress but my breasts had gaffer's tape on them. And the sides were attached to my skin because it was too big and they couldn't take it in because of the way it was made. So, during filming, I'd wear sweats until the last minute, then put on the dress on the set.'[56]

Paris wears the gown during Carver's cocktail party. It is these scenes that reveal Hemming's meticulous attention to detail to complement the other design elements in the film. Hemming chose to dress the extras performing as waiting staff in newspaper-print dresses and suit jackets (Figure 10.2). Hemming explained her inspiration behind them:

> I found a photograph of a woman lying down on the floor, with a load of newspapers covering her private parts. I said to the producer, Barbara Broccoli, 'I would like to create [*Playboy*] Bunny Girls, but with newspapers.' Every piece which is on [the costumes] had to be made up by my assistants from friends photograph albums, so we could not be accused of stealing copyright, with ten pages of fictional news stories. We had them printed on calico and chose girls with large cup sizes to wear them.[57]

The newspaper-print cocktail dress was strapless with a corseted bodice, a sweetheart neckline and a pleated-panel skirt. The skirt has an underskirt of white tulle to emphasize shape. For the male jacket, it was structured with semi-peak lapels, long sleeves and a single-button fastening.

The character of Wai Lin was played by Malaysian actress Michelle Yeoh, renowned for performing her own stunts in *Yes, Madam* (1985), *Police Story 3: Supercop* (1992) and *Holy Weapon* (1993). Thus, the producers and studio 'were absolutely [against] forcing her into becoming a cleavage-and-thigh revealing girl', in keeping with the character's profession, a secret agent employed by the Chinese People's External Security Force, and the Chinese equivalent of Bond.[58] Therefore, Hemming took the similar approach to designing 'working' costumes for Natalya

FIGURE 10.2 The 'newspaper print' jacket worn during Elliot Carver's cocktail party. *Tomorrow Never Dies* directed by Roger Spottiswoode © Eon Productions/MGM 1997. All rights reserved.

in *GoldenEye*. Because of Wai Lin's action sequences, Yeoh needed to be dressed in clothes that allowed her to fight, run and ride pillion on a motorbike, and so Hemming dressed her in a distinctive red Prada leather jacket, white cropped T-shirt, black jersey cotton trousers and cream-coloured pumps sourced from No Name for the motorbike scene. The metallic silver floor-length halter-neck gown worn by Wai Lin during Carver's cocktail party was designed by Hemming, as was the brown leather catsuit. For the catsuit, Hemming created a mood board that demonstrates the two key inspirations behind its design, namely Cathy Gale's and Emma Peel's leather outfits worn in *The Avengers*. Noting that the catsuit was to be a one piece, the 'mahogany' leather was sourced from the leathermaker Alma. The legs of the catsuit were to include 'a slight flare or bootcut trouser to cover high heel', and Hemming paid particular attention to the shoulders, writing on two images 'I love these shoulders and jacket back detail, could it work seams wise?' and: 'This shoulder shape – almost padded. Lovely seaming and collar shape.'[59]

The World is Not Enough (1999)

Brosnan's third Bond film, *The World is Not Enough*, was directed by Michael Apted and budgeted at around £62 million: the first Bond film to break the $100 million-budget barrier. This film has more references to the 1960s Bond films than the two previous Brosnan films, specifically *Thunderball* and *On Her Majesty's Secret Service*, and offers interesting insights into gender politics, particularly through costume and dress. The script was originally written by Neal Purvis and Robert Wade, and Purvis was credited with the idea that the villain should be female.[60] It was then passed to Dana Stevens, the first woman to be involved with a Bond script since Johanna Harwood, who worked on *Dr. No* and *From Russia With Love*.[61] Stevens worked on the script for three weeks, and restructured the character of Elektra King (Sophie Marceau). Bruce Feirstein was then employed to polish the script before the production began shooting. Apted explained that 'the boys [Purvis and Wade] did the story, Dana did the women and Bruce did the Bond'.[62]

In keeping with her approach to Brosnan's previous Bond films, Hemming explained that she wanted to

> keep him classic looking and sophisticated – sort of lost in time – and not to make him fashionable [   ] you won't feel like he's a fashion victim of any kind. Because of that, I try to find a kind of modern tailoring but with a Savile Row feel about it and not go in the way of Armani or [Hugo] Boss.[63]

Furthermore: 'Although the essential attitude of the clothing is similar to previous films, there is a subtle introduction of a minimalist touch [for example] the one button closure on the jacket of the three-piece suit that Bond wears for a meeting in M's office.'[64] Beyond this, Brosnan's wearing of the suits also appears more relaxed than in *GoldenEye* and *Tomorrow Never Dies*.

In *The World is Not Enough*, Bond wears seven suits, a ski suit, and a blue Russian Atomic Energy Agency uniform. In order of appearance, the tailored items include a charcoal wool suit worn with a blue cotton shirt and navy silk tie with a brown chevron design, a dark charcoal three-piece suit with blue pinstripe worn with a white shirt and distinctive tie with a geometric pattern in red, silver and gold over a black background, a grey cheviot tweed suit with a blue windowpane pattern and a white shirt and a woven black tie, a charcoal double-breasted overcoat, a midnight blue dinner suit made from a wool and mohair blend with a white shirt, and a beige herringbone Irish linen suit with a blue shirt. Hemming had wanted to dress Bond in the linen suit during *Tomorrow Never Dies*. Bond is not the only person to wear Brioni-tailored clothes in the film: Moneypenny wears a double-breasted chalk stripe trouser suit and a single-breasted tartan jacket with black trousers, and for M's costumes, Hemming took a slightly different approach to that of the other characters, particularly the 'Bond girls', in the film:

> I think it's a little different with Judi Dench because M comes from the real world. She comes from MI6 where people actually exist. The Secret Service is a bit of a man's club so I tried to make her look polished, pretty, nice and womanly to combat any feeling of a masculine head of security [...] She's not a costume creation.[65]

Elektra King is of English-Azerbaijani descent, and is described in in the first half of the script as having a 'china doll face' which is both 'fragile and proud', that she is 'beautiful, elegant', 'brave and vulnerable' and has a 'fragile figure'.[66] After Bond is sent on a mission to protect her, the description of Elektra begins to change, including in her costumes: 'more vibrant than we have ever seen her, living up to her name. She is impossibly glamorous in a sparkling dress that fits like a second skin. Her hair is full and tumbling, her eyes are fiery and wild.'[67] The costume reflects the subtle transformation of her character from 'damsel in distress' into the film's lead villain. Based on this, Hemming explained her approach: '[Elektra] has a leaning towards the East, so we've added little ethnic ingredients to all her costumes. We always tried to go for an option with embroidery on it, or some jewellery. Just keep pushing her in that direction so that it adds an extra dimension to that character when you watch the film.'[68] The costume that Hemming designed for Elektra in the casino scene was inspired by the cartoon character Jessica Rabbit in *Who Framed Roger Rabbit?* (1988). The red floor-length fitted gown has two spaghetti straps and a scalloped sweetheart neckline (Figure 10.3). It was constructed by hand, featuring a built-in *brassière* and corset, and included intricate embroidered detailing. The colour, Hemming explained, was selected to

FIGURE 10.3 Elektra King's 'Jessica Rabbit'-inspired gown. *The World is Not Enough* directed by Michael Apted © Eon Productions/MGM 1999.

'help portray the character's inner angle and wrath beginning to seep out from her composed character as well as her flamboyant side'.[69] In Hemming's costume concept, the designer writes that the gown is made from 'red beaded net over black stretch see-thru net – no seams under bust or on cups, all shape from cutting and piecing lace', and that the stole made to accompany the dress is made from 'metallic gold and red silk with velvet border'.[70] The shoes were sourced from Gina, and made from gold and red snakeskin leather with gold plated soles; Hemming explained that Gina made this pair of shoes especially for Marceau to wear in the scene.[71]

After it has been revealed that Elektra is the film's main villain, Hemming dresses the character in another key costume, worn when Elektra sexually torments and tortures Bond; straddling him while using a feminine-looking and ornate torture chair with a garotte. In the costume design for Elektra's two-piece costume in this scene, Hemming has written that it includes a 'see-thru bodice' with fabric purchased from Joel 'designed by Ungaro' and a lilac-coloured 'slip, wrap around skirt' made from a satin-silk fabric by Versace.[72] Five copies of the dress were made. The bodice is made from delicate floral lace, and includes long bell sleeves. It is worn with a circular lilac skirt made from sheer silk that is cut on the bias with asymmetric seams and a front slit allowing Elektra to straddle Bond on the torture device.

Unlike M, Dr Christmas Jones (Denise Richards) demonstrates regressive gender politics. If M is 'not a costume creation', as Hemming put it, then Jones certainly embodies one, as is ironically highlighted by her costume which makes direct reference to another fictional and pixelated character as with Elektra, in this case Lara Croft, the star of the *Tomb Raider* franchise (Figure 10.4). In the script, Jones is described as being: 'a beautiful American girl', 'mid-twenties', with 'shortish hair, hot right now. In one movement she unzips and steps out of the [radiation]

FIGURE 10.4 Dr Christmas Jones's *Tomb Raider*-inspired attire. *The World is Not Enough* directed by Michael Apted © Eon Productions/MGM 1999.

suit, revealing a khaki sports bra, cut-off shorts, heavy duty boots. She has a deep tan and an incredible figure.'[73] On Hemming's main costume design for Jones, it is headed: 'Nuclear de-commissioning underground [costume] aka Laura [*sic*] Croft.' Hemming's description includes an 'olive drab airtex French Connection vest cropped and stonewashed over a black La Perla bra', 'nylon swim shorts' sourced from Thomas Mann, a 'webbing belt' with 'mini Geiger counter' and 'Caterpillar boots and socks'.[74]

Created by Toby Gard of Core Design, Croft's 'classic costume' in the first three *Tomb Raider* videogames (1996–98) was a turquoise tank top, light brown combat shorts, white socks and calf-high boots. Jones's surname is possibly another direct reference to Croft, in that the character, an aristocratic English archaeologist, was based in part on the character Dr Indiana Jones (Harrison Ford). Jones's forename was allegedly inspired by Christmas Humphreys QC, the lead prosecutor in the Derek Bentley case, based on Purvis and Wade's work on the script for *Let Him Have It* (1991).[75] This is a somewhat unconvincing argument, particularly as it appears to have been used solely for the cringeworthy joke and final line in the film. In the draft script, Jones quips: 'You know James ... I think Christmas is coming early this year,' but in the realized film this is switched to allow Bond the final line: 'I thought Christmas only comes once a year.'[76]

Croft's gender discourse and reception is debatable: on the one hand, the character is celebrated as a feminist hero who is central to and leads narratives, yet on the other, is perceived to be a character created to embody men's desires whom they can control, including the alleged creation of a 'naked Lara' patch for the early videogames, Charlie Brooker's derogative sketch 'Lara Croft's Cruelty Zoo' in *PC Zone* that was subsequently banned, and the soft-core parody porn film *Womb Raider* (2003). The same cannot be argued for Jones's character, especially when compared to Natalya and Wai Lin in Brosnan's previous films. This imbalance in

Jones's treatment is demonstrated when compared alongside these characters' costumes. Hemming dressed Natalya and Wai Lin in costumes that directly referenced their jobs without sexualizing them. However, with Jones, as Toby Young quipped: 'It's a safe bet that she's the only member of that profession who has a tattoo on her midriff and wears hot pants and a boob tube beneath her radiation suit.'[77] Indeed, Hemming admitted making Jones 'sexy' was her main approach to costuming the character:

> When we first see Denise Richards, she gets out of a protective white suit she wears when working in a nuclear facility. If she were a real nuclear physicist she'd probably wear a pair of tracksuit bottoms and a T-shirt underneath, but we went for a pair of really tight shorts and a cropped vest because she has to act in that for the rest of the sequence. And we wanted a more sexy look.[78]

The critical reception of *The World is Not Enough* was mixed, and in terms of costume, it was Richards who received the most focus. For example, Jami Bernard believed that: 'Denise Richards is a disappointment as a second "Bond girl". Although it's endearing that she plays a nuclear physicist who wears tank tops and micro-shorts to handle plutonium, the dialogue confounds her [...] Perhaps the joke is that Bond, unrepentant letch that he is, can still have his bimbos as long as they sport a PhD and little else.'[79] Summing up most reviewers' thoughts, Rob Deters and Jeff Hammer stated: 'Ever wonder what scientists wear under those white suits you use to protect yourself from radiation? Apparently skin-tight tank tops and hot pants are the dress code in the nuclear community.'[80] Whether because of, or in spite of, the inspiration of Croft behind Hemming's costuming of Jones, Hemming was later hired to design the costumes for the first film adaptation of the *Tomb Raider* franchise, *Lara Croft: Tomb Raider* (2001), and stated, apparently without irony: 'It was a hard one. You've got an actor [Angelina Jolie] trying to play the role of someone who already exists in everyone's mind. You have to make her look fashionable and original, but keep within the preconceptions and avoid upsetting anyone.'[81]

Die Another Day (2002)

Although it was not recognized as such at the time of the film's release, *Die Another Day*, directed by Lee Tamahori and budgeted at £98 million ($142 million), was to be Brosnan's last Bond film. As *Die Another Day* was to be released forty years after *Dr. No*, it includes many references to previous Bond films, including *Dr. No*, *Goldfinger*, *On Her Majesty's Secret Service* and *The Spy Who Loved Me*, and many costume decisions made by Hemming and the wardrobe team honour Connery's

Bond films. The costume process took three months prior to the film commencing production.[82]

Brosnan wears more Brioni clothing in *Die Another Day* than his other films, including sportswear and shirts as well as the suits. Bond wears five two-piece suits, namely a navy birdseye-woven suit, a dark tan linen suit, a grey pinstripe suit, a midnight blue dinner suit and a charcoal worsted suit. Over the grey pinstripe suit, Bond wears a navy cashmere double-breasted guards' overcoat, and with the charcoal suit he wears a navy single-breasted overcoat. According to Karen Kay, thirty copies of each suit were made, with Brioni 'dedicating one master tailor and his team to Brosnan for eight months'.[83] At the beginning of the film, Bond wears a tan suede jacket made by the General Leather Company with matching trousers. Underneath the jacket, Bond is dressed in a brown leather gilet with a zip fastening and a grey cotton shirt made by R.M. Williams, over which Bond wears a charcoal-coloured knitted crew neck top labelled Hanro of Switzerland. The dark brown leather and canvas lace-up boots were provided by Kurt Geiger. The distinctive blue Hawaiian shirt with embroidered patterns was custom made by Brioni. Bond wears the shirt partially unfastened to expose the white vest that he wears beneath, and these items are accompanied by navy linen trousers.

The film includes the most direct reference to suits and tailoring than Brosnan's others: on Bond entering the Peninsular Hotel in Hong Kong, the character asks Mr. Chang, a Chinese intelligence agent masquerading as the hotel's manager, to 'send up my tailor'. In the script direction, the scene that follows is described: 'A FABULOUS ARRAY OF SHIRTS on the huge bed. Two brand new suits hang on a closet door. We find Bond in the bathroom, towel around his waist, finishing Phillishaving that beard off.'[84] Brioni provided the cellophane-wrapped shirts that appear in this scene. Chang's surname, and the setting of the scene in the Peninsular Hotel, is a direct reference to the Chinese tailor, Mr. Chang, who moved from Fenghua to Shanghai to train under a master shirtmaker before leaving for Hong Kong in 1949. In 1953, Chang set up his first tailoring shop, Ascot Chang, and in 1963 opened his first branch in the Peninsular Hotel. The tailoring firm has since become one of Hong Kong's leading tailors.

The film's villain, Gustav Graves (Toby Stephens), is based heavily on Sir Hugo Drax's character in Fleming's *Moonraker*. Besides both having red hair, blue eyes and undergoing plastic surgery, Drax is described by Bond in the novel as being 'a national hero' and 'a sort of superman', who is popular with the public.[85] As a modernized version of Drax, Stephens's portrayal of Graves is updated to reflect Sir Richard Branson, similar to how the script describes the character in a *Vanity Fair* article, 'Gustav Graves: King of Diamonds', as being an 'action man-businessman [...] Ballooning, mountaineering, chariteering', that Bond reads when on-board a British Airways flight.[86] Indeed, Graves's entrance in *Die Another Day* via a Union Jack-parachute landing in front of Buckingham Palace to receive a knighthood emphasizes that characterization, and ironically references *The Spy*

Who Loved Me. Graves as Colonel Moon later taunts Bond that he modelled his transformation on Bond's personality: 'We only met briefly, but you left a lasting impression [...] I chose to model the disgusting Gustav Graves on you. Oh, just in the details. That unjustifiable swagger, the crass quips, the self-defence mechanism concealing such inadequacy'. This quotation, as well as the character's back story of having been sent by his father, General Moon, to study at the universities of Oxford and Harvard, sums up the basis in which Hemming approached costuming Graves's luxury wardrobe, which was 'very traditional – classic but very modern. He wears suits by Gucci and Dolce & Gabbana and also a Vivienne Westwood overcoat. He had all the modern, expensive designer-wear, including Prada shoes and cufflinks by Tateossian. We didn't make him try and look unusual, just really chic and svelte'.[87] Hemming's decision to dress Graves in expensive costumes is reflective of how Drax's clothing is described in Fleming's novel on Bond's initial meeting with the character in Blades:

> Bond concluded his inspection with Drax's clothes which were expensive and in excellent taste – a dark blue pinstripe in lightweight flannel, double-breasted with turnback cuffs, a heavy white silk shirt with a stiff collar, an unobtrusive tie with a small grey and white check, modest cufflinks, which looked like Cartier, and a plain gold Patek Philippe watch with a black leather strap.[88]

Graves wears two suits in the film: a two-piece dark pinstripe suit tailored by Gucci on arriving by parachute outside Buckingham Palace, and an elegant black, double-breasted, two-piece dinner suit tailored by Dolce & Gabbana during the Ice Palace cocktail party, which Spaiser argues was inspired by men's suit fashions of the 1930s, similar to Hemming's inspiration for Bond's suits in *Tomorrow Never Dies*.[89] This enhances Graves being a reflection of Bond. The suit jacket was tailored with straight shoulders, a clean chest and a supressed waist, and is close fitting with no vents. Underneath the jacket a white dress shirt is worn, fastened with a black satin bowtie. The suit trousers have wide legs tapering to the bottom with a silk braid on the side of each outer leg. When outside the Ice Palace to introduce Icarus's power, Graves wears the full-length charcoal-coloured fur-trimmed overcoat sourced from Vivienne Westwood.

Jinx Johnson's (Halle Berry) main costume pieces in *Die Another Day* include three different-coloured bikinis, a silk wrap dress with a floral print, a fuchsia pink evening gown adorned in diamonds and a burgundy mock-leather 'action suit'. Hemming described Jinx's character as 'enigmatic, mysterious and incredibly sexy, so I wanted to dress her quite saucily'.[90] The bikinis were created for Berry by La Perla. Directly referencing Honey Ryder's entrance in *Dr. No*, Jinx emerges from the sea in a two-piece swimsuit as Bond watches on through binoculars (Figure 10.5).[91] According to Hemming, 'Halle and I both agreed that she didn't suit a white bikini like the one Andress wore,' so the designer requested a colour to

FIGURE 10.5 Jinx Johnson exiting the sea in a bikini reminiscent of Honey Ryder. *Die Another Day* directed by Lee Tamahori © Eon Productions/MGM 2002. All rights reserved.

suit Berry's skin tone instead, and La Perla provided one in orange.[92] This is at odds with Jinx's final costume in the film: an ivory bikini. It is more likely that although the orange bikini and the scene it appears in is a homage to Andress, the choice of colour reflects the prominent scheme that Hemming used to costume Jinx. Ten versions of the orange bikini were made, and Patrick Whittaker and Keir Malem were employed to construct the white leather belts with individual 'J' fastenings that were worn with it. Three copies of the belt were created, each costing £400 and taking three days to hand-make.[93]

Jinx is then costumed in a wrap dress designed by Hemming. Twenty-five identical copies of the dress were made for Berry and her stunt double, Amanda Foster. The dress is sleeveless with straps and a V-neck, cut to emphasize the bust. Flowers and leaves are appliquéd onto the wrap closure of the dress. It is made from a rose-pink silk fabric, printed with stylized leafy flowers in dark pink, peach and taupe, with embroidered and turquoise beaded detail to the flowers. The script directs the following:

102. EXT. CLIFF EDGE – CONTINUOUS
The fire behind her, Jinx walks purposefully toward the cliff-edge behind the clinic. Strips off her dress, revealing a two-piece swimsuit and the HARD DRIVE in a plastic pouch, strapped to her body.[94]

In this scene, Jinx is dressed in a bright pink bikini, both to complement the wrap dress and also to connect with Jinx's next costume piece in the film, the fuchsia pink evening gown. It is in this scene that there is also a small reference to *Tomb Raider*, albeit in a more positive, progressive, way to that of the regressive depiction of Jones in *The World is Not Enough*. When Jinx dives backwards off the edge of a high wall and lands in the ocean as the clinic's guards shoot at her from above, it directly echoes a cutscene in *Tomb Raider* (1996) when Croft escapes from the villain, Jacqueline Natla, and her henchmen by swan-diving off the top of a cliff.

Jinx's cyclamen diamond-encrusted pink gown worn during the Ice Palace cocktail party was the best 'borrow' of the film, according to Hemming, who persuaded Donatella Versace to make the dress 'in the style which I had seen in a magazine, but in the colour and with the effect that we wanted for the film [...] I think it will be a "Wow!" thing.'[95] The colour was chosen to foreground the colourways of 'purply-pink' that Hemming envisaged for Jinx's character. The floor-length, halter-necked backless gown is structured to highlight the jewels that are placed in a geometric diamond-shaped pattern, with diamond-encrusted straps crossed at the back. The fuchsia pink silk sandals with a four-inch heel that were made to match the gown were sourced from Gina, with Hemming deciding to retain the connection with the shoemaker from *The World is Not Enough*. Berry said of wearing the gown:

> I get to wear some glamorous costumes in the role of Jinx [...] I'm more at home with the fashion gowns, whereas the army fatigues and combats are a bit difficult because you have to wear them believably and look comfortable in them [...] The glamorous gowns were the easy part.[96]

Describing the gown as 'like wearing a Ferrari', Berry later paid tribute to this costume by wearing an Atelier Versace '007-inspired' gown to the 2013 Academy Awards ceremony: 'I wanted to go as a "Bond girl", and this is what Donatella came up with,' Berry explained.[97]

On Hemming's costume design for Jinx's tightly-fitted burgundy mock-leather action suit, she writes that the shoulders should be made of 'mesh or punched leather' and that it was a 'biker-type' inspired suit.[98] Hemming also provided Whittaker and Malem with a sketch of how the 'knife belt' could work, advising on the design that the 'black dots are brass studs' and the 'dotted line is outline of knives'.[99] Whittaker and Malem made four copies of the bespoke, six-knife black scabbard belt. It is this costume that leads Miranda Frost (Rosamund Pike) to deliver the derogatory remark to Jinx before imprisoning her in the Ice Palace: 'That's pretty good tailoring. I hope it doesn't shrink when it gets wet.'

Against Jinx, Miranda Frost plays the bad 'Bond girl'. In an earlier script draft, the character was to be called Gala Brand, named after the character in Fleming's *Moonraker*. In the novel, Brand is a policewoman assigned from Special Branch and is working undercover as a personal secretary to Drax. In the script, Brand's character is similar to the novel: an intelligence operative who is assigned a mission by MI6 to gather information on Graves through posing as his publicist. However, Brand's character evolved in later versions of the script, replacing Damian Falco (Michael Madsen) in the double agent role, and the character's name was changed. There are many references to Brand's character as being 'icy' in the script, and presumably this was why the name 'Miranda Frost' was chosen after the name of Gala Brand was discarded, for example:

> BOND
> (pleasant)
> Are you going to Iceland?
>
> GALA
> (icy)
> You should know when to back off, Mister Bond.

And she storms off. Bond watches her go. She really is a fine figure of an ice maiden.[100]

The icy description is made in direct reference to Brand in the novel, in which Fleming describes her as having a 'frigid indifference' towards Bond, and of wearing a 'severe evening dress' in 'charcoal black grosgrain with full sleeves' and a 'wrapover bodice'.[101]

Inspired by the synonyms of 'icy' to describe Brand's character in the script, Hemming explained that Frost 'had a much more cool and hard look', and therefore Armani 'was the obvious choice to bring a cool, elegant Grace-Kelly style glamour to the character'.[102] Armani provided a tailored silver suit for Frost to wear during the scene that she discusses her and Bond's mission with M. The jacket has wide lapels with a single notch, and is worn with a knee-length skirt. On this outfit, Pike stated that it helped her to get into character: 'They [the suit combination] are the ultimate in pared-down polished perfection. They made me feel very grown up and confident.'[103] Frost wears another Armani outfit when she reveals herself as being a double agent to Bond. It is a fur-lined, full-length coat, made from taupe leather and rabbit fur. It has slashed hip pockets, and is fastened with hooks and eyes. It is cinched at the waist with a matching leather sash belt, and is worn with a matching fur stole. For Frost's fencing and sportswear, Hemming commissioned Angels to make the items with the brief that they were to emphasize the 'extremes' of her character and were 'modern, up-to-date, almost sci-fi, fencing clothes'.[104] The fencing outfit was worn with white doeskin lace-up boots, of which five pairs were provided by Gina. Hemming designed the couture black sports *brassière* worn by Frost in her final scenes and fight with Jinx. This *brassière*, accompanied with a pair of loose white sports trousers, is particularly reminiscent of the combat costumes worn by Buffy Summers (Sarah Michelle Gellar) in the television series *Buffy the Vampire Slayer* (1997–2003), especially in cut and structure. This look proves particularly ironic after Jinx impales Frost through the chest with a dagger embedded in a copy of Sun Tzu's *The Art of War* (c. fifth century BC).

The clearest allusion to the 'icy' description comes in the form of Frost's blue and crystal evening gown worn during the cocktail party, and directly contrasts in colour and style to that of Jinx's. It included Swarovski hanging crystals in the shape of icicles and snowflakes on the neckline that were designed to catch the light from the chandeliers used in the scene to emphasize the character's movement and personality. On Hemming's costume design, she writes that it is an adaptation of a Jenny Packham dress with the fabric sourced from Joel, the same company who provided the fabric for Elektra's dress.[105] The column-shaped, asymmetrically shouldered, floor-length gown is cut off-the-shoulder, and designed to emphasize Pike's curves, with the gown flaring slightly out towards the hem. The gown is worn with a white fur stole to encapsulate glamour and the character's expensive taste in fashion. The jewellery worn by Frost was also provided by Swarovski, including a crystal ring worn on Frost's right hand. Gina provided the silver and leather crystal shoes to be worn with the gown.[106]

It was the Ice Palace cocktail party that provided to be the 'biggest challenge' for Hemming to costume:

It was a situation where we had to make hundreds of people look extremely glamorous. We decided on a really silvery, icy palate and we knew that the crowd were to be in evening wear but, at the same time, they had to look warm and comfortable. We spent considerable time sorting wonderful synthetic fur fabrics and, at the same time, a number of makers supplied us with real fur coats – which I have never had done before.[107]

For the outfits worn by the extras, fifty gowns were provided by Escada, and new designs were sourced from Amanda Wakeley, Jenny Packham, Ben de Lisi and Helen David. Furthermore, Fendi provided fifty pieces of couture. For the extras' jewellery, the production borrowed a selection from Tiffany & Co. Hemming noted on filming of the cocktail party scenes: 'It was a big dollar day. A lot of crowd, a lot of jewellery, a lot of evening wear, a lot of fur.' With a similar attention to detail that Hemming paid in costuming the extras who played waiters and waitresses in Elliot Carver's cocktail party in *Tomorrow Never Dies*, Hemming arranged for the waiters and waitresses in the Ice Palace cocktail party scenes to have roller-skates to provide the viewer with the impression that they were ice-skating.

As with *The World is Not Enough*, reviews of *Die Another Day* were mixed. Owing to the series of Austin Power film spoofs produced since 1997, as well as the action film starring Vin Diesel as Xander Cage in *xXx* (2002), critics recognized that this Bond film had to deliver to audiences appreciative of these types of film. Nicholas Barber felt that although the film 'takes an agreeable vacation in the Sean Connery period, allowing Brosnan to stroll around a sunny Caribbean island in his summer casuals', and that Berry 'enlivens' the film on her entrance in a bikini, the film was ultimately 'too disjointed, too self-referential, too loud and too long – arguably the worst of the Brosnan Bonds'.[108] Barber quipped that *Die Another Day* 'is a fluffed opportunity to assert that nobody does it better'. Similarly, Anthony

Quinn felt the film was disappointing, and apart from the 'suave command' of Brosnan in the role of Bond, and Berry, who 'handles [the role] nonetheless with grace and insouciance that the film could use more of', the rest of the cast left little to be desired.[109] For Quinn, Graves 'looks as if he's doing a bad impersonation of Rik Mayall's Alan B'stard', and Pike disappointed in that after 'she initially promises a streak of feminine feistiness', it didn't take long before her character 'is thawing between the sheets with Bond'. Peter Bradshaw offered a mixed review: although Brosnan offered a 'decent' portrayal of Bond and Berry 'is perhaps the classiest in Bond history [Berry] looks jaw-droppingly sexy as she emerges from the waves in a retro-Ursula Andress bikini, and gives the whole thing a touch of real style', the pace and the digitized stunts were disappointing.[110] Walker praised Brosnan's performance: 'Not a hair out of place, not a wrinkle in his Brioni suit.'[111]

Although it was expected that Brosnan would likely continue in the role of Bond with another film, there was a four-year hiatus following *Die Another Day*, and it was during this period that Eon Productions acquired the rights to film Fleming's *Casino Royale* from Sony Pictures. Therefore, it was decided by the production company to go in a different direction than that of the Bond films established with Brosnan. Thus, the actor hung up his Brioni suits with good grace, and the search to find an actor to reboot Bond began.

Notes

1 Garth Pearce, *The Making of GoldenEye* (London: Boxtree Limited, 1995), 1.
2 Tim Cooper, 'A piercing new insight into the Brosnan Bond', *Evening Standard*, 8 June 1994, 3.
3 Susannah Herbert, 'Brosnan to make a new man of Bond', *Daily Telegraph*, 9 June 1994, 6. The 'Windsor knot' is from Fleming's novel, and the 'red wine with fish' is from the film adaptation of *From Russia With Love*; Herbert conflates the two in her quotation.
4 Abigail Wild, 'Glamour to dye for', *Glasgow Herald*, 20 November 2002, 14.
5 Eon Productions, '*GoldenEye* Production Notes', 1995, 13.
6 Pearce, *The Making of GoldenEye*, 87.
7 Eon Productions, 14.
8 Pearce, *The Making of GoldenEye*, 89.
9 Robert Newman, 'Bond is Back', *Observer*, 25 November 1995, 7.
10 Baz Bamigboye, 'GoldenEye', *Daily Mail*, 23 January 1995, 6.
11 Mike Ellison, 'Really, Mr. Bond, this sort of thing isn't very British', *Guardian*, 23 January 1995, 22.
12 David Lister, 'Bond girls edge slowly towards maturity', *Independent*, 23 January 1995, 3.
13 Ibid.
14 Quentin Letts, 'The name is Bond – Giovanni Bond', *Daily Telegraph*, 22 August 1995, 17.

15 Bonhams, 'Lot 177: Pierce Brosnan from *GoldenEye* 1996', *The Angels Star Collection of Film & TV Costumes* auction, 6 March 2007, www.bonhams.com/auctions/15337/lot/177/ (accessed 2 June 2020).

16 Spaiser, 'Basted for Bond: Examining Pierce Brosnan's Brioni clothes', *The Suits of James Bond*, 13 July 2015, www.bondsuits.com/basted-for-bond-examining-pierce-brosnans-brioni-clothes/ (accessed 2 June 2020).

17 Greg Williams, *Bond on Set: Filming Die Another Day* (London: Boxtree, 2004), 44.

18 Spaiser, 'A military jacket and vest in Archangel in *GoldenEye*', *The Suits of James Bond*, 17 May 2015, www.bondsuits.com/a-military-jacket-and-vest-in-archangel/ (accessed 3 June 2020).

19 Eon Productions, 14.

20 Pearce, *The Making of GoldenEye*, 88.

21 Eon Productions, 14.

22 Sophie Laybourne, 'Bond girls back on target', *Daily Telegraph*, 30 January 1995, 15.

23 Pearce, *The Making of GoldenEye*, 88.

24 Eon Productions, 14.

25 Alan Jones, 'Bond girls for the 90s: *GoldenEye*', *Cinefantastique*, November 1995, 6. Despite Scorupco arguing to the contrary, Natalya did in fact wear an ivory cotton bikini with matching sarong in *GoldenEye*, which also featured heavily in the film's publicity material and promotional shots.

26 Pearce, *The Making of GoldenEye*, 88.

27 Laybourne.

28 Eon Productions, 14.

29 Lindy Hemming's mood board for this dress can be viewed in Cosgrave, Hemming and McConnon, *Designing 007*, 86.

30 Eon Productions, 14.

31 Cosgrave, Hemming and McConnon, 160.

32 Laybourne.

33 BFI, S17929: Michael France and Jeffrey Caine with revisions by Bruce Feirstein, *GoldenEye*, second polish, 22 December 1994, Sc. 108.

34 Pearce, *The Making of GoldenEye*, 89.

35 Brenda Polan, 'Miss Moneypenny, how you've changed!', *You Magazine, Mail on Sunday*, 7 November 1995, 42.

36 Ivan Waterman, 'Premium Bond', *Today*, 8 November 1995, 7.

37 Rachel Kelly, 'The name's Bond, Samantha Bond', *The Times*, 24 November 1995, 19.

38 Pearce, *The Making of GoldenEye*, 89.

39 For a close analysis of M, feminism and post feminism, see Peter C. Kunze, 'From masculine mastermind to maternal martyr: Judi Dench's M, *Skyfall* and the patriarchal logic of the James Bond films', in Lisa Funnell (ed.) *For His Eyes Only: The women of James Bond* (Colombia: Colombia University Press, 2015), 237–45.

40 Adam Mars-Jones, 'James Bond, agent of change', *Independent*, 23 November 1995, 8.

41 Christopher Tookey, 'A premium Bond', *Daily Mail*, 8 November 1995, 6.

42 Georgia Brown, 'Oi Boys', *Village Voice*, 28 November 1995, 64.

43 Nigel Andrews, '*GoldenEye*', *Financial Times*, 23 November 1995, 21.

44 Brigit Grant, 'Deadly but dull', *Classic Magazine, Sunday Express*, 26 November 1995, 49; Quentin Curtis, 'But where's the Aston Martin?', *Independent on Sunday*, 26 November 1995, 13.

45 Philip French, '*GoldenEye*', *Observer*, 26 November 1995, 14.

46 Pearce, *The Making of Tomorrow Never Dies* (London: Boxtree, 1997), 42.

47 Ibid.

48 Spaiser, 'A midnight blue dinner suit back in time in *Tomorrow Never Dies*', *The Suits of James Bond*, 30 December 2011, www.bondsuits. com/a-midnight-blue-dinner-suit-back-in-time-in-tomorrow-never-dies/ (accessed 3 June 2020).

49 Pearce, *The Making of Tomorrow Never Dies*, 43.

50 Ibid.

51 Bruce Feirstein and Simon L. Aturif, *Tomorrow Never Dies*, first draft screenplay, 23 August 1996, 38.

52 Ibid., 105.

53 Pearce, *The Making of Tomorrow Never Dies*, 47.

54 Rachel Urquhart, '*Vogue*'s View: The new conservatives', *Vogue*, 1 September 1995, 248.

55 Pearce, *The Making of Tomorrow Never Dies*, 46.

56 Colin Wilson, 'Teri's private eyeful', *Mail on Sunday*, 14 December 1997, 33.

57 Pearce, *The Making of Tomorrow Never Dies*, 46.

58 Betty Goodwin, 'Conservative never dies', *Los Angeles Times*, 8 January 1998, www. latimes.com/archives/la-xpm-1998-jan-08-ls-5965-story.html (accessed 4 June 2020).

59 Cosgrave, Hemming and McConnon, 176.

60 Iain Johnstone, *The World is Not Enough: A Companion* (London: Boxtree, 1999), 31.

61 Melanie Williams has written on Johanna Harwood's involvement with the Bond films in her chapter 'Her Word Was Her Bond: Johanna Harwood, Bond's First Woman Screenwriter', in Steven Gerrard (ed.), *From Blofeld to Moneypenny: Gender in James Bond* (Bingley: Emerald Press, 2020), 117–28.

62 Johnstone, 35.

63 Geoff Freeman, '*The World is Not Enough* Final Production Notes', July 1999, 68.

64 'Style 11-15', *Associated Press*, 15 November 1999.

65 Freeman, 68.

66 Neil Purvis, Robert Wade and Dana Stevens, *The World is Not Enough*, second draft screenplay, n.d., 15.

67 Ibid., 45.

68 Freeman, 68.

69 Vivian Hendriksz, 'Dressing 007: Costume is first reading the script', *Fashion United*, 22 October 2014, https://fashionunited.uk/v1/fashion/designing-007-costume-design-is-first-reading-the-script/2014102213913 (accessed 5 June 2020).

70 Cosgrave, Hemming and McConnon, 88.

71 Freeman, 68.

72 Cosgrave, Hemming and McConnon, 165.

73 Purvis, Wade and Stevens, 59.

74 Meg Simmonds, *Bond by Design*, 256.

75 Johnstone, 32.

76 Purvis, Wade and Stevens, 131.

77 Toby Young, 'It's the hottest Christmas on record: Denise Richards is raising temperatures as Bond bombshell Dr Christmas Jones', *Evening Standard*, 29 November 1999, 29.

78 Freeman, 18.

79 Jami Bernard, 'Her Majesty's suave secret servant', *New York Daily News*, 19 November 1999, 66.

80 Rob Deters and Jeff Hammer, '*The World is Not Enough*: Thin on charm and substance', *University Wire*, 22 November 1999.

81 Wild.

82 Freeman, '*Die Another Day* final production notes', Eon Productions, August 2002, 58.

83 Karen Kay, 'Meet the real star of 007', *Evening Standard*, 20 November 2002, 25.

84 BFI, Lindy Hemming Collection, LHE/39/7: Purvis and Wade, *BOND XX*, draft screenplay, 10 October 2001, 22.

85 Fleming, *Moonraker*, 19.

86 BFI, LHE/39/7: 43.

87 Freeman, 93.

88 Fleming, *Moonraker*, 48.

89 Spaiser, 'Gustav Graves in 1930s-inspired black tie', *The Suits of James Bond*, 27 December 2016, www.bondsuits.com/gustav-graves-1930s-inspired-black-tie/ (accessed 7 June 2020).

90 Freeman, 93.

91 BFI, LHE/39/7: 31.

92 Kay, 24.

93 Ibid.

94 BFI, LHE/39/7: 39.

95 Freeman, 92.

96 Ibid., 58.

97 Alexandra De Rosa, 'Halle Berry's best red carpet looks', *In Style*, 23 May 2014, www.instyle.com/fashion/clothing/halle-berrys-best-red-carpet-looks-ever (accessed 7 June 2020).

98 Cosgrave, Hemming and McConnon, 178.

99 Ibid., 179.

100 BFI, LHE/39/7: 51.

101 Fleming, 127, 128.

102 Kay, 24.

103 Ibid.

104 Ibid.

105 Cosgrave, Hemming and McConnon, 207.

106 Kay, 24.

107 Freeman, 92.

108 Nicholas Barber, 'Nobody does it better? Not on the strength of this, James old boy', *Independent*, 24 December 2002, 10.

109 Anthony Quinn, 'Beyond salvation', *Independent*, 22 November 2002, 8.

110 Peter Bradshaw, '*Die Another Day*', *Guardian*, 15 November 2002, 13.

111 Alexander Walker, 'Licence to chill', *Evening Standard*, 20 November 2002, 51.

11 SLICK TRIGGER SUITS: DANIEL CRAIG (2006–08)

After Brosnan's licence to kill had been revoked for allegedly being 'too old' to play Bond, Eon Productions began to consider the next actor to play 007.[1] A casting memo was leaked to the British press around September 2005 on who Eon Productions *didn't* want to play Bond: Eric Bana was 'not handsome enough', Hugh Jackman 'too fey', Colin Farrell 'too sleazy' and Ewan McGregor 'too short'.[2] On 15 October 2005, Daniel Craig was announced as the sixth actor to step into Bond's shoes at the official Eon Productions press launch for *Casino Royale*, having arrived on a speedboat wearing a Brioni suit. This was followed by the announcement from director Martin Campbell that Craig 'will play a tougher, grittier and darker 007'.[3] This was not without incident: the press complained that Craig had worn a life vest over his suit when arriving on the speedboat, to which Craig dryly quipped: 'I should have worn orange armbands. It would have been a much better look.'[4]

Craig previously appeared in *Lara Croft: Tomb Raider* (2001) and *Layer Cake* (2004), and Barbara Broccoli explained her reasons as to why he had been offered the role: 'I saw Daniel in *Our Friends in the North*. I saw him in *Elizabeth*, just walking down the hallway. I thought "My God." He does have extraordinary presence. Just look at the body of work. He can be a character actor but he can also be a leading man. And a star. It's a pretty unique thing.'[5] Craig himself was initially hesitant to accept the role, given his fear of being typecast as Bond: 'I said I was very honoured but I couldn't actually consider this. In a fantasy, yes. But not in reality. We sat around the table and discussed things. I told them that Bond needed to change. Even if it fails you have to turn it around.'[6] Craig later explained that the main reason he agreed to play the role was a line in Neal Purvis's and Robert Wade's script, polished by Paul Haggis: 'Do I look like I give a damn?' in response to a bartender asking the character if he would like his Martini 'shaken or stirred'.[7]

Casino Royale (2006)

Sony Pictures, the distributor of *Casino Royale*, were conscious of the strong fan base for the Bond films, writing in its 'Domestic [American] Marketing Strategy' document that:

> The biggest risk with *Casino Royale* is that people are very connected to their view of James Bond as a suave, sophisticated brains-over-brawn secret agent with a tux and a martini. It will be crucial to present an image of Craig as Bond that will be acceptable to the Bond fan, while moving in the direction of a contemporary action hero for the newer Bond audience without alienating the core.[8]

Sony's marketing strategy concluded that the key strengths of *Casino Royale* included:

> Audience members like the fact that the film promises to be darker, edgier and more serious than the more fantastical tone of the most recent Bond films. Knowing that *Casino Royale* will tell the origins of James Bond heightens interest among moviegoers. The large majority of people are undeterred by the fact that *Casino Royale* introduces a new actor in the role of Bond. In fact, many are open to the idea or hope that a new Bond will invigorate the franchise.

However, noting that the 'Bond brand and the Bond character are entirely indistinguishable', the strategy document warned 'it is imperative that Daniel Craig walks a fine line between new and classic as to not polarize audiences. Craig's re-interpretation must balance the need to make Craig feel more modern and relevant against the core audience's desire to see the Bond they know – or see Craig at least *become* the Bond they know'.[9]

To assist this strategy, Hemming was again employed as the costume designer for *Casino Royale*, and rather than commissioning a new tailor for Craig's Bond, Eon Productions remained with Brioni. In keeping with Hemming's approach to tailoring Brosnan, she wanted Craig 'to look contemporary but classic, too'.[10] Due to Craig's skin tone and colouring, Hemming decided to 'use mainly blue, to be honest. Nearly everything he has got is navy, pale blue, grey, mid-grey and black. But then I almost never use colour on Bond because colour dates everything.' Spaiser has compared the difference in shape, structure and cut between Brosnan and Craig's Brioni suits, explaining that although the jackets 'still have the same strong Roman shoulders,' Craig's jackets 'have a closer fit through the body'.[11] The trousers, however, have a fuller cut through the leg, and the button stance and gorge are higher than that of Brosnan's suits. Generally, Craig's Brioni suit jackets in *Casino Royale* have straight, padded shoulders, roped sleeve-heads, medium lapels and a lean chest with suppressed waist. The details include flapped pockets and four cuff buttons on the sleeve. In the film, Craig wears five Brioni-tailored suits, including a light grey linen suit, a navy suit, a charcoal blue suit, a black dinner suit and a three-piece navy suit at the end of the film. In keeping with Sony's marketing strategy in that the audience should see the new Bond go from earning his '00' status and developing into the 'recognizable' Bond at the film's finale, Hemming consciously addressed this: 'In the first part of the film, Bond is working undercover in Madagascar and he's dressed very casually, but by the time he meets Vesper on a train, he's beginning to look something like the 007 we all know.'[12]

In Fleming's *Casino Royale*, there is limited description offered on Bond's clothing, except for a dark blue pyjama coat. Such is the case with the shooting script for the film, with little specific description or direction of Bond's clothing except: 'no tuxedos in vacation casinos anymore, he sports a simple polo shirt', at the country club in the Bahamas.[13] This description reflects the updating of the novel. The black shirt was sourced from Macy's house brand 'Alfani', and paired with plain-weave linen trousers from Ted Baker's 'Larked' range. The best-dressed character in this scene is Solange Dimitrios (Caterina Murino), who wears a Jenny Packham coral-coloured silk evening gown with a cowl neckline, which Lindy Hemming explained was selected to reflect Solange's character 'who was exotic, hot and fiery', and was dyed in a colour of Hemming's choosing.[14] It is floor-length and cut on the bias with a slit at the front. The gown is backless with a latticed ribbon adornment tied in a bow at the base of the back. The straps of the gown are detailed with tiny beads of differing shades of red, coral and gold.

There is also no specific mention of the since-infamous blue swimming trunks worn by Bond in the script, sourced from La Perla's 'Grigioperla Lodato' range from its spring/summer 2006 collection. Hemming made the decision to dress Craig in trunks owing to his physique, and to playfully flip the traditional gaze of the audience from the 'Bond girls' to Bond:

> I knew that he would look really sexy in them [. . .] why should it always be the girls in bikinis?! I meant it to be like that. It's a joke between us all that there is often someone coming out of the sea in a Bond film and I said 'Well, if someone's coming out of the sea, they have to look as sexy as Ursula Andress.'[15]

Bond's swimming trunks that emphasize Craig's athletic torso were generally well-received by critics. For example, Anthony Quinn thought that Craig looked 'very good in skimpy swimming trunks', and Daniel Doyle, the menswear buyer for Liberty, London believed: 'In my opinion it's the tight short that conveys real style and is easier for a lot of guys to wear – Daniel Craig springs to mind.'[16] This did not however prevent a small number of derogatory comments, typically from male critics, with Nigel Andrews writing: 'When the waves part for the traditional Bimbo Emergent shot, hallowed by past Aphrodites such as Ursula Andress and Halle Berry, the bimbo-turned-himbo is Craig himself.'[17] Although there is little in the way of description offered on Bond's clothing in the script, there are, however, other fashion references, including the traditional jest when Bond breaks into M's (Judi Dench) house. Unfortunately, Bond's line 'I should have stuck to my cover, Mr. Sandy Bizet, Fashion Buyer. [Regarding newspaper] "Fashion Buyer kills Terrorist." That may just have fooled them,' did not make the final cut of the film, likely due to Craig's desire to depict a more serious and grittier Bond.[18]

The script offers more description regarding the female wardrobe, particularly in the case of Bond's love interest, Vesper Lynd (Eva Green), which draws heavily on Fleming's description in the novel. Vesper is described as wearing:

> Round her neck she wore a plain gold chain of wide flat links and on the fourth finger of the right hand was a broad topaz ring. Her medium-length dress was of grey *soie sauvage* with a square-cut bodice, lasciviously tight across her fine breasts. The skirt was closely pleated and flowed down from a narrow, but not thin, waist. A handstitched black *sabretache* rested on the chair beside her, together with a wide cart-wheel hat of gold straw, its crown encircled by a thin black velvet ribbon which tied at the back in a short bow. Her shoes were square-toed of plain black leather.[19]

In the script, Vesper wears 'a no-nonsense but well-fitted suit'.[20] In the film, this was translated to an Armani black trouser-suit cinched at the waist with a wide black leather belt. The suit is made from heavy fabric, and the jacket is slim-cut with trousers that are long and loosely fitted. The lapels of the jacket are raised to frame her neck and enhance the Algerian love knot necklace that became a key part of the narrative at the end of the film and *Quantum of Solace*. Sophie Harley designed the necklace, and was commissioned to do so because she created wedding jewellery for Hemming's daughter. The necklace was made using 'ancient goldsmithing combined with contemporary techniques', and the brief was to create 'four interconnecting rings' for the necklace: 'It was to be called an "Algerian love knot" [which] I think is something to do with one of the spies who bought it for [Vesper], but [the term] doesn't exist in jewellery terms. They let me run loose with it'.[21] Harley revealed that Campbell 'loved' the necklace, and asked that she design Vesper's earrings. Harley made about ten copies of the necklace for both *Casino Royale* and *Quantum of Solace*. Bond wears his navy suit that has a subtle grey pinstripe during these scenes, with a white cotton Brioni shirt that includes a thick white twill stripe with alternate blue and grey pinstripes. The collar is fastened with a burgundy tie that has yellow polka dots with a white pin dot in each centre.

In the novel, Fleming makes reference to the flirtation and growing attraction between Bond and Vesper which is developed through clothing, with specific reference to Vesper's black velvet dress. Vesper initially asks Bond: 'Do you mind if we go straight to dinner? [...] I want to make a grand entrance and the truth is there's a horrible secret about black velvet. It marks when you sit down. And, by the way, if you hear me scream tonight, I shall have sat on a cane chair.'[22] During dinner, Bond tells Vesper: 'I can't drink to the health of your new frock without knowing your Christian name,' and persuades her: 'And now have you decided what you would like to have for dinner? Please be expensive [...] or you'll have let down that beautiful frock.'[23] In the script, Purvis and Wade adopt a similar approach, beginning with Bond and Vesper sizing up the others fashion choices and character over dinner on the train to Montenegro:

103. INT. DINING CAR, TRAVELLING – NIGHT.

> BOND
>
> About you?
> > (studies her, enjoying this)
> Well. Your beauty is a problem.
> You worry that you won't be taken
> seriously...
>
> VESPER
>
> Which one can say of any attractive
> woman with two brain cells.
>
> BOND
>
> True, but this one overcompensates
> by wearing slightly masculine
> clothing and being more aggressive
> than her female colleagues, which
> gives her a somewhat prickly
> demeanour and, ironically, makes
> her less likely to be accepted and
> promoted by her male superiors,
> who mistake her insecurity for
> arrogance.

Vesper responds caustically to Bond:

> VESPER
>
> By the cut of your suit you went
> to Oxford or wherever, and actually
> think human beings dress like that.
> But you wear it with such disdain,
> that my guess is that you didn't come
> from money and all your school
> chums rubbed that in your face
> everyday [...] MI6 looks for
> maladjusted young men who'd give

little thought to sacrificing others
in order to protect Queen and
country. You know, former SAS
types with easy smiles and expensive
watches –
     (re: his)
 – Rolex?

BOND
– Omega.

VESPER
– beautiful.[24]

The mention of Bond's Omega watch in this scene works as both a jest about watches worn by former Bonds as well as deliberate product placement.

In the script, the pair continue their flirtation through costume and dress. On alighting the train, both Bond and Vesper wear overcoats to mirror one another, yet they still oppose each other in relation to costume through structure and the colour of costume worn beneath. Vesper's is a fitted navy trench coat with Juliet sleeves and a belt cinched at her waist to accentuate her figure. Bronwen Cosgrave notes: 'It's pretty, peaked shoulders are the hallmarks of Gucci designer Frida Giannini.'[25] Bond is wearing is a navy herringbone raincoat, which he removes in a later scene, revealing the charcoal blue suit made from worsted wool with a subtle weave of charcoal grey and navy underneath. The shirt is made of pale blue cotton with light grey stripes, and has a moderate spread collar and French double cuffs on the sleeves. It is fastened with a tie that has a blue and white checkerboard pattern. During these scenes, Vesper wears a tailored cream suit made from gaberdine, which was made by the film's wardrobe department based on Hemming's design. The single-breasted jacket has notched lapels, and is worn with a wide patent leather black belt. It is a variation of the Armani suit previously worn by Vesper on the train. The pencil skirt is hemmed at the knee. Both of the suits worn by Vesper in *Casino Royale* are chosen to portray a conservative character that conceals a secretive and passionate psychology. Hemming wanted the two suits worn by Vesper to be reflective of Katharine Hepburn's style.[26]

In the scenes that Bond and Vesper prepare for the poker game in their hotel suites, the script draws heavily upon costume and develops the pair's relationship through dress:

113. INT. BOND & VESPER'S SUITE – VESPER'S BATHROOM – EVENING.
[…] The bathroom door opens and James swings a garment bag into the room, hangs it on hook on the back of the door.

BOND
Something I picked up at a little
place nearby.

VESPER
Something you expect me to wear?

BOND
I need you looking fabulous, so
that when you walk up behind me
and kiss me on the neck, the players
across from me will be thinking
about your neckline and not about
their cards. Do you think you can
handle that?

VESPER
I'll try my best.[27]

In the novel, Fleming affords Vesper's dress a rich description: 'Her dress was of black velvet, simple and yet with the touch of splendour that only half a dozen *couturiers* in the world can achieve. There was a thin necklace of diamonds at her throat and a diamond clip in the low vee which just exposed the jutting swell of her breasts.'[28] Vesper admits to Bond that she obtained the dress and a suit from a friend 'who is a *vendeuse* with Dior [...]'; 'otherwise I couldn't possibly have competed with all these people [in the restaurant].'[29] In the film, the dress Bond provides Vesper with is a backless aubergine silk jersey gown sourced from Roberto Cavalli (Figure 11.1). It is inclusive of a rhinestone-studded plunging neckline,

FIGURE 11.1 Vesper's Roberto Cavalli evening gown provided by James Bond. *Casino Royale* directed by Martin Campbell © Eon Productions/MGM/Columbia Pictures 2006. All rights reserved.

reminiscent of Fleming's description of diamond necklace and 'plunging vee'. For continuity, the Art Department built a Cavalli boutique in the hotel set to indicate where Bond would have obtained Vesper's gown.[30] Five copies of the gown were made, given the amount of action the costume received.

Cosgrave argues that the 'Bond girls' in *Casino Royale* are 'adorned by one of the most fashion-forward wardrobes [. . .] Indeed, the "costumes" are so of the moment that *Casino Royale* demands to be seen purely for its style pointers. How to look chic on the beach, at the baccarat table, and in the bedroom – such is the sartorial tutorial of *Casino Royale*.' Cosgrave explained that Hemming 'gleans their stand-out pieces straight out of *Vogue* [. . .] the coveted clothes are Roberto Cavalli eveningwear, Giorgio Armani suits and bespoke shoes by Gina'. Hemming remarked that her approach was to discuss with the manufacturers and 'style people' what they would be producing for their next collections, and

> we go and see them and see what samples they've got and what they are going to be making. Often with designers like Versace and Dolce & Gabbana, they were willing to make me things in different colours out of their own collections because they know they would get big exposure just about the time when their own clothes are out. It's fantastic for them.[31]

On the cost of costuming the cast from designer labels, Hemming used the example of the Armani leather jacket worn by Craig in the film:

> The jacket was $4,000 when I saw it in Los Angeles [. . .] so I talked to Armani and they said 'yes, yes, okay, we'll make it for you.' And I thought 'oh no, we'll never be able to afford this.' [Twenty-five copies of the jacket were needed] You can see how the budget goes up. But do you know, they made them for me in the factory and they only charged me something like €400 each.

In the novel, Bond is briefly described during the baccarat game as wearing a 'thin, double-ended black satin tie', and a 'single-breasted dinner jacket coat over his heavy silk evening shirt'.[32] In the script, Bond's costume worn during the poker game (Figure 11.2) is used to further the flirtation between Bond and Vesper continuing on from the previous scene:

114. HIS BEDROOM
where he stops dead. He sees . . .
A GARMENT BAG
Lying on his bed.

115. BACK IN VESPER'S BATHROOM.
He pushes open the door, the garment bag hung from his finger. She doesn't turn from the mirror.

BOND
I have a tuxedo.

VESPER
I've seen it. There are tuxedos,
dear, and there are tuxedos. This
is the latter. And I need you
looking like a man who belongs
at that table.

BOND
(how?)
... It's tailored.

VESPER
Oh, I sized you up the moment we
met.[33]

Bond's dinner suit was, according to Hemming, tailored to be 'an understated, classic black tuxedo finished off with black ottoman silk trimmings, pure horn buttons and opaque grosgrain lapels'.[34] The buttons on the dinner jacket are actually silk-covered, however the trouser buttons are made from horn. The jacket has silk-faced peak lapels. The trousers have single-reverse pleats and straight legs with a silk stripe on the outside legs. They are held up with white silk braces fastened with brass fittings made by Albert Thurson for Gieves & Hawkes. The use of braces is similar to Dalton's wearing of a dinner suit in *The Living Daylights*, and is reflective of the similarities between both actors' performances as Bond. Beneath the jacket, Bond wears a shirt and tie that was sourced from Turnbull and Asser, in which 'the company designed a unique, long-pointed collar that is glamorous without being

FIGURE 11.2 'Becoming James Bond' with the Brioni dinner suit provided by Vesper. *Casino Royale* directed by Martin Campbell © Eon Productions/MGM/Columbia Pictures 2006.

ostentatious. Other subtle details include the mitered double cuffs and the concealed front placket – a slit in the garment which hides the mother-of-pearl buttons underneath. Bond's hand-knotted bowtie is made from raw Shantung silk, a fabric that offers a wonderful, tactile texture.'[35] Craig was reportedly impressed by the evening suit, exclaiming: 'A Brioni evening suit is a wondrous thing to behold. You put it on and it's like wearing silk gloves.'[36]

During the poker game, the villain Le Chiffre (Mads Mikkelsen) is costumed in a flamboyant Brioni black velvet dinner jacket with black shirt, crushed velvet waistcoat, and black wool trousers, the jacket reminiscent of other male film villains, denoted by their wearing of a crushed velvet smoking jacket in film, for example Roger Simmons (Richard Chamberlain) in *The Towering Inferno* (1974). Hemming interpreted the character as 'a menacing man who lives in a twilight world. He's not flashy, he's secretive. He isn't a man who is much interested in clothes, but what he wears is expensive and luxurious. His Brioni evening suit is velvet, to emphasize richness.'[37] The jacket has straight, padded shoulders with grosgrain silk facings on the wide peaked lapels. It is fastened with two buttons and has a welt breast pocket with silk trim and two jetted hip pockets. The waistcoat is fastened with four velvet-covered buttons, as with the jacket. Beneath the waistcoat, Le Chiffre wears black dress shirt sourced from Turnbull & Asser which has a spread collar, a hidden placket and double cuffs, and is fastened with a black silk bowtie. The wool trousers contrast with the velvet jacket and waistcoat and have straight legs and single-reverse pleats. By selecting the suit and shirt from the same source as Bond's, this works to offer a mirror between the hero and the villain during the poker game.

The poker game continues over the course of two nights, including much drama beyond the high stakes being played at the table. Because of this, Vesper is dressed in a black silk Versace gown with a boned bodice, strapped back and fishtail skirt, which is paired with a beaded black lace bolero for the second evening of the game. Although the costumes worn by Solange and Vesper in the film were applauded as being highly stylish and forward-looking in terms of fashion trends, Le Chiffre's girlfriend Valenka (Ivana Milličević) was not. This is a deliberate reflection of her character in that she is dark, dangerous and has psychopathic tendencies. Hemming elected to dress Valenka in 'snake-like' dresses that reveal much of her skin, the most distinctive of which is the brightly-coloured, yellow Roberto Cavalli fishtail dress, decorated with rhinestones between the bust, and cut to show most of her midriff that she wears during the poker game. Hemming explained: 'In contrast to the other women, she is blonde and her character is tense – a villain's girlfriend and possibly a murderer, looking like a model and very confident. You saw clothes that I describe as almost without clothes.'[38]

There are two key items of costume in *Casino Royale* following Bond winning the poker game and subsequent torture at the hands of Le Chiffre in the film, the first also being one of the most distinctive pieces in *Casino Royale*: Vesper's red *crêpe* wrap dress which is knee-length, sleeveless and has a modest V-neck. It is one of Hemming's own designs, and the extras used in the crowded St Mark's Square scenes were asked not to wear items of red clothing so that Vesper could remain distinctive. Hemming explained that this dress was her 'small tribute to *Don't Look Now* [1973]'.[39] The dress is accompanied by a slim red leather belt and a red crochet cardigan. By this point in the film, Vesper has omitted wearing her Algerian love knot necklace having fallen in love with Bond. It is vastly different from Vesper's previous costumes, which were conservative and typically understated in colour excepting the evening gown provided by Bond, and therefore the choice of red works to reveal Vesper's passionate nature that had been previously shielded from Bond. The other significant item of clothing that appears in the final scenes of *Casino Royale* is Bond wearing a navy three-piece suit. The suit's fabric has a subtle light grey stripe made from lightweight worsted wool. The trousers have a darted front and turn-up cuffs at the bottom. Beneath the jacket, the shirt is made from light blue cotton, fastened with a honeycomb-patterned tie in blue and white colours. It is here that Bond fully transitions into the well-tailored spy that audiences expect to see in keeping with Sony's marketing strategy.

Casino Royale was well received by critics, with Craig's performance particularly celebrated and aligned with both Fleming's Bond and Connery simultaneously. On Craig, Philip French suggested that he is 'the most athletic and agile 007 since Connery', and is 'one of only two Bonds (the other being Timothy Dalton) to hint at an inner life'.[40] Roger Clarke stated immediately that 'Craig is very good indeed: everything about his performance shows cunning and grace [...] His slightly brutish Anglo-Saxon face is a strange and bony one, and, like the dinner jacket he's forced to wear, is bespoke when it comes to anxiety. This is a Bond that feeds on anxiety and is alive with inadequacies and flaws.'[41] Wendy Ide praised that the 'immensely enjoyable' *Casino Royale*: 'answers its critics with an insouciant sneer and a self-confident swagger [...] Craig brings a brutally efficient physicality to the role and a thrilling element of sadistic cruelty – his is a Bond you feel gains real job satisfaction from his licence to kill.'[42] The *Guardian* similarly praised that 'Daniel Craig has shown himself to be fully capable of taking on a British icon: a man of cool, cruel determination, mesmerising sex appeal and a fatally destructive way with women [...] Craig is a fantastic Bond.'[43]

Quantum of Solace (2008)

In September 2006, it was reported that Brioni would be launching a limited edition 'Brioni for James Bond' dinner suit to coincide with the release of *Casino Royale*, retailing at $6,000. It was sold in Brioni's flagship stores and select retailers, including Harrods, Bergdorf Goodman Men, Neiman Marcus and Lane Crawford. Reminiscent of the marketing approach of Montague Burton in the mid-1960s, the Brioni dinner jacket was described as finished with black ottoman silk trimmings, pure horn buttons and opaque grosgrain peak lapels. The real customisation, however, is on the inside. The jacket is lined in a special silver '007' print and will include a personalised, numbered label. That's just the beginning. A series of espionage features [include] a gun holster in the left lapel, waterproof document holders in the shoulders, hidden pockets in the plackets and a knife case fold, sealed with Velcro, in the lining of the sleeve.[44]

The gadgets listed sound particularly gimmicky, and it is unusual that Brioni would choose to market such a suit. For context, it was widely reported at the time that bespoke tailoring firms were struggling to attract new customers, and that established customers were ordering fewer suits, due to the world-wide financial crisis in 2007/2008. Catherine Caines reflected that 'designers have to fight harder to convince consumers the worth of investing thousands in a suit, and what better marketing coup than dressing a superhero?'[45] Regarding the latter, Simon Brooke reported: 'As designers and luxury houses look for new ways to create excitement around their brands and maximise exclusivity, limited editions are increasingly popular, especially for the hard-to-reach male consumer.'[46] In Brooke's article, James Beattie, a City of London trader, revealed that he purchased one of the 'Brioni for James Bond' dinner suits: purely for the pleasure of saying that he owned one, rather than to wear it. It was this dinner suit that would cause tension between Brioni and Eon Productions, the most significant 'tailoring war' in the franchise to date: one directly between Eon Productions and Brioni, rather than between tailoring firms or critics.

Dave Lackey explains that Brioni had no formal arrangement with Eon Productions: 'The fashion house provided all of Bond's wardrobe in exchange for the right to use his name in public relation materials.'[47] Therefore, excepting these materials, such as glossy images in collection catalogues and posters in stores, Brioni was *not* permitted to use the Bond brand through creating and marketing Bond-themed products so as to make financial gain. This differs from the product placement deals agreed between Eon Productions and other companies, for example Ford, Jaguar, Bollinger, Heineken, Smirnoff and Omega. Therefore, the 'Brioni for James Bond' dinner suit can be understood to be in direct violation of said arrangement. Eon Productions are famously protective of the Bond brand, and have often vigorously pursued lawsuits against companies unaffiliated with the 'official' franchise. An example of this was the Intellectual Property case between Fabergé and Eon Productions in 2003. Fabergé had former links to Bond, notably being referenced in Fleming's short story 'The Property of a Lady' and the film *Octopussy*, and Fabergé wanted to capitalize on these links with a jewellery range titled 'From Russia With Love'. The trademark application was challenged by Danjaq Ltd, who claimed that 'shoppers would presume that the jewellery was official Bond merchandise' and believed 'the application undermined its own *From Russia With Love* computer games trademark.[48] The International Property Office ruled in favour of Fabergé on the basis that 'the public can tell the difference between film references and official products'.

Although there is no evidence to suggest a lawsuit was filed against Brioni by Eon Productions, likely due to the unfavourable attention it would attract, the production company's wrath became quickly evident. Rumours that Bond would not be dressed in Brioni for *Quantum of Solace* arose early in 2008, with Simon Goodley questioning: 'Does Bond not trust his tailor? I see that Daniel Craig has been strutting his stuff at the Oscars wearing a suit from Dunhill.'[49] There was brief speculation that Dunhill might possibly tailor Craig for *Quantum of Solace*, with Lackey alleging that the actor 'had convinced Eon Productions to use the label in the new film', however the reporter also noted that at a GQ Man of the Year photoshoot, 'the actor refused an entire rack of designer suits and insisted on a Tom Ford bespoke suit'. Indeed, it was announced by *The Times* on 10 March 2008 that: '007 has switched allegiances. James Bond is forsaking tuxedos made by the heartbreakingly expensive Brioni. Tom Ford has won the licence to twill.'[50]

Tom Ford, formerly the creative director for women's wear at Gucci and Yves Saint Laurent, opened up his first menswear store on Madison Avenue, New York, in April 2007 and it has been alleged that Craig was one of his first clients. According to Eon Productions, the decision to hire Tom Ford to supply Bond's suits had nothing to do with tensions that may have arisen between the company and Brioni, but rather the establishment of Craig in the role of Bond. According to Keith Snelgrove, director for product placement: 'It was time for a change and, whereas Brioni is very polished, this new Bond is edgier and darker [...] Tom Ford's tailored suits work better for him.'[51] Snelgrove's argument would have been more persuasive had it not been the very same point raised pre-publicity by Sony for *Casino Royale* in that Craig was to play a 'grittier' and 'more edgy' Bond, and Eon Productions chose to retain the services of Brioni.

Lackey suggested that it was Louise Frogley, the costume designer for *Quantum of Solace*, who made the decision to 'sever ties with Brioni and forge a new clothing partnership'.[52] Lindsay Pugh, the wardrobe supervisor for *Quantum of Solace*, argued that the reason for choosing Tom Ford was: 'The Brioni suits were too relaxed [...] The way that Daniel wears his clothes required something sharper. For us, it was the perfect partnership – Tom Ford understood exactly what we needed, and worked hard to give us what we wanted, while staying within his own design.'[53] However, Frogley has contradicted this argument, stating:

Everything goes through Eon Productions [...] and they are very precise about their marketing and what they will use and the conditions its under [...] I was trying to solve a problem and I was just seeing all this great stuff Tom Ford was doing. I knew the relationship with the previous tailors had come to an end with Bond and they were looking for another house to take over, and I contacted Ford.[54]

The positive press surrounding the decision to hire Tom Ford could not completely quash speculation as to why the outfitter had been selected over Brioni. Hugh Rifkind was 'sent on a mission' by *The Times*, echoing 'Observer' in 1970, to question Eon's decision to hire Tom Ford and 'revoke' Brioni's 'licence to kit'. Rifkind interviewed Hemming and Antonella De Simone, co-chief executive of Brioni, and both 'insisted' that Brioni did not 'pay for the privilege' to dress Bond, with De Simone declaring: 'This is not our policy [. . .] we were chosen for our art, never for money. We want to be discreet and elegant. Outside the glamour and the noise.'[55] This, of course, disregards the selling of Brioni's *Casino Royale* dinner suit. De Simone further stated: 'there has never been a Brioni advertisement featuring Brosnan or Craig'; yet, of course, there was. Certainly, Eon Productions learnt from its experience with Brioni, when the latter's 'discretion was beginning to fade': from *Quantum of Solace*, Tom Ford and Eon Productions have a mutual agreement in place regarding product placement.

Beyond the problems relating to the decision as to who would tailor Bond's suits for *Quantum of Solace*, the production of the film was beset with another, more serious, problem, namely the 2007–2008 Writers Guild of America strike, which led to the film's director, Marc Forster, and Craig having to re-work and polish the script treatment which had been originally drafted by Purvis, Wade and Haggis. Nonetheless, the main unit production shooting of *Quantum of Solace* started on 3 January 2008 at Pinewood Studios, followed by location shooting in Panama, Chile, Italy and Austria, with filming complete on 21 June 2008.

Regardless of the issues surrounding the script and Bond's suits, *Quantum of Solace* is more commanding and visually impressive than *Casino Royale* in its style and design. Craig explained that he and Forster 'knew that we wanted to make the most stylish Bond movie we could [. . .] we have taken a very stylistic concept of what Bond movies were and added a modern feel'.[56] To achieve this, the production design for *Quantum of Solace* is based completely around a monochromatic black and white colour scheme which works to highlight striking contrasts between individual characters and the film's narrative. For Tom Ford's approach towards tailoring Craig, Frogley explained that the actor 'has quite a large face, so we had to make sure that the suit and shirt collars were in proportion [. . .] you also need to think about the fabric – it can't pucker around the shoulders or collar even very slightly, because on camera it would really stand out'.[57] In terms of the fabric colour and style for Craig's suits, shirts and other items of clothing, Pugh argued that the wardrobe department decided to do so in a 'slightly Sixties way': 'We wanted to strengthen Bond's image and, with variations on the [film's] monochrome theme, gave him a sharper look – it's a sort of uniform', and the entire costume scheme of black, white and silver-grey for the rest of the cast was designed to enhance Bond's.[58] Ford stated that his company 'made about 420 pieces for eleven costume changes. For each scene, we made three suits that were perfect, three suits that were bloodied, blown up and had been in a pool – and then we had to make most of those different permutations for the stuntmen as well.'[59] Del Smith has explained the process behind tailoring suits today for a film production:

> The tailors that get chosen today are usually picked because the stylist/costume designer knows them. Another factor is that filmmakers are likely to go with whoever is willing to pay and are able to tailor suits as quickly as possible for a production [...] the stylist would normally expect a tailor to turn around the order in about three weeks. Then you have to arrange fittings with the actors, and it's not unusual to only get two with an actor due to their availability. Often, you'll have to turn up to a studio to conduct the fitting and wait for the actor to become available.

Because of this process, Smith argues that it is highly likely that Craig's Tom Ford suits are made-to-measure rather than bespoke, as with Brosnan's and Craig's Brioni suits: 'This is partly because of the amount of [suits] they need to make, and because it is unlikely that Daniel Craig would have visited Tom Ford's workshop [for fittings] which he would need to do if they were bespoke.'

In the pre-credit sequence, Bond is involved in a car chase that follows on immediately from the final scenes in *Casino Royale*. There is a significant continuity error here: Bond is not dressed in his three-piece Brioni suit worn at the end of *Casino Royale*, but rather a two-piece Tom Ford suit. Besides this, the main differences between the suits include the fabric: in *Casino Royale* the suit's stripes are light grey and in *Quantum of Solace* they are light blue pinstripes. Furthermore, they have a different silhouette. Spaiser explains the key differences: 'The Brioni suit jacket has straight shoulders with a healthy amount of shoulder padding whereas the Tom Ford suit jacket has much softer pagoda [Cifonelli] shoulders, which have a slight concave shape,' and the Tom Ford jacket has a more defined waist.[60] Furthermore, the trousers have a slimmer cut. The shirt is lighter in shade, and the tie has a different pattern of blue and black squares, rather than honeycomb, both sourced from Tom Ford. There has been much speculation among Bond fans as to why there is such an obvious costume continuity error present in the opening scene, ranging from *Quantum of Solace* employed a different costume designer leading to a reinterpretation of Bond's image, that it was deemed more appropriate to dress Bond in a two-piece suit given the Italian climate, or due to the lack of a script. However, given the issues between Eon Productions and Brioni, it is most likely that the decision was made for a completely fresh start.

Following this scene, Bond's suits work to develop his character and the relationships he has towards others and their costumes, particularly M. Their monochromatic clothes mirror and oppose each other alternately throughout the film to reflect M's initial mistrust of Bond that develops into their understanding and mutual trust of each other by the end of *Quantum of Solace*. In their first scenes together, Bond wears a navy wool overcoat over a charcoal suit, revealed in the following scene. The overcoat has Cifonelli shoulders and a darted front and suppressed waist to give the coat an athletic silhouette. In direct contrast, M is dressed in a black, single-breasted, knitted woollen jacket inclusive of a distinctive wide spread collar, under which she wears a white shirt with a wide notched collar. The fabric of Bond's and M's costumes reflects the opposition between the two in particular. In the scene that follows, Bond, M and Bill Tanner (Rory Kinnear) walk through corridors and down the stairs in MI6, and it is here that the monochrome colour scheme becomes distinctive. Bond has removed his overcoat, and the audience receives a full view of his Tom Ford 'Regency model' dark charcoal grey suit made from mohair and wool. Bond wears a white folded pocket square in the breast pocket of the jacket, which would become a costume trope in Craig's later films. The fitted shirt is made from white cotton and has a moderate spread collar and double cuffs, fastened with an aubergine tie that has white pin dots.

Bond meets the film's main villain, environmentalist entrepreneur Dominic Greene (Mathieu Amalric) and his former girlfriend, Camille Montes (Olga Kurylenko), in Haiti. Bond is dressed casually in a Tom Ford black polo shirt and white Levi 306 Sta-Prest denim jeans. Camille is the most distinctively dressed in these scenes, wearing clothes directly at odds with the monochrome colour scheme which she later comes to adopt. Pugh explained that for the female wardrobe 'we wanted toned-down starkness with unfussy lines and no frills [...] we didn't want costume pieces we just went to the shops'.[61] Although many items were sourced from Prada, Camille's costume was sourced from Jasper Conran's spring/summer 2008 range. It is comprised of a rust orange nylon leotard with ruched bodice and spaghetti straps, and a full pleated skirt of bronze shot silk with zip fastening at the back. Camille wears a chunky gold-coloured chainmail necklace with a stylized fish pendant. Comparatively, Greene is casually dressed in a loose-fitting white linen shirt inclusive of ribbed patterning, and light tan cotton twill trousers. This is consistent with the way Greene is costumed throughout the majority of the film, namely in a range of colourful and patterned tropical shirts made of silk with open collars accompanied with light-coloured chino trousers. On the brief occasions when he wears tailored suits, in the opera sequence and during his fundraising party, he wears a 'Q' lapel pin on his jacket lapel reflecting his membership of the underground organization Quantum.

Bond tracks Greene to Bregenz, Austria, where Greene attends a performance of Giacomo Puccini's *Tosca* (1900). It is during these scenes when the monochrome design is at its most stylish in terms of costume. Not being appropriately attired to attend the opera, Bond steals a midnight blue dinner suit from the wardrobe department backstage. Spaiser believes that the mohair-cashmere dinner suit takes its influence from the Anthony Sinclair-tailored dinner suit that Connery wears at the Les Ambassadeurs Club in *Dr. No*.[62] As with Connery, Craig's jacket has a shawl collar, with jetted pockets, double vents and gauntlet cuffs, all faced with black silk. The shirt and tie are also reflective of Connery's costume as well: the white shirt has a spread collar, double cuffs and a pleated front, and the black silk bowtie is diamond shaped. Both Connery's and Craig's jackets also include a white linen pocket square placed in the breast pocket.

Travelling with Mathis (Giancarlo Giannini) on an overnight Virgin Atlantic flight to Bolivia, Bond sits at the first-class bar drinking several Martinis and lamenting over his relationship with Vesper, whilst wearing a dark brown mohair suit with a hopsack weave in dark and light brown. Bond's shirt is made of white cotton with a spread collar and double cuffs, and is fastened with a tie including small squares detailed in dark brown and tan. On landing in Bolivia, Bond meets Agent 'Strawberry' Fields (Gemma Arterton), a British consulate MI6 field-operative. Fields is costumed in a tan-coloured Burberry trench coat that is belted and suede knee-high boots in russet brown that reflect the colour of her hair. As with Camille's costume, Fields's breaks away from the monochromatic theme. Arterton explained: 'I didn't know what was going to happen with my costume – originally they wanted me to look quite prim and ordered, but we [Arterton and Frogley] also wanted to make my character to look a bit wild and a bit unkempt to reflect her character: trying to be something that she can't maintain.'[63] Arterton further elucidated that in her introductory scene she wore the trench coat, boots and little else beneath: 'So it's like she's kitted out but being really filthy at the same time!' This is also reflected in the 'stripper' inuendo present in the scene's dialogue:

Bond Fields, when is the next flight to London?

Fields Tomorrow morning.

Bond Well then, we have all night.

Fields If you attempt to flee, I will arrest you, drop you off in jail and take you to the plane in chains, understand?

Bond Perfectly. After you.
[Behind Fields's back]

Mathis I think she has handcuffs.

Bond I do hope so.

Indeed, in the scenes that follow when Bond, Fields and Mathis check in to their hotel, it does not take long for Bond to seduce Fields in their hotel suite under the guise of searching it. This leads to a minor costume jest within the film after Bond has received information that Greene is to hold a fundraising party in the evening and invites her to attend. Stroking her naked back in the bedroom, Bond asks Fields:

Bond Do you want to go to a party?

Fields A party? But I have nothing to wear . . .

Bond We'll fix that.

Reminiscent of Bond purchasing Kara's opera coat and gown in *The Living Daylights* and Vesper's gown in *Casino Royale*, it is implied that Bond obtains Fields's dress in the hotel's boutique, and is therefore another connection between Dalton's and Craig's Bond. Sourced from Prada, it is a black silk and wool shift dress with a silver-grey panel and bow detail at the front, reflecting the influence that Bond has had on Fields following sexual intercourse as, in contrast with her previous attire, it is in keeping with the monochromatic theme. The dress formed part of Prada's 2007 autumn/winter range. Fields wears a prasiolite (green amethyst) necklace made by Leslie Schifft. Arterton thought her Prada dress was 'beautiful, very Audrey Hepburn, but it is something Bond had brought for me so it is really top end. It's Prada and it fits like a glove [. . .] it's streamlined but again there's this cute thing going on.'[64]

Bond attends Greene's fundraising party wearing a midnight blue mohair dinner suit. This is accompanied with a plain white cotton shirt that includes a spread collar and double cuffs, fastened with a blue and white tie woven in a basket weave. Camille, too, is present at the party, dressed in a black Prada dress. Originally, it was intended that Camille was to be dressed for the party in a black trouser suit, however Frogley realized that

> we were designing the costume to fit the stunts and it seemed to me that we were putting the cart before the horse. People took it for granted that it had to be a certain way but when we actually looked at it carefully, we questioned why we were designing a trouser suit with arms for a glamorous party set in a hot country – it didn't make sense.[65]

Believing that 'Prada had the best looks', Frogley explained that the company 'was incredibly helpful and made 20 identical dresses for us in one week'. Although the dress was created as a 'one-off' for *Quantum of Solace*, Prada makes a variation of this dress every season. Camille's 'exclusive' dress is made from *crêpe*, cut with a

FIGURE 11.3 James Bond's and Camille Montes's monochromatic costumes. *Quantum of Solace* directed by Marc Forster © Eon Productions/MGM/Columbia Pictures 2008. All rights reserved.

sweetheart neckline and includes thick black cotton twill tape shoulder straps with an appliqué *crêpe* rose attached. The dress is ruched at the left side and fastened as a bow at the back, and the skirt is pleated. The reason behind the idea of costuming Camille in a trouser suit was because it was to be worn across four scenes following the party: when Bond and Camille fly across the Bolivian desert, after being ejected from the plane and parachuting into a sink-hole, on discovering Greene's plot to blockade Bolivia's fresh water supply and blackmail General Medrano (Joaquín Cosío), and crossing the desert to arrive back at Bond's hotel. It is these two outfits which are the focus of the marketing strategy for *Quantum of Solace* and are reminiscent of Bond and Anya walking across the Egyptian desert in *The Spy Who Loved Me* (Figure 11.3).

Following the pair's arrival at the hotel, Bond discovers Fields's fate: Greene and his Quantum associates arranged for her to be killed by drowning and smothering her in crude oil, in direct allusion to Jill Masterson's visually distinctive murder by gold paint in *Goldfinger*. M's costume in these scenes are designed to be in total opposition to that of Bond's, believing that Bond has become a threat to both friend and foe (Plate 14). M wears a cream jacket with wide lapels, white linen shirt and tan-coloured trousers as she orders Bond to disarm and end his mission. She does however soften towards Bond later in the scene, stating that he is 'still her agent' and orders him to be 'watched' believing him to know something.

The film's final scenes take place in Kazan, Russia, after Bond has tracked down Vesper's former lover, Yusef Kabira (Simon Kassianides), a member of Quantum who seduces women to obtain information for the organization and was indirectly the cause of her death. Bond and M have come to reflect each other in their costume choices, both in terms of colour and fabric (Figure 11.4). The costumes work to demonstrate that Bond and M have come to an understanding and can finally mutually respect and trust one another: this is reflected in their

FIGURE 11.4 James Bond's and M's mirrored monochromatic costumes. *Quantum of Solace* directed by Marc Forster © Eon Productions/MGM/Columbia Pictures 2008. All rights reserved.

monochromatic mirroring in their individual costumes. Bond wears a double-breasted, knee-length black herringbone wool greatcoat which is belted at the back. A brown and black glen plaid scarf, also sourced from Tom Ford, is worn around his neck. M wears a black trench coat, fastened but not belted over her outfit, including a wide-collared white shirt. The pair's monochromatic costume is heightened as they stand discussing the case surrounded by falling snow. The film ends with Bond having achieved closure over the death of Vesper: he walks away from M, having agreed to return to MI6, dropping the Algerian love knot in the snow before the camera fades into the film's credits.

Notes

1 Neal Symons, 'Australian actor turns down licence to thrill', *The Times*, 13 August 2005, 26.

2 John-Paul Flintoff, 'Bond Bombshell', *The Sunday Times Magazine*, 8 October 2006, 391.

3 'Daniel Craig takes on 007 mantle', *BBC News*, 14 October 2005, http://news.bbc.co.uk/1/hi/entertainment/4337224.stm (accessed 15 February 2020).

4 *Becoming Bond*, documentary, directed by Rob Done (USA: Special Treats Productions, 2006).

5 Flintoff, 393.

6 Ibid., 394.

7 George Simpson, 'James Bond: Daniel Craig *Casino Royale* ULTIMATUM "I refused, what was the f***ing point?"', *Express*, 30 December 2019.

8 Sony Pictures, '*Casino Royale* Domestic Theatrical Marketing Strategy', 16 June 2006, 2. https://search.wikileaks.org/?q=Casino+Royale+domestic+marketing+strategy (accessed 13 February 2020).

9 Ibid., 4.

10 '*Casino Royale* costume designer interview – Lindy Hemming', *MI6 HQ*, 9 December 2006, www.mi6-hq.com/sections/articles/bond_21_lindy_hemming_interview.php (accessed 13 February 2020).

11 Spaiser, 'Basted for Bond: Examining Daniel Craig's Brioni clothes', *The Suits of James Bond*, 19 July 2015, www.bondsuits.com/basted-for-bond-examining-daniel-craigs-brioni-clothes/ (accessed 18 February 2020).

12 Christopher Bray and Nick Foulkes, 'Dressed to kill; Barbara Broccoli calls Daniel Craig's Bond "a tough guy in a dinner jacket." But getting his look right proved the wardrobe team's toughest mission', *Mail on Sunday*, 29 October 2006, 42.

13 Neal Purvis, Robert Wade and Paul Haggis, *Casino Royale*, final revised shooting script, 13 December 2005, 21.

14 'New *Casino Royale* Bond girl dress is best seller for designer', *MI6 HQ*, 25 December 2006, www.mi6-hq.com/news/index.php?itemid=4582 (accessed 25 February 2020).

15 '*Casino Royale* costume designer interview – Lindy Hemming'.

16 Simon Brooke, 'Briefer encounters', *Financial Times*, 28 July 2007, 7.

17 Nigel Andrews, 'A daft, devout determination to be debonair', *Financial Times*, 16 November 2006, 15.

18 Purvis, Wade and Haggis, 16.

19 Fleming, *Casino Royale* (1953; London: Penguin Books, 2009), 32, 33.

20 Purvis, Wade and Haggis, 40.

21 'Sophie Harley and the magic of the Algerian love knot', *From Tailors With Love* podcast, directed by Pete Brooker, 17 July 2019, www.bondsuits.com/from-tailors-with-love-sophie-harley-and-the-algerian-love-knot/ (accessed 25 February 2020).

22 Fleming, 52.

23 Ibid., 53.

24 Purvis, Wade and Haggis, 42.

25 Bronwyn Cosgrave, 'The name's Cavalli . . .', *Financial Times*, 18 November 2006, 44.

26 '*Casino Royale* production notes', *Cinema Review*, 2006, www.cinemareview.com/production.asp?prodid=3741 (accessed 25 February 2020).

27 Purvis, Wade and Haggis, 51.

28 Fleming, 51, 52.

29 Ibid., 58.

30 '*Casino Royale* production notes'.

31 '*Casino Royale* costume designer interview – Lindy Hemming'.

32 Fleming, 50, 51.

33 Purvis, Wade and Haggis, 51, 52.

34 Bray and Foulkes.

35 Ibid.

36 Ibid.

37 '*Casino Royale* production notes'.

38 Ibid.

39 '*Casino Royale* costume designer interview – Lindy Hemming'.

40 Philip French, '*Casino Royale*', *Observer*, 19 November 2006.

41 Roger Clarke, '*Casino Royale*', *Sight & Sound*, January 2007.

42 Wendy Ide, 'Craig gambles with the winning hand', *The Times*, 16 November 2006, 16.

43 '*Casino Royale*', *Guardian*, 10 November 2006, 9.

44 Courtney Colarita, 'Brioni launching Bond tux', *DNR*, 25 September 2006, 8.

45 Catherine Caines, 'Designer fitted for heroism', *The Australian*, 16 July 2008, 16.

46 Brooke, 'Get it while you can', *Financial Times*, 4 August 2007, 7.

47 Dave Lackey, 'The race to dress Bond', *Financial Post* (Canada), 19 April 2008, FW Z.

40 Matthew Moore, 'For once, the Russians get the better of Bond', *Daily Telegraph*, 2 July 2009, 13.

49 Simon Goodley, 'Does Bond not trust his tailor?', *Daily Telegraph*, 28 February 2008, 8.

50 'Dressed to Kill', *The Times*, 10 March 2008, 16.

51 Brooke, 'The name's Ford, Tom Ford', *Financial Times*, 25 October 2008, 44.

52 Lackey.

53 Jessica Fellowes, '007 and his girls are back with a crisp new look', *Daily Telegraph*, 22 October 2008, 25.

54 Caines.

55 Hugo Rifkind, 'Dressed to sell', *The Times*, 10 March 2008, 80.

56 John Hiscock, 'How we made Bond beautiful', *Daily Telegraph*, 24 October 2008, 32.

57 Brooke, 'The name's Ford, Tom Ford'.

58 Fellowes.

59 Adam Tschorn, '007's tailor is Ford, Tom Ford', *Pittsburgh Tribune Review*, 7 July 2008.

60 Spaiser, 'Comparing Daniel Craig's navy pinstripe suits', *The Suits of James Bond*, 7 May 2015, www.bondsuits.com/comparing-daniel-craigs-navy-pinstripe-suits/ (accessed 25 February 2020).

61 Fellowes.

62 Spaiser, 'A familiar dinner suit in *Quantum of Solace*', *The Suits of James Bond*, 14 November 2011, www.bondsuits.com/a-familiar-dinner-suit/ (accessed 25 February 2020).

63 Devin Zydel, 'Gemma Arterton is Fields, Agent Fields: the *Quantum* girl who "thinks she can control Bond"', *Commander Bond*, 18 November 2008, http://commanderbond.net/5822/gemma-arterton-is-fields-agent-fields.html (accessed 25 February 2020).

64 Ibid.

65 Ibid.

12 'YOU TRAVEL WITH A *TUXEDO*?': DANIEL CRAIG (2012–15)

It was during the production of *Skyfall* that Daniel Craig significantly developed his own agency over the way his Bond was dressed. It had been Lindy Hemming for Craig's first outing as Bond in *Casino Royale*, and with *Quantum of Solace*, it was Eon Productions' dispute with Brioni that led to Louise Frogley needing 'to solve a problem' and selecting Tom Ford to design Craig's wardrobe in collaboration with the actor. For *Skyfall*, costume designer Jany Temime was recommended by the film's director, Sam Mendes, to design the wardrobe. Temime's notable credits included designing the costumes for the *Harry Potter* film franchise from *Harry Potter and the Prisoner of Azkaban* (2004), and *Bridget Jones: The Edge of Reason* (2004). Temime explained her role: 'When you get to do a Bond, you take with you all that makes Bond. When I was designing, I knew I was going to have a suit, a sportswear outfit, a bathing suit, a tuxedo. But the interesting thing we had to do was make it new and fresh and especially in 2012 with the fiftieth anniversary.'[1] Tom Ford remained Eon Productions' tailor of choice for *Skyfall*, and Temime outlined some of the costume suggestions Craig made in relation to his suits, namely 'a slim fitting suit tailored very near the body [...] Daniel wanted a suit you could forget – a suit that wasn't on top of his body, but *moving with* his body.'[2] Other recommendations put forward by Craig included: 'I want a tab trouser, slim fit, and light jackets with little padding.' For her own creative agency, Temime explained that Tom Ford was 'fantastic', and, echoing Hemming's approach:

I wanted Bond to look perfect all the time, so I chose Tom Ford shirts that had a tab under the collar – great for action scenes – and light blue and sky blue colours, because they go wonderfully with Daniel's eyes. I also wanted a tie you could forget; I didn't want Bond to be the guy with a tie that has a little square on it. Those are too loud, and you'll just remember the wrong design.

Albeit similar in how Hemming selected colours to suit Craig's tone and palette, Temime in this quotation is attempting to distinguish her work from that of former costume designers employed on the Bond films. Regarding Craig's trousers for *Skyfall*, Temime noted that they 'were flat-fronted and beltless – [wearing belts] are so nineties', in direct reference to how Hemming and Frogley styled Craig. In relation to Craig's agency over other areas, Craig 'personally selected and insisted upon' his personal stylist, Richard Davies, for promotional activities, including the Britannia Awards on 7 November 2012, a BAFTA Q&A on 8 November 2012, and *Jimmy Kimmel Live* on 9 November 2012.[3] This included three outfit changes priced at $1,000 'per look' and shipping for fitting; both items coming to a total of $3,944.85 (£2,465). Davies worked on the production of *Skyfall*, credited as an assistant designer along with Vivienne Jones.

Skyfall (2012)

Principal photography for *Skyfall* began on 7 November 2011 in London and was completed in early June 2012. Locations included Turkey, Japan and second unit shooting in Shanghai, China, before filming was completed at Pinewood Studios. The film opens in Istanbul with Bond and a female agent (Naomie Harris) – who is revealed to be Eve Moneypenny at the end of the film – in pursuit of a mercenary, Patrice (Ola Rapace). Bond wears a black and white sharkskin suit. In keeping with Craig's request, the jacket is very close-fitting with straight but narrow shoulders, and has narrow-legged trousers with a low rise and turn-up cuffs at the bottom. Underneath the jacket, Bond wears a white shirt fastened with a grenadine weave tie that has a black and silver check pattern, and the jacket includes a folded white pocket square in the breast pocket. It is over the course of these scenes that Bond lands in a train carriage and straightens his cufflinks, offering visual humour to the scene. Temime explains that the cufflink adjustment was Craig's idea and 'it was so perfect'.[4] The cufflinks for *Skyfall* were specially designed by Tom Ford, and included the Bond family crest to reflect the film's plot and Bond's familial connections in order to add a personal touch.[5]

After the opening credits, Bond, presumed to have been shot dead by Moneypenny, is revealed to be alive and staying on a Turkish island. It was for these scenes that Craig informed Temime that he wanted 'to look really shoddy', and so she elected to dress him in a leather jacket from Levi's Vintage 'Menlo' range: 'an old-fashioned style that you'd forget easily', and the jacket appears suitably distressed by the wardrobe department as per Craig's request.[6] Bond wears the jacket with a light blue shirt with a grey floral pattern sourced from Zara, khaki-coloured chinos from Topman, and brown suede desert boots, also from Zara. On Bond's return to London and breaking into M's flat as he did in *Casino Royale*, he wears the same dishevelled outfit. M informs Bond that his apartment has been sold and possessions placed in storage, and thus Bond decides to stay in a hotel. The following morning, Bond is escorted to the new MI6 headquarters for a debrief and to undertake a fitness assessment to be declared fit for active duty, which, as Christopher Laverty wittily puts it, occurs presumably after 'an unseen trip to Selfridges [and a] stop off at Crockett & Jones'.[7] After Bond's physical assessment, in which he wears a royal blue tracksuit, Bond wears a glen check suit in a mid-grey and black weave which Tom Ford refers to as 'Prince of Wales' check, but which is not the same Prince of Wales check fabric used for the three-piece suit worn by Connery in *Goldfinger*. With the suit, Bond wears a sky blue cotton shirt beneath the jacket, fastened with a tie with alternating square checks in blue, black and grey. Bond wears a pocket square tucked in his breast pocket that matches the shirt colour. The pocket square is a particular signature of Bond's suits in *Skyfall*, and is perhaps ironic, given that this was a costume trope of Christopher Walken's villain, Max Zorin, in *A View to a Kill*.

On arriving in Shanghai to track down Patrice, Bond masquerades as a chauffeur. Temime explains that Bond's coat was Craig's idea, telling her: 'I want to have a blue peacoat. I know Billy Reid makes very nice ones'.[8] The navy coat was made from wool and has peak lapels, a single vent and natural horn buttons for fastenings. Billy Reid provided twenty coats for this scene: five large and fifteen medium, the medium size jackets being used for the 'hero' shots and the large size jackets for movement and stunt work. It is rumoured that Craig later purchased a version of the coat for himself.[9] With the peacoat, Bond wears a black V-neck John Smedley sweater, slim-legged trousers made with a shark-grey wool from Acne's 'Wall Street' range, a white dress shirt and a peaked cap. After returning to his hotel room, Moneypenny arrives having been sent by M to update Bond on his mission and 'check-up on him'. In this scene, Bond is shirtless and flirts with Moneypenny, allowing her to shave his face and neck with a cutthroat razor. The scene cuts to fireworks showering over the Floating Dragon Casino, providing an allusion to sex in direct reference to Alfred Hitchcock's *To Catch a Thief* (1955). Under the fireworks, Bond travels on a dragon-shaped boat under an archway to reach the entrance of the casino, wearing a midnight blue dinner suit (Figure 12.1). Made from wool, the jacket has a shawl collar which is faced in black satin-silk. It has straight and narrow shoulders with roped sleeve-heads and is fastened with one button, also covered in silk. It is lined with navy silk. The matching trousers are trimmed on the outside seam with a black silk stripe. Bond wears the suit with a white cotton shirt, pleated black silk cummerbund and a black grosgrain bowtie.

Back at MI6 Headquarters in London, Bond wears a suit made of charcoal serge with a light blue rope stripe. The jacket is single-breasted and includes a pale blue pocket square folded in the breast pocket that matches the colour of his shirt. Bond's tie is made from a dark blue grenadine weave. After Bond travels with M to his family estate in Scotland, known as 'Skyfall', Bond changes from his suit to casual clothing more suited for the weather. He wears a Barbour 'X To Ki To'

Beacon Heritage sports jacket designed by Tokihido Yoshida. The jacket is made from 6oz Sylkoil waxed cotton and is olive in colour. It includes the distinctive Burberry tartan lining and has a single welted chest pocket and two lower-back poacher pockets. Post the release of *Skyfall*, Barbour released a version of this jacket in July 2013 renamed 'Dept. B Commander' in direct reference to Bond, and the jacket was reflective of how Craig wore it in *Skyfall*, namely without the detachable hood. Underneath the jacket, Bond wears a 'Blue Wave'-coloured N.Peal round-necked cashmere sweater from its 'Oxford' range. The corduroy trousers were sourced from All Saints. With this outfit Bond wears a Tom Ford scarf around his neck, which, according to Temime was, 'very expensive [. . .] made from the finest cashmere,' and was Craig's idea: 'He wanted [it] to look as though he had found the scarf in the Bond's family home [to reflect] the human side of his character [. . .] He wanted to show that Bond needed some sort of protection. It was a psychological thing, something that was supposed to be from his family.'[10]

When *Skyfall*'s villain, Raoul Silva (Javier Bardem), introduces himself to Bond, he is dressed in a Thom Sweeney ivory three-piece suit with a brown waistcoat, floral-patterned Prada shirt and Jeffrey West 'Marriot Brogue Cricket Chelsea' boots. On the Prada shirt, Temime noted that she was 'addicted' to it, 'because it had just the right level of lightness and expensiveness. I'm not going to call it "bad taste" – the graphic of that shirt is beautiful – but it's not Bond; a gentleman wouldn't wear that [. . .] I did [Silva's] entire costume around that shirt.'[11] On selecting this suit and the rest of Silva's wardrobe, Temime explained that her impression of his character was that he 'is slightly nouveau riche, and I wanted to show that he did his best to impress Bond', and that the Silva 'was one of the most difficult characters to establish for me [. . .] he's your traditional Bond villain. And then I wanted to create my villain. When you're working with an actor like Javier Bardem, you've got to work together. I've got to give him a costume that will help him create that villain.'[12] Over Bond's and Silva's interactions with one another, their costumes adopt another trope which has become familiar in Craig's Bond films: the villain being dressed in light colours and Bond dressed in dark to provide an ironic flip between hero and villain. For Silva's other key costume in *Skyfall*, when he is disguised in a police officer's uniform, Temime explained that she originally intended him to wear an ordinary uniform, however: 'Mendes complained that he [Bardem] looked too drab. He wanted him to stay in nouveau riche character. That meant refitting Bardem more stylishly along with all the other extras so they would match.'[13] On Silva's uniform, this includes a collar number on the lapels of 'JH 101'. The clearest image of how the uniforms are stylized in the film is in the crowd scene when Bond is faced with a host of extras dressed as police: the hat worn by the female police officer is particularly distinctive.

Bond first views the bad 'Bond girl', Séverine (Bérénice Marlohe), in Shanghai. After Patrice dies falling from the skyscraper, Bond looks to the apartment opposite and sees Séverine standing and gazing steadily back at him. Séverine wears a fitted black shift dress with a Florentine neckline and square back sourced from L'Wren Scott's 2012 collection, chosen for its 1940s silhouette. The dress has three-quarter length sleeves and is hemmed at the knee. Her waist is cinched with a wide leather belt that has the unusual design feature of a buckle fastening at the front and back. The painting that Séverine stands next to is Amedeo Modigliani's expressionist portrait of Lunia Czechowska, *Woman with a Fan* (1919) (Plate 15). The inclusion of this painting here is a direct reference to the placement of Francisco Goya's *The Duke of Wellington* (1812–14) in Dr. No's lair. Goya's portrait was included in *Dr. No* at the suggestion of the script assistant, Johanna Harwood, due to the painting having been reported as stolen from the National Gallery on 21 August 1961. The Modigliani painting was stolen in May 2010 from the Modern Art Museum in Paris, along with four others, reported to be collectively worth £89 million. The paintings were stolen by Vjeran Tomic who was arrested for the crime the following year and nicknamed 'Spider-Man' by the press for 'clambering into posh Parisian apartments and museums alike, to steal valuable gems and works of art', offering a rather witty reference to Sony as well as *Dr. No*.[14]

It is Séverine's black backless gown which is the most distinctive costume in the casino scene (Figure 12.2). In the script, there is a slight indication of the style of dress that the character is supposed to wear: 'A woman is standing at the top of the stairs. Her back to Bond. Backless dress. He'd recognise her anywhere.'[15] Temime designed Séverine's dress with some input from Marlohe, and based the style on Rita Hayworth's black dress in *Gilda*, similar in silhouette to the gown worn by Helga Brandt in *You Only Live Twice*. The dress took six months to create, meaning that work would have begun in May 2011, and therefore it is Temime who had the agency over the way in which the dress looked rather than the scriptwriters. It features 60,000 Swarovski crystals, Swarovski being an official licensee for *Skyfall*. The dress included a corseted bodice, a sheer back which was covered with 'tattoo-effect' transfers, and a floor-length satin-silk skirt with sheer side panels. Temime revealed that:

We had to make six different versions of the body, so that Bérénice could change twice a day during filming. Each time she changed we had to sew the body onto the main part of the dress while she was wearing it – it was so delicate [. . .] The first time you see the dress is from the back so you see this beautiful tattoo-effect across the sheer fabric – which we dyed to match her skin tone, to suggest that she was naked. This is my 'Bond girl' and she had to look fantastic.[16]

As with Silva, it is notable that Temime often refers to the characters as 'hers' in interview, with the exception of Craig's Bond. This is in keeping with the designer's desire to distance herself from previous wardrobe teams that have worked on earlier Bond films. Marlohe explained that her input inspired the gowns 'tattoo effect':

> I was lucky, I could see the dress before [it was complete], and I just thought that some changes should be done because it had to fit my idea about the Séverine character. I'm very happy with the result because it is exactly what I had in mind: a bit dangerous and 'dragonesque', with the tattoos and the long scary nails. [. . .] I was inspired by the Chimera.[17]

Séverine reminded Temime of Ava Gardner and film noir: 'I wanted her to look sexy and exceptional and dark.'[18] It is during the scenes between Bond and Séverine when the dialogue between the pair offers recognition towards the fashion-led banter typical of Bond films and is similar to the discourse between Bond and Vesper in *Casino Royale*:

Séverine   Would you mind if I asked you a business question?

Bond   Depends on the question.

Séverine   It has to do with . . . death.

Bond   A subject in which you're well versed.

Séverine   And how would you know that?

Bond   Only a certain kind of woman wears a backless dress with a Beretta 70 strapped to her thigh.

Séverine   One can never be too careful when handsome men in tuxedos carry Walthers.

Beyond the characters' flirtation through dress, the dialogue offers another reference to *Dr. No* and Fleming's novels in that the Beretta 70 was the model issued to replace the previous version, and the one which Bond uses before it is replaced with his Walther PPK at M's request. It also invites direct comparison

FIGURE 12.2 Séverine's 'tattoo' evening gown. *Skyfall* directed by Sam Mendes © Eon Productions/MGM/Columbia Pictures 2012. All rights reserved.

with Pam Bouvier in *Licence to Kill*, who wore a Beretta strapped to her thigh under the 'Rip Away Hem Dress'. As with *Licence to Kill*, it also humorously references Geoffrey Boothroyd's description of the gun that he offered to Fleming in their correspondence: 'I dislike a man who comes into contact with all sorts of formidable people using a .25 Beretta. This sort of gun is really a lady's gun, and not a really nice lady at that.'[19]

When Bond joins Séverine on her yacht, *Chimera*, she wears a satin-silk night robe, created by Belgian lingerie designer Carine Gilson, which was 'Number 12' in the designer's 2011 summer collection. The floor-length, cream-coloured robe is made from silk sourced from Lyon, France, and is patterned with scalloped black Chantilly floral lace appliquéd onto the front and sleeves. The collar is V-necked and shaped by pin-tucking the bust and back and is tied at the waist with a belt. On arriving in 'Dead City', Séverine is costumed in a fitted Donna Karan ruby red jersey dress. It has capped sleeves and a low-cut surplice neckline. The dress is draped and gathered under the bust on the left side and is knee-length.

Initially a field agent, Moneypenny wears a beige Belstaff jacket from the 'New Selsey' range, which is in a fitted 'biker-style' with a buckled funnel collar, lots of pockets, zipped cuffs, and is fastened with a concealed front zip and press studs. Beneath the jacket, Moneypenny is dressed in a white shirt, and her black leather trousers are sourced from J Brand. She wears an Omega Aqua Terra watch on her wrist in keeping with *Skyfall*'s brand promotion. When Bond subsequently meets Moneypenny in the MI6 headquarters, she is dressed in a white sheer silk blouse with black leather piping on the collar and pocket fastenings over the bust, a mustard yellow pencil skirt and black suede-heeled ankle boots, the colours reflecting her indecisiveness over whether to return to fieldwork.

During her flirtation with Bond in his Shanghai hotel room, Moneypenny is dressed in a red silk blouse with cloverleaf lapels, red pencil skirt and a wide tan leather belt fastened with a gold buckle before changing into her most distinctive costume in *Skyfall*. In the casino, Moneypenny is dressed in an Amanda Wakeley gown from the designer's 2011 collection. Yellow-gold in colour, the *crêpe* satin-silk gown is cut on the bias and floor-length with visible fold-and-stitch detailing. The original dress was strapless, however three slim and interconnected spaghetti shoulder straps were added to the bodice for the film. Wakeley, who previously provided dresses for Halle Berry and Rosamund Pike in *Die Another Day*, explained that she was approached by Temime to provide Harris's dress: 'Since much of the film takes place in London, I think that Jany was interested in working with an iconic London designer. We could have designed something special for the movie, but when Jany and I looked through the collection together, there were a number of dresses that really seemed to fit the brief.'[20]

Wakeley was pleased to offer the dress for the film, and also provide two shift dresses for Judi Dench, explaining: 'I am a huge fan of James Bond [...] For our brand it is great global exposure [...] I think it is wonderful for Amanda Wakeley in that it conveys the breadth of our design reach, from glam evening to more understated day wear.' At the end of *Skyfall*, Moneypenny takes off her overcoat to reveal a light blue Roland Mouret 'O'Hara' *crêpe* wool dress. It is a fitted, knee-length dress with fold-and-pleat detailing around at the rounded neck. It has capped sleeves with asymmetric seams, a back vent, and is fastened with a gold zip at the back. This dress is representative of Moneypenny adopting a more conservative role after declining active service and the partaking of fieldwork, namely becoming the secretary to M's replacement, Gareth Mallory (Ralph Fiennes). It is Moneypenny going from field agent to secretary that reflects Eon Productions' sleight of hand in relation to gender politics that is particularly evident in both Brosnan's and Craig's Bond films.

Gareth Mallory is introduced in *Skyfall* as the chairman of the Intelligence and Security Committee. In the script, there is a small direction offered on Mallory's costume: 'Impeccably tailored. Trim and controlled.'[21] In the film, Mallory wears items of clothing tailored by Timothy Everest. He first wears a dark grey suit, of which his jacket is draped over a chair. The flat front, high-waist trousers have a slim, tapered cut, and are held up with *fleur-de-lys*-embroidered navy braces, produced by Albert Thurston. Mallory's cotton shirt is deep sky blue with a moderate spread collar fastened with a navy tie that includes a woven lattice pattern in purple. When Mallory first meets Bond, their suits work to directly contrast with one another in order to demonstrate their initial wariness of each other. Mallory wears a more traditional three-piece chalk-stripe suit in mid-blue. The suit jacket has straight, padded shoulders with roped sleeve-heads, and the jacket is cut with a lean chest. The waistcoat has six buttons worn with five of the buttons fastened. Beneath it, Mallory wears a light blue shirt fastened with a navy tie that has large white polka dots with a navy pin dot in the centre of each. At the end of the film, Mallory is dressed in the most traditional suit he wears in *Skyfall*:

a double-breasted navy suit, made from heavy woollen flannel cloth including soft grey chalk stripes, worn with a mid-blue shirt fastened with a red ribbed silk tie. This costume works to affirm his status as the new 'M' and Bond's superior. By way of comparison, Bond in these scenes is dressed in a navy herringbone suit and a light blue shirt that is fastened with a mid-grey and dark navy tie. This works to demonstrate the pair's mutual respect for one another that has grown over the course of the film, similar to *Quantum of Solace*.

The other MI6 character that Bond is introduced to in *Skyfall* is Q (Ben Whishaw) during the scene based in the National Gallery. The script offers the following direction in relation to Q's costume: 'A slender young man in his twenties, dressed in an elegant suit, moves in next to Bond.'[22] This scene offers a good example of Temime applying her own agency. The designer explained that with Q:

> I had very little time to establish a character [...] When Q arrives in the museum, I wanted Bond to think he's just a nerd or a student – that's why I used a duffle coat. But first, I put glasses on Ben Whishaw. What he had on was very expensive, like the Margiela jacket he wears under his duffle coat. They were modish, nerdy, expensive clothes that nobody else would recognise – except for another computer wizard.[23]

Q's duffle coat is a coffee brown-coloured fishtail parka coat with a hood sourced from Pretty Green. The original hood included a detachable faux fur trim, however this was removed for the film. In the scenes based in MI6, Q wears a mustard-coloured V-neck cardigan that formed part of the Dries van Noten autumn/winter 2011 range. It is fastened by a front zip, and the collar has a dark blue and red stripe. His white Reiss shirt has a light grey pencil stripe detail and he wears a dark blue knitted silk tie from Zara and Hentsch Man plaid trousers in navy and plum.

According to Sony's marketing strategy for *Skyfall*, the key challenges for the film were recognized as being to find 'novel ways' to 'eventize' the film and communicating how the film would build upon the franchise, with Sony noting that the anniversary year as well as Bond's appearance in the Olympics Opening Ceremony would work to help this.[24] For the post-production marketing related to fashion and costume, Sony's strategy aimed 'for significant breakout campaigns along a broad spectrum of subjects: Style and Fashion/Travel/High Tech/Fitness.'[25] 'Editorial Ideas' for fashion marketing included women for the first time since *On Her Majesty's Secret Service*: 'Pump up female interest via glossy fashion spreads/ profiles of "Bond girls" Naomie Harris and Bérénice Marlohe, and take advantage of the high-style special shoot photography by Gavin Bond.'[26] It is from *Skyfall* onwards that it can be understood that both Eon Productions and Sony were keen to actively promote Bond through lifestyle and fashion more than previous Bond films since 1970.[27] As part of this, Sony outlined how to approach international promotion partners:

Pitch only to partners who can reflect the **themes/values** of [the] Bond brand including:

- Lifestyle
- State-of-the-art technology
- Action
- Witty humour
- Villains
- 'Bond girls'[28]

To help promotional campaigns, Sony noted the established consumer beliefs surrounding the character were: 'Bond is original and the epitome of cool/I want to be just like James Bond,' with the desired consumer effect being: 'I want to buy products that are associated with Bond and *Skyfall*/To live the Bond lifestyle/ Aspirational.'[29] Sony's 'Marketing Strategy' document notes that two out of seven 'confirmed partners/licensees' were UK retailer Harrods, offering 'Point of Sale (POS) materials throughout the estate,' which would be 'visible to 1.7 million visitors', with the store offering 'print and online promotional support'.[30] Omega continued to have a sponsorship partnership with the brand, with a '$15MM [million] Media Commitment', producing TV advertisements that featured Craig and Marlohe as brand ambassadors, and creating two special watches; a fiftieth anniversary version, released on 22 February 2012, and a limited-edition *Skyfall* watch to be released at the same time as the film. The limited-edition male watch retailed at around $4,760. In terms of 'placed brands' within the film, Tom Ford is listed under 'apparel', and Swarovski is listed as a 'licensee', permitted to offer a fiftieth anniversary collection '*Skyfall* piece' with Marlohe to feature in its promotional campaign.[21] Because both are listed in the document as a 'global partners' Sony requested: 'please refrain from pitching to partners in the following categories', including apparel, jewellery and watches.[31]

Spectre (2015)

Following the success of *Skyfall*, Mendes returned to direct *Spectre* and a similar cast and crew were employed to produce the film, including Temime, and Tom Ford retained its contract and sponsorship to tailor Craig's suits. The script was written by John Logan, Neal Purvis and Robert Wade, and Jez Butterworth was employed to polish it. The pre-production process behind *Spectre* was not without issue, as was leaked in November 2014 by WikiLeaks, who released two versions of the script and various email correspondence between Sony executives and Eon Productions; the former displaying frustration with the latter over the script and budget for *Spectre*, reported to be between $220 and 275 million. Keen on keeping the production cost of *Spectre* down, Jonathan Glickman wrote to Broccoli and Wilson:

> We are currently facing a budget that is far beyond what we anticipated and are under immense pressure to reduce the number to $250M net of rebates and incentives. This is not about 'nickel and diming' the production. As of now, our shooting period is $50M higher than *Skyfall* and the current gross budget sits in the mid-$300Ms, making this one of the most expensive films ever made. We recognize that this movie needs to build on the past few films – and there are expectations we must meet for the audience. Still, we must find further cuts.[32]

To do this, Glickman suggested finding 'further' financial incentives to film in Mexico, saving $3 million by not filming sequences in Italy, having a second unit shoot Bond's arrival at Mr. White's 'Alpine Chalet' in Austria, reducing the number of train carriages from four to three in Morocco and 'dropping rain' from the film's finale.

Regardless of the issues over the script and the budget, the film began main production shooting on 14 December 2014, and principal photography was completed on 5 July 2015. Filming took place at Pinewood Studios and on location in London, Austria, Rome, Mexico City and Morocco. To differentiate Craig's *Spectre* wardrobe from the one he wore in *Skyfall*, Temime explained that: 'I wanted a very special [shirt] collar for *Skyfall*, with a tab under it. I dropped this for *Spectre* using a slightly bigger collar instead, just to update it.'[33] On the suits themselves, for both films the jackets are cut fashionably short and have a very suppressed waist. Spaiser believes that the key differences in the suits for *Spectre* are that the jackets have a fuller chest, wider shoulders and fuller sleeves.[34] The trousers are similar in that they are low rise, narrow-legged, with a flat front and turn-ups. Craig wears two different styles of Tom Ford suit for *Spectre*: the 'O'Connor' model and the 'Windsor' model. The 'O'Connor' model is the main suit type worn by Craig in the film. Craig wears two 'Windsor' model suits. Both jacket models include straight shoulders with roped sleeve-heads, and are tailored to have a lean chest and a suppressed waist. The jackets are short in length and have a single vent. The key differences between the two types of suit are that the 'O'Connor' model has narrow lapels and the 'Windsor' has medium-wide peaked lapels. The pockets on the 'O'Connor' jacket are slanted and flapped, and the 'Windsor' jacket includes a right-hand ticket pocket and straight, flapped pockets on either side. The 'O'Connor' jacket includes four cuff buttons on the sleeves and the 'Windsor' jacket includes five.[35] As well as Tom Ford, Craig also expressed a desire to be costumed in Brunello Cucinelli for *Spectre*, and Temime obliged.

The film opens with scenes taking place in Mexico during a Day of the Dead festival. Temime noted of the costumes in these scenes: 'We went to Mexico and found amazing people there. It is their culture, so they had to teach me. I told them 'please do it your way.' And then they worked for six months but the results were breath-taking.'³⁶ Anna Terrazas, the costume supervisor in Mexico, explained: 'Each jacket was created per person, the dresses. We're really trying to make them all different, and always bringing [the theme of] death into these costumes.' Costume supervisor Kenny Crouch revealed the extent of fully costuming the extras in these scenes:

> [It's] quite unique now to do it in costume. With CGI these days, you can do no more than five or six. So the trick is to [dress the extras] fast. There's a minimum amount of time to get anybody ready. We did it this morning in seventy-five minutes for 1,500 [people]; that's twenty a minute. I mean, that's some game.

For this scene, the Day of the Dead costumes are mainly coloured in black and white with accents of red, as denoted in the script:

1. EXT. STREET, MEXICO – LATE DAY
In this sea of RED and BLACK, we pick up a MAN IN A WHITE SUIT AND BLACK MASK, who is moving against the stream. This is MARCO SCIARRA. An assassin [. . .] Bond is dressed in all black, and is masked too. His arm is round a shapely MASKED GIRL.³⁷

As with *Skyfall*, Temime decided to continue with the deliberate and ironic contrast between the villain and Bond in *Spectre*. Bond's Day of the Dead costume consists of a black lightweight frockcoat that is calf-length with a flared skirt, and includes a white pattern in the shape of a skeleton painted onto the fabric. The skeleton's ribcage appears on the chest of the coat, with the vertebrae printed on the black silk tie. The ribcage, vertebrae and hip bones are painted on the rear of the coat. The coat-tails include leg bone patterning and the sleeves have arm bones printed on the sides. Bond also wears black leather gloves, a skull mask and carries a skull-headed cane. Temime explained:

> He had to look like James Bond in a crowd. We fitted different coats on him before I found an early twentieth-century coat that we remade before painting on the skeleton. I then found a top hat and we had a mask specially made because it had to be articulated. You had to see his eyes in close up – Daniel's eyes are very recognisable.³⁸

By comparison, Sciarra (Alessandro Cremona) wears a silk three-piece suit in cream, with a charcoal grey shirt and red silk cravat.

The following scenes offer a reference towards a previous Bond film, when Estrella (Stephanie Sigman) takes Bond to her hotel room and Bond strips off his Day of the Dead costume to reveal a blue Prince of Wales check suit beneath, in direct reference to the pre-credit sequence in *Goldfinger*: 'Now she turns and crawls onto the bed in her slip, expecting him to follow. But she turns to see him standing at the opened window, dressed now in a suit.'[39] The suit is one of the four 'O'Connor' models. With the suit, Bond wears a white shirt fastened with a medium-blue silk tie. After Bond leaves through the window, climbs over the balcony railings and walks over the rooftops he adjusts his cufflinks, which since *Skyfall* has become one of Craig's costume tropes.

Bond wears his second 'O'Connor' suit on meeting M and subsequently Q at MI6 Headquarters. It is a grey herringbone suit with a track stripe, made with a blend of worsted wool, mohair and silk. Bond wears this suit with a white cotton shirt fastened with a medium-dark grey tie on meeting M. He subsequently changes into a sky blue cotton shirt fastened with a dark navy tie when attending Q's mechanical workshop the following morning. This costume ensemble is worn beneath a three-quarter length, navy herringbone Tom Ford Chesterfield coat that is made from a cashmere and silk blend. After Bond travels to Rome, he attends Sciarra's funeral wearing a black double-breasted Tom Ford overcoat that is made from brushed wool and is quite military in its structure. It has wide peak lapels, is fastened with eight black horn buttons, and is hemmed below the knee. It is belted at the back in order to create a structured and close silhouette. Underneath the coat, Bond wears a three-piece black herringbone suit in the 'Windsor' model. It has wide peaked lapels and straight, sharp shoulders, inspired by Tommy Nutter's suits, and the trousers have a flat front and narrow, straight legs with plain hems. Bond wears the suit over a white cotton shirt with a point collar that is fastened with a black silk tie with woven checks. Temime said of the shirt that 'the collar is more Italian style: it is Bond in disguise', and elucidated:

> I changed some details for the suit as [Bond] was in a lot of different situations so the suit had to reflect the situation that he was in. There is a scene in Rome and he had to look like one of the other Italians so we had to disguise him to fit in with the other Italian men there.[40]

Bond disguises himself further by wearing black leather gloves, from the aptly-named 'Fleming' range sourced from Dents, and 'Havana'-coloured sunglasses from the Tom Ford 'Snowden' range.

When Bond travels to Morocco to visit L'Americain with Dr Madeleine Swann (Léa Seydoux), he wears a tan lightweight jacket sourced from Matchless, London. The jacket is loose and waistless with a zip fastening. With the jacket, Bond wears khaki cotton chinos sourced from Brunello Cucinelli that are similar to his Tom Ford trousers in that they are narrow-legged with a flat front. Beneath the jacket Bond wears a Tom Ford navy polo-neck cotton shirt. On discovering the location of Blofeld's (Christoph Waltz) lair, Bond and Madeleine travel on a train to reach the remote location. It is these scenes that form the most stylish and fashionable part of the film. In the script, *Spectre* was to originally include a longer scene between Madeleine and Bond in her compartment, reminiscent of *From Russia with Love*:

119. INT. MADELEINE'S COMPARTMENT, TRAIN – DAY

[…] Inside a compartment, Bond unzips his luggage. Madeleine watches as he removes a tightly rolled up dinner jacket. Unrolls it once more. Opens the door. A GUARD is passing.

> BOND
>
> Can you see if the Valet can press this for me?

> GUARD
>
> Yes, Sir.

He leaves.

> MADELEINE
>
> You travel with a *tuxedo*?

Bond frowns, almost slightly confused.

> BOND
>
> Of course.[41]

In the final film this scene is omitted, however for continuity *Spectre* does include the moment when Bond hands a suit bag to a passing guard and asks 'Would you press this for me? Thank you,' on way to Madeleine's carriage. The script directs:

128. INT. DINING CARRIAGE, TRAIN – NIGHT

Bond sits in the dining booth, immaculate in his white dinner jacket. Madeleine approaches. Looking stunning. She sits opposite him.[42]

Temime has explained her approach towards Bond's ivory dinner jacket as being silk because: 'I wanted something very sensual. Bond is in Tangier, Morocco, so I went for a 1930s feel. There have been Bonds in white tuxedos before but this shape is new. We used Crockett & Jones shoes, which have the shape I want. The leather is perfect, and they fit Daniel perfectly.'[43] The suit ensemble is from the 'Windsor' range. The jacket is single-breasted and Bond wears black woollen trousers trimmed on the outside seam with a black satin-silk stripe. Underneath the jacket he wears a white cotton dress shirt provided by Tom Ford with a pleated front and double cuffs, a black pleated silk cummerbund and a black bowtie (Plate 16). The trousers are held up using white braces, and the jacket is adorned with a red carnation. Temime noted: 'It was very hard to do better than the *Skyfall* blue tuxedo but I took my inspiration from Humphrey Bogart in *Casablanca* (1942) and Morocco. Daniel added the red carnation buttonhole.'[44] Temime later denied that she was inspired in any way by Connery's ivory dinner jacket worn in *Goldfinger*, however it appears that Craig was by adding the red carnation. Given that there was a previous allusion to *Goldfinger* in relation to costume at the beginning of *Spectre*, it is likely that the dinner suit worn by Connery would have almost certainly informed the one worn by Craig, even if only on a subliminal level. This suit was prominently used in the film's promotional materials. As Porteous noted in relation to *Octopussy*, as a costume designer 'you don't confess to anything'.

On alighting the train in the middle of a desert, Bond wears an unstructured light brown jacket and a pair of light khaki cotton trousers, both sourced from Brunello Cucinelli, made from a wool, silk and linen blend. It is reminiscent of Dalton's tan-coloured suit in *The Living Daylights*. The white shirt and rust-coloured tie made from a knitted silk blend were sourced from Tom Ford. After arriving at Blofeld's lair, Bond and Madeleine are escorted to their bedrooms before being invited to join Blofeld for drinks, reminiscent of *Dr. No*. This leads to the final distinctive costume scene in *Spectre*. The script notes that Bond's clothing is prepared by Blofeld:

142. INT. HIS BEDROOM – DAY
Bond enters a magnificent bedroom [. . .] A suit is laid out on his bed.

142A. INT. HOUSE – LATE AFTERNOON
Bond waits for Madeleine at the foot of the stairs. He is still – defiantly – in his own suit.[45]

In the film, Bond choses to wear the suit provided by Blofeld instead of defying Blofeld by wearing his own suit as the script indicates. This scene caused correspondence between the Sony executives concerned with the rising cost of *Spectre*, with Amy Pascal asking Glickman 'are we doing the Bond puts on a tux twice?'[46] Elizabeth Cantillon replied: 'I'm glad you said that about the tux (something easy as opposed to this budget). It's so clever in the last draft when she [Madeleine] says, "you travel with a tux?" And [Bond] does. It's great. Maybe [there] doesn't have to be another tux in [Blofeld's] lair?' suggesting a potential cost saving.[47] As Bond wears both suits in the film, it is therefore not a cost saving *per se*, however it does mean that neither suit provided for *Spectre* was wasted. The suit is the 'O'Connor' model, made from blue sharkskin fabric. With the suit, Bond wears a white cotton shirt with a point collar that is fastened an 'ink'-coloured, dark navy silk tie. Bond wears a folded white pocket square in the breast pocket of the jacket.

In the final scenes of *Spectre*, Bond wears a three-piece suit, reminiscent of the suit he wears on 'becoming Bond' at the end of *Casino Royale*. Again, it is the 'O'Connor' model, made from a wool, silk and mohair blend in dark charcoal with a slight

Damier check patterning. Bond wears the jacket with a six-button waistcoat and a sky blue cotton shirt with a point collar that is fastened with a black silk tie. Bond wears a folded pocket square in the breast pocket of his jacket to match his shirt.

Temime's approach towards costuming Blofeld was: 'I wanted to keep it simple, abstract, because the man is so bad that you don't need much detail. All the menace is in his mind.'[48] Timothy Everest tailored Blofeld's Nehru-style jackets in bottle green, navy and midnight blue silk with a velvet collar. They have a rounded Nehru collar, single-button fastening and welt hip pockets, reminiscent of Kamal Khan in *Octopussy*. With the Nehru jacket, Blofeld wears a navy Wooyoungmi shirt with black rubber lace effect on the collar and cuffs that are fastened with a button, and pale grey Margiela trousers with a drawstring waist. Blofeld's shoes are from the 'Fiandra Slipper' range designed by Bottega Veneta that are made from dark navy woven leather. Blofeld wears these shoes without socks. The reason for a sockless-villain was, according to Waltz, a purely practical one, and nothing to do with the direction in the script or character interpretation from Temime: 'Have you ever worn socks in the desert? It's kind of hot [...] It was about 105 degrees,' though, of course, Craig wears socks when playing Bond in these scenes.[49] By not electing to wear socks, however, Blofeld's costume reflects Franz Sanchez in *Licence to Kill* in another connection between Dalton's and Craig's Bond films.

When Bond tracks down Madeleine, who is working at the Höffler Klinik in Austria, the character is initially costumed in a black sheer sleeveless silk blouse that has a high circular collar with a pussy-bow fastening and black trousers. The outfit is accessorised with a wide black leather belt and Madeleine wears low-heeled ankle boots. Later, Madeleine wears the outfit with a grey *crêpe* Theory Lanai blazer which is collarless with structured shoulders and a sharply cut opening. On Madeleine's work outfit, Temime explained that the character

is a professional woman. She's a psychologist; she has an important job at the clinic. So she has clothes that we would wear to go to work [...] Ultimately, I just wanted to show that you can be very sexy every day, feeling good and feeling powerful and being yourself from eight o' clock in the morning. Being confident in your skin, having a powerful job – that makes you a 'Bond girl'.[50]

For the scenes in L'Americain, Madeleine wears a white cotton shirt dress with a gold button front-fastening. It is V-necked with short circular-capped sleeves that include turn-ups and is cinched at the waist with a thin white leather belt. Madeleine wears the outfit with low-heeled sandals fastened with an ankle strap.

The dress worn by Madeleine during the train sequence that is reminiscent of *From Russia With Love* was selected by Temime as she 'didn't want a "red carpet" evening dress but something that could be rolled up in a suitcase, dressed up or dressed down. Something sexy and simple,' which also works for continuity (Figure 12.3).[51] Stating that she wanted the dress to be 'nostalgic,' Temime explained

that: 'This is the first time that she catches Bond's attention, so I wanted the dress to be more like a second skin for her and also as simple as possible because of the situation.'[52] The dress was part of the 'Salma' range for Ghost in a 'Dusty Green' shade, available to purchase in the UK department store John Lewis. It is a lined satin floor-length gown with a boat neck, capped sleeves and a cowl back. With the dress, Madeleine wears champagne glitter-coloured Jimmy Choo 'Ivette' sandals.

For the scenes hosted in Blofeld's lair, the script offers the following direction in relation to Madeleine's costume: 'On the bed, a single beautiful dark blue dress, which catches the light.'[53] It also notes that Madeleine 'looks stunning' after changing into it. The dress in the film is a cream-coloured dress with blue scalloped lace overlay sourced from the Australian brand Lover which formed part of its 'Venus' range. It has an 'illusion' neckline, an asymmetrical hemline, short sleeves and a hidden zip fastening at the back. On meeting Blofeld, who shows Bond and Madeleine a meteor in his observatory, the script originally included a quip from Madeleine regarding her clothing, omitted from the final film, but reflective of her character as promoted through her costumes:

INT. OBSERVATORY – LATE AFTERNOON

OBERHAUSER
It's strange because I feel I know
you so well after all these years.

MADELEINE
You may know my dress size but you
don't know me.[54]

The secondary 'Bond girl', Lucia (Monica Bellucci) and the widow of Sciarra, is costumed in funeral clothes, and the script affords the following direction: 'Centre-stage, the WIDOW (LUCIA), black veil covering her face – the funeral service clearly over. The black clothes in stark contrast to the white marble steps.'[55] Temime explained that for Lucia, she was inspired by Sophia Loren, and the character: 'had to be dressed like an iconic Italian star; elegant and sculptural against the clean 1930s architecture.'[56] However, Temime was limited in what she could clothe the character in for the scene, given that Lucia was dressed for a funeral:

> I had to design something demure but still oozing of sexiness. To do that, I decided to add some mystery to the traditional black. The most important thing in the costume is the veil attached to the hat. I wanted Bond to look at her and not immediately know who she was, because it's a surprise for him like it is for us, and it creates a moment of suspense where you slowly discover her.[57]

This is not dissimilar to the approach used to costume Madame Boitier in *Thunderball*. Lucia wears a distinctively cut black coat which is made of wool. The lapels are wide and curved, and the coat has a plain front-buttoned closure and full-length sleeves. The coat is three-quarter length with a cinched waist and flares out from the waist to the hips. Underneath the coat, Lucia wears a fitted black knee-length jersey dress with long sleeves and two slashed sections above the chest. From the back, the main design feature of the dress is a scooped silk detail, dyed to the colour of Bellucci's skin tone, inclusive of black web detailing that reflects her veil worn during the funeral and making her dress appear as though it is backless. With this outfit, Lucia wears a pair of matte black leather Christian Louboutin 'So Kate' shoes that have five-inch stiletto heels.

Timothy Everest continued to tailor M's suits as with *Skyfall*, the brief of which was: 'to contemporise M from heavy worsted wools and flannels to a more modern, medium weight Super 120's worsted wool and baby cashmere coatings. The basis of the character's wardrobe is still predominantly classic, two-piece Prince of Wales [check] with blue overcheck.'[58] In his office, M wears a double-breasted three-piece navy suit with light grey pinstripes. Spaiser explains that the jacket: 'has a classic Savile Row cut with straight shoulders, roped sleeve-heads, a full chest, a nipped waist and medium-wide peaked lapels,' and the trousers have a plain front and tapered legs.[59] M's shirt is a mid-blue cotton shirt and his tie is navy with a slight pink detail. By comparison, Max Denbigh, codename 'C' (Andrew Scott), wears a black and grey glen check two-piece suit, sourced from Burberry. Spaiser notes that: 'The suit jacket has an English silhouette with straight shoulders and roped sleeve-heads. The chest is lean with a close fit and the waist is suppressed,' though the suit is not as tightly-fitted as Bond's.[60] The suit trousers are similar to Bond's in that they are slim-fitting and flat-fronted. The shirt that Denbigh wears with the suit is ecru with stripes and is fastened with a black tie that has asymmetric white polka dots. The suits worn by the three men in this scene work to reflect the differences in their individual characters (Figure 12.4): M's is the most traditional

FIGURE 12.4 Different suit styles in *Spectre*. Directed by Sam Mendes © Eon Productions/MGM/Columbia Pictures 2015. All rights reserved.

in terms of design, even though Timothy Everest worked to modernize the character's look. Denbigh's suit is more fashionable and modern in terms of design than that of M's, though is Burberry as opposed to Bond's Tom Ford suit in this scene. Although Denbigh proports to have a more modern outlook than that of M and Bond towards the Security Services ('We're going to bring British Intelligence out of the Dark Ages and into the light'), it is Bond's suits that can be deemed the most fashionable in this scene, given the tighter-fitting cut of his Tom Ford suits.

Moneypenny's costumes continue to be more conservative in style and colour in keeping with the final scenes of *Skyfall*. Harris explained her character's wardrobe choices: 'But I think she's constrained by working in a quite conventional office environment, so she has to wear traditional office wear and then brighten it up with some colourful, quirky touches.'[61] Temime concurs: 'In the case of Moneypenny, we had seen her already last time, but now she is working in the office. She has a tough job, working in the Secret Service, so we dressed her up like that—and I used colours for her.' Moneypenny wears a dark blue, fitted, knee-length cotton dress and kitten-heeled shoes with a wide ankle strap. When she visits Bond at his apartment in the evening, she wears a woollen blue coat in a lighter shade of blue than her dress. The coat has notched lapels, a two-button fastening and one back vent. It is hemmed two inches above her dress.

As with Moneypenny, Temime continues Q's character development from *Skyfall* by electing to costume Whishaw in expensive yet 'nerdy' clothing. In *Spectre*, Q wears a Maison Margiela suit in his mechanical workshop. It is a semi-solid brown colour, inclusive of light brown, dark brown, red and blue threads, and the jacket has straight shoulders and a clean chest. The collar is made of pinwale corduroy, and the sleeves have matching corduroy elbow patches. Beneath the jacket, Q wears a Kenzo 'Graphic Trees' shirt in a cobalt blue colour, made from cotton, that is fastened with a knitted burgundy tie, possibly made from silk. The scene in the mechanical workshop also affords for Omega watch product placement, as noted in the script:

29. INT. Q'S MECHANICAL WORKSHOP – DAY

Q

But you <u>can</u> have this.

He hands Bond an understated, black-strapped OMEGA WATCH.

BOND

What does it do?

Q

It tells the time. Might help with
your punctuality issues.[62]

The watch that Q offers Bond is an Omega Seamaster 300 *Spectre* limited edition watch with a 'steel on NATO strap', retailing at £4,750.

Generally, the press offered positive reviews towards Craig's more 'serious' and 'gritty' performances in *Quantum of Solace*, *Skyfall* and *Spectre*, and Adam Tschorn in particular was impressed with the Tom Ford suits in *Quantum of Solace*: 'Neither distinctly British nor Italian nor even European, [Bond is] a sartorial chameleon who blends in everywhere in the world while simultaneously standing out as the sharpest looking man in the room.'[63] However, since Craig began to have more agency over the way he was dressed in *Skyfall* and *Spectre*, not everyone was impressed with the change in Bond's sartorial style in relation to the tighter-fitting Tom Ford suit models. Roger Stone believed:

The problem with *Skyfall* in a nutshell? Daniel Craig's slim-cut suits are too tight, too narrow shouldered and too small. At five-foot-ten, they make him look smaller [...] 007 shouldn't be wearing suits better suited to Pee-wee Herman or Curly Howard in *The Three Stooges*. Craig's suits are so tight they pull everywhere and it's most unflattering. A suit should have clean lines, and Mr. Craig's suits don't. The suits violate all principles of good tailoring.[64]

Adam King, co-founder of the bespoke tailoring firm King & Allen, similarly complained after the release of *Spectre* that Craig's 'jackets were too tight [and] were far too short. This is Bond, not the Arctic Monkeys circa 2011! [...] I noticed puckering all the way down the back seam of the jacket. That's nothing to do with fit – that's poor-quality stitching.'[65] It has since been confirmed in 2019 that Tom Ford will continue to suit Craig's Bond in *No Time To Die* in 'made-to-measure' tailored clothing.[66] Given that Craig has very much established his agency over how Bond should be dressed since *Skyfall*, it is likely that the character will continue to be fashionably rather than classically dressed in his tight-fitting, second-skin suits in *No Time To Die*.

Notes

1 Bill Desowitz, 'Immersed in movies: Costume designer Jany Temime talks *Skyfall*', *indiewire*, 21 December 2012, www.indiewire.com/2012/12/immersed-in-movies-costume-designer-jany-temime-talks-skyfall-200262/ (accessed 29 February 2020).

2 Stelios Phili, 'Style Reconnaissance: *Skyfall*'s Jany Temime on Daniel Craig's wardrobe requests, the first Bond villain to wear Prada, and the deal with Javier Bardem's blond hair', *GQ*, 9 November 2012, www.gq.com/story/jany-temime-skyfall-interview-james-bond-style-daniel-craig (accessed 29 February 2020).

3 Richard Davies, 'Vendor Request Form', 2 January 2013, https://wikileaks.org/sony /docs/03_03/MKTGFIN/PO-PDF/Richard%20Davies109.pdf (accessed 29 February 2020).

4 Phili.

5 Rob Sharp, 'Dressing like James Bond', *Christie's*, 15 February 2016, www.christies.com/features/How-to-dress-like-James-Bond-7042-1.aspx (accessed 29 February 2020).

6 Phili.

7 Christopher Laverty, 'Review: *Skyfall*', *Clothes on Film*, 16 October 2012, https://clothesonfilm.com/review-skyfall/ (accessed 29 February 2020).

8 Phili.

9 'Pretty Green fishtail parka', *James Bond Lifestyle*, 22 November 2012, www.jamesbondlifestyle.com/product/pretty-green-fishtail-parka (accessed 1 March 2020).

10 Desowitz.

11 Phili.

12 Desowitz.

13 Phili.

14 Agence France-Presse, '"Spider-Man" burglar on trial over $100m Paris art theft', *Guardian*, 30 January 2017, www.theguardian.com/world/2017/jan/30/spider-man-burglar-on-trial-over-100m-paris-art-theft (accessed 1 March 2020).

15 Greg Williams, *Bond on Set: Filming Skyfall*, (London: Dorling Kindersley Limited, 2012), 70.

16 Sarah Karmali, '*Skyfall*'s designer on dressing a Bond girl', *Vogue*, 25 October 2012, www.vogue.co.uk/gallery/skyfall-costume-designer-jany-temime-on-dressing-bond-girl-berenice-marlohe (accessed 1 March 2020).

17 Remmert van Braam, 'Interview with Bérénice Marlohe', *James Bond Lifestyle*, www.jamesbondlifestyle.com/news/interview-bérénice-marlohe (accessed 1 March 2020).

18 Karmali.

19 Geoffrey Boothroyd to Fleming, 23 May 1956 in Fergus Fleming, *The Man with the Golden Typewriter*, 141.

20 Ella Alexander, 'Amanda Wakeley: How I dressed Bond girls', *Vogue*, 23 October 2012, www.vogue.co.uk/gallery/amanda-wakeley-dresses-skyfall-bond-girls (accessed 1 March 2020).

21 Williams, 36.

22 Ibid., 52.

23 Phili.

24 Sony Pictures, 'International Theatrical Marketing Strategy: *Skyfall*', September 2012, 2, 3. https://wikileaks.org/sony/docs/01/Market/MP_MARKET/MKT%20Columbia/ FINANCEIRO/BUDGETS/BUDGETS%20SUBMETIDOS/BUDGET%20-%20 SKYFALL/SKYFALLInternational%20Theatrical%20Mktg%20Strategy%20FINAL.pdf (accessed 29 February 2020).

25 Ibid., 21.

26 Ibid., 23.

27 Sarah Gilligan has researched the fashioning of Craig's Bond and the brand promotion of his films in her chapter 'Branding the new Bond: Daniel Craig and designer fashion', in Robert G. Weiner, B. Lynn Whitfield and Jack Becker (eds), *James Bond in World and Popular Culture: The Films Are Not Enough*, 2nd edn (Newcastle upon Tyne: Cambridge Scholars Publishing, 2011), 76–85.

28 Sony Pictures, 27.

29 Ibid., 29.

30 Ibid., 31.

31 Ibid., 32.

32 Jonathan Glickman to Broccoli, Wilson and Peter Oillataguerre, 8 November 2014, https://wikileaks.org/sony/emails/emailid/69288 (accessed 3 March 2020).

33 Sharp.

34 Spaiser, 'The differences between the *Skyfall* and *Spectre* Tom Ford O'Connor suits', *The Suits of James Bond*, 10 November 2015, www.bondsuits.com/differences-between-the-skyfall-and-spectre-oconnor-suits/ (accessed 3 March 2020).

35 Spaiser, 'Basted for Bond: Examining Daniel Craig's Tom Ford clothes in *Spectre*', *The Suits of James Bond*, 29 October 2015, www.bondsuits.com/basted-for-bond-examining-daniel-craigs-tom-ford-clothes-in-spectre/ (accessed 9 March 2020).

36 *Day of the Dead Festival*, featurette, directed by Sam Mendes (USA: Sony Pictures, 2015).

37 John Logan, Neal Purvis and Robert Wade, *Spectre*, third revised shooting script, 1 December 2014, 1.

38 Sharp.

39 Logan, Purvis and Wade, 2.

40 'The costumes of *Spectre*', *007.com*, 2 December 2015, www.007.com/the-costumes-of-spectre/ (accessed 4 March 2020); Alice Cuffe, '*Spectre* wardrobe secrets: Costume designer Jany Temime on dressing James Bond', *International Business Times*, 3 December 2015, www.ibtimes.co.uk/spectre-wardrobe-secrets-costume-designer-jany-temime-dressing-james-bond-1525246 (accessed 4 March 2020).

41 Logan, Purvis and Wade, 82, 83.

42 Ibid., 85.

43 Sharp.

44 'The costumes of *Spectre*'.

45 Logan, Purvis and Wade, 95.

46 Amy Pascal to Glickman and Elizabeth Cantillon, 9 November 2014, https://wikileaks.org/sony/emails/emailid/69288 (accessed 3 March 2020).

47 Cantillon to Pascal and Glickman, 10 November 2014, ibid.

48 Sharp.

49 Spaiser, 'Blofeld's navy Nehru jacket in *Spectre*', *The Suits of James Bond*, 7 November 2016, www.bondsuits.com/blofelds-navy-nehru-jacket-spectre/ (accessed 9 March 2020).

50 Raquel Laneri, 'The Bond girls have a whole new look', *Refinery 29*, 30 October 2015, www.refinery29.com/en-us/bond-movie-costume-designer-jany-temime-interview (accessed 4 March 2020).

51 'The costumes of *Spectre*'.

52 Katie Davidson, 'How the Bond girls got a modern reboot for *Spectre*', *Style Caster*, 2016, https://stylecaster.com/jany-tamime-spectre/ (accessed 4 March 2020).

53 Logan, Purvis and Wade, 95.

54 Ibid., 98.

55 Ibid., 28.

56 'The costumes of *Spectre*'.

57 Laneri.

58 'Following on from *Skyfall*, Timothy Everest reprises the role as tailor', *Timothy Everest*, 2 October 2015, https://timothyeverest.co.uk/spectre/ (accessed 4 March 2020).

59 Spaiser, 'M: Double-breasted chalk stripe suit in *Spectre*', *The Suits of James Bond*, 16 February 2016, www.bondsuits.com/m-double-breasted-chalk-stripe-suit-in-spectre/ (accessed 4 March 2020).

60 Spaiser, 'Max Denbigh's grey glen check suit', *The Suits of James Bond*, 5 March 2016, www.bondsuits.com/max-denbighs-grey-glen-check-suit/ (accessed 4 March 2020).

61 Davidson.

62 Logan, Purvis and Wade, 24.

63 Adam Tschorn, 'James Bond takes a *Quantum* leap in luxury', *Los Angeles Times*, 16 November 2008.

64 Roger Stone, 'James Bond and the sartorial tradition', *Huffington Post*, 26 November 2012, www.huffpost.com/entry/skyfall-james-bond-sartorial_b_2192261 (accessed 10 October 2020).

65 Adam King, 'Why were Daniel Craig's suits so ill-fitting in *Spectre*?', *King & Allen*, n.d., http://kingandallen.co.uk/journal/2015/daniel-craigs-ill-fitting-suits-in-spectre/ (accessed 10 October 2020).

66 'Insider', 'Tom Ford dresses 007 in *No Time To Die*', *007.com*, www.007.com/tom-ford-dresses-007-in-no-time-to-die/#:~:text=James%20Bond%20to%20wear%20made,Craig%20as%20the%20iconic%20character (accessed 10 October 2020).

CONCLUSION

The twenty-five Eon Productions James Bond films, produced over nearly sixty years, form the longest running continuous franchise in cinema history. Analysing these films through costume has afforded the opportunity to research this small but significant area through three key themes: agency, labour and the costumes themselves. Furthermore, it has allowed for understanding how the processes and costs behind costuming film have adapted over an extended period of time in the British film industry from the early 1960s to the present.

Fashioning James Bond has demonstrated the different agencies behind costume decisions, particularly in relation to the tailoring of James Bond's suits. For *Dr. No*, the decision to employ Anthony Sinclair as Sean Connery's tailor was made by the film's director, Terence Young, and this was the same approach adopted by Peter Hunt, the director of *On Her Majesty's Secret Service*, in employing his personal tailor Dimitrov 'Dimi' Major to create George Lazenby's suits. Roger Moore, however, was instrumental in the decision to use his personal tailors, owing to his sustained interest in the menswear fashion industry. Moore has had most bespoke tailors throughout his tenure as Bond, all employed on the actor's recommendation: Cyril Castle, Angelo Vitucci and Douglas Hayward. Following Moore, Timothy Dalton wore made-to-measure suits on the recommendation of the costume designers Emma Porteous and Jodie Tillen, based upon Dalton's own request to distance himself from Moore's fashion-conscious Bond and owing to his interpretation of Fleming's novels. Upon the casting of Pierce Brosnan for *GoldenEye*, the costume designer, Lindy Hemming, made the executive decision to dress the character in Brioni, expressing a desire for Bond to return to the 'classic' and 'traditional' suitings afforded to Connery. Hemming remains the only costume designer to date who has had significant agency over the way Bond is dressed in the films. Daniel Craig was first tailored by Brioni for *Casino Royale* in keeping with Eon Productions' contract with the firm and Hemming's recommendation, however owing to issues that arose between the production company and Brioni, Louise Frogley suggested Tom Ford provide Bond's suits in order to 'solve a problem' for *Quantum of Solace*. From *Skyfall* onwards, Tom Ford has been contracted to provide Craig's suits. However, the actor has also developed significant agency over the way that they are cut and structured, making key suggestions to Jany Temime, the costume designer for *Skyfall* and *Spectre*. Although Suttirat Anne Larlarb has replaced Temime as the costume designer for *No Time To Die*, Tom Ford remains Eon Productions' 'tailor of choice', and Craig has retained his own agency over the way he is to be costumed.

Although both Moore and Craig have possessed more agency over the way that they have been costumed, there is a perception that their more 'fashionable' suits have dated quicker than the ones worn by the other Bond actors. It should be noted that Moore was often referred to as one of the 'best dressed men' in the 1980s: there is much retrospective exaggeration applied by critics over the amount of flared trousers, safari suits and fashion faux pas that Moore wore throughout his tenure as Bond.[1] Similarly, Craig was named as best dressed in *GQ*'s 'Men of the Year' survey in 2007 for wearing Brioni suits in *Casino Royale* and in 2008 for wearing Tom Ford suits in *Quantum of Solace*.[2] However, since Craig has gained more agency and has worn tighter-fitting suits at his own request, he has, ironically, dropped down the list.

In relation to the tailors and menswear outfitters employed to provide suits for film, Del Smith has outlined the difference in approach to tailoring a suit for a film character versus tailoring a suit for a private client:

> When I tailor a suit for a client, I need to get to know them and their personality to understand what they want for a suit, for example what they need it for and where they intend to wear it. I work with the client personally to create a suit that will make them look and feel good. When you tailor a suit for film, you need to compliment the actor's physique, but also tailor it to suit the personality of the character that they are playing, which can be difficult if you haven't seen the script or know the source material. You also need to know the types of scenes that the suit will be worn in, for example if the suit is to be worn in an action sequence it needs to be tailored with heavier fabrics to be robust against any action that it may receive. You also need to be informed about the scene's lighting and colour scheme in order to tailor the suit in the right cloth, colour and weight.

This, of course, relates to the theme of labour, and in the Bond films there are several examples of when a costume designer has not been employed on the production of a Bond film at all, and therefore the role of designing, making and sourcing costumes goes to the wardrobe supervisor, wardrobe master or wardrobe mistress. Furthermore, there is also a gendered imbalance between such a perception that costume is 'women's work' and the salaries afforded to different roles.

To understand this theme, relevant sources have shed light on the labour and process involved in creating various wardrobe items. The role of the designer has adapted over the production of the Bond films: less time is now afforded to designing costumes and commissioning a costumier such as Bermans and Nathans, later Angels, to make them, and from Dalton's films onward, many costumes are sourced from leading fashion houses instead. Similarly, it is clear that the process of sourcing Bond's suits has changed over time, as indeed is the way in which they are produced. Until Moore's last Bond film, *A View to a Kill*, the suits were bespoke through the commissioning of a tailor. After the casting of Dalton, this changed as Eon Productions needed to source a larger volume of suits in a shorter period of time, and therefore Bond's suits have since been made-to-measure or off-the-peg. This has not been without incident: tailors have not been reticent in offering their views on Bond's suits, beginning with Domenico Caraceni in 1962. These 'tailoring wars' have involved irritation expressed between different tailors hired to provide Bond's suits, for example the alleged disagreement between Sinclair and Major; the umbrage taken by the British press and Savile Row tailors over the hiring of Brioni in the 1990s; and has come full circle in the most recent 'tailoring war' between Eon Productions and Brioni over the production of a 'James Bond for Brioni' dinner suit. To date, and despite frequent claims to the contrary, a Savile Row tailoring firm has never been employed to provide Bond's suits. This is also similar with the sourcing of costumes for other characters: although costumes were in part always sourced from costumiers and fashion houses since *Dr. No*, more emphasis is now placed on selecting costumes based on recent fashion collections including from Giorgio Armani, Versace and Prada since the 1990s.

From the sources available, *Fashioning James Bond* has mapped how costume designers have approached the process of designing costume from script to screen and their individual design imperatives. Similarities between how different costume designers approach their role include collaborative discussion with the director, production designer, art director, hair and make-up artists in order to develop the costumes from the script, and harmonize the costumes between the different characters and a film's design elements. The majority of costume designers will first read the script for inspiration before preparing initial preparatory sketches for further discussion and development. This book has analysed the designs produced by the different costume designers where available, revealing that these renderings are works of art in their own right beyond their purpose of demonstrating a designer's interpretation of the character and the costume assigned to them. One interesting design aspect that has become evident on comparing costume sketches is that when grouped and compared in relation to gender, it is often the men who produce the more whimsical, lyrical and sketchier costume designs, such as Anthony Mendleson, Donfeld and Jacques Fonteray, and the women who consistently produce the more staccato and exacting line drawings with colour encapsulated within the figures, as can be understood from the designs produced by Beatrice Dawson, Julie Harris, Porteous and Hemming. In terms of how different designers approach psychology, Jocelyn Rickards, the first full-time costume designer to be employed on a Bond film, believed that costume offers a 'visual signpost' for a character's background, and similarly, Hemming explained that costume design is about 'looking at people and trying to understand what they do'. Colour is recognized as important by all of the designers, particularly by Harris and Porteous. Where there can be inconsistencies in terms of approaches towards costume design is how the input of the actor or actress is interpreted. For example, Donfeld believed that the actress 'should never inflict her opinion on the dress designer'. By way of comparison, Temime in particular elected to work collaboratively with the cast, and the designer has explained in interview how both Javier Bardem and Bérénice Marlohe had an input in how their costumes were designed for *Skyfall*. Furthermore, Grace Jones had significant agency over the way her character, May Day, was costumed in *A View to A Kill*, and insisted to Porteous that she be costumed by Azzedine Alaïa and Lawrence Easden. Compared with any other actor or actress besides Moore, it is Jones who has possessed the most agency over the way her character was costumed in a Bond film to date.

Training has also varied, with Marjorie Cornelius having little experience in costume design prior to working on *On Her Majesty's Secret Service*, although this film is arguably the most lavishly costumed of all the Bond films. Since Elizabeth Waller was hired as the costume designer on *For Your Eyes Only* having previously worked for the BBC, the majority of designers, including Porteous, Tillen and Hemming, have designed costumes for television prior to transferring their skills to film productions; Tillen transferred her experiences of costuming *Miami Vice* directly onto *Licence to Kill*, an image consistently referred to throughout the film's critical reception. In relation to inspiration, it is certainly true that this is where designers are particularly and consistently secretive. As summed up by Porteous, they have a variety of influences, however 'you don't confess to anything', although some influences can become evident when analysing the variety of costumes designed and sourced for different characters. An example of this is in Hemming's approach towards the female characters in Brosnan's films: often, Hemming takes inspiration from cartoon or pixilated fictional characters, including 'Cruella de Ville meets Morticia Addams' and Snow White for Xenia Onatopp, Jessica Rabbit for Elektra King and Lara Croft for Dr Christmas Jones. Similarly, designers will often seek to distance themselves from another designers' work on previous Bond films, and this is particularly evident in interviews conducted with Porteous, Hemming and Temime: often, Temime will refer to the characters as being 'hers' – 'my villain', 'my "Bond girl"' – and has denied being influenced by Connery's costumes in *Goldfinger* despite the similarities between the creative use of suits in the pre-title sequence for both *Goldfinger* and *Spectre*, and the ivory dinner jacket with red carnation worn by Bond in these two films.

Finally, one key difference in terms of labour rather than agency in relation to wardrobe personnel is in the gender pay difference. Using the examples of *Dr. No* and *From Russia With Love*, the male wardrobe masters were paid more than the female costume designers and the wardrobe mistresses employed on these productions. This is consistent with pay afforded for different wardrobe personnel during the 1960s in relation to gender. Besides pay, there has also been an imbalance in the way that different wardrobe roles have been credited in the Bond films, for example Tessa Prendergast was afforded a credit as the costume designer on *Dr. No* despite Prendergast only being involved with the production when on location in Jamaica, specifically assisting in the creation of Ursula Andress's bikini. However, John Brady and Eileen Sullivan were both uncredited for their roles despite making the bulk of the costume decisions for the film. It is also notable that the costume designers who have been employed on the Bond films have become more vocal about their work and the process of creating wardrobe in contemporary interviews: since the employment of Porteous, who was also the first costume designer to be employed on consecutive Bond films, she, alongside Tillen, Hemming, Frogley and Temime have been interviewed about their creative agency and the decisions they have made toward the design of the Bond films. Previous designers have reflected on their role in the Bond films, including Rickards, Mendleson, Harris and Fonteray, but only retrospectively. This can be directly mapped onto a rising interest in costume both critically and in academia since the late 1980s following the publication of Elizabeth Leese's survey on the role of costume in the broader contexts of film production, particularly in relation to British and Hollywood cinema.

A further example of the interconnected themes of agency and labour has been demonstrated in *Fashioning James Bond* through analysis of the different roles afforded to members of the wardrobe team in order to realize the costumes from the script to the final film. Elizabeth Nielsen defines the differences between the various wardrobe roles as split between the designer, and the 'costume manufacturing workers' whom she terms as 'costumers' and 'artisans', including the role of the cutter, fitter, figure maker, draper, finisher, tailor, beader, milliner and shoemaker, recognizing that they 'understand the designers ideas, use dyes expertly and have an almost instinctive command of colour values [...] It takes years of refinement of their skills before costumers can transform a sketch into the living garment of colour, shape, personality, and authenticity on screen.'[3] As an example of this in the Bond films, one of Harris's designs for Solitaire's costumes in *Live and Let Die* is of a completely different fabric, cut, colour and silhouette to the one that was made for the film, and therefore an analysis of the design versus the final costume allows for a further understanding of the process behind realizing a costume specification and the individual creative agencies of the wardrobe department, including the 'signature' of the designer versus the 'signature' of the maker. There are, of course, reasons behind the changes to costumes beyond the different agencies involved. This could be due to the set design, for example Eunice Gayson's original gown sourced for the casino scene set in Les Ambassadeurs Club in *Dr. No* blended in with the gold and brown background, and therefore Gayson and Sullivan had to source a new gown for this scene. Alternatively, another reason for change is the sourcing of available fabric, for example Della Churchill's wedding gown in *Licence to Kill*. Two copies had to be made, and therefore seventeen metres of material needed to be sourced. Tillen explained that 'lengths of [the material] had to be collected from different places around the USA', and that 'panic broke out for two long days in the costume department when they were still short of three metres.'[4]

This leads into the final theme of the book, the costumes themselves. In *Fashioning James Bond*, character groupings have been analysed in order to understand how costume contributes to the overall look and style of the Bond films, including Bond, the villains and the 'Bond girls'. Often, these groupings conform to how these characters are intended to look so as to conform to a particular stereotype, for example in the suits worn by Bond, the Asian influence afforded to the villains in relation to Mao and Nehru jackets in particular, and the bikinis worn by the 'Bond girls'. However, there are rare occasions when costume is used to assist in the breaking of this, for example Bond's swimming trunks in *Casino Royale* that work to flip the gaze normally fixed upon 'Bond girls' in their bikinis. Similarly, the common perception of 'Bond girls' being sexually enhanced by their wearing of bikinis or low-cut evening gowns is broken with characters such as Tatiana Romanova, Tilly Masterson, Pussy Galore, Natalya Simonova, Wai Lin and Dr Madeleine Swann, who are defined more by their costumes that reflect their professional job roles as opposed to their sex appeal.

Costumes also work to market and promote the Bond films beyond the texts themselves, particularly since the release of *Goldfinger*, and have assisted in the internationalization of Bond as a brand. This is in part owing to the promotion of Bond as an icon promoted in 1960s lifestyle magazines which focused on fashion, alcohol and travelling to exotic locations as personified in both the novels and the films. The character of Bond was particularly well received in America, Britain, Europe and Japan, and this caused many different 007-labelled fashion products to be marketed to these countries including cufflinks, shirts, shoes, suits and ties. However, *Fashioning James Bond* has revealed that these attempts have often failed and that Bond ironically does not provide a 'Midas touch' to the firms involved. For example, Montague Burton did not manage to capitalize on *Goldfinger*'s box-office success, and for the release of *On Her Majesty's Secret Service*, Eon Productions attempted to target the female fan audience by working with Arts Galore and Berkertex Bride to create a version of Tracy di Vincenzo's wedding ring and outfit. Neither of these attempts were deemed to be successful, and it was not until after Craig's debut as Bond that Eon Productions would revisit marketing and promoting the films through fashion brands in earnest, including Orlebar Brown, Crockett & Jones and The London Sock Exchange. This is in part due to the marketing of Craig's films that particularly invites comparison with Connery's Bond, but also because of the rise of fan blogs, 'influencers' and lifestyle websites that particularly promote how to emulate Bond through fashion and style products. Eon Productions have also advanced and professionalized how they work with different fashion brands in relation to product placement in the films and the marketing strategy following their release. These new firms' success, however, remains to be seen.

Thus, *Fashioning James Bond* offers a methodology with which to approach future analysis and research into the costuming of film, including the agency, process and labour behind how costumes are produced from script to screen. Piecing together the different primary sources, including interviews with designers and wardrobe personnel, and reviewing the script, budgets, costume designs, call sheets, daily progress reports, final cost reports, critical reception, trade papers, lifestyle magazines and marketing materials where available, has been a time consuming though thoroughly rewarding process. By utilizing an empirical methodology, it allows for this book's research into costuming the Bond films to be nuanced by understanding the process from script to screen, and the interpretation of the designer versus the realized costumes as they appear in the final film. Most designers have reflected on the budget they were afforded and their ability to be particularly creative on the Bond films in which they worked, including Mendleson believing that it was 'no hardship' to work in the Bahamas during the production of *Thunderball*, Harris explaining that 'money was of no object' and Porteous believing: 'You can probably get more of an outlet on a Bond film. You can really go to town.' Though a small amount of academic work has previously focused on the role of the costume designer, much more research needs to conducted in understanding the other roles assigned to those working within wardrobe departments and the outsourcing of work to costumiers, which this book begins to address. Furthermore, *Fashioning James Bond* highlights other avenues of research to understand agency, labour and costume more broadly, including an analysis of costume within national cinemas, as well as research into the connected roles of costume, make-up and hair, all of which work in tandem to realize a character as they are presented within a film. In relation to Bond, the focus on this book has been on the Eon Productions films, a series likely to continue beyond the coronavirus-delayed *No Time To Die*. Thus, the analysis of fashion, costume and gender in the James Bond films will return.

Notes

1 'The debonair prince', *Daily Mail*, 5 July 1982, 14; 'Gold for Daly in slimline stakes', *Daily Mail*, 27 December 1984, 5.

2 'Daniel Craig tops *GQ*'s best dressed list', *FashionUnited*, 31 March 2008, https://fashionunited.uk/news/fashion/daniel craig-tops-gq-s-best-dressed-list/2008033133819 (accessed 25 October 2020).

3 Nielsen, 'Handmaidens of the Glamour Culture: Costumes in the Hollywood Studio System', in Gaines and Herzog (eds), *Fabrications*, 161.

4 Hibbin, *The Making of Licence To Kill*, 28.

APPENDIX: FRANK FOSTER FILMOGRAPHY

Year	Film Title	Actor(s)
1957	*The Good Companions*	Paddy Stone, Irving Davies
1957	*Blue Murder at St Trinian's*	George Cole
1958	*Dracula*	Christopher Lee
1958	*The Man Inside*	Jack Palance
1958	*No Time to Die/Tank Force*	Victor Mature
1959	*Mary Peach*	Peter Finch
1959	*The Hound of the Baskervilles*	Christopher Lee, Peter Cushing
1959	*I'm All Right Jack*	Ian Carmichael, Terry-Thomas, Richard Attenborough, Peter Sellers
1959	*Suddenly Last Summer*	Montgomery Clift
1960	*The Grass is Greener*	Cary Grant, Robert Mitchum
1960	*Tunes of Glory*	Alec Guinness
1960	*Two-Way Stretch*	Peter Sellers, Lionel Jeffries, David Lodge, Bernard Cribbins
1960	*Let's Make Love*	Yves Montand
1960	*The Entertainer*	Laurence Olivier
1961	*The Singer not the Song*	Dirk Bogarde
1962	*Lawrence of Arabia*	Peter O'Toole, Omar Sharif
1962	*Billy Budd*	Terence Stamp, Peter Ustinov
1962	*Only Two Can Play*	Peter Sellers
1962	*Road to Hong Kong*	Bing Crosby, Bob Hope
1962	*Lolita*	James Mason

Year	Film Title	Actor(s)
1962	***Dr. No***	**Sean Connery, Bernard Lee**
1963	*The V.I.P.s*	Richard Burton
1963	*Tom Jones*	Albert Finney
1963	*The Pink Panther*	Peter Sellers, David Niven, Robert Wagner
1963	*The Servant*	Dirk Bogarde, James Fox
1963	*The Leopard*	Alain Delon
1963	*Billy Liar*	Leonard Rossiter, Tom Courtenay
1963	***From Russia With Love***	**Sean Connery, Bernard Lee, Robert Shaw, Pedro Armendáriz**
1964	*My Fair Lady*	Rex Harrison, Jeremy Brett
1964	*The Yellow Rolls-Royce*	Rex Harrison
1964	*Guns at Batasi*	Johnny Leyton
1964	*First Men in the Moon*	Lionel Jeffries
1964	*Hot Enough for June*	Robert Morley, John Le Mesurier
1964	*The Beauty Jungle*	Ian Hendry
1964	*The Pumpkin Eater*	Peter Finch
1964	*Woman of Straw*	Sean Connery, Ralph Richardson
1964	***Goldfinger***	**Sean Connery, Gert Fröbe, the pilots of 'Pussy Galore's Flying Circus'**
1964	*Dr Strangelove or: How I Learned to Stop Worrying and Love the Bomb*	Peter Sellers
1965	*Those Magnificent Men in their Flying Machines*	Terry-Thomas
1965	*The Intelligence Men*	Eric Morecambe and Ernie Wise
1965	*The Great Race*	Tony Curtis
1965	*Lord Jim*	Peter O'Toole
1965	*Carry On Cowboy*	Sid James, Jim Dale, Kenneth Williams
1965	*The Knack . . . And How to Get It*	Michael Crawford, Ray Brooks
1965	*Darling*	Laurence Harvey
1965	***Thunderball***	**Sean Connery**

1966	*Carry On Screaming*	Kenneth Williams
1966	*Arabesque*	Gregory Peck
1966	*Modesty Blaise*	Dirk Bogarde
1966	*Torn Curtain*	Paul Newman
1967	*Casino Royale*	Peter Sellers, William Holden, Orson Welles
1967	*Far From the Madding Crowd*	Peter Finch
1967	*Half a Sixpence*	Tommy Steele
1967	*To Sir With Love*	Sidney Poitier
1967	***You Only Live Twice***	**Sean Connery, Donald Pleasence, Charles Gray**
1968	*Shalako*	Jack Hawkins, Sean Connery
1968	*Chitty Chitty Bang Bang*	Gert Fröbe
1968	*Oliver!*	Mark Lester
1969	***On Her Majesty's Secret Service***	**George Lazenby, Telly Savalas**
1969	*The Prime of Miss Jean Brodie*	Robert Stevens
1969	*The Night of the Following Day*	Marlon Brando
1969	*Women in Love*	Alan Bates
1969	*The Assassination Bureau*	Oliver Reed
1970	*The Only Game in Town*	Warren Beatty
1970	*Entertaining Mr. Sloane*	Harry Andrews, Peter McEnery
1970	*The Man Who Haunted Himself*	Roger Moore
1971	***Diamonds Are Forever***	**Sean Connery, Charles Gray**
1971	*Villain*	Richard Burton, Ian McShane
1971	*Klute*	Donald Sutherland
1972	*Mutiny on the Buses*	Reg Varney
1973	***Live and Let Die***	**Roger Moore, Jane Seymour, Yaphet Kotto**
1974	*Murder on the Orient Express*	Albert Finney
1974	***The Man With the Golden Gun***	**Roger Moore, Christopher Lee**
1976	*The Cassandra Crossing*	Richard Harris

Year	Film Title	Actor(s)
1976	*The Sicilian Cross/Street People*	Roger Moore
1976	*Shout at the Devil*	Roger Moore
1977	**The Spy Who Loved Me**	**Roger Moore, Curt Jürgens, Richard Kiel, Walter Gotell, Geoffrey Keen**
1978	*Force 10 From Navarone*	Harrison Ford
1978	*The Medusa Touch*	Richard Burton
1978	*The Big Sleep*	Robert Mitchum
1979	*Escape to Athena*	Roger Moore, David Niven
1979	**Moonraker**	**Roger Moore, Richard Kiel, Walter Gotell, Geoffrey Keen**
1980	*Airplane!*	Robert Hays
1980	*The Mirror Crack'd*	Rock Hudson
1981	**For Your Eyes Only**	**Roger Moore, Topol, James Villiers, Walter Gotell, Geoffrey Keen**
1983	**Octopussy**	**Roger Moore, Louis Jourdan, Steven Berkoff, Walter Gotell, Geoffrey Keen**
1985	**A View to a Kill**	**Roger Moore, Christopher Walken, Geoffrey Keen**
1985	*The Shooting Party*	John Gielgud, James Mason

GLOSSARY

Agal Typically made of goat hair, an *agal* is a black cord accessory, used to keep the *ghutrah* in place on the wearer's head.

A-line skirt A skirt that is fitted at the hips and is cut to widen out towards the hem, so-named due to its shape being reminiscent of a capitalized 'A'.

Angel sleeve A long, very wide sleeve that hangs loose from the shoulder of a dress or gown.

Appliqué A cutout decoration fastened or overlayed onto a larger surface or piece of material.

Art silk A term shortened from 'artificial silk', often used to line suit jackets.

Ascot collar A long, wide band collar with two ends that are brought to the front and looped over one another.

Balmacaan A coat originating from Inverness in Scotland, that has raglan sleeves that extend fully in one piece from a Prussian collar, and is typically made of tweed or gabardine fabric.

Band gale ka An Indian coat that is short with a fitted neck; an earlier version of the Nehru jacket.

Barchetta pocket 'Barchetta' meaning 'little boat' in Italian, referring to the welt of a breast pocket that is curved similarly like the shape of a boat.

Baste Tacking material with long, loose stitches in preparation for sewing.

Bell sleeve A typically long sleeve that is fitted around the shoulder and upper arm, flaring out to the wrist in the shape of a bell.

Bespoke suit A suit made from a new pattern that has been especially created for the individual wearer, with no modification or use of a base pattern. A bespoke suit includes multiple fittings with a client during the creation process that is used to achieve the final suit.

Bias-cut To be cut 'on the grain' of a fabric: instead of following the straight weave, the bias-cut places the pattern at a forty-five degree angle on the woven fabric. It is used to accentuate the body line and create more curves or soft drapes in the completed garment.

Bisht An Arabian traditional long cloak that is typically made from wool and ranging in colour from white, beige and cream to darker shades of brown, grey and black and worn over a *thobe*, the word deriving from Persia meaning 'to go on one's back'.

Blouson jacket A casual jacket that has a close or fitted waistband that causes the body of the jacket to blouse out over the waistband.

Bolero jacket A short, open-fronted jacket that is typically collarless with long sleeves and is hemmed above the waist.

Bombachas A pair of loose, baggy trousers that are gathered tightly at the ankle and are worn for riding and outdoor work. Worn especially in Argentina and Uruguay.

Bouffant sleeve A sleeve that is gathered widely at the sleeve cap to create a 'puff' and is fitted closely from beneath to a narrow cuff at the wrist.

Box pleat Created from two knife pleats (two folds of equal width) facing away from one another to give a wide, vertical pleat. Inverted box pleats are sewn in reverse.

Brandebourgs A knot-shaped pass, also termed a 'frog fastening' that was initially used on officers' uniforms. Term originates from Brandenburg in Germany.

Bullet brassière A conical shaped and spiral stitched brassière that was particularly popular in the 1950s.

Cagoule A lightweight, hooded and thigh-length waterproof jacket.

Camp collar A soft, double-notched and one-piece collar that is sewn directly to the body of a shirt, allowing it to lay flat.

Chantilly lace A delicate, machine-made bobbin lace of silk made from a fine hexagonal mesh ground and pattern.

Cheese-cutter cap Also known as a 'flat cap'; a rounded cap with a small, stiff brim at the front.

Chesterfield coat A knee-length overcoat with simple vertical seams, no side-back piece and a velvet collar, named after George Stanhope, 6th Earl of Chesterfield.

Chiripa A menswear garment formed by wrapping a woollen blanket around the hips, originating from Argentina.

Chino trousers A pair of trousers made from a coarse twilled cotton fabric known as 'chino' cloth.

Cifonelli shoulder A highly-stylized and constructed shoulder line of a jacket that has a concave contour sloping down from the shoulder and rising up again towards the arm. So-called due to its shape resembling the roof of a pagoda. Also known as a 'pagoda shoulder'.

Circular skirt A skirt made from a circle of fabric with an opening in the centre for the waist so that the skirt is very full but hangs from the waist without darts, pleats or gathers.

Cloverleaf lapels A one-piece lapel with rounded corners on the lapel and collar that resembles the shape of a cloverleaf.

Cocktail cuff A turn-back cuff designed with a combination of a button closure and a distinctive cutaway foldback.

Cod costume A costume piece that is created to be interchangeable with another in order to deceive the audience.

Constructed-shelf brassière A brassière that is constructed to sit under the bust with double layers placed between the breast and outer brassière material to enhance and showcase cleavage, normally without or with limited padding.

Cowl neckline A neckline created from loosely draped fabric that falls in rounded folds around the collarbone.

Crêpe de chine A soft, fine, sheer fabric made from silk.

Daks tops Created by Simpsons of Piccadilly, London. Side adjustors placed on the trouser waist that can be tightened via a metal adjustor enabling trousers to remain in place without the need for a belt or braces and thus ensuring the line of the suit is not disrupted.

Décolleté neckline A plunging neckline, the French term 'décolleté' meaning 'to expose the neck'.

Diaphanous A sheer or transparent piece of fabric.

Dishdasha A long, typically white, robe with long sleeves, traditionally worn by men from the Arabian Peninsula.

Double-breasted jacket A coat or jacket with wide, overlapping front flaps and two symmetrical columns of buttons, typically tailored with peaked lapels.

Empire line A style of clothing, typically a dress or gown, that is characterized by a high waistline cut beneath the bust and a low, scooped neckline, fitted bodice, and a gathered skirt that is long and loosely fitted.

Filigree pattern An ornamental and intricate metalwork, typically made from gold or silver with tiny beads or twisted threads, and arranged in an artistic motif.

Fish-tail skirt A long skirt that is tightly fitted from the waist to below the knee before flaring out in an exaggerated way towards the hemline.

Fit-and-flare silhouette A silhouette of a dress that has a fitted upper body (fit) and a full skirt (flare).

Florentine neckline A moderately low, wide and angular neckline that is rectangular in shape.

Forward pleat A pleat that opens inwards towards the trouser fly seam, associated with English-style tailoring.

French seam A seam that encloses a seam allowance on the inside of a sewn item so that no raw edge is visible. Commonly used on sheer fabrics.

French double cuffs A long, folded cuff that is typically squared with buttonholes to be fastened with cufflinks.

Frogmouth pocket A pocket that is situated horizontally across the front of the trouser instead of a vertical slit. So-termed for its resemblance to the mouth of a frog.

Funnel collar A large, wide collar which stands away from the neck and the face and typically opens at the front that resembles the shape of a funnel.

Furisode Meaning 'swinging sleeve' in Japanese; a kimono that is distinguished by its long, hanging sleeves.

Gauntlet cuff A turnback cuff that is narrow at the wrist and flares outwards to resemble the cuff of a gauntlet.

Ghutrah A traditional Arabian headscarf typically fashioned from a white square scarf made from cotton, and held in place by an *agal*.

Gilet A light, sleeveless and padded jacket that resembles a waistcoat, that can be hemmed between waist and knee-length. Are typically straight-sided rather than fitted.

Gorge The seam that attaches the collar of a suit jacket to the body of a lapel to create a distinguishing feature.

Gusset A diamond or triangular shaped insert in a seam to provide expansion (breadth) or reinforcement to reduce stress on a garment, typically used for shoulders, underarms and the crotch seam for swimwear and lingerie in particular.

Hacking pocket A slanted hip pocket of a suit jacket that is placed up towards the sternum at an angle as a stylistic variation of a straight pocket. A hacking pocket is typically flapped.

Halter-neck A garment held up by a strap that runs from the front of the bodice to fasten around the back of the neck with the upper back and shoulders uncovered.

Inverness coat A waterproof, sleeveless outer-coat originating from Scotland in the 1850s that includes a long cape hemmed to the same length as a sleeve with the arms emerging from armholes beneath the cape.

Jetted pocket A pocket that is formed as a slit bordered by two thin strips of fabric (welts) that is visible on the facing of the jacket with the pouch hanging inside.

Juliet sleeve A long sleeve that is gathered in an exaggerated and puffed way at the sleeve cap and tightly tapers down from above the elbow to the cuff. It is similar in shape to the 'leg of mutton' sleeve but is created from two parts.

Kaftan A light-weight and loosely fitted garment traditionally made from cotton or silk and worn as a coat or as an overdress that has long sleeves and is hemmed at the ankle.

Kanzashi Hair ornaments made from a range of materials including lacquered wood, gold or silver-plated metal, tortoiseshell, silk and folded cotton. Used in the creation of traditional Japanese hair styles.

Khamak A distinguished and complicated embroidery artwork originating from Kandahar, Afghanistan that uses delicate silk stitches on fine woven cloths of cotton or wool fabrics.

Kick pleat A short, inverted pleat placed at the back of the base hem of a narrow skirt to create a 'kick' and allow the wearer more freedom of movement.

Lamé Meaning 'metal plate' in French. A woven or knitted fabric made from thin ribbons of metallic fibre and typically gold or silver in colour. Used for evening wear, theatrical and dance costumes, as well as costumes in futuristic or science-fiction genres.

Leg of mutton sleeves A sleeve that has a full sleeve cap tapering down towards the wrist, so-called as the sleeve resembles a mutton's leg in shape. Similar to a 'Juliet sleeve' although made from one piece of fabric rather than two.

Made-to-measure suit A suit created from a blend of bespoke and ready-to-wear techniques, with the 'standard' pattern modified by a firm to fit an individual wearer, with an initial fitting to take a client's measurements and a final fitting for alterations after the suit has been created.

Mandarin collar A small, close-fitting, stand-up collar, usually about one inch high with front edges that do not quite meet. Typically used on Mao and Nehru jackets.

Mao suit A modern Chinese suit developed from the *Zhongshan* suit, and a form of national dress with political overtones. Normally includes four pockets with a button fastening, and a five-button fastening down the centre.

Maxi-dress A casual and informal dress that is typically formfitting at the top, flowing loosely out towards the ankle.

Mitered cuff A barrel cuff with a notch ('miter') cut from each corner side above the button closure at a 45-degree angle; based on the woodwork term 'mitered joint'.

Napoleon collar A turnover, open-fronted collar that is fairly rigid in construction and cut high in order to frame the wearer's neck and lower head.

Naval battledress A retired style of military uniform worn by the British Navy, c.1943–45.

Nehru jacket A hip-length tailored coat with a Mandarin collar, modelled on a *sherwani* and named after Jawaharlal Nehru, Prime Minister of India between 1947 and 1964.

Neapolitan shoulder A style of jacket shoulder originating from Naples that has a sloped, soft and rounded shoulder which is achieved through a lack of padding, pleated sleeve-heads and *spalla camicia* ('shirt shoulder').

Norfolk jacket A loose-fitting, single-breasted tweed jacket with box pleats and either a belt or half-belt ('Half Norfolk').

Notched lapel A lapel sewn on to the collar of a jacket at an angle, creating a concave notch (triangle) between the two. Commonly used on single-breasted jackets.

Obi A broad sash worn around the waist of a Japanese kimono.

Panné velvet A crushed velvet created by the fabric's pile being flattened in the same direction.

Papaha A Russian high fur hat shaped like a cylinder, typically made from karakul sheep skin.

Patch pocket The simplest variation of a pocket: made from a 'patch' in the same fabric as the garment, and stitched directly onto the surface, thus its construction is highly visible. Patch pockets can be open or flapped.

Peacoat A short, double-breasted overcoat made from coarse woollen cloth, generally navy in colour.

Peak lapel The tips of a peak lapel point upwards, extending beyond the collar to create a stylized gorge. Commonly found on double-breasted jackets.

Peignoir A light dressing gown or *négligée*, typically made from diaphanous fabric such as chiffon, the French word *'peignoir'* translating as 'bathrobe'.

Pencil skirt A slim-fitting skirt with a straight and narrow cut, typically hemmed at the knee, which is sewn to be closely fitted.

Peplum A short overskirt or ruffle attached to the waistline of a jacket, blouse or dress. Derived from the Greek word πέπλος ('*péplos*').

Pince-nez A pair of glasses with a nose clip instead of earpieces.

Piping A trim or edging created by sewing a thin strip of folded fabric (for example, bias binding) into a narrow tube before attaching it to the edge of a piece of fabric. Used to define or reinforce the lines of a garment.

Piqué weave A style of weaving commonly used in cotton yarn which is defined by raised parallel cords or fine ribbing to create geometric designs in the fabric.

Placket An opening or slit in a garment that allows the wearer to put the garment on. Commonly used in shirts, skirts and trousers, and fastened with buttons.

Poncho A sleeveless garment made from thick woollen cloth with a slit in the centre for the head that when worn drapes over the chest, originating from South America.

Prussian collar A high, upright, military-style collar.

Ready-to-wear Can also be termed 'off-the-peg'; an item of clothing that has been made and purchased in standardized sizes and not made especially to fit a particular person.

Reverse pleat A pleat that opens out towards the trouser pocket, associated with Italian tailoring.

Ruching A gathering overlay of fabric strips that are pleated, fluted or gathered together to create a 'ripple' effect.

Safari suit A casual suit with typical features including epaulettes, a self-belt and four flapped patch pockets. Made from light material and typically worn in warmer climates. Originally created to be worn on safari tours in South Africa.

Sari A garment traditionally worn in the Indian subcontinent, made from a strip of unstitched cloth ranging from four to nine metres in length that is draped over the body in various styles.

Sensu A Japanese folding fan typically decorated with calligraphy and symbolic patterns.

Shalwar kameez A Punjabi outfit that consists of a tunic (*kameez*) that is loose-fitting and knee-length with long sleeves, and trousers (*salwar*). The *salwar* are tailored to be long and loose-fitting with narrow hems above the ankles that are stitched to reflect cuffs.

Shawl lapels A lapel that is tailored to have a continuous curve without a seam between the collar or lapel.

Sheath silhouette A dress or gown that fits close to the body and is achieved though being straight-cut and often nipped at the waist with no waist seam. The bodice and the skirt are joined together by combining the skirt darts into one dart.

Shift dress A dress or gown where the cloth falls straight from the shoulders to the hem and is darted around the bust. Typically features a high scoop or boat neckline.

Shiromuku A Japanese mostly-white wedding ensemble worn by the bride in traditional wedding ceremonies. The ensemble consists of a *furisode* kimono with a trailing hem (*kakeshita*), a broad *obi* (*maru/fukuro*) worn around the waist and a *uchikake* cloak over the kimono. Accessories include a wedding hood (*Wataboshi*) and traditional headgear (*tsunokakushi*).

Shirring Created by sewing multiple rows of parallel stitching in a piece of fabric to gather material, usually in the sleeves, bodice or yoke.

Single-breasted jacket A coat or jacket which has a narrow overlap and only one column of buttons, typically tailored with notched lapels.

Sirwal A pair of trousers that are gathered by a drawstring at the waist or hip, and have loose, baggy legs that are gathered closely at the ankle, typically worn in Muslim countries. Colloquially termed 'harem trousers/pants'.

Sleeve-head A thick strip of fabric or batting used to lift and support the sleeve cap and enhance the sleeve's drape.

Smoking jacket An informal lounge jacket dating from the 1850s, typically including a shawl collar and turn-up cuffs, and made from velvet, silk, or a combination of both.

Sombrero A straw hat with a distinctive high pointed crown, a wide brim with a slightly upturned edge and a chin strap, originating from Mexico.

Spread collar A collar that has wider points that are angled ('spread') outwards instead of pointing down as with a 'forward point' collar.

Surplice neckline A neckline created when fabric from one side of the shoulder crosses and overlaps the fabric from the other side at the front, and then is sewn down in the seam.

Sweetheart neckline A neckline with a concave bottom edge that resembles the shape of the top half of a heart, and used to accentuate the bust.

Thagiyah A white skull cap worn over a *ghutrah*.

Thobe An ankle-length, long-sleeved and tunic-like garment worn beneath a *bisht* by men typically from the Arabian Peninsula.

Triaxial weave Composed of three sets of yarns that intersect and interlace with each other at 60-degree angles.

Tsunokakushi A Japanese wedding headpiece worn as part of a bride's traditional *Shiromuku* ensemble. It is made from a rectangular piece of cloth and covers the bridal high topknot of the hair, often made from white silk.

Tyrolean hat A hat traditionally made with green felt, with a crown that tapers to a point and a sloping brim roughly the size of the wearers hand. Typically includes a band with a 'brush' made from the beard of a chamois goat. Originates from Tyrol in the Swiss Alps.

Tyroler A German-Swiss folk costume developed by Alpine peasants, also termed a *dirndl*, generally regarded as traditional dress for women based in the Alps. The dress is formed of a close-fitting bodice with a low neckline and a high-waisted skirt. The bodice is worn over a white blouse, and an apron is worn over the skirt.

Unstructured suit A suit jacket with minimal canvas, very little lining and a thin shoulder, creating a lightweight and breathable jacket.

Welt pocket A bound, flat pocket finished with a welt (a strip of fabric used to cover or bind one or both edges of a pocket opening) or a reinforced border along the edge of a piece of fabric.

Wing-tab collar A high, stiff shirt collar that includes a concealed tab to keep the collar wings together to prevent them from flapping upwards.

Windsor knot A particular way that a tie is knotted to create a triangular knot with the wide end of the tie draping in front of the narrow end, attributed to Edward, Duke of Windsor.

'Windsor look' A particular menswear style promoted by Edward, Duke of Windsor which he termed 'dress soft', and flamboyantly involved bold use of colour, texture, pattern and the 'breaking' of fashion codes, for example wearing patterned shirts fastened with striped ties and trousers with cuffed hems.

Yoke A shaped pattern piece that forms part of a garment, normally fitting around the neck and shoulders or the hips to provide support to looser parts of the garment. A yoke can also be used for definition as part of a design detail.

Yukata A Japanese casual kimono that is unlined and typically made from cotton commonly worn during the summer months.

Yūzen A Japanese dye resist technique used to decorate a kimono.

FILMOGRAPHY

Dr. No. United Artists/Eon Productions. 1962.
Director: Terence Young. *Producers*: Harry Saltzman and Albert R. Broccoli. *Costume Designer*: Tessa Welborn. *Wardrobe Master*: John Brady. *Wardrobe Mistress*: Eileen Sullivan. *Wardrobe Assistant*: Patricia Baden. *Tailor*: Anthony Sinclair.

From Russia With Love. United Artists/Eon Productions. 1963.
Director: Terence Young. *Producers*: Harry Saltzman and Albert R. Broccoli. *Costume Designer*: Jocelyn Rickards. *Wardrobe Master*: Ernie Farrer. *Wardrobe Mistress*: Eileen Sullivan. *Tailor*: Anthony Sinclair.

Goldfinger. United Artists/Eon Productions. 1964.
Director: Guy Hamilton. *Producers*: Harry Saltzman and Albert R. Broccoli. *Costume Designer*: Beatrice Dawson. *Wardrobe Supervisor*: Elsa Fennell. *Wardrobe Master*: John Hilling. *Wardrobe Mistress*: Eileen Sullivan. *Tailor*: Anthony Sinclair.

Thunderball. United Artists/Eon Productions. 1965.
Director: Terence Young. *Producer*: Kevin McClory. *Executive Producers*: Harry Saltzman and Albert R. Broccoli. *Costume Designer*: Anthony Mendleson. *Wardrobe Master*: John Brady. *Wardrobe Mistress*: Eileen Sullivan. *Tailor*: Anthony Sinclair.

You Only Live Twice. United Artists/Eon Productions. 1967.
Director: Lewis Gilbert. *Producers*: Harry Saltzman and Albert R. Broccoli. *Wardrobe Master*: Brian Owen-Smith. *Wardrobe Mistress*: Eileen Sullivan. *Wardrobe (Second Unit)*: Roy Ponting. *Tailor*: Anthony Sinclair.

On Her Majesty's Secret Service. United Artists/Eon Productions. 1969.
Director: Peter Hunt. *Producers*: Albert R. Broccoli and Harry Saltzman. *Costume Designer*: Marjory Cornelius. *Wardrobe Mistress*: Jackie Cummins. *Wardrobe Master*: John Brady. *Wardrobe Assistants*: Janet Dodson and Jimmy Smith. *Tailor*: Dimitrov Major.

Diamonds Are Forever. United Artists/Eon Productions. 1971.
Director: Guy Hamilton. *Producers*: Albert R. Broccoli and Harry Saltzman. *Wardrobe Supervisors*: Elsa Fennell and Ted Tetrick. *Wardrobe Master*: Ray Beck. *Costumers*: Kent James and Mina Mittelman. *Miss St. John's Costumes*: Donfeld. *Tailor*: Anthony Sinclair.

Live and Let Die. United Artists/Eon Productions. 1973
Director: Guy Hamilton. *Producers*: Harry Saltzman and Albert R. Broccoli. *Costume Designer*: Julie Harris. *Wardrobe Supervisor*: Laurel Staffell. *Wardrobe Master*: John

Hilling. *Wardrobe Mistress*: Joanna Wright. *Wardrobe Assistant*: Colin Wilson. *Tailor*: Cyril Castle.

The Man with the Golden Gun. United Artists/Eon Productions. 1974
   Director: Guy Hamilton. *Producers*: Albert R. Broccoli and Harry Saltzman. *Wardrobe Supervisor*: Elsa Fennell. *Wardrobe Master*: Tiny Nicholls. *Wardrobe Assistants*: Evelyn Gibbs and Colin Wilson. *Tailor*: Cyril Castle.

The Spy Who Loved Me. United Artists/Eon Productions. 1977.
   Director: Lewis Gilbert. *Producer*: Albert R. Broccoli. *Wardrobe Supervisor*: Rosemary Burrows. *Fashion Consultant*: Ronald Paterson. *Tailor*: Angelo Vitucci.

Moonraker. United Artists/Eon Productions and Les Productions Artistes Associes. 1979.
   Director: Lewis Gilbert. *Producer*: Albert R. Broccoli. *Costume Designer*: Jacques Fonteray. *Wardrobe Master*: Jean Zay. *Wardrobe Mistress*: Colette Baudot. *Tailor*: Angelo Vitucci.

For Your Eyes Only. United Artists/Eon Productions. 1981.
   Director: John Glen. *Producer*: Albert R. Broccoli. *Costume Designer*: Elizabeth Waller. *Wardrobe Master*: Tiny Nicholls. *Wardrobe Mistress*: Marina Dreckcr. *Wardrobe for Miss Bouquet and Miss Harris*: Raemonde Rahvis. *Tailor*: Douglas Hayward.

Octopussy. MGM-United Artists/Eon Productions. 1983.
   Director: John Glen. *Producer*: Albert R. Broccoli. *Costume Designer*: Emma Porteous. *Wardrobe Master*: Tiny Nicholls. *Tailor*: Douglas Hayward.

A View to a Kill. MGM-United Artists/Eon Productions. 1985.
   Director: John Glen. *Producers*: Albert R. Broccoli and Michael G. Wilson. *Costume Designer*: Emma Porteous. *Wardrobe Supervisor*: Renate Wienert. *Wardrobe Master*: Tiny Nicholls. *Additional Wardrobe, Grace Jones*: Azzadine Alaïa. *Tailor*: Douglas Hayward.

The Living Daylights. MGM-United Artists/Eon Productions. 1987.
   Director: John Glen. *Producers*: Albert R. Broccoli and Michael G. Wilson. *Costume Designer*: Emma Porteous. *Wardrobe Supervisor*: Tiny Nicholls. *Wardrobe Master (Second Unit)*: Don Mothersill. *Suits provided by*: Bermans and Nathans, Lambert Hofer, Benjamin Simon, Ralph Lauren and Paul Simon.

Licence to Kill. MGM-United Artists/Eon Productions. 1989.
   Director: John Glen. *Producers*: Albert R. Broccoli and Michael G. Wilson. *Costume Designer*: Jodie Tillen. *Wardrobe Supervisors*: Hugo Peña and Barbara Scott. *Wardrobe Supervisor (Florida)*: Robert Chase. *Wardrobe Master (Mexicali)*: Enrique Villavicencio.

GoldenEye. MGM-United Artists/Eon Productions. 1995.
   Director: Martin Campbell. *Producers*: Michael G. Wilson and Barbara Broccoli. *Costume Designer*: Lindy Hemming. *Wardrobe Supervisors*: Renate Wienert and John Scott. *Wardrobe Masters*: Nigel Egerton and Colin Wilson. *Wardrobe Assistants*: Dan Grace, Tim Guthrie, Jenny Hawkins and Lester Mills. *Wardrobe*: Janie Green. *Tailor*: Brioni.

Tomorrow Never Dies. MGM-United Artists/Eon Productions. 1997.
   Director: Roger Spottiswoode. *Producers*: Michael G. Wilson and Barbara Broccoli. *Costume Designer*: Lindy Hemming. *Assistant Costume Designer*: Maria Tortu.

Wardrobe Supervisors: John Scott and Mutita Na Songkla. *Wardrobe Master*: Colin Wilson. *Wardrobe Mistress*: Jenny Hawkins. *Wardrobe Assistants*: Dan Grace, Lester Mills, Sophie Norinder, Livia Pascucci and Berenice Wright. *Costumer*: Suzy Freeman. *Costume Cutter*: Lee Clayton. *Tailor*: Brioni.

The World is not Enough. MGM-United Artists/Eon Productions. 1999.
   Director: Michael Apted. *Producers*: Michael G. Wilson and Barbara Broccoli. *Costume Designer*: Lindy Hemming. *Assistant Costume Designers*: David Crossman and Jacqueline Durran. *Wardrobe Supervisor*: John Scott. *Wardrobe Masters*: Dave Croucher, Dan Grace and Colin Wilson. *Wardrobe Mistresses*: Helen Mattocks and Jane Petrie. *Wardrobe Assistant*: Lester Mills. *Tailor*: Brioni.

Die Another Day. MGM/Twentieth Century-Fox/Eon Productions. 2002.
   Director: Lee Tamahori. *Producers*: Michael G. Wilson and Barbara Broccoli. *Costume Designer*: Lindy Hemming. *Assistant Costume Designer*: Guy Speranza. *Wardrobe Supervisor*: Graham Churchyard. *Wardrobe Masters*: Anthony Brookman, Dave Croucher and Colin Wilson. *Wardrobe Mistresses*: Anabel Campbell-Yates and Helen Mattocks. *Wardrobe Assistants*: Heather Banta, Henry Christopher, Sally Puttick, Tom Hornsby, Laura Johnson and Justine Warhurst. *Wardrobe*: Tina Kalivas. *Costume Design Assistant*: Andrea Cripps. *Costume Coordinator*: Martin Mandeville. *Costume Breakdown Artist*: Emma Walker. *Costume Buyer*: Jeeda Barford. *Costume Makers*: Jacqueline Mulligan and Dominic Young. *Costume Maker (Academy Costumes)*: Sam Brown. *Special Costumes*: Whitaker Malem. *Military Costumer*: Peter k. Christopher. *Costume Assistants*: Gabriella Loria, Debbie Scott and Sunny Rowley. *Tailor*: Brioni.

Casino Royale. MGM/Columbia Pictures/Eon Productions. 2006.
   Director: Martin Campbell. *Producers*: Michael G. Wilson and Barbara Broccoli. *Costume Designer*: Lindy Hemming. *Assistant Costume Designers*: Gabriela Horská, Gabriella Loria and Maria Tortu. *Wardrobe Master (Second Unit)*: Brendan Handscombe. *Wardrobe Mistress (Crowd)*: Jenny Hawkins. *Costume Supervisor*: Dan Grace. *Costume Supervisor (Czech Republic)*: Hana Kucerova. *Costume Coordinator*: Dita Valentinova. *Costume Breakdown*: Stephen Kill. *Costume Buyer*: Jeeda Barford. *Costumers*: Jirina Eisenhamerova and Maria Hubackova. *Costumer (Bond)*: Mark Sutherland. *Stand-by Costumer*: Lee Croucher. *Costume Assistant*: Amanda Trewin. *Daily Costume Assistant*: Harriet Lyons. *Costume Ager/Dyer*: Steven Porch. *Seamstress*: Larisa. *Costume Department Assistant*: Anna Hinds. *Tailor*: Brioni.

Quantum of Solace. MGM/Columbia Pictures/Eon Productions. 2008.
   Director: Marc Forster. *Producers*: Michael G. Wilson and Barbara Broccoli. *Costume Designer*: Louise Frogley. *Assistant Costume Designer*: Jenny Hawkins. *Wardrobe Master (Crowd)*: Brendan Handscombe. *Wardrobe Assistant*: Diana Wyand. *Costume Supervisor*: Lindsay Pugh. *Costume Supervisor (Crowd)*: Charlotte Child. *Costume Coordinator*: Sheena Wichary. *Costume Buyer*: Gabriella Loria. *Costume Buyer (Panama)*: Regina Calvo. *Costumer*: Javier Arrieta. *Costumer (Bond)*: Mark Sutherland. *Costumers (Crowd, Austria)*: Max Jones, Sophia Spink, Nathalie Karni and Justine Warhurst. *Costume Assistants*: Valeria Perucci, Maurizio Torti and Maite Tarilonte. *Costume Assistant (Second Unit)*: Lucilla Simbari. *Costume Makers*: Liberty Kelly and Jacqueline Mulligan. *Costume Maker (Panama)*: Magali Telliol. *Costume Cutter*: Dominic Young. *Costume Runner*: Perry Goyen. *Tailor*: Tom Ford.

Skyfall. MGM/Columbia Pictures/Eon Productions. 2012.

  Director: Sam Mendes. *Producers*: Michael G. Wilson and Barbara Broccoli. *Costume Designer*: Jany Temime. *Assistant Costume Designers*: Richard Davies and Vivienne Jones. *Assistant Costume Designers (Crowd)*: Joe Hobbs and Emily-Rose Da Silveira. *Wardrobe Supervisor*: Gordon Harmer. *Wardrobe Master*: Paul Yeowell. *Wardrobe Mistress*: Joanna Campbell. *Wardrobe Assistants*: Russell Barnett, Teddy George-Poku, Carin Hoff, Bob Van Hellenberg Hubar, Yasemin Kascioglu, Kate Laver, Yvonne Otzen and William Steggle. *Wardrobe Assistants (Fethiye)*: Ezgi Acar, Ece Akten, Hulya Iri and Gaye Ömür. *Wardrobe Assistants (Turkey)*: Feride Aydin, Ayse Cam, Hilal Cimen, Filiz Dana, Buket Demirel, Ozgur Can Demirhan and Secilay Dogan. *Costume Supervisor (Turkey)*: Funda Buyuktunalioglu. *Costume Illustrator*: Warren Holder. *Costume Coordinator*: Sanaz Missaghian. *Costume Buyer*: Michelle Philo. *Costumer*: Chan Chi Wan. *Costumier (Bond)*: Neil Murphy. *Costume Assistant*: Heidi McQueen-Prentice. *Daily Costume Assistant*: Samantha Keeble. *Costume Makers*: Helen Beasley, Sue Bradbear and Yvonne Meyrick-Brook. *Cutter*: Gary Page. *Textile Artists*: Nicola Belton, Sacha Chandisingh and Joanna Weaving. *Breakdown Daily*: Laura Renouf. *Principal Dresser (Dailies)*: Sarah Tiffin. *Costume Trainees*: Sekina Baker and Jemma Jessup. *Tailor*: Tom Ford.

Spectre. MGM/Columbia Pictures/Eon Productions. 2015.

  Director: Sam Mendes. *Producers*: Michael G. Wilson and Barbara Broccoli. *Costume Designer*: Jany Temime. *Assistant Costume Designers*: Richard Davies and Vivienne Jones. *Assistant Costume Designer (Crowd)*: Françoise Fourcade. *Wardrobe Supervisor*: Joanna Campbell Lynch. *Wardrobe Master (Second Unit)*: Paul Colford. *Wardrobe Mistress (Second Unit)*: Karen Beale. *Wardrobe Mistress (Crowd)*: Sarah Brest. *Wardrobe Assistants (Mexico)*: Julien Boisselier and Mariana Escárzaga. *Wardrobe (Crowd, Austria)*: Carina Mayer, Marlies Mayringer and Theresa Pultar. *Wardrobe*: Jimena Tenorio. *Costume Supervisors*: Abderrahim Benkhayi and Ken Crouch. *Costume Supervisor (Mexico)*: Anna Terrazas. *Costume Supervisor (Italy)*: Stefano De Nardis. *Associate Costume Supervisor (Italy)*: Claudio Manzi. *Costume Illustrators*: Lucy Calder and Jessica Goodall. *Head Breakdown Artist*: Laura Renouf. *Costume Coordinator*: Claire Watson. *Costume Buyer*: Sara Khabir. *Assistant Buyer*: Lauren Kilcar. *Key Costumer*: Adil Arbouch. *Costumers*: Bob Van Hellenberg Hubar Jnr, Sunny Rowley and Gisela Sanchez. *Costumer (Daily)*: Mark Lord. *Principal Costumier*: Kevin Pratten. *Costumier*: Dougie Hawkes. *Costumier (Bond)*: Neil Murphy. *Daily Crowd Costumier*: Gabriella Morpeth. *Costume Assistants*: Amine Benkhayi, Max Brennan, Maria Garcés, Lee Kenny, Ana Velia Lopez, Robyn Manton and Charlotte Sadler. *Costume Assistants (Italy)*: Carlotta Moricci and Maurizio Torti. *Costume Assistant (Crowd)*: Katia Folco. *Head Costume Maker*: Sue Bradbear. *Costume Maker*: Eniko Karadi. *Junior Costume Maker*: Alex Cox. *Speciality Costume Makers*: David McLaughlin Rebecca Sellors and Susanne Morthorst Staal. *Head Costume Painter*: Arturo Lazcano. *Principal Cutter*: Gary Page. *Principal Stand-by*: Lynsey Harris. *Principal Costume (Dailies)*: Jessica Phillips. *Costumes (Dailies)*: Steve O'Sullivan and Billy Pritchard. *Crowd Costume Runner (Mexico)*: Lyndsey Wardrop. *Principal Costume Trainee*: Lucy Brookes. *Costume Trainee*: Viviana Crosato. *Costume Trainee (Italy)*: Aurora Bresciani. *Costume Trainees (Crowd)*: Liz Essex and Crystel Tottenham. *Tailor*: Tom Ford.

BIBLIOGRAPHY

Albion, Alexis. 'Wanting to be James Bond'. In *Ian Fleming & James Bond: The cultural politics of 007*, edited by Edward P. Comentale, Stephen Watt and Skip Willman, 202–24. Bloomington: Indiana University Press, 2005.

Amis, Kingsley. *The James Bond Dossier*. London: Jonathan Cape Limited, 1965.

Bennett, Tony and Janet Woollacott. *Bond and Beyond: The Political Career of a Popular Hero*. Basingstoke and London: Macmillan Education Limited, 1987.

Black, Jeremy. *The Politics of James Bond: From Fleming's Novels to the Big Screen*. Westport: Praeger Publishers, 2000.

Bouzereau, Laurent. *The Art of Bond: From storyboard to screen, the creative process*. London: Boxtree, 2006.

Broccoli, Albert R. with Donald Zec. *When the Snow Melts: The autobiography of Cubby Broccoli*. London and Basingstoke: Boxtree, 1998.

Bruzzi, Stella. *Undressing Cinema: Clothing and identity in the movies*. London and New York: Routledge, 1997.

Bruzzi, Stella and Pamela Church Gibson (eds). *Fashion Cultures Revisited: Theories, explorations and analysis*. 2nd edn. Abingdon and New York, 2013.

Buckton, Oliver (ed.). *The Many Facets of Diamonds Are Forever: James Bond on page and screen*. Maryland and London: Lexington Books, 2019.

Castaldo Lundèn, Elizabeth. 'Barbarella's wardrobe: Exploring Jacques Fonteray's intergalactic runway'. *Film Fashion & Consumption* 5, no. 2 (2016): 185–211.

Chancellor, Henry. *James Bond: The Man and His World*. London: John Murray, 2005.

Chapman, James. *Licence to Thrill: A cultural history of the James Bond films*. 2nd edn. London and New York: I.B. Tauris, 2007.

Chapman, James. 'The Trouble with Harry: The difficult relationship of Harry Saltzman and Film Finances'. *Historical Journal of Film, Radio and Television* 34, no. 1 (2014): 43–71.

Church Gibson, Pamela. 'Film Costume'. In *The Oxford Guide to Film Studies*, edited by John Hill and Pamela Church Gibson, 36–42. Oxford: Oxford University Press, 1998.

Cook, Pam. *Fashioning the Nation: Costume and identity in British cinema*. London: British Film Institute, 1996.

Cook, Pam and Claire Hines. 'Sean Connery *Is* James Bond: Re-fashioning British masculinity in the 1960s'. In *Fashioning Film Stars. Dress, culture identity*, edited by Rachel Moseley, 147–59. London: British Film Institute: 2005.

Cork, John and Bruce Scivalli. *The James Bond Legacy*. London: Boxtree, 2002.

Cosgrave, Bronwen, Lindy Hemming and Neil McConnon (eds). *Designing 007: 50 Years of Bond Style*. London: Barbican International Enterprises, 2012.

Drazin, Charles. *A Bond for Bond: Film Finances and Dr. No*. London: Film Finances Limited, 2011.

Duncan, Paul (ed.). *The James Bond Archives*. London: Taschen, 2015.

Edlitz, Mark. *The Many Lives of James Bond: How the creators of 007 have decoded the superspy*. Guilford and Connecticut: Lyons Press, 2019.

Fashionary. *Fashionpedia: The visual dictionary of fashion design*. Hong Kong: Fashionary Limited, 2020.

Field, Matthew and Ajay Chowdhury. *Some Kind of Hero: The remarkable story of the James Bond films*. Stroud: The History Press, 2015.

Fleming, Fergus (ed.). *The Man with the Golden Typewriter: Ian Fleming's James Bond letters*. London and New York: Bloomsbury, 2015.

Fleming, Ian. *Casino Royale*. 1953. Reprinted. London: Penguin Books, 2009.

Fleming, Ian. *Live and Let Die*. 1954. Reprinted. London: Penguin Books, 2009.

Fleming, Ian. *Moonraker*. 1955. Reprinted. London: Penguin Books, 2009.

Fleming, Ian. *Diamonds Are Forever*. 1956. Reprinted. London: Penguin Books, 2009.

Fleming, Ian. *From Russia With Love*. 1957. Reprinted. London: Penguin Books, 2009.

Fleming, Ian. *Dr. No*. 1958. Reprinted. London: Penguin Books, 2009.

Fleming, Ian. *Goldfinger*. 1959. Reprinted. London: Penguin Books, 2009.

Fleming, Ian. *For Your Eyes Only*. 1960. Reprinted. London: Penguin Books, 2009.

Fleming, Ian. *Thunderball*. 1961. Reprinted. London: Penguin Books, 2009.

Fleming, Ian. *The Spy Who Loved Me*. 1962. Reprinted. London: Penguin Books, 2009.

Fleming, Ian. *On Her Majesty's Secret Service*. 1963. Reprinted. London: Penguin Books, 2009.

Fleming, Ian. *You Only Live Twice*. 1964. Reprinted. London: Penguin Books, 2009.

Fleming, Ian. *The Man with the Golden Gun*. 1965. Reprinted. London: Penguin Books, 2009.

Fleming, Ian. *Octopussy and the Living Daylights*. 1966. Reprinted. London: Penguin Books, 2009.

Flusser, Alan. *Style and the Man: How and where to buy fine men's clothes*. New York: HarperStyle, 1996.

Fonteray, Jacques. *Costumes pour le cinema: Carnet de dessins*. Paris: Imprimé, 1999.

Frenk, Joachim and Christian Krug (eds). *The Cultures of James Bond*. Trier: Wissenschaftlicher Verlag, 2011.

Funnell, Lisa (ed.). *For His Eyes Only: The women of James Bond*. London and New York: Wallflower Press, 2015.

Funnell, Lisa. 'Reworking the Bond girl concept in the Craig era'. *Journal of Popular Film and Television* XLVI, no. 2 (2018): 11–21.

Funnell, Lisa and Klaus Dodds. *Geographies, Genders and Geopolitics of James Bond*. London: Palgrave Macmillan, 2017.

Gaines, Jane M. and Charlotte Herzog (eds). *Fabrications: Costume and the Female Body*. London and New York: Routledge, 1990.

Gayson, Eunice with Andrew Boyle and Gareth Owen. *The First Lady of Bond*. Cambridge: Signum Books, 2012.

Gerrard, Steven (ed.). *From Blofeld to Moneypenny: Gender in James Bond*. Bingley: Emerald, 2020.

Germanà, Monica. *Bond Girls: Body, fashion and gender*. London and New York: Bloomsbury, 2020.

Gilligan, Sarah. 'Branding the new Bond: Daniel Craig and designer fashion'. In *James Bond in World and Popular Culture: The films are not enough*, edited by Robert G. Weiner, B.

Lynn Whitfield and Jack Becker, 76–85. 2nd edn. Newcastle upon Tyne: Cambridge Scholars Publishing, 2011.

Harper, Sue. *Women in British Cinema: Mad, bad and dangerous to know*. London and New York: Continuum, 2000.

Helfenstein, Charles. *The Making of On Her Majesty's Secret Service*. USA: Spies LLC, 2009.

Helfenstein, Charles. *The Making of The Living Daylights*. USA: Spies LLC, 2012.

Hibbin, Sally. *The Making of Licence to Kill*. New York: Salem House, 1989.

Hines, Claire (ed.). *Fan Phenomena: James Bond*. Bristol and Chicago: Intellect, 2015.

Hines, Claire. *The Playboy and James Bond: 007, Ian Fleming and Playboy Magazine*. Manchester: Manchester University Press, 2018.

Hollander, Anne. *Sex and Suits: The evolution of modern dress*. New York: Alfred A. Knoff, 1995.

Jeffers McDonald, Tamar. *Hollywood Catwalk: Exploring costume and transformation in American film*. London: I.B. Tauris, 2010.

Johnstone, Iain. *The World is Not Enough: A companion*. London: Boxtree, 1999.

Jones, Grace with Paul Morley. *Grace Jones: I'll never write my memoirs*. London: Simon & Schuster, 2015.

Jones, Stephanie. "'Mr. Bond, I've been expecting you": The Cinematic Inaugurations of a New James Bond'. *International Journal of James Bond Studies* 1, no. 1 (2017), https://jamesbondstudies.ac.uk/articles/abstract/10.24877/jbs.6/.

Leese, Elizabeth. *Costume Design in the Movies: An Illustrated Guide to the Work of 157 Great Designers*. 1976. Reprinted with foreword by Julie Harris. London and New York: Dover Publications, 1991.

Levy, Shawn. *Dolce Vita Confidential: Fellini, Loren, Pucci, Paparazzi, and the Swinging High Life of 1950s Rome*. London: Weidenfeld & Nicolson, 2016.

Lindner, Christoph (ed.). *The James Bond Phenomenon: A critical reader*. Manchester and New York: Manchester University Press, 2003.

Lindner, Christoph (ed.). *Revisioning 007: James Bond and Casino Royale*. London and New York: Wallflower Press, 2009.

MacGregor, Trish and Rob MacGregor. *The Making of Miami Vice*. New York: Ballentine Books, 1986.

Mankiewicz, Tom and Robert Crane. *My Life as a Mankiewicz: An insiders journey through Hollywood*. Kentucky: University Press of Kentucky, 2012.

McInerney, Jay, Nick Foulkes, Neil Norman and Nick Sullivan. *Dressed to Kill: The suited hero*. Paris and New York: Flammarion, 1995.

Moniot, Drew. 'James Bond and America in the Sixties: An Investigation of the Formula Film in Popular Culture'. *Journal of the University Film Association* 28, no. 3 (1976): 25–33.

Moore, Roger with Gareth Owen. *My Word is My Bond: The autobiography*. London: Michael O'Mara Books, 2008.

Moore, Roger with Gareth Owen. *Bond on Bond: The ultimate book on over 50 years of 007*. London: Michael O'Mara Books, 2015.

Moseley, Rachel (ed.). *Fashioning Film Stars: Dress, culture, identity*. London: British Film Institute, 2005.

Nadoolman Landis, Deborah. *Film Craft: Costume design*. Lewis: Ilix, 2012.

Pearce, Garth. *The Making of GoldenEye*. London: Boxtree Limited, 1995.

Pearce, Garth. *The Making of Tomorrow Never Dies*. London: Boxtree Limited, 1997.

Pearson, John. *The Life of Ian Fleming*. London: Jonathan Cape Limited, 1966.

Pedersen, Stephanie. *Bra: A thousand years of style, support and seduction*. Newton Abbot: David and Charles, 2004.

Rickards, Jocelyn. *The Painted Banquet: My life and loves*. London: Weidenfeld, 1987.

Rubin, Steven Jay. *The James Bond Films: A behind the scenes history*. London: Talisman Books, 1981.

Sellers, Robert. *The Battle for Bond: The genesis of cinema's greatest hero*. Sheffield: Tomahawk Press, 2007.

Simmonds, Meg. *Bond by Design: The art of the James Bond films*. London: Dorling Kindersley, 2015.

Soter, Tom. *Bond and Beyond: 007 and other special agents*. New York: Image Publishing, 1993.

Spaiser, Matt. *The Suits of James Bond*. www.bondsuits.com/. 2010–.

Spicer, Andrew. 'Sean Connery: Loosening his Bonds'. In *British Stars and Stardom: From Alma Taylor to Sean Connery*, edited by Bruce Babington, 218–30. Manchester: Manchester University Press, 2001.

Street, Sarah. *Costume and Cinema: Dress codes in popular cinema*. London: Wallflower Press, 2001.

Strong, Jeremy (ed.). *James Bond Uncovered*. London: Palgrave Macmillan, 2018.

Thomas, Sarah. 'The New Brutalism: Agency, Embodiment and Performance in Daniel Craig's 007'. *Journal of Popular Film & Television* 46, no. 1 (January/March, 2018): 34–45.

Tornabuoni, Lietta. 'A popular phenomenon'. In *The Bond Affair*, edited by Oreste Del Buono and Umberto Eco, 13–34. London: Macdonald, 1966.

Verheul, Jaap (ed.). *The Cultural Life of James Bond: Specters of 007*. Amsterdam: Amsterdam University Press, 2020.

Walker, Alexander. *National Heroes: British cinema in the Seventies and Eighties*. London: Orion, 2005.

Williams, Greg. *Bond on Set: Filming Die Another Day*. London: Boxtree, 2004.

Williams, Greg. *Bond on Set: Filming Skyfall*. London: Dorling Kindersley Limited, 2012.

Williams, Melanie. 'The Girl You Don't See: Julie Harris and the Costume Designer in British Cinema'. *Feminist Media Histories* 2, no. 2 (2016): 62–74.

Magazine, Newspaper and Trade Sources

Cinema Retro, Daily Mail, Daily Mirror, Daily Telegraph, Drapery and Fashion Weekly, Esquire, Evening Standard, Financial Times, Guardian, Illustrated London News, Independent, Independent on Sunday, Kinematograph Weekly, Ladies Home Journal, Life, Los Angeles Times, Mail on Sunday, Men's Wear, Monthly Film Bulletin, Motion Picture Herald, News of the World, New York Times, Observer, Playboy, Rolling Stone, Screen International, The Stage, Starburst, The Sunday Times, Style for Men Weekly, Style Weekly, Sunday Express, Sunday Mirror, Sunday Telegraph, Tailor & Cutter, Tatler, Television Mail, The Times, Today's Cinema, Variety, Vogue, Washington Post.

INDEX